Aging without growing old

Take Charge of Your Health as Your Years Increase

Judy Lindberg McFarland

with Laura McFarland Luczak
Foreword by Douglas Walter McFarland M.D.

NOTICE: The material in this book is intended solely to report the experiences of Judy Lindberg McFarland, and those of her mother, Gladys Lindberg, and what they have learned in more than a half of century of study and work in the field of nutrition. There is no intention to diagnose any medical condition or to prescribe medication, or to suggest treatment for any medical ailment or disease condition. Judy McFarland is not a physician and does not purport to act as a physician. Any reader who suffers from any medical condition should consult his or her physician.

Library of Congress Cataloging-in-Publication Data

ISBN 1-888848-08-1

Library of Congress Catalog Card Number:
96-62079

Published by WESTERN FRONT LTD., Palos Verdes, CA.
Cover Design/Book Design/Typography: Karen Ryan
Printing: BookCrafters, Chelsea, MI
Manufactured in the United States of America

Dedication

I dedicate this work to the memory of my mother,

Gladys Melcher Lindberg,

a pioneer in the field of nutrition

whose incredible insights and loving counsel

put thousands on the path to robust health.

And to the memory of my father,

Walter Harold Lindberg,

whose vision, brilliance, and hard work

gave Mother a platform from which to teach.

TABLE OF CONTENTS

Foreword

Growing up in the McFarland household was not your average experience. Nowhere in the cupboard would you find cookies, candy, white bread, or processed foods. The refrigerator had no bologna, American cheese, soft drinks, margarine, or ice cream. My friends would say that there was nothing to snack on at my house! Instead, I snacked on fruits, nuts, trail mix, and an occasional treat such as homemade peanut butter candy or powdered milk candy.

The importance of health and of eating right was impressed upon me by my family at an early age, but most other people I encountered never appeared concerned about nutrition. It seemed that people were only interested in their health when they became ill. If one tried to eat good foods or take vitamins, he or she was considered a "health nut."

Our summer vacations were also different. As part of our vacations, we often went to various cities to attend nutrition conventions. During each convention, so many people would want to talk to my grandmother, Gladys Lindberg, that they often stood in line! I concluded that she must be famous, and I was right—my grandmother was famous in nutrition circles. I came to realize that being a McFarland was unique, from the food we ate, to the fact that my grandmother always wore pink.

I learned at a young age about taking vitamins and drinking protein shakes, but it was while I was a teenager that I began to recognize the depth of my grandmother's convictions about healthy eating. As I drove her home from work every Saturday, she told me about the people she had counseled that day and about their terrible physical problems, for which physicians had no cure. The hours she spent speaking with people at the nutrition store were more than mere business hours to her—she was deeply concerned about the good health of her clients.

My mother and grandmother worked together closely in their crusade for good health. On many occasions, my mother would read to me the thank-you letters that she and my grandmother had received from people whose lives and health had been turned around as the result of following the program my grandmother and mother had developed. The secret of the program created by my grandmother and mother was simple, and it is something I experienced firsthand in my childhood and teen years: a variety of good natural foods, vitamins and mineral supplementation, and no junk foods.

In college, I began to realize why people such as my mother and grandmother had a difficult time reaching and convincing a wide audience about the benefits of nutrition and supplements. Physicians, scientists, professors, and educators would not accept evidence and arguments that foods and vitamins could improve one's health, and this is an attitude that has been perpetuated by the popular press as well. I was often surprised at how my professors would deride brilliant scientists, such as Linus Pauling, for their "unconventional" views on vitamins.

In medical school, I again was surprised at how little time was spent on nutrition and preventive medicine. Although my medical interests led me to the field of Emergency Medicine, I readily understand how people can be frustrated with modern medicine. After years of living unhealthy lives, so many people are terrified to see their health fall apart in the "golden years"—and this is compounded when they see no effective treatments or cures offered by their doctors. As a physician, I realize that modern medicine has provided me with an education in diseases and how to treat them, but far less information on how to *prevent* them. In my work within the Emergency Department, I see patients with strokes, heart attacks, emphysema, cirrhosis of the liver, diverticulitis, and many other problems that are testament to poor prevention.

Modern medicine in the United States has focused on the treatment of disease with surgery or medications, but has left the "achievement of optimal health" largely unresearched. The average American's high-fat diet, inadequate exercise, and abuse of alcohol and tobacco have prevented millions from achieving their full health potential. As a nation, we are now beginning to recognize the importance of weight loss, exercise, a healthy diet, and the value of vitamin and mineral supplements. We are also realizing the limitations of current medical treatments to cure disease and help us reach optimal health. I believe the future breakthroughs in medicine will come in the field of prevention and reaching optimal health, not from the manufacturing of a new pill. I also believe that people such as my grandmother, who began her pioneering work in nutrition more than fifty years ago, are to be thanked for enlightening and empowering us to live healthier lives.

This book is easy to read and it should be easily understood by people of all backgrounds. Thousands of people have benefited tremendously from the Lindberg Nutrition program, with results that confirm the nutritional basis for many of their ailments.

The Lindberg Nutrition program is not a new fad that will be gone tomorrow. I believe you will be surprised at the amount of current scientific findings on vitamins and supplements that has never reached the popular media—findings that support the program recommended in this book.

For anyone seeking to take charge of their health—and to optimize their health—this book is an excellent resource.

— **Douglas Walter McFarland, M.D.**

Preface

The music of *Pomp and Circumstance* marked the beginning of a wonderful occasion for our family. Seated in the auditorium on the campus of the University of California at Los Angeles, my family felt great pride as we watched the dignified professors and guests move down the aisle, followed by the graduating class. I finally caught sight of the handsome, smiling face of my youngest son, Douglas Walter McFarland, M.D. He had completed years of study and there, in his academic cap and gown, he looked every inch "our son, the doctor."

I couldn't keep tears of joy from flowing as the ceremony continued. I was thrilled for Douglas, knowing how hard he had worked to earn his degree. I had no doubt that he would be an exceptional physician. Mingled with my joy was a twinge of sadness, however. I grieved that my precious mother, Gladys Lindberg, had not lived to share this special moment with us. She had passed away just two years before. My thoughts flashed back to her life. I visualized her beauty, grace, and charm. She always was elegantly dressed in her favorite pink-colored outfits. I saw her surrounded by familiar groups of clients at one of the Lindberg Nutrition stores, patiently listening to health complaints and then stating, "I am not a doctor and cannot treat disease, but healthy people don't have that, so let's make you healthy."

Mother once had a desire deep in her heart to be a physician, but that was not her lot in life. Instead, she raised three sickly children through the 1930s Depression and World War II. Her experiences not only compelled her to want to see people well, but made her a deeply compassionate person. And, what she discovered with her amazing scientific mind about sickness and health placed her forty years ahead of her time in the field of nutrition.

The course of my mother's life was drastically altered by what started out to be, by all appearances, a childhood bout with the flu. My sister Janice developed a high fever one night and there was nothing Mother could do to help her. Janice had these spells frequently, and that night, while Janice's body waged war against the fever racking her body, Mother knelt beside her and prayed for knowledge about how to keep her child well. She fell asleep beside her and, in the morning, Janice's body was cool. Mother knew her prayers had been answered. She also realized almost instantly that nearly all the food we ate had been highly processed, preserved or devitalized in some way. Thus, with an insatiable drive, she began the quest of her life—to make and keep her family healthy. She started with an organic garden in our backyard.

Our lives changed dramatically as Mother improved our eating habits. She read everything she could find about nutrition and vitamins, and she applied what she learned to our family. Neighbors began to see the results in us, and came to her for advice.

Mother had a great ability to read complicated medical text-books and then translate that information into simple terms so that the ordinary person could understand it. She loved reading about the tremendous scientific work of unsung medical heroes. As she read, she classified and compiled information to use in developing her own personal nutrition programs.

Gladys Lindberg never promised to cure anybody of anything. She simply listened to the health problems that people brought to her, and then she taught people how to eat properly and how to supplement their diet in order to create the favorable cir-cumstances in which health might flourish. The fact that so many people had astounding results after following her dietary suggestions was the proof of her expertise.

She read of the wonderful pioneering doctors, and their results with nutritional substances. In surveying the past, Mother set about to glean the best nutritional practices of the past and to apply them to the present and future of her family. She had no desire to go back to her "hard life" in the little town of Peck, Idaho, nor to revert to a primitive lifestyle, but she did desire to bring the best nutritional qualities of the past into modern-day living.

In comparing real-life people with the medical case studies, Mother concluded that much higher amounts of the then called Minimum Daily Requirement, (now the RDAs) of vitamins A, C, E, (the antioxidants) and the known B-complex vitamins should be taken. She also began to realize the value of the "wonder foods" of her day, including brewer's yeast, yogurt, cod liver oil, powdered milk, black-strap molasses, lecithin and other natural foods. These became the mainstay of her nutritional programs.

Mother was determined to find a nutritious regimen for her family, and then, to make that regimen palatable and even tasty. She began very simply by putting certified raw milk in a blender, then adding bananas, or other seasonal fruit, and concentrated orange juice or blackstrap molasses. Lastly, in would go the brewer's yeast, raw liver powder, bone meal, calcium, vitamin C, and lecithin. She created a health drink she named the "Serenity Cocktail." She would say "all of these nutrients keep us serene."

As far as I'm concerned, those original drinks tasted terrible. We children tried to rebel, but gradually we accepted the fact that Mother was trying to do the right thing for us. When Mother gave us a drink, we developed all types of ways of "getting it down." And soon we went from being sickly kids to energetic youngsters!

Mother's Friend and Fellow Pioneer: Adelle Davis

One of the significant events in my mother's early years of studying and experimenting came when she heard Adelle Davis lecture at a department store in downtown Los Angeles. Adelle was giving a series of lectures while promoting her first book, *Vitality Through Planned Nutrition*.

After the lecture, Mother introduced herself and enthusiastically shared with Adelle her own experiences, subsequent findings, and the results in her children's lives. She concluded, "I've been doing with my family all the things you talked about."

Thus began a lifelong friendship with Adelle. Mother and Adelle got together frequently to discuss what was new in the field of health. Both were pioneers in applied nutrition and they learned much from each other. Both had a commitment to raising people's consciousness about nutrition. Good health was the passion of their lives.

I often went to Adelle's home on Sundays with Mother and Dad while Adelle was writing her best-selling book, *Let's Eat Right to Keep Fit*. Mother happily contributed many examples. In fact, when I read Adelle's book, it sounds like Mother talking. Adelle wanted to dedicate the book to Mother, but my father wouldn't allow it, desiring to protect Mother from some of the very negative press Adelle was receiving. Adelle was highly controversial in those days with her revolutionary ideas. She was promoting the use of vitamins, little-known and little-discussed at that time.

More people around the world have been turned on to nutrition by Adelle Davis' books than by any other writings. Mutual affection and admiration always characterized our family's relationship with Adelle.

Vitamin and Mineral Packs at the Dining Room Table

When neighbors saw the remarkable change in our lives, word began to spread quickly. Soon, Mother had relatives, neighbors, and friends coming to her regularly for advice on what to do to help their children and themselves become healthier.

Word of her program spread across the Los Angeles area. She was asked so often about the vitamins and minerals she was giving us, that she began to buy them wholesale in quantities of a thousand at a time. There were very few health food stores in that era. Then, when friends stopped in for advice, she'd hold a class around the dining room table and those who wanted to try the program would count out their own vitamins, put them into white envelopes, and pay Mother exactly what the vitamins had cost her. Mother had great satisfaction in seeing people's health improve from week to week! As her "clients" came back for more vitamins and minerals, she'd share the new information she had learned. Her process was a continual one of learning and applying, then teaching others how to apply the best and most recent health research.

Today, you can find clear plastic packs of vitamins and minerals just about everywhere, and they began with Mother! What is their origin?

One of Mother's clients was a blind woman who could not distinguish between the envelopes of the various vitamin and mineral tablets. So Mother spread out a hundred small squares of wax paper on the dining table, put a daily supply of about six vitamins and minerals on each square, and then twisted the squares into packets so this woman could take just one packet a day. The woman loved the idea, and so did her friends.

After trying many variations of doing this by hand for approximately fifteen years, my brother Bob, who had a knack for engineering, designed a machine that allowed the tablets to drop into little cellophane packets, which were then sealed.

Why multiple tablets in a packet? Because no single pill could contain a high enough potency for her formulas without becoming too large to swallow. She never agreed with the one-tablet-a-day concept.

Finally the day came when, after observing for a long time what was happening around our dining room table, my father said, half jokingly, "Gladys, this has become a business. You must get this out of the house." And get it out of the house he did, in 1949. My father, Walter Harold Lindberg, had a unique business ability, coupled with perseverance and hard work. He took the initiative and found the location for our first store. It was his idea to call it the Lindberg Nutrition Service. He said, "Our service will be Gladys giving her time to help people become nutrition-wise, and it will be free advice." Our motto was "Keep in the Pink" —referring to the natural color of good health—and our stores and labels were all pink in color. Mother wore only pink clothes and drove a pink car.

A Program That Has Stood the Test of Time

The principles of nutrition presented in this book *work*. They are easily applied. They can be put into use by virtually any person. Furthermore, most of these principles have been tested and proven over time. Some of the research reported in this book is fairly recent, and some of it is innovative and on the cutting edge of medical and scientific study. But the general principles and suggestions regarding health and good nutrition have stood the test of time.

Good health achieved first through knowledge and then through action became a crusade for her. The baton was passed to me, and I gladly accepted it.

What I know about nutrition was not necessarily gained in a classroom. I do have a Bachelor of Science degree in Foods and Nutrition from Pepperdine University. Most of what I know was learned at the elbow of my mother.

Mother regularly attended lectures and had discussions with the most noteworthy nutritional experts and researchers over a forty-year span. These experts became personal friends. Fortunately for me, Mother didn't drive, so I became her chauffeur. From the time I was a teenager, I also attended the lectures and seminars that she attended. I was involved in conversations that my mother had with Adelle Davis, Dr. Carlton Fredericks, Dr. Lester Morrison, Gayelord Hauser, and other greats in the field of nutrition.

I saw Mother's clients return to her over the months and I saw first hand how their health improved from visit to visit. I felt Mother's love and compassion for these precious people and I saw how rewarding her work was to her. What a wonderful heritage I received from her!

Helping yourself and your loved ones stay healthy and

achieve optimal health is one of the most important things you can do in life. I truly believe that there's nothing more important that I can do than to help people learn how to have more vitality and energy to do what God has intended for them. I can't begin to tell you how gratifying it has been for me to help individuals turn their lives around, prevent common ailments, and in some cases, experience renewed health even after having years of health problems.

In following my mother's example, I also began reading the classic works of early researchers. I became part of a group that started the American Nutrition Society in the South Bay area of California, and served as the group's program chairman and president for many years. I've also been involved in our industry many, many years, served on the Board of directors of the National Nutritional Foods Association (NNFA), and on the Golden West regional board of the NNFA. At the 1996 NNFA national convention in Nashville, I was honored with an award for ongoing and continued support for the nutrition and health industry. I stay current with nutritional and scientific literature, and attend lectures and seminars across the nation, and even in other parts of the world.

Television Notables Believe in Nutrition

In 1981, Pat Robertson, host of the TV program "The 700 Club" did a feature on Gladys Lindberg and Lindberg Nutrition shortly after our first book, *Take Charge of Your Health*, was released. They showed our retail stores and the 100,000 square-foot warehouse of Nature's Best, our distribution company. (Nature's Best is now owned by my brother's family.) I was on the program with Mother and the first question Pat asked was, "How did a little lady like you start such a fantastic business?" She then gave her testimony on how she got started. Pat Robertson is very interested in keeping the body as "God's temple"—in good health—and he continues to bring nutritional information to his television audience.

About the same time, Mother and I appeared on television with the dynamic Regis Philbin. We fixed a Serenity Cocktail drink with brewer's yeast, protein, whey, lecithin, and a banana, all mixed with certified raw milk. Regis was so dear, he even said it tasted good! Regis is the popular co-host of "Live with Regis and Cathy Lee." He has always been an advocate of vitamin and mineral supplements, and to this day, he and his wife Joy use our vitamin packs. It was fun to hear him say recently on his TV program, "I take my

Lindberg Varsity Pack every day along with my niacin."

In January of 1993, I was invited to be a guest on "The Doctor's Night" on Trinity Broadcasting Network (TBN), a national (almost world-wide) television program. The hosts were Paul and Jan Crouch, along with five medical doctors and myself. We had a great three hours of answering viewers' questions about nutrition.

Since that time, I have been invited to do many of these very popular prime-time television programs, and always count it as an honor to participate. My part on the shows is to discuss proper nutrition and how to build health and improve our sense of well-being. It's always amazing to me how the switchboard at their station lights up with calls from people all over the world who want to know more. In this book I've tried to answer many of the most frequently asked questions from these television programs, knowing that they are the most common and relevant to a wide variety of people.

It has also been a wonderful experience being a frequent guest on Carol Lawrence's television program on TBN, "The Carol Lawrence Show." Carol is a beautiful and vivacious actress, singer and dancer who is a big advocate of good nutrition.

My daughter Laura and I were regular weekly guests for almost two years on the TBN television program, "Doctor to Doctor." We prepared nutritious recipes and cooked each week. This was a great experience for us, and I can't thank Laura enough for helping me "pull it all together." We receive thousands of letters as a result of these educational programs. People are in such need of information about nutrition, and they are eager to learn!

I recently attended a National Health Federation convention in Pasadena, California, where Dr. William Lane of *Sharks Don't Get Cancer* had asked me to share a booth to pass out our *Nutrition Express* catalog, which carries his products. I was amazed and thrilled to hear so many wonderful stories about how my mother's advice had saved their lives. One dear man started to weep as he told me his story. What a tremendous heritage Mother has left me!

And Now, Our Children—The Third Generation.
Our children have joined my husband, Don, and me in our family business of helping people find abundant health. Three of our children work directly with us. Our daughter Laura also received her Bachelor of Science degree in Foods and Nutrition from

Pepperdine University. She has worked in our store, helped set up mail-order with her Dad, helps me with lectures, appears on television with me, and is by my side just as I was by my mother's side. Our son Gary is Director of Operations and buyer for Lindberg Nutrition and Nutrition Express. Dan is our Marketing Director. Douglas is our physician specializing in emergency medicine.

Though the number keeps changing, I am currently the proud grandparent of ten, one granddaughter and nine grandsons. How blessed we are to be "Pappa Don" and "Nonnie" to these beautiful and healthy grandchildren.

There are no "magic bullets." When we discuss the subject of aging, we must lay the nutritional foundation for lasting health. As much as we may dream about the "magic bullet" that will prevent aging or the degenerative diseases that usually accompany growing old, there is no such pill, yet. But there is a tremendous amount of information available to you, to help you along this anti-aging path. I make no claims in this book that any one nutrient, vitamin, mineral, hormone or practice will help every person, immediately, and all the time. *All* the nutrients your body needs must be supplied in sufficient and balanced quantities in order for your body to be properly nourished. But... there is a whole nutrition program that will help you achieve optimal health now, and for the rest of your life!

Acknowledgement

My precious family has been so supportive throughout the writing of this book, reading and re-reading chapters, proofing drafts and making suggestions. I first want to thank my husband, Don, for his unconditional love, encouragement and support for this project.

I also thank my son Douglas, who has given me critical medical advice on several chapters. He was raised in a family believing in, and using nutritional supplements, even though he was not taught this type of preventive or nutritional medicine at the university or medical school.

My daughter Laura will always have a special place in my heart for sticking with me to the final word of the final chapter. She really knows how to get a job done. Not only has she been by my side as we attended many educational seminars and conferences, she has worked in our business and stayed abreast of the most recent nutritional information. I am forever indebted to you, Laura.

Several others have helped me in writing this book. I want to thank Helen Hosier and Norm Rohrer for getting me started in the very early stages, and Frank Murray for his contribution toward this manuscript. Thank you, Dr. Jan Dargatz, a very professional and patient editor who put up with so many changes. I also want to acknowledge and thank Marcia Zimmerman, C.N., Richard Passwater, Ph.D., Dan McFarland, B.A., and Carol McFarland, B.A., M.Ed., for taking time out of their busy schedules to read the manuscript and offer their suggestions.

There is a very special group of my dear friends that have been praying for the message in this book and for me, as I completed this project. May God bless all of you.

My publisher from Western Front, Cliff Ford, has been a dear friend and a gem to work with as he helped birth this book.

There were many who I have looked to as authorities that I have had the honor of knowing. These experts, from my mother's generation, are gone now, but I want to acknowledge them: Adelle Davis (author), Carlton Fredericks, Ph.D. (author), Gaylord Hauser (pioneering nutritionist), Lester Morrison, M.D., D.Cs., F.A.C.P. (arteriosclerosis research), Linus Pauling, Ph.D. (vitamin C), Evan Shute, M.D. (vitamin E), Broda Barnes, M.D., Ph.D.

(thyroid), Robert Bingham, M.D. (arthritis) and Robert Mendelsohn, M.D. (author). We all have benefited from their numerous accomplishments and their pioneering spirit.

Now there are new "stars" from my generation, experts in the field of health, who have become family friends or friends I have made from our industry. They include: Richard Passwater, Ph.D., Betty Kamen, Dr. William Crook, Joseph Pizzorno, N.D., Stephen Langer, M.D., Julian Whitaker, M.D., Eric Braverman, M.D., Dr. Patrick Quillin, Udo Erasmus, Lendon Smith, M.D., Dr. Donald Brown, Stephen Foster, Michael Murray, N.D., Frank Varese, M.D., Abram Hoffer M.D., Ph.D., Hans Kugler, Ph.D., William Lane, Ph.D., Earl Mindell, R.Ph., Ph.D., Jeffrey Bland, Ph.D., Janet Zand, L.Ac, O.M.D., Steven Schechter, N.D., Maureen Salaman, Richard Casdorph, M.D., Michael Corrigan, Dana Ullman, Marcia Zimmerman, Ann Louise Gittleman, Frank Murray, and many, many others.

These are the new stars, the ones I still have the opportunity to learn from. You will find many of them referenced in this book.

Chapter 1

Aging

Let's Slow It Down

Holding Back the Hands of the Biological Time Clock

"We shouldn't think of growing older as a time of physical
degeneration, senility or becoming cantankerous.
Our goal should be to maximize our vitality,
doing what contributes to optimum health,
so we can maintain our zest for living."
— **Gladys Lindberg**

My mother, Gladys Lindberg, had a simple test for establishing the true age of a person. She would tell you to pick up the skin on the back of your hand, and to pull it up taut, hold it for a few seconds, and then let go. If your skin snapped back, Mother declared you to be young, regardless of your chronological years. If your skin "crawled" back, you were old. Truly old skin may take a minute or more to return to normal. Mother, of course, loved to show her customers how elastic her own beautiful skin was. Check yours. Compare your skin with younger and older friends. Later, I will discuss how to keep your skin young and elastic.

We each have two ages: our **chronological age**—which involves the celebrating of birthdays and passing of years, and our **biological age**—which reflects the rate at which we are getting older. Everybody ages at the same chronological rate, but people *do not* age at the same biological rate. You will find the skin-test comparison interesting, especially with those who smoke and drink alcohol. The goal of nearly everybody I know is to reduce the rate at which they age biologically!

My husband and I were high school sweethearts and continued dating throughout college. Don received a football scholarship to the University of Southern California, and we didn't marry until 1955, after college. Several years ago, we went to our 40th high school reunion and were looking forward to meeting our friends from long ago. When we arrived at the hotel, Don said he was going to ask directions to the ballroom, but I assured him we would find our friends without difficulty. Well .... we found a ballroom with lots of celebrating, happy, senior citizens. Don hesitated before going in, saying, "This can't be our class, they look too old." Of course it was our group!

We realized very quickly how fast the years had flown. I had never thought much about our own aging until we attended that party and saw many of our long-lost friends. We were all about the same chronological age (except the "new" wives of several of the men), but we certainly had many different biological ages. Some looked great, but others I recognized only by the high school photo on their name tag. What caused the difference in the aging of our friends?

Is There an Aging Clock?

Aging is influenced by many factors, including genetics, lifestyle and what has been called an "aging clock." This aging clock regulates specific changes at various times throughout our lives. An example of this internal time clock would be when our bodies start producing hormones that control our growth and sexual development, a time called puberty. Another example of this internal time clock would relate to women and menopause. Women enter menopause at different ages, from early forties to mid-fifties.

At the time of mid-life, for both sexes, our body starts to wind down. A signal is sent by the level of our hormones that we are past our prime. Our body is now more vulnerable to various illnesses and degenerative diseases.

An important aspect of aging is the decline of key physiological functions—vision impairment with cataracts, glaucoma; brittle bones and dowager humps (usually associated with osteoporosis or osteoarthritis); weaker muscles and loss of strength; diseases that shorten life (such as cancer, heart disease, diabetes); a weakened immune system; senility or memory loss; and the list goes on.

Many of these conditions are not necessarily true signs of aging, but rather, the result of combinations of long-term nutritional deficiencies, and decreases in our natural hormone levels. Physical activity and our positive mental attitude play an important part in preventing this "disease" of aging.

Holding Back the Hands of the Biological Time Clock

In the mid-sixties, Dr. Leonard Hayflick published an interesting paper in which he concluded that human cells have a definite number of cell divisions built into their genetic code. In other words, our cells are capable of reproducing themselves only so many times. This conclusion, in turn, suggested that there was a limit to the human life span.[1] The idea of a biological time clock was born.

Several years later, however, at the Miami Symposium on Theoretical Aspects of Aging, a researcher reported that only in certain cell cultures did cells stop dividing, while in others, they continued to divide. This researcher also noted that cells that had stopped dividing could be stimulated to divide again.[2]

Other scientists picked up on this possibility, and in 1976, a researcher reported that red blood cells in a culture with partial vitamin E deficiency were destroyed eight to ten percent faster than cells with adequate vitamin E.[3] Another scientist enriched human cells in a test tube with vitamin E and found that he could prolong the cells' life span for as many as 120 generations of cell division, compared to a span of 50 generations for untreated cells![4] Vitamin E was apparently acting as an antioxidant in this experiment.

Today, the findings seem to point toward a two-sided truth: on the one hand, we do have a biological clock within each cell, which limits its age. On the other hand, we can intervene in this cell mechanism and add time to the clock, as the researchers did with vitamin E. There is more valuable information on vitamin E as an antioxidant in Chapter 3.

Cell Function is the Basis of all Life. As we grow older, trillions of body cells reproduce countless times, and in the course of reproduction, gradually change. To reduce biological aging, our goal is to maintain the reproduction of our cells with minimal deterioration or change.

Every cell has a limited life. It performs its function in the body, then reproduces itself and dies. At any given time, thousands of your cells may be dying, while thousands more are being born, some faster than others. Fat cells, for example, reproduce slowly, while skin cells reproduce approximately every ten hours.

Only one type of cell doesn't follow this pattern—the cells of your brain. You were given your lifetime supply of brain cells at the time of your birth. When these cells become worn out and die, they are never replaced. Scientists tell us that by the age 35, a person is losing 100,000 brain cells a day. I always wonder who is counting! Fortunately, the initial supply is so great that this loss is scarcely noticeable.

Do We Have Control Over Aging? Much of aging has to do with our lifestyles, choices and personal environment. The good news is that this is something over which we do have some control. A number of things cause damage to our cells, such as ultraviolet light, X-rays, smoking, alcohol, lack of exercise, chemicals in our foods, processed or oxidized fats, and many other factors. But damage to cells can be minimized in many ways, as you will see throughout this book. Scientists are increasingly focusing their research on the entire process of aging and are defining it as an instant by instant destruction of weakened, undefended cells that on a massive scale leads to the degeneration of the body and even the mind.

It is Easier to Say What Aging is Not. It is not senility and poor health. These are conditions generally brought on by chronic malnutrition and inattention to what the body needs to maintain its vigor at any age. Unfortunately, senility and aging are often equated. The truth is that everybody ages, but only some become senile. Senility is not inevitable. Memory loss, inability to store new information, and certain personality quirks associated with senility can be postponed, if not prevented, as you will see.

Just as senility is not inevitable, neither are most chronic degenerative diseases. A person can age without many of the conditions we have come to assume are inescapable. Yes, we can slow down and in many cases, prevent this physical and even mental degeneration. Yes, we can slow down this whole aging process, and even restore our youthful zest for living and loving. So let's get started!

The Value of Scientific Research and Medical Studies

Throughout this book you are going to find numerous references to scientific research and medical studies. Some of the studies are very recent, others are classic studies. Just because a medical study is old doesn't make it invalid. Some twenty-five years ago, I heard distinguished physicians discuss studies that linked a folic acid deficiency to gross birth defects. And yet, this finding has been reported recently as if this fact was just discovered.

I recently attended a conference at the National Institute of Health in Bethesda, Maryland and heard a young Ph.D. from a renowned University speak about vitamin E. The information presented was very basic, and "surface level" as far as I was concerned. After the lecture, I asked this young researcher if she had read any of the classic vitamin E studies conducted by Drs. Wilfrid and Evan Shute of Canada. She had never heard of them. How sad to miss out on their wealth of knowledge! Their research on vitamin E was presented widely in the 1950s, 60s and even the 70s. They worked with 38,000 cardiac patients and documented tremendous benefits of vitamin E in preventing heart disease and heart attacks. Their research stands as valid today as it was back then. "New research" touting that vitamin E can prevent heart disease is only now gaining the attention it should have thirty years ago.

Living on This Side of Disease. An overwhelming number of people, young and old, simply don't feel well. They do not have an obvious illness, yet they do not feel good on a consistent basis. They are living in the twilight zone of health—without a major problem or life-threatening disease, yet with a multitude of minor problems that keep them from experiencing the full vitality and energy of health. They are, indeed, "living on the edge of disease."

"Healthy People Don't Have That." In my nutritional counseling when I hear most of my clients' list of symptoms and ailments, I quickly tell them, "healthy people don't have that, let's make you healthy."

What is it that healthy people don't have? Perhaps first and foremost, they don't have major degenerative diseases—cancer, heart trouble, crippling arthritis, osteoporosis, mental illness, senility or Alzheimer's, diabetes, emphysema, arteriosclerosis (hardening of the arteries), atherosclerosis (fatty deposits in arteries), and others.

Research statistics tell us that degenerative diseases are responsible for more than 70 percent of all deaths in this country. I once heard former Surgeon General C. Everett Koop say that "dietary imbalances" are the leading preventable contributors to premature death in the United States. This is borne out by the Centers for Disease Control, which has stated that 54 percent of heart disease, 37 percent of cancer, 50 percent of cerebrovascular disease (pertaining to the blood vessels of the brain), and 49 percent of atherosclerosis is preventable through lifestyle modification. In all, some 1.6 million deaths a year may be related to poor nutrition! As startling as these figures may be, there is great hope for people willing to take charge of their health. Most people are aging too rapidly and are dying from something that can be prevented! Many are finding there is a great deal they can do to help themselves.

We need to recognize that the degenerative diseases that are rampant today were hardly known before the Industrial Revolution, which brought people from farms into the cities. People in past generations faced major killers that were more commonly associated with germs, parasites, or viruses—diseases such as smallpox, influenza, plagues, and diphtheria. These have almost all been conquered, thanks in large part to the discovery of antibiotics and modern means of refrigeration and sanitation.

The major causes of aging and degenerative diseases are associated generally with the absence or lack of some substance from our system. Stated in other terms, the person with any of these diseases is generally missing something that would otherwise keep him or her well. That "something" is nearly always associated with things people can take into their bodies, and in many cases, it is something related to nutrition. In very simple terms, *malnutrition* is a significant cause of aging and degenerative diseases which is often the lack of certain vitamins, minerals, or trace elements.

Our goal, then, is to make sure that we take into our bodies all that we need to maintain excellent health and eliminate those things from our diet that we know damage our health. It sounds simple, and in many ways it is. Unfortunately, there is much confusion about what constitutes an "adequate diet"—a diet that promotes total health and a feeling of well-being, strength, energy and vitality. One nutritionist says one thing, another contradicts. One book reports certain findings, and another refutes its claims.

You Are Unique! No two individuals have the same genetic code, cellular structure or hormone balance. We all take individualized routes through life, encountering different environments and stressors. Despite our unique nutritional differences, our goal of good health is the same.

Good health is far more than simply the absence of disease. Your body is always trying to make you well. It is constantly in the process of making trillions of new cells. These cells have to reach into your blood stream to obtain more than fifty chemicals: amino acids (the building blocks of protein), fatty acids, minerals, trace elements, vitamins, and enzymes. These chemicals must come from the food we eat, the water we drink, and the air we breathe. When our food is hydrogenated, homogenized, refined, microwaved, preserved, emulsified, pasteurized, chemicalized, colored, bleached, and sterilized, something is lost. In many cases, it is *health* that is lost!

You are unique, with an individually determined biochemical heredity pattern. The exact amount of each nutrient that you need is as distinct as your fingerprint or voice print. When you experience a health problem, your body is sending you a signal that your body cells are ailing. They are not being provided with the nutrients they need to sustain and propagate healthy cells, tissues, and organs.

Your body may be able to get along without a particular nutritional substance for days, weeks, months, even years, but if the pattern continues, you will eventually develop a health problem. Some people will develop problems sooner than others. Some will develop more severe problems than others. But eventually, all of us are subject to problems if we don't provide our bodies with the materials needed for rebuilding healthy cells.

Many fail to understand the role of nutrition and unknowingly deprive themselves of optimum health. Their minor abnormalities, left uncorrected, frequently lead to more serious disease. Recognizing subtle deviations from good health and taking steps to correct them early is preventive medicine at its best. And that's what this book intends to help you accomplish.

Maintaining a Zest for Living. I often see clients who have been customers of ours for almost fifty years. My mother, Gladys Lindberg—a pioneer in the field of nutrition—put them on a program, and they have stayed on it through the decades. Why? Because it worked for them. They look great, are feeling well, and are aging with grace. They are free of disease. So they return again and again to continue doing what they know works so well for them. They often tell me amazing stories about how their health was radically transformed years ago by Mother's advice.

They Can't Kill Me Now. One woman came into our store recently with her darling mother, who was visiting in southern California from Alabama. The mother had been a mail-order customer for more than thirty-five years. When she came to visit her daughter in Los Angeles, she insisted on coming to our store to meet me, primarily because I was Gladys Lindberg's daughter.

I found this spry little woman—with steel gray hair—pushing her own shopping cart through the store. She told me how she once had been so sick that her doctors had said there was no hope for her. She said, "I had everything wrong that could go wrong. They just gave up on me. I came to see Gladys Lindberg and she saved my life." She went on to inform me that she is now 96 years old. "They can't kill me now," she said with a twinkle in her eye. "I just go on and on." And off she went, buzzing through our store pushing her cart and loading it up with products that had been recommended to her "way back in the fifties."

When I meet women such as this, I know that the medical establishment would label her story as "anecdotal evidence," but to me, it is a miracle. This woman was not a part of a double-blind, cross-over study. Still, she is enjoying good health at age 96. As far as I'm concerned, she is the beneficiary of the best nutritional wisdom Mother had to offer . . . and which I am delighted to share with you in this anti-aging book.

Don't Change a Thing. Another woman called to ask me if she should change what she had been taking, which was our special athletic vitamin and mineral packets. This is the packet that was originally designed for amateur and professional athletes. In talking with her, I discovered she was driving her own car, working in her yard and took complete care of herself as her husband had passed away the year before. She still had all her mental faculties, and had no real complaints, but was just "moving a little slower." In ordering her vitamins, she wondered if she should change what she was doing. She said she had been faithful in following Gladys Lindberg's advice for more than thirty-five years. Her voice sounded quite young so I finally asked, "How old are you, honey?"

She replied, *"Eighty-nine."*

I immediately responded, *"Don't change a thing!"*

The higher potencies in these vitamin and mineral packets

worked for her. I am sure at eighty-nine we would all love to still be driving our car, and be completely independent.

They Have Aged Without Growing Old. Such people as these have aged without growing old. Nutrition has played a major role in preventing their physical and mental deterioration. Many of the senior citizens we see have maintained a zest for living, loving, working, and growing. They are still striving to be the very best they can be.

We have always maintained that you can improve with age—that you can retain an attractive appearance and vitality while enjoying optimum health. But health is not something that just happens. It is an ongoing investment that involves your total lifestyle.

Let's Build You Up! My role as a nutritional counselor is to discuss a person's eating habits, and to suggest dietary changes that may help to encourage good nutritional practices, including supplementation of all the essential vitamins, minerals, herbs, the natural hormones and even the single amino acids when necessary. Exercise also fits into this formula, along with prayer. I try to inspire my clients to take charge of their own health, and when they build up their health, many of their physical and emotional problems will also improve, and many times even disappear.

Make a decision today that you are going to strive for optimal health—the best health you can possibly have, and that you are going to seek to become healthy through natural and nutritional means. You can enjoy greater health at any age, so let's make you healthy! You can take charge of your health . . . and slow down the aging process . . . beginning now!

Chapter 2

The Significance
of Vitamins, Minerals and Herbs

Important Nutrients
for Health and Healing

"When the missionary zeal took hold of me,
I was thrilled to read the works of the
pioneering doctors. Their tremendous
results helped chart my path and open my eyes
to this whole field of nutrition."
— **Gladys Lindberg**

The late Albert Szent-Gyorgyi, M.D., Ph.D., was a brilliant researcher who received the Nobel Prize for Physiology and Medicine as well as the Albert Lasker Prize for his theory of muscle contraction. One of his classic statements was, "the whole idea of a vitamin is a paradox and difficult to digest. Everybody knows that things we eat can make us sick, but it seems utterly senseless to say that something which we have *not* eaten could make us sick. And this is exactly what a vitamin is: *A substance which makes us sick and even die by not eating it.*"[1]

I believe this statement is one that truly reflects the great importance of vitamins. If we do not obtain the vitamins or minerals we need from our food supply or in supplement form, we can become sick and even die. The Scriptures tell us: "My people are destroyed for lack of knowledge" (Hosea 4:6). Classic examples of this in history are diseases that caused a tremendous amount of suffering and millions of deaths for "lack" of a certain vitamin, and the knowledge that it was needed.

Today, researchers know that each of the diseases below is the result of a deficiency of an important molecule in the organs and tissues of the body.

- **Scurvy.** In the 1700s, British sailors perished for the lack of knowledge that ascorbic acid or vitamin C prevented scurvy. It was not until 1928 that Dr. Szent-Gyorgyi was able to obtain pure vitamin C, and not until 1939 that it was named ascorbic acid and recognized as a possible dietary deficiency.
- **Beriberi** results from an insufficient supply of the vitamin B1 (thiamin). The word beriberi means "extreme weakness" in the Singhalese language. It was common in Asia where the diet was

limited to white rice in which the B1 was refined out.

- **Pellagra** is caused by an insufficient supply of vitamin B3 (niacin) and results in dermatitis, diarrhea, and dementia (confusion and memory loss).
- **Pernicious anemia** results from an insufficient amount or absorption of vitamin B12 (cobalamin). An intrinsic factor is essential for the absorption of vitamin B12.
- **Rickets** is caused by a lack of vitamin D in the diet or insufficient exposure of the skin to sunlight.
- **Goiter** can be prevented by taking the mineral iodine.
- **Anemia** is treated and prevented by taking iron.
- **Osteoporosis** can be prevented by taking calcium and vitamin D.
- **Spina Bifida** and other birth defects can be prevented if the expectant mother takes the B-vitamin, folic acid.

The causes of these diseases may be obvious to many, but we also need to be able to recognize subclinical deficiencies, or "pre-disease" symptoms, and reverse trends before they develop. The more we learn about these deficiency symptoms, the more we are equipped to take charge of our health and the health of our loved ones.

Many people are finally realizing that the average American diet is far from adequate and actually causes some of the diseases we face today. Some of the diet-induced diseases that have become major killers are heart disease, many forms of cancer, diabetes, osteoporosis, arthritis, and premature aging. Other conditions such as allergies, obesity, chronic fatigue, impotence, birth defects, and so forth can also be directly related to nutritional imbalances in our bodies.

In all, deficiencies of certain vitamins and minerals can be involved in the death of millions of Americans annually. You only need to walk into any nursing home to see outright evidence of deficiencies—especially scurvy—that have not been recognized, and therefore, are not being corrected.

Scurvy in This Day and Age?

I am sure you have seen older people who have deep red bruising (sometimes almost purple) on their hands and arms. They may even tell you they don't know why any slight bump or scrape seems to cause it. Their gums bleed easily, especially when they brush their teeth. Wounds don't heal, their skin is rough, and their muscles waste away. In my mother's old classic medical books there are examples of scurvy and the symptoms appear identical. We all know scurvy has been conquered . . . or has it?

In these classic books the recommendation is always vitamin C. I often wonder what these older people must be doing or taking that is destroying their vitamin C, or what is increasing the need for vitamin C in their bodies.

This story is tragic to me because everyone thinks scurvy is from the old days. Information reported in the *Journal of the American Medical Association* stated, "Scurvy is a disease that can mimic other more serious disorders . . . and because clinical features of scurvy are no longer well appreciated, scorbutic patients are often extensively evaluated for other disorders."[2]

Michael Rosenbaum, M.D., said, "Most physicians believe that everyone gets all the vitamin C they need, so they fail to suspect scurvy when faced with the symptoms. The symptoms of scurvy can mimic the symptoms of cardiovascular disease, arthritis, infectious disorders, and many other common illnesses usually treated by means far more expensive than vitamin C supplementation." He went on to say, "A lot of illness and unnecessary medical treatment might be prevented by making sure everyone got plenty of vitamin C in their diets."[2]

If you see your loved ones with these symptoms, recommend vitamin C with bioflavonoids and Pycnogenol® or grape seed extract on a daily basis.

Vitamins

Vitamins are not the fuel, but they are like the ignition switch that sparks the fuel and keeps the engine running.

A vitamin is a group of organic compounds that, in very small amounts, are essential for normal growth, development and metabolism. With a few exceptions, they cannot be synthesized or made in the body, and must be supplied by the diet. Vitamins are produced by living material, such as plants and animals, as compared to minerals that come from the soil. Lack of sufficient quantities of any of the vitamins produces specific deficiency diseases. In fact, if a substance does not produce a deficiency symptom when it is removed from the diet, it is not considered a vitamin.

Each vitamin functions in many diverse roles and always with other essential nutrients. They participate in a variety of life-building processes, including the formation and maintenance of blood cells, hormones, all the cells and tissues of the body, and even the creation of our genetic material.

Vitamins Contain NO Calories. Vitamins are not used as sources of energy as some believe. They contain no calories, and they cannot make you fat. They are used to form enzymes that are biologic catalysts in many metabolic reactions within the body. Several vitamins help convert the calories in carbohydrates, protein, and fat into usable energy for the body. In other words, vitamins are not the fuel, but they are like the ignition switch that sparks the fuel and keeps the engine running. When vitamins are not present in sufficient quantity, metabolism ceases or is impaired.

Classifications of Vitamins
Vitamins are generally classified as water-soluble or fat-soluble vitamins.

Water-Soluble Vitamins dissolve in water and are not stored by the body to any great extent. These include vitamin C, or ascorbic acid, and all the B-vitamins.
- B1—Thiamin
- B2—Riboflavin
- B3—Niacin, which includes niacinamide and nicotinamide
- B6—Pyridoxine, which includes pyridoxal and pyridoxamine
- B12—Cobalamin
- Folic Acid
- B5—Pantothenic Acid
- Biotin
- Choline*
- Inositol*
- PABA*—Para-amino-benzoic acid

* *While essential vitamins for humans, these are not officially recognized as B-vitamins, but are considered part of the "B-complex" family.*

NOTE: *Niacin can be made in the body from the amino acid, tryptophan.*

The Fat-Soluble Vitamins dissolve in fat and in substances that dissolve fat. These vitamins are stored in the fatty parts of the liver and other tissues. The fat-soluble vitamins are:

- Vitamin A
- Vitamin D
- Vitamin E
- Vitamin K

Note: *Vitamin D is called "the sunshine vitamin" because when the ultraviolet rays from sunlight hit the skin, a form of cholesterol in the body is converted into vitamin D.*

What Increases Your Need for Vitamins? When you perspire, take diuretic drugs (such as high blood pressure medication), or have diarrhea, you lose an abnormal amount of water-soluble vitamins. Stress and exertion also deplete the body of these valuable nutrients. Actually, our supply of these vitamins is constantly being diminished by the activity of our own bodies. Therefore, if we are to maintain even reasonably good health, these vitamins have to be replaced on a routine basis.

A variety of factors can cause a person to expend, excrete, or malabsorb certain vitamins and minerals. Some of these are:

• tobacco	• salt	• estrogen
• sugar	• rancid fats	• cortisone
• mineral oil	• antibiotics	• aspirin
• antacids	• tranquilizers	• sleeping pills
• surgery	• sickness	• accidents
• diuretics	• laxatives	• polluted water
• fluoride	• pesticides	• food additives
• polluted air	• pregnancy	• extreme cold
• extreme heat	• nursing	• oral contraceptives
• emotional strain	• prescription drugs	• chlorinated water

Any one of these factors can cause the body to need an increase in vitamins and minerals. . . and most people today encounter one or more of these factors on a daily basis! We also must consider other factors that impact our lives today:

- the kinds of food you eat.
- how these foods are prepared or processed.
- the physical, mental, and emotional stress you experience.
- the environment in which you live and work, and the contaminants to which you are exposed.
- your unique, individually determined biochemical heredity pattern or genetic code.
- the type and amount of exercise you do, or do not do.
- the quality of soil in which your food was grown.
- the type of water you drink—distilled water has had all the minerals removed.

All of these factors affect your unique requirement level for any particular vitamin or mineral.

"Do I really need to take vitamin and mineral supplements?" This is a question I hear often. The good news is that I hear this question less today than several years ago. The general public is becoming much more informed about the need for vitamins and minerals. Many people now come to me with a list of products they have "heard about," eager for more information or advice related to their specific health concerns.

Still, a great many people seem to feel that they can get all of their daily requirements for vitamins and minerals from a "well-balanced diet" without taking additional supplements.

The diet we tend to think about as being well-balanced is one that came from our nation's agricultural heritage. Our great grandparents came from the farm, where they performed hard physical labor all day and consumed between 4,000 and 5,000 calories per day. They got their milk right from the cow and their fruit and vegetables from the garden. They ground their own whole grains and ate five or six times a day. They didn't need vitamin or mineral supplements because they received enough of these nutrients from the large amounts of natural and fresh foods they consumed.

Can't Burn all Those Calories. Most of us today can't consume those large amounts of natural and fresh foods like our ancestors. We don't do as much physical labor so we can't burn the extra calories or we'll gain weight. The food we eat today varies considerably in the amount of nutrients it contains, the way it is grown, the chemicals sprayed on it, how it is processed, and very often, in the way we store or prepare foods in our own kitchens.

Our farm-fed ancestors didn't eat the processed, man-made, synthetic fast food we consume today. For the most part, they did not need to supplement their diets. The foods of today are not the foods of our ancestors.

Not Getting the Minimum RDAs. Furthermore, the United States Department of Agriculture has stated that as many as one out of every two Americans are not getting the minimum RDAs (Recommended Dietary Allowances) as the result of their current diet. Even though these guidelines reflect a minimal level, one-half of our population falls below minimum![3]

In addition to that reported fact, government statistics have shown that fat consumption has increased by 30 percent and sugar consumption by 50 percent in the past several decades. The average American consumes approximately 120 pounds of sugar each year, which is about 1/3 pound a day.[4] Remember this is per every man, woman and child. Average means that some are eating less but many Americans are eating even more.

Top ten items purchased in grocery stores ranked by dollar volume as listed in the Top Ten Almanac are as follows:[5]

1	Marlboro® cigarettes
2	Coca Cola Classic®
3	Pepsi Cola®
4	Kraft® Processed Cheese
5	Diet Coke®
6	Campbell's® soup
7	Budweiser® beer
8	Tide® detergent
9	Folger's® coffee
10	Winston® cigarettes

You'll note there's not one whole food on this list! If the most popular purchases are nicotine, sugar, caffeine, and sodium-rich processed foods ... what can we expect in the way of health?

Other Studies Show:

- *Time* magazine has reported that only about nine percent of Americans manage to consume five servings a day of fruit and vegetables, according to the National Center for Health Statistics.
- A 1989 USDA survey of 21,500 people showed that over a three-day period, not one of them consumed 100 percent of the RDA for ten nutrients—the RDA already being too low, in my opinion.
- Surveys have shown that on the average, an elderly person takes between six and nine prescription drugs a day, many of which can rob the body of vitamins and minerals in a variety of ways such as increasing urinary excretion, blocking absorption, binding to nutrients and deactivating them, destroying nutrients, causing nutrients to be used up more rapidly, and increasing loss of nutrients in the stool.[6]

It seems the most intelligent decision a person can make today is to begin to take vitamin and mineral supplements on a daily basis.

When clients tell me they can't afford vitamins, which cost less than a cup of coffee or a soft drink, I tell them they can't afford not to take them! Vitamins and minerals are our best anti-aging insurance policy. I believe you'll agree with me as you read the tremendous research in the rest of this book.

The Safety of Vitamins

As we and others in the nutrition field fought the proposed legislation designed to require prescriptions for vitamins, the very popular radio commentator Paul Harvey joined in the fight. At stake was our right to sell, buy, and take the vitamins we want. The forces against the free access to vitamins claimed the American public was wasting its money on vitamins. The public said back, "It is my money to spend as I see fit." The tactic of the anti-access group then changed its emphasis to say that vitamins are dangerous and toxic. This has been their message for a number of years. At the core of this issue is if vitamins are turned into prescription drugs, pharmaceutical companies could charge a great deal more for them. Is it economics, far more than science, that fueled their concern?

When it comes to the safety of vitamins, Paul Harvey wrote in one of his columns:

- A recent eight-year study at 72 poison control centers revealed that sleeping pills and tranquilizers killed 460 people.
- Analgesics led to 715 deaths.
- Anti-depressants accounted for 805 fatalities.
- Cardiovascular drugs killed another 360.
- There were 2,500 people killed by accidental or intentional overdose of drugs.
- During that same eight years the number of people killed by vitamins was zero!
- There were no reported fatalities from taking vitamins either by children or adults.
- All suggest that vitamins, whatever their benefits, are 2,500 times safer than drugs.

Meanwhile, doctors who do recognize benefits from vitamin therapy are recommending them to overcome high cholesterol, to reduce cancer risk, to prevent or relieve many chronic health problems.[7]

Within the scientific community, Dr. Linus Pauling was a great champion in proclaiming the safety of vitamins, even when they are taken in large amounts. Side effects occur very infrequently and are rarely serious, and those which do occur often relate to factors other than the vitamins themselves.

Vitamins and Minerals Are Safe and Effective

Julian Whitaker, M.D., the very informed physician whom I have appeared with many times on the Trinity Broadcasting Network program "The Doctor's Night", wrote recently, "According to detailed analysis of all available data, there are over 10 million adverse reactions yearly from FDA-approved, over-the-counter, and prescription drugs. We are not talking about mild nausea or headaches. Between 60,000 and 149,000 people die per year from adverse drug reactions, according to the *Journal of the American Medical Association*. Each year, more Americans die after taking prescription drugs than died in the entire Vietnam war. This constitutes a real public health issue." [8]

Dr. Whitaker makes a very important point. "Only a single death related to a vitamin supplement was reported in the United States by the American Association of Poison Control Centers (AAPCC) in 1990. Only one death! After investigation by Citizens for Health, there is good reason to question whether this death was attributable to the supplement, as the young man suffered paranoid schizophrenia and was also taking six major drugs at the same time, along with the vitamin niacin." Whitaker said, "I personally would wager that his death was attributable to the six drugs that caused his liver damage." [9]

Abram Hoffer, M.D., Ph.D., said in the *Journal of Orthomolecular Medicine*: "Vitamins which are safe even in large doses have not been acceptable to the medical profession, and their negative side effects have been consistently exaggerated and over-emphasized, to the point that many of these so-called toxicities have been invented, without there being any scientific evidence that these side effects are real." [10]

A Growing Acceptance for Vitamins and Minerals

I had the honor of meeting Dr. Abram Hoffer, a Canadian psychiatrist and editor-in-chief of the *Journal of Orthomolecular Medicine*, one evening at an Alternative Cancer Treatment seminar. Dr. Hoffer is one of the pioneering medical doctors in the area of nutrition. He stated that almost every modern, acceptable treatment we see in medicine today seemed to require forty or more years of use and study before it became widely accepted. Dr. Hoffer said he started the clock in 1957 when he first published a paper describing the use of large doses of vitamin B3 (niacin) for the treatment of acute schizophrenia. He projected that by the year 1997 this information would become recognized as the best treatment for schizophrenia and that orthomolecular medicine would be accepted by the medical profession. Well, it hasn't happened yet! Indeed, the field of orthomolecular medicine stems from this paper of Dr. Hoffer's, as well as several others like it.

Dr. Hoffer and B6. Dr. Hoffer has also researched vitamin B6 (pyridoxine) and first published his studies on this important vitamin in 1975. He believes that 75 percent of people who are severely ill with mental disorders need much larger amounts of B6.

He writes: "As well as being mentally ill, these patients may have constipation and abdominal pains, unexplained fever and chills, morning nausea (especially if pregnant), low blood sugar, impotence or lack of menstruation, and nerve symptoms such as amnesia, tremor, spasms, and seizures. About one-third of all schizophrenic patients suffer from this need for very large amounts of the vitamin."[11]

Orthomolecular Medicine. It was actually Dr. Linus Pauling who defined the term "orthomolecular" and placed his immense scientific prestige and knowledge behind the concept. Orthomolecular medicine means using certain nutrients in much larger amounts than is customary to satisfy the excessive need for the nutrients at various sites in the body. Dr. Pauling's work on vitamin C has been one of the major factors in swaying public opinion—and the opinions of those in the scientific community—to take vitamins more seriously. Dr. Pauling first studied the impact of vitamin C on colds and flu, then in the treatment of cancer, and finally in the role vitamin C plays in preventing hardening of the arteries. I once heard Dr. Pauling say at a conference that if he had started his research with heart disease instead of cancer, he would have found the cure for heart disease. You will read more in the "Heart" chapter about Pauling's work, especially how vitamin C prevents the oxidation of fats in the arteries and is one of the main antioxidant vitamins.

Minerals

Just as with vitamins, never underestimate the importance of minerals to your total well-being.

People often think of minerals as relating only to teeth and bones, but minerals also preserve the vigor of the heart and brain, as well as the muscles and the entire nervous system. About five percent of your total body weight is mineral matter. They are found in your bones, teeth, nerve cells, muscles, soft tissues, and blood.

Minerals are important in the production of hormones and enzymes, in the creation of antibodies, and in keeping the blood and tissue fluids from becoming either too acidic or too alkaline.

Some minerals, such as sodium, potassium, and calcium, have electrical charges that act as a magnet to attract other electrically charged substances to form complex molecules, conduct electrical impulses along nerves, or transport substances in and out of the cells. In the blood and other fluids, minerals regulate the fluid pressure between cells and the blood. Minerals also bind to proteins and other organic substances and are found in red blood cells, all cell membranes, hormones, and enzymes, the catalysts of all bodily processes.[12]

Minerals are Essential for Human Health. The essential major minerals (sometimes called macro-nutrients or nutrients needed in larger amounts) include the following:

- calcium
- phosphorus
- potassium
- sulfur
- sodium
- chloride
- magnesium

Other essential minerals (also called micro-nutrients or trace elements) are found in the body in only small amounts. The most important trace elements are:

- iron
- zinc
- selenium
- manganese
- copper
- cobalt
- iodine
- molybdenum
- chromium
- boron
- vanadium[13]

Still other essential trace elements that appear to be important for other warm-blooded animals (although not specifically studied thoroughly in human beings yet) are such minerals as fluorine and silicon. Generally we have no problem getting enough of these in our diets. Still other trace amounts of the following minerals are usually found in the body, but little is known about how they affect the maintenance of normal bodily processes at this time: arsenic, barium, bromine, cadmium, germanium, strontium, gold, silver, aluminum, tin, nickel, bismuth, and gallium—several of these are actually known to be toxic, so their presence in the body may not reflect an element of health.

Mineral Deficiencies

Mineral or trace element deficiencies occur much more often than vitamin deficiencies. Those at increased risk for mineral deficiencies are people who eat low-calorie diets, the elderly, pregnant women, vegetarians, those who take certain drugs, including diuretics, and those living in areas where the soil has been depleted of certain minerals.

Vitamins are usually present in foods in similar amounts around the world, but this is not true for minerals. Geologic conditions make certain areas rich in minerals and trace elements, while the soil in other areas of the world are scarce in minerals and trace elements.

Minerals can work either together or against each other. Some compete for absorption. When this happens, a large intake of one mineral can actually produce a deficiency of another. This is especially true of the trace minerals iron, zinc, and copper. Some minerals can enhance the absorption and use of other minerals, as in the case of calcium, magnesium and phosphorus which all work together well.

Absorption of minerals is generally dependent on the body's particular needs.

Herbs

We often refer to herbs as "God's first pharmacy." Herbs have been valuable sources of natural medicine for thousands of years. They have had a remarkable history of curative effects, especially when used in a proper way.

Every plant on this earth is part of God's creation and has a purpose. One of the best arguments for saving the rain forest is that they may contain as yet undiscovered plants that may help to cure cancer, AIDS, and other killer diseases. Even as we must keep an eye to the future, we also know that a number of well-researched herbal products are already available today. Herbs known in various parts of the world—but which still have not been researched or accepted in our nation—may be valuable in treating various diseases. While herbal medicine is not the focus of this book, I do believe we should use the most researched herbal products when necessary.

In other chapters we will discuss a number of herbs, such as alfalfa, astragalus, cat's claw, echinacea, golden seal, garlic, ginkgo biloba, ginseng, hawthorn berry, valerian root, etc.

Mother Nature's Remedies

The leaves, flowers, bark, berries, or roots of plants are fast becoming the treatment of choice for millions of Americans. In fact, more than $1.6 billion worth of herbal products are sold each year in the United States alone.[14] Packaged as capsules, tablets, teas, concentrated extracts, tinctures, and salves, these botanicals, as they are also called, are a natural and safe alternative to drugs. The medicinal herbs are those valued in the treatment and prevention of illness. Herbs have been found to help in a variety of conditions, including viral infections such as influenza.

Herbs as Pharmaceutical Agents. Herbs contain powerful pharmaceutical agents. In fact, an estimated one-third of our pharmaceutical drugs are derived from plants. As an example, white willow bark led to aspirin, the opium poppy is the basis of the opiate narcotic drugs, the foxglove herb gave rise to Digitalis®, the heart drug; and more recently, the Pacific Northwest yew tree has been used to make Taxol®, a drug used to treat ovarian cancer. Two of the most useful chemotherapy drugs, Vincristine® and Vinblastin® are derived from the common plant Madagascar periwinkle (*Vinca rosea*).[15] French oncologist Dr. Leon Schwarzenberg has said that "twenty-eight of the thirty-two most commonly used modern chemotherapeutic drugs were discovered by chance and are derived from plants."[16]

A number of other drugs are extracted from plants. A danger arises, however, when the extracts no longer have the herbal components in their natural state.

Herbs as Preventive Measures. The medicinal herbs are valued not only for their ability to treat illness but also for their capacity to prevent illness, which is why some are recommended as a preventive measure. Herbs have great potential to improve the quality of a person's life, especially when they are combined with proper diet, nutritional supplements, rest, exercise, and a healthy mental, emotional, and spiritual approach to living. Many herbs are referenced throughout this book in connection with specific ailments.

Chapter 3

Building Immunity

and Longevity with Antioxidants

Live a Long Life by Preventing the Killer Diseases

"Every minute in your body, three billion cells die
and three billion cells are created! To properly replenish
these cells, your blood needs to contain forty
different chemicals, including oxygen, hormones,
enzymes, vitamins, and minerals. When any of these
are lacking, your body cannot make the necessary
repairs, and if deficiencies are not corrected,
disease will result and we age."
— **Gladys Lindberg**

Every day we're bombarded with substances that can cause damage to our bodies at the cellular level.

We are exposed repeatedly, and almost constantly in some cases, to unnecessary X-rays, radioactivity, the effects of a diminishing ozone layer in our atmosphere, smog, chemical products that give off volatile fumes, and even chemical dumping. Our homes are filled with toxic substances such as asbestos, vinyl chloride, and formaldehyde (found in plywood, particle board, paints, plastics, and detergents). We use dangerous chemical "bug bombs" to rid our homes of pests, and in the process, contaminate every area of our homes with toxic chemicals.

Alternative Medicine—The Definitive Guide explains how the radiant energy emitted by computer screens, television sets, microwave ovens, fluorescent lights, high voltage electric power lines that go over some of our homes, electric heating in the ceilings of some homes, and even the energy from electric blankets and heated water beds can interfere with the body's own electric field.

Perhaps the most widespread pollutant over which we have control is tobacco smoke, which has been cited repeatedly as a contributing cause of cancer . . . and still, people smoke.

Potential Dangers. Added to these potential dangers are preservatives and chemical additives in our foods, agricultural pesticides, chemical sprays, food processing, cured and processed meats and the tremendous amounts of sugar added to our food. Even mercury amalgam fillings in our teeth have been linked to a weakening of the immune system.

Then, if we add mental stress which we're subjected to everyday, it's easy to understand why "living" can be hazardous to one's health!

Regardless of the arguments that might be drawn related to the impact of any pollutants or energy sources, the net effect of *all* these forces striking our bodies from within and without on a daily basis must be seen as staggering. At no other time in history has the human population been bombarded by so many factors on a consistent basis, all of which "run down" our battery. Is it any wonder that we are seeing such a rapid increase in cancer, tumors, leukemia, infertility and congenital birth defects?

All of these pollutants weaken the body's ability to function, and in turn, make the body more susceptible to foreign invaders. These attacks ultimately impact the health of the individual cells in our body. What does exposure to these environmental toxins do to a cell? It causes free-radical damage which is one of the main theories on aging at the cellular level.

What Is a Free-Radical?

A free-radical is a molecule that has lost a vital piece of itself—one of its electrically charged electrons that normally orbit in pairs. To restore balance, the free-radical frantically tries to steal an electron from a nearby molecule or give away its unpaired electron. In doing so, it wreaks molecular havoc, careening into protein, fat, and the genetic DNA of cells, disfiguring and corroding them. If the target is fat, the radical can set off wildly destructive chain reactions that break down membranes, leaving cells to disintegrate. If the radical hits protein, it can destroy the cell's ability to function. If it hits DNA, it can cause mutations that incite cells to aberrant behavior. Over time, free-radical damage leaves the body aged and diseased.

In an analogy, Bruce N. Ames, Ph.D., University of California at Berkeley, likens the production of free-radicals to the smoke and soot by-products produced by a wood-burning fireplace. To carry the analogy further, the waste of a wood-burning fire is easily channeled away from your home's interior by your fireplace chimney, but in the body, free-radical by-products are not so easily eliminated. Certain free-radical scavengers must help remove these harmful free-radicals from the body.

They Grind us Down. Dr. Ames has said, "We need free-radicals to live, but they're also the bane of our existence.

Through free-radical reactions in our body, it's as though we're being irradiated at low levels all the time. They grind us down." He has calculated that each of our cells endures ten thousand oxidative hits every day from errant free-radicals, but that most of these cells are immediately repaired.[1]

The point to be made, of course, is that even if we lived in a pure environment, our own bodies would produce free oxygen radicals. There simply is no way to avoid their presence within the body.

Many free-radicals are produced in our personal environment, such as sunlight, smog, high altitude, exposure to X-ray, toxins in food and water, pollen, ozone, molds and dust, and so forth. We can't avoid free-radicals. They are everywhere. What we can do is attempt to diminish their impact on the body.

Causes Degenerative Diseases. Free-radical damage can impair the immune system, and result in various types of cellular damage. As might be expected, such cellular damage is associated with many of our degenerative diseases, Lou Gehrig's disease, arthritis, Alzheimer's disease, some types of cancer, heart attacks, hardening of the arteries, Parkinson's disease, cataracts, cerebral vascular changes that we know as senility, and many others.[2]

What Can We Do? Free-radicals are rendered harmless by antioxidants. Antioxidants are the "saviors" in this process. An antioxidant is a substance that can donate a sought-after electron to a free-radical without becoming dangerous itself. An antioxidant that comes into contact with a free-radical puts an end to the rampage of cellular and bodily destruction.

Antioxidants—They Can Prolong Life

Antioxidant literally means "against oxidation." Antioxidants are the good guys that continually combat the harmful effects of oxidation in the body. They are constantly on duty to render wayward free-radicals harmless. The net result of their work is that they prolong the life of cells, and thus, prolong life itself.

In the laboratory, antioxidants have been shown to prolong the life of mice. Denham Harman, M.D., who developed the free-radical theory of aging more than 40 years ago, discovered that sick old mice actually seemed to get younger when given massive doses of vitamin A. Although Harman has shown that resistance to disease decreases with age, these older mice developed fewer infections and their immune systems improved dramatically.[3]

I like to think of antioxidants as the "good guys" in the war against aging. They can prevent or repair damage to the cells. They are important nutrients in detoxifying the body and cleaning up harmful wastes. Your body makes special antioxidant enzymes, but you can also get many antioxidants in foods and nutritional supplements.

The major antioxidants are:

• Vitamin A • Vitamin C • Vitamin E • Selenium • Beta-Carotene

---

Other excellent antioxidants include:

- Bioflavonoids
- Ginseng
- Molybdenum
- Zinc
- L-Cysteine
- Melatonin
- Copper
- Ginkgo Biloba
- Pycnogenol®
- B-vitamins
  (*folic acid, riboflavin, B12*)
- Garlic
- Manganese
- Echinacea
- Milk Thistle
- Wheat and Barley Grass
- CoQ10 (*Coenzyme Q 10*)
- Alpha-Lipoic Acid
- Glutathione
- Grape Seed Extract
- Pine Bark Extract
- DHEA
- Carotenoids (*lycopene, beta-carotene, alpha-carotene, cryptoxanthin, lutein/zeaxanthin*)

Many of these antioxidants will be discussed in more detail throughout this book.

Knowing the Value of the Antioxidants for our Immune System

There are several thousand research articles in medical literature on the value of the antioxidants. I want you to see how we can incorporate this information into our lives.

Two antioxidants are variations of vitamin A:

■**Vitamin A**—known as retinol or retinyl. It is always found in animal products—such as liver, milk, eggs, butter, cream, and fish liver oil.

■**Carotenoids**—which we see most commonly as beta-carotene, is converted to vitamin A once inside the body. Typically found in carrots, sweet potatoes, and many other vegetables and fruit characterized generally by yellow/orange pigment. The body converts beta-carotene into vitamin A. We will first discuss vitamin A and then go back to carotenoids.

Dr. Sheldon Hendler reported, "Note that those with hypothyroidism and some with diabetes may not be able to efficiently convert beta-carotene to vitamin A and may thus assume a yellowish pigmentation in the skin even at lower doses. This pigmentation is not harmful in itself and will fade once beta-carotene intake is stopped or reduced."

"Those who note yellowish pigmentation while taking beta-carotene in moderate dose ranges and who have not previously been diagnosed as diabetic or as having hypothyroidism should be tested for these conditions."[4] Dr. Hendler also said he has seen a number of cases where low-dose beta-carotene supplementation has unmasked these diseases.

Carotenoids
Fruit and Vegetable Antioxidants

Virtually all carotenoids work as antioxidants to rid the body of potentially cell damaging free-radicals. High blood levels of carotenoids are usually associated with a lower risk of degenerative disease. Recent research suggests that carotenoids lower the risk of certain cancers such as lung, stomach, cervix, breast, oral and bladder cancer. According to cancer researcher, Gladys Block, Ph.D., an extensive and unimpeachable analysis of nearly 200 studies from 17 countries showed that eating fruit and vegetables regularly slashed your chances of getting cancer in half.

In at least twenty-one population-based studies, there is a 20 to 50 percent reduction in risk for many, but not all, cancers among those who are in the top quarter of fruit and vegetable intake, as compared to those in the bottom quarter. The researchers found the survival rates were much higher for women with lung cancer, endometrial cancer, cervical dysplasia (a precancerous condition of the uterine cervix), and they were less likely to develop pancreatic cancer.[5]

Carotenoids also appear to enhance the immune system and protect against age-related ailments such as stroke and heart disease.[6] Scientists have discovered more than 500 carotenoids; only 40 to 50, however, are found in the American diet, and only about 14 are actually absorbed and found in the bloodstream. See chart on next page for major carotenoids.[7]

Phytonutrients. Sometimes also called *phytochemicals*, either term simply refers to plant-derived nutrients. Carotenoids are phytonutrients, the nutritional elements that occur naturally in fruit and vegetables, giving them their distinctive yellow, orange and red colors. Green leafy vegetables are also high in carotenoids, but chlorophyll hides the yellow and orange pigments. Vegetables rich in carotenoids include carrots, tomatoes, sweet potatoes, broccoli, spinach and kale.

You may have heard the recent campaign to convince Americans to eat five servings a day of fruit and vegetables. As far as I am concerned, that's a minimum! Place your emphasis on organically grown fresh fruit and vegetables for maximum benefit.

Deeply colored fruit and vegetables are a sign that flavonoids and antioxidants are present! Red grapes and red onions have much more antioxidant value than green grapes and white onions. Blueberries contain an exceptionally high concentration of antioxidant flavonoids, as do strawberries, blackberries, bing cherries and boysenberries. Look for dark, richly colored fruit and vegetables in your market!

THE OTHER ANTIOXIDANTS:

Antioxidant	Potential Benefits	Where to Get it
Alpha-Lipoic Acid	Extends the effects of other antioxidants, including vitamins E, C, and glutathione.	Red meat, (possibly yeast).
Carotenoids *lycopene*	Reduces the risk of certain cancers and cardiovascular disease.	Tomatoes, guava, watermelon, apricots, pink grapefruit.
lutein *zeaxanthin*	Prevents age-related macular degeneration (an eye disease resulting in blindness.)	Spinach, broccoli mustard & collard greens, kale, hot chilies.
beta-carotene	Limits oxidation-type reactions and neutralizes free-radicals inside the cell; protects lipoproteins against oxidative damage.	Carrots, spinach, kale, sweet potatoes, tomatoes, papaya, apricots, melons.
alpha-carotene	Inhibits the production of skin, liver and lung cancer cells.	Pumpkin, cantaloupe, yellow & red peppers, carrots, corn.
cryptoxanthin	High levels are associated with a significant reduction in cervical cancer risk.	Peaches, tangerines, oranges, papaya, nectarines.
bioflavonoids	Decreases risk of cardiovascular disease and some cancers; enhances the effects of vitamin C.	Onions, buckwheat, most fruit, including grapes, plums, apples, cherries, white rind of citrus fruit.
Selenium	Reduces the risk of some cancers; enhances the effects of vitamin E.	Fish, liver, garlic, asparagus, Brazil nuts, mushrooms.[8]

Important Studies on the Value of Carotenoids in Relation to Cancer

- Scientists found that women with lung cancer who loaded up on vegetables nearly doubled their survival time compared with those eating the least amount of vegetables. They found that tomatoes, oranges, and broccoli appeared to improve survival times the most.[9]
- Deep colored fruit and vegetables were a major deterrent to endometrial cancer. Others found tomato eaters were five times less likely to develop pancreatic cancer.[10]
- A study over a 19-year period showed that a diet with low beta-carotene consumption caused a seven-fold increased risk of lung cancer.[11]
- Beta-carotene reversed the progression of premalignant lesions in the mouth.
- Post-menopausal women with a high intake of vitamin C reduced their risk of breast cancer by 16 percent, and vitamin C, vitamin E, and beta-carotene were also linked to protection against cervical cancer.[12]

There are many, many other studies that have associated carotenoids with a lower rate of cancer. It sounds to me as if the nutritional advice given for the last 40 years of "eat your dark green and yellow vegetables" and "drink your carrot juice" has had more merit than some have given it!

No adverse effects have been reported in people who have taken natural forms of beta-carotene for many years.[13]

Vitamin A (Retinol) Provides Valuable Protection

Even in the early days of vitamin research, discoveries pointed to the amazing infection-fighting properties of vitamin A (retinol, or retinyl), derived from fish liver oil. An early sign of vitamin A deficiency is damage to the linings of respiratory, digestive and urogenital tracts. Vitamin A helps to maintain protective barriers against infectious organisms entering the body by preserving the integrity of the skin and mucous membranes. This is why all good parents gave their children cod-liver oil (a natural source of vitamin A), it kept their children well.[14]

A vitamin A deficiency also increases susceptibility to viral, bacterial, and protozoal infections and makes these problems worse and more often fatal. In sum, vitamin A is vital to the health of our immune system![15]

Protective Against Cancer. Not only does vitamin A protect against infection, it appears to be one of the most important protective nutrients against cancer. Whether it is a result of its antioxidant properties or its ability to impact the organs and cells of the immune system, vitamin A appears to be one of our strongest allies against degenerative diseases which cause aging.[16]

- Since the 1920s, a deficiency in vitamin A has been linked to the development of cancerous tissues, particularly in the lining of the respiratory, gastrointestinal, and genitourinary tracts.[17]
- In a study of 16,000 men, a deficiency of vitamin A was clearly associated with an increased risk of cancer, independent of age or smoking habits. The authors of this study concluded that measures should be taken to increase serum-retinol levels in men and women as a possible means of reducing cancer.[18]
- Breast cancer patients with higher blood levels of vitamin A responded twice as well to chemotherapy as women with lower levels. Scottish researchers reported an association between improved chemotherapy response and higher vitamin A levels for patients with cancer of the breast, cancer of the bowel, and melanoma.
- Studies revealed that men with prostate cancer had low levels of vitamin A.[19]
- Lung cancer patients who were given extremely high doses of vitamin A for three weeks had increased cellular immunity.[20]

Extensive Surgery. Similar studies have shown that vitamin A is very helpful in stimulating immune function that is often suppressed with extensive surgery. Cancer patients received 1.5 million IUs, while surgical patients were given 300,000 to 450,000 IUs daily, just before major surgery, and for seven days after surgery. These patients showed increased T-cell activity several days after surgery, while the control group showed the usual immunosuppression. They had no signs of toxicity from these mega-doses, which of course were given under medical supervision and only for a short period.[21]

Is Vitamin A Toxic? The *American Journal of Clinical Nutrition* has reported that in adults, vitamin A toxicity is uncommon at doses less than 100,000 IU per day. In cases of genuine toxicity, when vitamin A is stopped, the symptoms generally are relieved within a short amount of time. In humans, five cases of birth defects have been reported in which the mother took high doses of vitamin A during pregnancy. However, the Journal reported, there was no clear cause-and-effect relationship between the vitamin A and the birth defect in any of these cases. The intake of high vitamin A may have been coincidental to other factors.[22]

According to the American Academy of Pediatrics, vitamin A toxicity generally does not occur unless someone consumes more than 1,000,000 IUs in a two to three-week period.[23]

Furthermore, you may find it interesting to know that the liver stores up to 1,000,000 IUs of vitamin A, so it is clear to see that this vitamin is vital to the body's health.

Symptoms of Overdose. It is important to recognize the symptoms of a vitamin A overdose, which includes chronic headache, vomiting, loss of hair, dryness of the mucous membranes, and liver damage. When the vitamin A is stopped, the condition clears up. For children and teens, cod liver oil is one of the best forms of natural vitamin A and D.

"There has never been a vitamin-caused fatality."
Biochemist Richard Passwater, Ph.D., says, "In fifty years of vitamin supplementation, there has never been a vitamin-caused fatality reported in an adult in the U.S., nor has there been a reported death of a child due to the accidental consumption of a jar of vitamins."[24]

Caution Urged with Vitamin A in Pregnancy. The *New England Journal of Medicine* reported in November 1995, that women who take large doses of vitamin A around the time of conception or early in their pregnancy run a higher than average risk of delivering infants with birth defects. This study was widely reported on all the television newscasts.

My two pregnant daughters-in-law called me in a panic, thinking they may have damaged their unborn babies since they were taking vitamin A. I reassured them that the vitamins they were taking only contained 7,500 IU of vitamin A in the form of fish oil, and the rest was from beta-carotene. I realized that a great many pregnant women must have felt fear about this also.

During the time of conception or during the first several months of pregnancy is the period considered the greatest risk. Taking excessive vitamin A at these times did not mean that a baby would definitely suffer defects, it only meant the risk was slightly higher.[25]

This study was based on women questioned from 1984 to 1987, so I question why it took over ten years for the information to be reported?

Vitamin A is essential for normal cellular differentiation and in regulating organ development in the fetus. The medical literature has also shown that a deficiency in vitamin A caused the same type of birth defect that excessive amounts may cause.[26]

According to one major survey, one-half of Americans consume 19 percent or less of the RDA for vitamin A, and one-fourth of the population consumes no more than 11 percent of the RDA.[27]

So, the conclusion drawn from the vitamin A and pregnancy study is, yes, there is a risk of taking too much vitamin A if you're pregnant, but the risk is generally overstated.[28]

The researchers recommended that pregnant women either limit their vitamin A consumption to 4,000 to 8,000 IU daily, or alternatively, take beta-carotene.[29] Beta-carotene is only converted into vitamin A when the body needs it, therefore, you do not have potential toxicity problems with this precursor to vitamin A.

Antioxidant Value
of Vitamin C for Geriatrics

Vitamin C is one of the most widely heralded antioxidants. The proper use of ascorbic acid (vitamin C) *throughout life* may provide the long-awaited breakthrough in geriatrics. Vitamin C can prolong the period of "vigorous and healthy maturity," not just the life span, according to Irwin Stone, M.D.[30]

Symptoms of Old Age. Years ago, Dr. Walter H. Eddy of Columbia University pointed out that many typical signs of old age are actually symptoms of subclinical scurvy! These include wrinkles or loss of skin elasticity, loss of teeth, and brittleness of bones. He theorized that the scurvy-preventing properties of vitamin C are required *even more* as a person ages, because absorption is often poorer with advancing years and much of this vitamin is destroyed by the intestine when the stomach fails to produce normal amounts of hydrochloric acid.[31]

Vitamin C:
Infections and Intracellular Cement

Vitamin C is easily destroyed by light and air, and is absent from most cooked or canned foods. Also, many of the blood-thinning drugs that older people take may interfere with vitamin C. Research has pointed toward the need to increase the vitamin C dosage as the years pass. You see, although you may be getting enough vitamin C to prevent scurvy in its grossest forms, you may lack sufficient vitamin C to ward off colds, to minimize aging, and to prevent cancer, infections, and other diseases.

Consider for a moment that most animals produce between 1,000 and 20,000 mg of vitamin C every day in their bodies, and animals do not have heart attacks and strokes. (Humans *do not manufacture vitamin C in their bodies and must obtain it from outside sources.*)

Vitamin C may well be one of the best life-extending and anti-aging products available to us, yet because it is so inexpensive and completely non-toxic, many people ignore its value.

Vitamin C is a potent broad-spectrum, non-toxic virus fighter when used in large doses. One of vitamin C's most important functions is the synthesis, formation, and maintenance of a protein-like substance called collagen. Collagen is the "cement" that supports and holds tissues and organs together, much like steel rods in reinforced concrete.

The late Fred Klenner, M.D., one of the pioneering authorities on the clinical application of vitamin C, regularly gave large amounts of vitamin C by injection to his patients with meningitis, encephalitis (inflammation of the brain), polio, viral pneumonia, pesticide contamination, and many other serious diseases. Many of Dr. Klenner's patients were not expected to live at the time he began giving them vitamin C therapy. However, with vitamin C given in massive amounts, sometimes around the clock, a good percentage of them recovered quickly and were discharged from the hospital in three or four days! Antibiotics had been given previously to these same patients without success.[32]

Virus Fighter. Dr. Irwin Stone has written about Dr. Klenner's work:"The main value of his work is in showing that any active viral disease can be successfully brought under control with ascorbic acid (vitamin C) if the proper large doses are used. It is inconceivable, but true, that Klenner's pioneering work has been almost completely ignored; no large-scale tests have been made to explore the exciting possibilities of his provocative clinical results."

Dr. Stone continued, "Millions of dollars of research money have been spent in unsuccessful attempts to find a non-toxic, effective virus fighter, and all sorts of exotic chemicals have been tried. All the while, harmless, inexpensive, and non-toxic ascorbic acid has been within easy reach of these investigators. More than *ten thousand studies* over the past four or five decades have shown vitamin C to be effective in battling a long list of human ailments. It might prove to be the 'magic bullet' for the control of viral diseases." [33]

The Role Vitamin C Plays. Through the years, a number of people have said that vitamin C is excreted in the urine and those taking large amounts of supplements are wasting their money. The man who won the Nobel Prize for Medicine in 1937 for his isolation of vitamin C and flavonoids, Albert Szent-Gyorgyi, M.D., Ph.D., was one of the most respected and honored biochemists of the 20th century. He contends that his research shows that vitamin C transduces protein into a living state and enables it to perform in our bodies. He has written, "The more ascorbic acid is available, the better the protein will work. . . . The ascorbic acid ingested by man is *excreted only partly with his urine. Its greatest part simply disappears!* What happened to it was a mystery. My studies indicate that it is incorporated into the living machinery!"[34]

This wise and honored scientist, who died at the age of 93, also discovered the flavonoids. He gave a friend with bleeding gums crude vitamin C from lemon and his condition cleared up. When the problem reappeared, he gave an even purer form of vitamin C and expected even better results. But the purer vitamin C did not work. Szent-Gyorgyi then isolated the *flavonoid* portion, the white part on an orange or grapefruit rind, gave it to his friend, and the problem cleared up. He named the flavonoids, vitamin P, but it was not considered a true vitamin and was abandoned.

Dr. Szent-Gyorgyi saw vitamin C as a cohesive force that holds living structure together. He said, "One should not wait for the application of this vitamin until one gets ill, trying to put the situation right by taking big doses. We should take it all the time." He also commented: "I strongly believe that a proper use of ascorbic acid can profoundly change our vital statistics, including those for cancer."[34]

Vitamin C and Cancer. Some significant studies have been done that show large doses of vitamin C have a life-extending effect for patients with advanced cancer, as well as a preventive effect. Gladys Block, Ph.D., epidemiologist at the University of California summarized more than 140 large-scale population studies on the relationship between vitamin C or vitamin C-rich foods and cancer. With possibly fewer than five exceptions, every study pointed toward a positive benefit from vitamin C, with more than 110 studies finding statistically significant reduction in the risk of virtually all kinds of cancer with a high intake of vitamin C.[35]

Cancer patients seem to have a much greater requirement for vitamin C than normal healthy individuals, apparently because all available vitamin C is mobilized by the body in its effort to boost natural resistance and repel invasive malignant growth.[36]

Vitamin C Dosages. The older we become, the less we are able to store and use vitamin C, and thus, we need to increase our intake of vitamin C.

Dr. Pauling recommended ten grams (10,000 mg) of vitamin C be taken daily for cancer patients. Most animals manufacture about this amount, calculated to the body weight of a human being. Pauling believed that if animals naturally make this amount, it is because they need it in these quantities to keep them in strong health. Timed release is not recommended in these high doses. The preferred way to take high doses (10 grams per day), would be to divide the vitamin C throughout the day. Make sure to take it with food. You may also use the buffered form in which minerals are combined with vitamin C to make it non-acidic. A healthy individual would do well with 3 to 6 grams of vitamin C a day.

Grape Seeds & Pycnogenols®
Contain Free-Radical Scavengers

A group of plant flavonols exert many health promoting effects. Related to bioflavonoids but possessing different health benefits, flavonols form unique condensed molecules that have a remarkable affinity for collagen protein, and act as powerful free-radical scavengers. Marcia Zimmerman, M.Ed., C.N., explained to me that because of their tendency to form highly active condensed clusters, Dr. Jacques Masquelier, the French scientist who discovered them, named them 'Pycnogenols.'[37] Since that time they have been referred to as *oligomeric proanthocyanidins* (OPCs), the American name, and *leukocyanidins* and *procyanadolic oligomers* (PCOs), the French name.

Although OPCs exist in many plants, as well as in red wine and dark grape juice, commercially available sources of OPC include extracts from grape seeds and the bark of the maritime (Landes) pine bark, trade-marked as Pycnogenol® by Horphag Overseas Ltd. There is also an entire complex of proanthocyanidins found in a variety of plants including pine bark, grape seed, lemon tree bark, peanuts, cranberries, and citrus peels.

Desirable Effects. OPC complexes are potent antioxidants and free-radical scavengers that help prevent "oxidative" damage, which has been linked to the aging process. Because of their antioxidant activity, OPCs are used in Europe to treat a number of ailments: vein and capillary disorders including venous insufficiency, varicose veins, capillary fragility, and vascular disorders of the retina. Perhaps the most significant use of OPCs will be in the prevention of atherosclerosis (hardening of the arteries from cholesterol deposits) and the resulting complications of heart disease and strokes.

In vitro (in a test tube or other equipment) studies measured the antioxidant activity of OPCs as 20 to 50 times stronger than that of vitamin C and vitamin E, respectively. From a cellular perspective, OPCs have the unique ability to cling to cellular proteins, strengthening and protecting them. This physical characteristic, along with OPCs ability to protect against both water and fat-soluble free-radicals, provides incredible protection to the cells against free-radical damage, according to Dr. Murray and Dr. Passwater.[38]

Lowers Cholesterol in Animals. In addition to preventing damage to the lining of the artery caused by cholesterol, OPC extracts have actually been shown to lower blood cholesterol levels and to shrink the size of cholesterol deposits in the arteries of animals. They also prevent destructive enzymes (elastase and collagenase) from eroding arterial walls, according to Dr. Passwater. Presumably they may exert similar benefits in humans.

The Value of OPCs (Grape Seed Extract and Pycnogenol®). Dr. Richard Passwater has said that they "can help protect you from approximately eighty diseases, including heart disease, cancer, arthritis, and most other non-germ diseases that are linked to the deleterious chemical action of free-radicals.... In addition to its antioxidant protection that slows the damage associated with aging, Pycnogenol® restores elasticity and smoothness to skin via its influence on skin protein formation. What is even more exciting is that Pycnogenol® is more than a powerful antioxidant, it nourishes blood cells, blood vessels, and the skin." [39]

OPCs are unique because they may help alleviate hay fever and other allergies by reducing histamine production, providing relief for allergy sufferers. They strengthen capillaries, prevent bruising, improve peripheral circulation, reduce varicose veins, and improve capillary resistance and permeability. These flavonols are also metal chelators.[40]

Recommended Dose. You will find several Pycnogenol® and grape seed extracts in your nutrition store. These are both excellent products and may be added to your nutritional program, along with your complete vitamin and mineral formulas. The current suggested dosage for both is 1 mg per pound of body weight, so a 130 lb woman would take three, 50 mg capsules.[41] Be sure to look for a high percentage of proanthocyanidin content on the label. Grape Seed extract is a popular choice for obtaining OPCs since it is less expensive than Pycnogenol®.

The Amazing Benefits of Vitamin E on Immunity

Vitamin E (*alpha tocopherol*) is a powerful antioxidant which seems to have a number of immune-protective and immune-stimulating effects. It protects against free-radicals and blocks some of the negative prostaglandins (a group of hormone-like fatty acids produced in small amounts in the body) that slow down the immune system. Vitamin E also protects cell membranes, thereby making them more difficult for viruses to attack.[42]

Aging and Immune Response. Aging is associated with changes in the immune response, which can contribute to increased incidence of infectious disease and tumors in the elderly. Although all aspects of the immune system are affected, the main alterations occur in the cellular area of the immune system.[43]

It Recharged Their Immunity. Nutritional manipulation of the immune system is the most practical way of delaying or reversing the age-associated changes in the immune system. A study reported at a seminar conducted by the N.Y. Academy of Science showed even though the immune response declined with age, it reverted almost to the level of young people after administering 400 to 800 IUs of vitamin E. A level of vitamin E greater than the RDA has been shown to enhance the immune system and reduce the incidence of age-associated diseases. For most of the healthy elderly subjects studied, it "recharged" their immunity, giving their bodies the ability to produce higher white cell counts when faced with infection. The proliferation of white blood cells that fight infection increased by 10 to 50 percent within thirty days. Some functions improved as much as 80 to 90 percent.[44]

Vitamin E and Cancer Protection. Vitamin E has been shown to lower the risk of breast cancer, epithelial cancer and cancer due to carcinogens. In fact, one study found that the group of women with the lowest blood serum level of vitamin E had four to five times the risk of developing stomach cancer, cancer of the pancreas, and cancer of the urinary tract.[45]

Another study showed that vitamin E levels in the blood were lower in the patients that developed lung and colorectal cancers than in the group that did not.[46]

Vitamin E Dosage. Many authorities agree that a person should take 400 IUs to 1,200 IUs of vitamin E from natural d-alpha tocopherol daily.

NOTE: If you have high blood pressure, you should consult your physician before increasing your intake beyond 800 IUs, due to its blood thinning properties. If you are using anti-coagulation drugs, or have a pre-existing hypertension condition, or any other medical problem, you should first consult your physician before taking larger doses of vitamin E supplements.

High Intensity Exercise and Free-Radicals. While we were attending a meeting of the National Nutritional Foods Association, my husband Don and I had the opportunity to meet Kenneth Cooper, M.D., founder of the Cooper Aerobics Center in Dallas, Texas, and the author of *Antioxidant Revolution*. Dr. Cooper is the father of the worldwide aerobics movement that started America running. He has found in recent years that high-intensity exercise, the type of training that athletes undertake, may actually produce an excess of free-radicals, which leads to disease. Many veteran distance runners have died of cancer, heart attacks, and other chronic diseases.

Dr. Cooper acknowledges that strenuous exercising generates large numbers of free-radicals as a by-product of deep or "heavy" breathing. He strongly recommends that those who exercise aerobically take the three major antioxidants: vitamins C, E, and beta-carotene as the most effective way to combat or reduce the production of free-radicals throughout the body. He has reported that vitamin E supplements prevent much of the free-radical damage, particularly to the DNA (deoxyribonucleic acid) where mutations can lead to cancer.[47]

Vitamin E Prevented DNA Damage. In a series of experiments at the University of Ulm, Germany, Gunter Speit, M.D., has found that only the consistent daily consumption of 1,200 IUs of vitamin E daily prevented DNA damage from exercise.[48] What valuable information for athletes or those of us involved in aerobics classes!

Dr. Cooper's extensive research has also shown that thirty minutes of low-intensity exercise three to four times a week is more healthy than strenuous exercise, and it can help reduce mortality from all causes. This amount of exercise sounds "livable" to me. More information on Dr. Cooper's program will be found in Chapter 7.

The Tremendous Benefits from Selenium

Selenium is a powerful antioxidant and a valuable protective agent against cancer, coronary artery disease, strokes, and heart attacks. It also plays a very important role in helping to reduce the incidence of many diseases associated with aging.[49]

Selenium can stimulate increased antibody response to germ infections when combined with vitamin E. In research conducted by Soviet scientists, this antibody response increased as much as thirty-fold in some studies.[50]

Selenium and vitamin E work together synergistically. Most researchers study the effects of only one nutrient at a time, and can easily miss the value of the combined effects. Generally speaking, vitamin E and selenium do not replace each other, but work best when taken together.

More than 400 research and scholarly articles have documented the role of selenium in cancer prevention. Many of these studies have found that people with low selenium levels also tended to have low vitamin E levels.

Protective Against Cancer. Studies in the early 1970s revealed that selenium was protective against cancer in laboratory animals. Dr. Gerhard Schrauzer of the University of California at San Diego and Dr. Richard Passwater conducted a series of experiments that showed an optimal selenium intake reduced the incidence of spontaneous breast cancer in susceptible female mice from 82 percent to

10 percent merely by adding selenium to their drinking water.

Dr. Schrauzer said: "If every woman in America started taking selenium (supplements) today, or had a high-selenium diet, within a few years the breast cancer rate would decline drastically."[51]

Dr. Schrauzer also remarked that if a breast cancer patient has low selenium levels in her blood, her tendency to develop metastases (other tumors spreading from the first) is increased, her possibility for survival is diminished, and her prognosis in general is poorer than if she had normal blood selenium levels.

I had the honor of meeting Dr. Schrauzer at an Alternative Cancer Treatment Seminar. His research results and recommendations should be shouted from the housetops! Everyone at the seminar agreed that all women should be taking selenium as a preventive measure.

And now finally, in December, 1996, the *Journal of the American Medical Association* (*JAMA*) researcher, Larry Clark, Ph.D., presented convincing evidence that supplemental selenium could reduce cancer death rates by as much as fifty percent. This study was the culmination of almost 40 years of research supporting the cancer-preventive aspects of selenium.[52]

In sum, selenium not only appears to be a preventive agent, but also a therapeutic agent in cancer treatment.

Selenium Dosage. A general recommendation is that people take 200 to 400 mcg (micrograms, not milligrams) daily as a supplement. Dr. Passwater has recommended giving 600 mcg per day to some patients with cancer. Even after taking this dose for years, patients had no toxic side effects. If you have cancer, suggest that your physician check your blood level to determine if you should take or increase your selenium. This is one trace mineral that you should not take more than is recommended. More is not necessarily better.

"New" Lipoic Acid Prevents Oxidative Damage

It has taken a long time for the concept of free-radicals to be accepted as a disease-causing agent. But, it was also a long time before Louis Pasteur's germ theory was widely accepted. A free-radical is just as deadly as a germ, but in a different way. Of course, neither one germ nor one free-radical presents a grave danger by itself. It's when these free-radicals multiply and create chain reactions that they cause damage over time, altering bodily functions and causing degenerative diseases which impact aging.

Your body's chemistry is dependent upon oxygen, and yet normal body processes—metabolism, respiration, and so forth—create harmful oxygen-containing molecules as by-products. Fortunately, we now have many antioxidants, including lipoic acid, to protect us against these byproducts of normal metabolism. In fact, antioxidants may eventually play a significant role in the treatment of arthritis, AIDS, diabetic retinopathy, and other health conditions.[53]

Lipoic acid, or alpha-lipoic acid, protects the liver and detoxifies tissues of heavy metals such as excessive iron and copper, and the toxic metals cadmium, lead, and mercury.

Lipoic acid also has the unique ability to enhance the antioxidant power of vitamins C, E, and glutathione (an amino acid) in the body, creating an antioxidant network that gives you more complete protection against damaging free-radicals. Unlike other valuable antioxidants, lipoic acid is both water and fat-soluble, so it can be used throughout the body.

An Exciting Antioxidant. Lipoic acid is an important link in the vital antioxidant network, and it is multifunctional. There are hundreds of studies over forty years revealing how lipoic acid performs many functions in the body, but it has only recently been noticed by the public. It has been shown to energize metabolism, to be a key compound for producing energy in the muscles, and it is important for everything we do, from physical activity to thinking. Lipoic acid unlocks energy from food calories and directs these calories away from fat production and into energy production.

The excitement about this nutrient can be seen in the many recent studies focusing on how lipoic acid improves the physique, combats free-radicals, protects our genetic material, slows aging, helps protect against heart disease, cancer, cataracts, diabetes, and many other diseases. It is also being studied in the treatment of Parkinson's disease and Alzheimer's disease. Lipoic acid is especially suited to protect nerve tissues against oxidative damage.[54]

Diabetes Link. Diabetics (both insulin and non-insulin dependent) will be excited to learn that lipoic acid has been used successfully for nearly thirty years in Germany, not only to normalize blood sugar levels, but to protect against the damage caused by diabetes. According to Dr. Passwater, it has reduced the secondary effects of diabetes, including damage to the retina, cataract formation, nerve and heart damage, and it also increases energy levels.

Study after study reported that lipoic acid safely regenerates damaged nerves, protects through its antioxidant and antiglycemic actions, and is the agent of choice for the prevention of diabetic complications, including neuropathy (damage to the peripheral nerves which connect the central nervous system), cardiomyopathy (any disease of the heart muscle), and retinopathy (disorder of the retina).[55]

Lipoic acid improves the blood flow in nerve tissues, improves glucose utilization in the brain, and improves basal ganglia function. The researchers observed no adverse effects from the high dosage of 600 mg per day of lipoic acid for diabetes.[56]

It is imperative that diabetics monitor their blood sugar levels closely and make appropriate adjustments to their medication.

Natural Sources. At this time the richest source of naturally-occurring lipoic acid is red meat. A dietary supplement may be important for vegetarians and those cutting down on red meat. It is also present in certain plants, such as potatoes. Under normal conditions, our bodies contain small amounts of lipoic acid, but it may not be a sufficient level to provide optimal protection from free-radicals.

Lipoic Acid Dosage. The typical preventive, daily supplementation range for healthy adults appears to be 20 to 50 mg. Higher amounts may be recommended by health care providers. There are no clinical, toxicological, or other studies that have shown a serious adverse effect from lipoic acid supplementation. It has been used for more than three decades at high dosages (300 to 600 mg a day) to treat diabetic neuropathy. A toxic dose, in animals of several species, has been noted but this dose translated to 30,000 to 37,500 mg (30–37.5 grams) for a 165-pound human.[57]

Lipoic acid supplementation is not recommended for pregnant women, until further studies are completed.

Zinc Promotes T-Cell Immunity

Zinc is an extremely important antioxidant mineral that is an immune stimulant, specifically promoting T-cell immunity. Individuals with low zinc levels have been found to have lowered resistance, atrophied thymus glands, and a reduced number of mature T-cells. Under these conditions, many immune functions are likely to be impaired, including anti-bacterial activity of your T-cells (from the thymus) and B-cells (from the bone marrow).

More than two hundred enzymes or "biologic catalysts" require zinc for their activity, including the enzymes involved in the production of nucleic acids DNA and RNA. In addition, zinc lends its hand to form the so-called zinc fingers, which allow proteins to bind specifically to nucleic acids. Zinc also plays a role in the structure and function of cell membranes.[58] Upon the first sign of cold and sore throat symptoms, zinc has the ability to shorten and decrease the severity of colds when taken in the form of zinc lozenges. However, it is more generally known as the "clear skin" mineral.

Benefits of Coenzyme Q 10

Coenzyme Q 10, more commonly referred to as CoQ10, appears to be a vital catalyst in the creation of the energy that cells need for life. Dr. Karl Folkers has shown that CoQ10 fights aging by stimulating immunity. Immunoglobulin or antibody G (IgG), the major antibody in the blood, rose significantly in patients receiving oral doses of 60 milligrams of CoQ10 daily. The rise of antibodies usually happened between one and three months after the treatment began.[59]

Breast Cancer: The treatment of breast cancer with CoQ10 was reported at the Eighth International Symposium on Biomedical and Clinical Aspects of Coenzyme Q 10, held in Stockholm, Sweden.

Knud Lockwood, M.D., and Karl Folkers, Ph.D., treated 32 "high risk" breast cancer patients with high doses of antioxidants, essential fatty acids, and CoQ10.

"No patient died and all expressed a feeling of well-being," wrote the researchers. "These clinical results are remarkable since about 4 deaths would have been expected. Now, after 24 months, all still survive; about 6 deaths would have been expected."

Six of the 32 patients showed partial tumor remission. In one, the dosage of CoQ10 was increased from 90 mg to 390 mg daily. Thirty days later, the tumor could no longer be felt, and 60 days later a mammogram could not detect any tumor at all.

Another high risk case was treated with 300 mg of CoQ10 after undergoing non-radical breast surgery. Three months later, no cancerous tissue could be detected.[60]

Heart and Brain: The most important information about CoQ10 is its heart protection quality which you can read about in Chapter 7.

In addition, CoQ10 has been linked to protection of the brain. Researchers believe it is important in protecting the cells' mitochondria, which may result in helping prevent degenerative brain diseases such as Alzheimer's disease, Lou Gehrig's disease, and gradual loss of memory and brain function usually associated with aging. CoQ10 is thought to be one of the few substances that can actually penetrate and restore vitality to the mitochondria, according to Dr. Denham Harman, a leading free-radical researcher.[61]

Unfortunately, the body's production of CoQ10 begins to decline around age twenty, often leaving people seriously deficient by middle age, when the body needs to fight off aging diseases.

Men, you may want to read about the importance of CoQ10 and impotence in Chapter 12.

CoQ10 Dosage. The recommendation is usually 30 to 60 mg a day, for generally healthy people. Some suggest 90 to 120 mg for those who want to prevent signs of aging or have heart problems.

One of the best aspects of CoQ10 appears to be that the substance has virtually no side effects. It is one of the safest substances ever tested, even at very high doses. No significant toxicity in animal or long-term human studies have been recorded.[62]

Glutathione
Is a Major Enemy of Free-Radicals

Glutathione is manufactured in the liver by three naturally occurring amino acids, *cysteine*, *glutamic acid* and *glycine*. Glutathione is a powerhouse antioxidant. A lack of it in the cells is considered by some researchers to be the foremost cause of premature aging. It protects every cell, tissue and organ in the body. In one study, those with 20 percent higher blood levels of glutathione had only one third the rate of arthritis, high blood pressure, heart disease, circulatory symptoms, diabetes, stomach symptoms, and urinary tract infections when compared to those with lower glutathione levels. Dr. Mara Julius, the author of this finding at the University of Michigan, said, "Even in very old age, people with the highest levels of glutathione bounce back from diseases and accidents the same way much younger people do. They are just more vigorous."[63]

The Anti-Aging Benefits of Glutathione
Jean Carper reports that glutathione:

- protects from cancer
- rejuvenates immunity
- blocks damage to the cells by breaking down free-radicals
- rejuvenates old and weak immune systems
- prevents lung injury from free-radicals
- fights against the free-radicals produced by rancid fat
- keeps blood cholesterol from oxidizing and becoming toxic
- cures some forms of Type II diabetes
- helps prevent macular degeneration
- maintains healthy immune function [64]

The Master Antioxidant: John T. Pinto of Memorial Sloan Kettering Cancer Center in New York calls glutathione the "master antioxidant" because it protects every cell, tissue, and organ in the body. He says, "If you deplete glutathione, the cell disintegrates and loses its immune activity. If you add glutathione to that ailing cell, it regenerates and becomes immuno-efficient."[65]

Glutathione protects the body against powerful natural and man-made oxidants. It helps the liver detoxify poisonous chemicals, and even helps protect the integrity of red blood cells. It helps prevent macular degeneration, and age-related eye disease.[66] It is also a neurotransmitter which you may read more about in Chapter 6.

Another researcher has noted that glutathione can deactivate at least thirty cancer-causing substances.[67] Glutathione works synergistically with vitamin C and selenium. Glutamine (an amino acid) also helps boost blood levels of glutathione. Digestive juices can break down supplemental glutathione into other substances, so we must make certain to consume the chemical building blocks that form glutathione in the body. In fact, taking the amino acid supplement glutamine is apt to boost your blood levels of glutathione much better than taking glutathione directly.

Douglas Wilmore, M.D., a professor of surgery at Harvard Medical School has researched glutamine, the amino acid which can boost glutathione levels, and says, "It's an awesome anti-aging agent, essential for anyone who is ill or under stress. It strengthens immunity, hastens recovery, and actually rejuvenates muscles weakened by wasting illnesses." He said to make sure you take it with vitamin C and selenium.[68]

How much to take? Glutamine is relatively inexpensive and readily available, and it greatly enhances the body's production of glutathione. Glutamine appears safe even in high doses. Daily doses of up to 40,000 mg have been taken under the supervision of a physician with no noticeable adverse effects, says Dr. Wilmore. A typical dosage among researchers who have studied this substance is 2,000 to 8,000 mg daily in tasteless powder form, and more if fighting an infection.[69]

Glutamine can be found in your nutrition store in 500 or 1,000 mg capsules or powder form.

Glutathione is found in whole fruit and vegetables, walnuts, orange juice, and fresh meat. Especially rich sources are raw avocado, watermelon, fresh asparagus, grapefruit, and baked acorn squash.

Important Herbs to Build Immunity

There are a number of herbs that appear to build immunity. A few important ones you may want to consider are these:

- Astragalus
- Echinacea
- Golden seal
- Cat's Claw
- Garlic
- Milk Thistle

Astragalus Is an Immune Stimulant

Astragalus (*Astragalus membranaceus*) is a commonly used traditional herb in Chinese medicine, used for three thousand years for its properties that produce resistance to disease. It is an immune system stimulant, and Chinese researchers have reported success in using it with cancer patients to offset some of the immune suppressing effects of radiation and Western cancer drugs.[70]

American researchers at M.D.Anderson Hospital and Tumor Institute in Houston, Texas, have been working with crude extracts and a specific active component of astragalus. The compound, a polysaccharide, has been shown to be highly effective in restoring immune functions to normal levels in test animals whose immune systems were suppressed by modern drugs.[71]

Astragalus is called an "adaptogen" and has been credited with producing long life for cells. Research shows that astragalus increases the strength of T-cells. It seems to protect the cells even when chemotherapy is used. When added to a cancer program, the survival time reportedly doubled among patients who received herbal therapy that included astragalus, as compared with those who received only standard chemotherapy and radiation.[72]

This herb also reportedly boosts the numbers and activity of T-cells, the roving white blood cells that eliminate bacteria and viruses. It is particularly effective in warding off flu and some respiratory infections.[73]

It is also used to increase resistance to disease, *but not while you are sick*. It is considered the best herb in Chinese medicine to strengthen resistance. Master herbalist Janet Zand recommends an echinacea and golden seal combination for one week, then switching to astragalus one week, alternating back and forth for increased resistance to infection, especially during the cold and flu season.

Echinacea:
A Significant Immune Stimulant

Echinacea (*Echinacea angustifolia* and *purpurea*) is also known as the Purple Coneflower. Researchers in Europe and the Far East have studied two varieties of this plant extensively and have found significant immune-stimulating properties.

Macrophages are the cells that kill and destroy bacteria, viruses, other infectious agents and cancer cells.[74] Echinacea increases natural killer cell activity, antibody binding, and levels of circulating white blood cells primarily responsible for defending against bacteria. It also exhibited interferon like properties, and is used in the treatment of influenza and herpes, strep throat and infected lymph glands.[75]

It is among the most powerful and effective remedies against all kinds of bacteria and viral infections. It has antibiotic, anti-viral, and anti-inflammatory-like properties, without any reported cases of toxicity.

Add echinacea to your list of herbal products to keep on hand. Herbalists advise *not* to use echinacea for a long period of time, otherwise it loses it effectiveness. It is better to alternate one or two weeks on, then one or two weeks off. Tinctures of echinacea are concentrated herbal extracts. Follow the instructions on the label.

Golden Seal
Has Good Antibacterial Properties

Another herb native to North America, golden seal (*Hydrastis canadensis*), has been used medicinally to soothe mucous membranes that line the respiratory, digestive, and genitourinary tracts. Its major compound, *berberine*, exhibits a broad spectrum of antibiotic activity. It also helps against bacteria, protozoa, and various fungi. Plus, it has been shown to activate macrophages (the cells that destroy bacteria, viruses, and tumor cells).[76]

Golden seal has been used in the treatment of infections involving the mucous membranes, such as strep throat, sinusitis, bronchitis and urinary tract infections. It helps in inflammation of the gallbladder and stimulates the secretion of bile.[77]

Generally speaking, golden seal is non-toxic, but it should not be used by pregnant women or for long periods of time. This is a potent herb for fighting bacterial infection, especially when combined with echinacea.

Cat's Claw May Be a "Wonder Herb"

Much is presently being written about cat's claw (*Uncaria tomentosa*). It is also known as '*una de gato*'. This unique herb is actually a high climbing vine found in the highlands of the Peruvian rain forest. It has been used for hundreds, perhaps thousands, of years by the Ashanica Indians for a wide range of health problems. According to research conducted in many nations, evidence suggests that cat's claw is beneficial in the treatment of cancer, arthritis, bursitis, rheumatism, genital herpes, herpes zoster, allergies, ulcers, systemic candidiasis, PMS, irregularities of the female cycle, environmental toxic poisoning, numerous bowel and intestinal disorders and organic depression.[78]

Brent W. David, D.C., has been working with cat's claw in the United States and has reported its remarkable ability to cleanse the entire intestinal tract and help patients who suffer from many stomach and bowel disorders, including Crohn's disease, diverticulitis, leaky bowel syndrome, colitis, hemorrhoids, gastritis, ulcers, parasites, and intestinal flora imbalance. In its healing ability and benefits to the immune system, cat's claw appears to have so many therapeutic applications that it far surpasses many well-known herbs.[79]

Don't Forget Garlic!

Our ancestors used roots and herbs in abundance. Garlic and onions, particularly, were staples. Germs do not like garlic; in fact, they cannot live in its presence. Ancient civilizations relied heavily on this bulb as a medication for indigestion, diarrhea, worms, skin diseases, dizziness, headaches, bronchitis, pneumonia, influenza, tuberculosis, infections and wounds, heart problems, arthritis, aging and even cancer. In recent years, people have rediscovered the medicinal merits of garlic in warding off colds and in the treatment of high blood pressure, strokes, and cardiovascular disease. Interestingly, countries where garlic is consumed in large quantities—Italy and Spain, for example—have a lower death rate from heart disease than America does.[80]

Milk Thistle for the Liver

Milk Thistle *(Silybum Marianum)* has been used for centuries for the treatment of liver problems. The active ingredient is a bioflavonoid mixture called *silymarin*. Research has demonstrated that it protects against liver toxins.[81] "Milk Thistle has been helpful in alcohol induced fatty liver disorders, chronic hepatitis (inflammation of the liver), chemically induced fatty liver disorders, cirrhosis or hardening of the liver, hepatic organ damage and psoriasis."[82]

The liver is one of the most important organs for filtering out toxins, and all of us are exposed to environmental toxins (smog, cigarette smoke, alcohol, preservatives, ozone, etc.). Look for capsules that contain a concentrated amount of silymarin, available at your nutrition store.

"Take Charge of Your Health" As you read this research about antioxidants building immunity, I hope you are convinced that it is time that you *Take Charge of Your Health* (the title of our previous book). New information about various vitamins, minerals, antioxidants and herbs is constantly reported in the news. It is one of the most exciting and rapidly growing fields of research. I encourage you to stay abreast of the information about these substances, and add them to your nutritional program. They may very well be the foremost key to your staying young biologically, even as your chronological years increase.

Chapter 4

Mirror, Mirror
on the Wall

Skin, Hair, and Nail Health

"No one wants to get old as we generally think of it—the muscles becoming soft, the bones brittle, a cantankerous personality, and a senile mind. While others have searched for the legendary "fountain of youth," I have been searching for something else—a way to help people stay healthy, energetic, and attractive. My search lead to nutrition."
—Gladys Lindberg

When you look in the mirror, what do you see? Do you see soft, supple, radiant, glowing, blemish-free skin? Or do you see age spots and new wrinkles?

The skin is the first "aging" sign we tend to see in ourselves. We all want to find ways to keep our skin beautiful, soft, and we hope, wrinkle free. We'll each get *some* wrinkles, but nobody wants them prematurely!

My mother, Gladys Lindberg, had the most beautiful skin for her age of any woman that I have ever seen. She far surpassed the "beauty experts" and "movie stars" in her beauty and grace. At age 85, she had a clear, peachy complexion and was virtually wrinkle free! She had no patchy brown spots or blemished skin. She never smoked and avoided the sun whenever possible. Mother started her quest for health when she was about 43 years old. She said her skin was blotchy and never radiant, but her program drastically changed the quality of her skin.

Important Advice for Skin Health

A woman recently came into our store looking for a "magic formula" for her deeply wrinkled skin. She was only in her mid-forties, but her skin had changed drastically over the last month. Being quite disturbed about the situation, she came to me wanting "that miracle cream."

I talked to her for a few minutes and discovered that she had been on a severe reducing diet for several months. She had followed a diet low in protein, and over the course of those months had lost her skin tone. Her skin had started to sag and wrinkle way beyond what would be normal for her chronological age. Most women want to be slim, but if you saw her, I'm sure you would agree, "not at that price!" Here are some things I told her that are important for healthy skin regardless of whether you're trying to lose weight or not.

Collagen—the Skin's "Cement"

Elastic skin is a sign that a person has ample *collagen*, the strong cement-like material that binds together the cells of your body. Collagen is a structural tissue and as such, it is replaced very slowly. Its strong white fibers, stronger than steel wire of the same size, and yellow elastic networks, called *elastin*, form the connective tissue that holds our bodies together. Collagen strengthens the skin, blood vessels, bones, and teeth. It is the intracellular cement that holds together the cells in various organs and tissues. It is made of fibrous protein. In fact, collagen comprises 30 percent of the total body protein.

Collagen is one of the most valuable proteins in the human body. A person who has been sick, or who has been on an extremely low-protein diet, very often sees the muscles in his or her arms and legs begin to sag, which is a sign that they have probably lost collagen.

Let's Start with Protein

The building blocks of protein are amino acids. Protein is not one substance, but literally tens of thousands of different substances. There are more than twenty amino acids, each of which has its own characteristics. In various combinations, these amino acids are capable of forming an almost limitless variety of proteins, each serving its own purpose.

Proteins are necessary for tissue repair and for the construction of new tissue. Every cell needs protein to maintain its life. Protein is also the primary substance used to "replace" worn out or dead cells:

- most white blood cells are replaced every ten days
- the cells in the lining of the gastrointestinal tract and blood platelets are replaced every four days.
- skin cells are replaced every twenty-four days. More than 98 percent of the molecules in the body are completely replaced each year![1]

Your muscles, hair, nails, skin, and eyes are made of protein. So are the cells that make up the liver, kidneys, heart, lungs, nerves, brain, and your sex glands. The body's most active protein users are the hormones secreted from the various glands—thyroxin from the thyroid, insulin from the pancreas, and a variety of hormones from the pituitary—as well as the soft tissues, hardworking major organs and muscles. They all require the richest stores of protein.

Next to water, protein is the most plentiful substance in your body. In fact, if all the water was squeezed out of you, about half of your dry weight would be protein. About one third of this protein would be in your muscles, a fifth in your bones and cartilage, a tenth in your skin, and the rest in your other tissues and body fluids.

Even hemoglobin is 95 percent protein. It's the protein in the red cells of the blood which carries oxygen from the lungs to the other parts of the body where it is used to burn molecules of food and produce energy.

How Much Protein a Day?

Many "experts" differ on the amount of protein needed in the diet. Some suggest very low amounts, some suggest much higher amounts, especially if body building. The following protein requirement chart is to be used only as a guideline for determining your protein requirement. You may need more, or you might be able to get by with slightly less. Your requirement depends on your percent of body fat, your weight and the physical activity you do. The higher your activity level, the more you will need to increase your dietary protein intake to repair and rebuild muscle.

If you are undergoing any type of severe stress (including the stresses of cancer, burns, radiation exposure, or pregnancy), you may need more. If you are susceptible to infections you may need more. Remember that antibodies, white blood cells, lymph cells, and everything our bodies use to fight infections, are made out of protein.

Daily Protein Requirements
For Men and Women Over 20*

Ideal Weight	Protein Needed	Safety Margin
80 lbs	40 grams	50 grams
111 lbs	50 grams	60 grams
133 lbs	60 grams	70 grams
156 lbs	70 grams	80 grams
178 lbs	80 grams	90 grams
200 lbs	90 grams	100 grams
222 lbs	100 grams	110 grams
244 lbs	110 grams	120 grams

Our calculations for this age group are based on the usual recommendation of 1 gram protein per kilogram (2.2 lbs) of ideal body weight, for sedentary individuals. However, adding 10 grams of protein to the above recommendation as a safety margin will ensure getting enough protein. Pregnant women should add an additional 20 grams and nursing mothers should add 40 grams of protein to the above recommendation. If you are physically active, exercising every day, figure 1 gram protein, per pound of lean (your ideal) weight.[2]

Three ounces of chicken yields approximately 20 grams of protein, 1/2 cup of water-packed tuna contains 28 grams, 8 oz low fat, plain yogurt has 12 grams. One egg provides 6 grams. An eight-ounce glass of low-fat milk has 8 grams. Remember, there are excellent protein powders that are alternatives to traditional protein foods. There are tips in the "Let's Put It All Together" chapter for getting all the protein you need for optimal health and beautiful skin.

We need to remember there is a balance of protein, fats and carbohydrates that Mother and I have basically taught. It is important to eat five times a day and include some form of protein at each meal or feeding. We have found this program has helped more people look and feel their best. This may be ideal for most people, but remember, we are "biologically different."

In our nutritional program I recommend a variety of complete protein foods, including fish, chicken, low-fat dairy, eggs, some red meat, quality protein powders and nutritional yeast. Also consume an ample supply of various fresh fruit and vegetables,

legumes which are complex carbohydrates, and includes the essential fatty acids. A strict fat free diet is not healthy for your skin. My
approach is this: You are not made of lettuce leaves. Your body is
made of protein which is essential for almost every cell in your
body, especially your skin, nails and hair.

Protecting Your Skin

As we discussed more thoroughly in the previous chapter on
antioxidants, we can protect our skin from free-radical damage, the
damage created when cells oxidize, by consuming antioxidants.
Beta-carotene, vitamin C, vitamin E, pine bark and grape seed
extract, and the trace mineral selenium are the antioxidants that
have been researched the most in their advantages to the cells.
Other nutrients that are good for our skin, hair, and nails are listed
below:

Vitamin B Complex. Most of the B-vitamins are related
to healthy skin. If you read the deficiency symptoms related to B-
vitamins, you quickly come to the conclusion: "take vitamin B-complex!" Roger Williams, Ph.D., discovered pantothenic acid (vitamin
B5) more than 50 years ago.[3] He found that chickens suffering from
"chick dermatitis" were cured quickly with pantothenic acid. Their
unhealthy skin and feathers were restored to health almost miracu-
lously. He suggested that people who had trouble with their hair
and skin might enjoy the same results from pantothenic acid. Dr.
Williams noted that of all the organs of the body, the skin is the first
organ that suffers from malnutrition. Other early indicators of malnutrition are found in the mouth, tongue, lips, and gums.[4]

Grape Seed Extract or Pycnogenols®. An antioxidant that comes from Pycnogenol® or grape seed extract has been
shown to be important in skin health. Dr. R. Kuttan and colleagues
have shown that Pycnogenol® binds tightly to skin collagen and
increases its resistance to enzyme degradation. It also helps repair
collagen.[5] For more information read Chapter 3.

Gamma-Linolenic Acid (GLA). GLA acts as an anti-
inflammatory agent with none of the side effects of anti-inflammatory drugs. It promotes growth of skin, hair, and nails. Evening

primrose oil, borage oil, and black currant seed oil are natural sources of GLA, in capsule form. There have been numerous studies showing the benefits of evening primrose oil in treating skin conditions. Other important fatty acids are called Omega-3 Fish Oils (EPA) which are found in cod liver oil and cold water fish such as salmon and sardines. Flax seed oil is also an excellent way to obtain a blend of Omega-3, Omega-6 and Omega-9 fatty acids.

Royal Jelly. This nutrient from the bee has an incredible effect on the skin, when taken as a supplement. Later we will discuss its application on the skin. It is rich in amino acids, vitamins, and pantothenic acid. Dr. M. Esperrois, of the French Institute of Chemistry, states that certain compounds in royal jelly often reverse the effects of normal aging of the skin, correcting darkening, wrinkling, and blemishes.

Doctors J. R. Lamberti and L. G. Cornero, researchers in Argentina, have said that royal jelly apparently delays aging by slowing the deterioration of collagen in those who use oral supplementation. Researchers at the University of Sarajevo found that royal jelly was a powerful anti-bacterial and anti-viral agent.[6] This product is available in capsule or jelly form at your nutrition store.

Silica. Silica or Silicon is a trace mineral, and next to oxygen, is the second most abundant element in the earth's crust. It is present in connective tissue, bone, skin, and fingernails. Silicon appears to be involved in the building and metabolism of these structures.[7]

Dietary sources of silicon include vegetables, whole grains, and seafood. The herb horsetail (*Equisetum arvense*) contains a large amount of silica. It has many uses in the body, such as preventing the hair from split ends and strengthening fingernails. Horsetail also helps facilitate the use of and retention of calcium in the body.[8]

There is a high-quality German liquid silica which is derived from quartz crystals that is a colloidal preparation of silica in a highly dispersible form. It is available at your nutrition store.

L-Cysteine. The sulfur-containing amino acids (methionine, cysteine, and taurine) will provide sulfur in concentrated and easily assimilated forms. Of these three amino acids, experts find that cysteine is the most effective in relieving skin problems. Robert Erdmann, Ph.D., said this isn't surprising, as a quarter of all the amino acids contained in collagen (the skin protein) are cysteine molecules. Without them, collagen would simply fall apart.[9]

All horny layers of the skin, including hair and fingernails, are high in cysteine. There is evidence that the high-sulfur proteins, cysteine being one of them, are missing in the hair of humans who have experienced abnormal hair loss. Preliminary findings indicate that daily supplementation of cysteine increases hair shaft diameter and hair growth density in certain cases of human baldness and hair loss.[10]

Carl C. Pfeiffer, Ph.D., M.D., said that egg yolks are rich sources of the sulfur amino acids, methionine and cysteine. Dr. Pfeiffer tells of the other minerals and vitamins in eggs and says, "The egg can thus be considered the ideal model of the exact nutrients to take with you to a desert island! The protein is complete, with all the essential amino acids, and the ratio of minerals is perfect for the purpose of growth. Eggs are the perfect food."[11]

Water. Of all the nutrients we will discuss in this chapter, water is the most important for beautiful skin. Your daily diet should include the equivalent of 8 to 10 glasses of pure water. This keeps enough moisture in your body. Caffeine and alcoholic drinks pull moisture out of your system.

The Skin's Two Biggest Enemies

Most of us know that the skin's biggest enemy is the **sun.** Regular exposure to ultraviolet rays erodes the elastic tissues in the skin causing a person to wrinkle prematurely. The ultraviolet energy from the sun produces free-radicals in the fats stored in the skin cell membranes. Years of sun exposure may lead to malignant melanoma, the most serious form of skin cancer—which has risen five to six fold around the world in recent decades! The second most common type of skin cancer is *squamous cell carcinoma*. It, too, is on the rise.

The next biggest enemy of the skin is **smoking cigarettes**. If you don't smoke, minimize your exposure to people who do. People who smoke a pack-and-a-half a day wrinkle about ten years sooner than a non-smoker. I am sure you can bring to mind several acquaintances who smoke—and generally, you will find that their skin is prematurely wrinkled, especially around the mouth and lips.

One cigarette destroys about 25 mg of vitamin C, the important nutrient for building collagen.[12] If you do smoke and can't quit, learn which antioxidants and nutrients you need to take to protect yourself from this damage.

Free-radical damage occurs any time a person is exposed to sun, smoke, environmental pollution, alcohol, and drugs. If you live in an area with high air pollution, if you drink alcohol, or if you are taking drugs of any kind, you need extra antioxidant protection.

Special Help for Skin Conditions

To help with various skin or hair conditions, we recommend a complete nutrition program which you will find in the last chapter, "Let's Put It All Together." In addition to the nutrients that are a part of that plan, some people need "extra" nutrients for specific areas of concern.

Age Spots. When you are deficient in vitamin E, fatty substances can turn into dark brown patches that are usually called "age spots." Some refer to these as "liver spots." We are most familiar with these darkened tissue patches when they appear on the face, arms, and back of the hands. Such deposits are not just on the surface skin, however. According to Roger J. Williams, Ph.D., the author of *Nutrition Against Disease*, these deposits can also be found in the brain, heart, adrenal gland, and other parts of the body. They are directly linked to a lack of vitamin E.[13] Williams recommends you not only increase your intake of vitamin E, but all of the antioxidants. It is especially important to take vitamin E *before* these "liver spots" begin to appear on your skin.

NOTE: *You must make sure, of course, that these "age spots" are not pre-cancerous lesions. If one of these brown spots pops up "out of the blue," or an old one suddenly changes shape, becomes raised, or bleeds, be sure to have a dermatologist take a look at it. You need to be certain it is not an early melanoma, a form of skin cancer.*

Wrinkles. Hans Selye, M.D., the original stress doctor, experimented with premature aging and found that wrinkles could be prevented with large amounts of vitamin E. It may be that the multiple stresses that induce aging cause cells in the lower layers of the skin to be destroyed. Bits of scar tissue then take their place and wrinkles result as the scar tissue contracts.

If wrinkles come from cells being damaged, the best prevention is to take all the antioxidants (especially A, E, C, selenium, CoQ10, grape seed extract or Pycnogenol®) and other nutrients to prevent healthy tissue from damage.

Eczema. Eczema is also called *atopic dermatitis* since the symptoms and therapies are similar to dermatitis. It may be caused by low adrenal function, irritants, allergies, or nutritional deficiencies. Symptoms usually consist of blisters, red bumps, swelling, oozing, crusting, scaling, and itching. Melvyn Werbach, M.D., in *Nutritional Influences on Illness,* reported several research studies in which patients took 3 to 9 grams of MaxEPA (Omega-3 fish oil) daily in divided doses, along with vitamin E. Other researchers used 2 grams, twice daily, of evening primrose oil after meals, while continuing on their regular medication. Results were noticeable in about 12 weeks and after 11 months, more than half were rated improved. If you add the mineral zinc to your diet, improvements could even be more dramatic. In one study, taking 50 mg of chelated zinc three times a day along with other nutrients resulted in full remission in all except one severe case.

The other nutritional supplements that have been shown to help are EPA/DHA from cod liver oil and cold water fish, flax oil, a "stress" B-complex, vitamins B6, A, C, E and the minerals magnesium and zinc. NOTE: *According to several researchers, if you have eczema, dermatitis or psoriasis, you may be low in stomach acidity and need to take hydrochloric acid tablets or capsules.*[15]

Dermatitis. Symptoms of dermatitis are similar to eczema and include itching, flaking, oozing, crusting, scaling, and thickening of the skin. It may be caused by an allergic reaction to certain foods or substances. The nutritional supplements recommended would be basically the same as for eczema with the addition of digestive enzymes, especially hydrochloric acid.[16]

Psoriasis. Psoriasis looks like patches of skin that are thickened and reddened and covered with scales. It usually does not itch and shows up most often on the arms, elbows, behind the ears, scalp, back, legs, and knees. Authorities suggest taking the essential fatty acids, evening primrose oil, vitamin A (fish oil), folic acid, B-complex, B6, vitamin C with bioflavonoids, zinc, lecithin and digestive enzymes.[17]

According to an article in the *Journal of the American Academy of Dermatology*, researchers found that the active ingredient in cayenne pepper (*capsaicin*) "topically applied, effectively treats pruritic psoriasis." This ointment reduced the severity of psoriasis including less scaling, thickness, and redness.[18] You can find this ointment in most nutrition stores.

Sunburns. A sunburn can be very damaging to the skin. Overexposure of the skin to the ultraviolet radiation in sunlight causes inflammation and burns. *First-degree* burns are when the skin reddens, affecting only the top layer. *Second-degree* burns create blisters and usually heal without scarring. *Third-degree* burns result in more severe damage to the skin. These burns are susceptible to infections and must be treated by a doctor. Secondary infections may follow once the skin has peeled.

Repeated overexposure to the sun and sunburns increases aging and the risk of skin cancer. Prevention is your best defense.

According to Drs. Evan and Wilfred Shute, vitamin E should be taken to aid in the healing process. Vitamin E may even be applied topically to the burn or scar.[19] Another popular topical remedy is to apply cool aloe vera gel liberally to the burned area. You may also mix the gel with vitamins A and E.

Vitamin C with bioflavonoids and zinc are also important for wound healing. Also try to consume high protein foods and be sure to supplement your diet with vitamin B-complex, especially pantothenic acid to help regenerate the body. NOTE: *With any serious burn, seek medical attention before applying anything to the skin.*

Acne. Acne is inflammation of the skin generally due to clogged pores. It may be worse at adolescence, just prior to menstruation as hormones change, when a person is under stress, or when the diet is poor. If you have this problem, add extra vitamin A (water-soluble from fish oil), beta-carotene, zinc, a "stress" vitamin B-complex, vitamin B6 (especially for acne associated with menstruation), essential fatty acids such as evening primrose oil, flax seed oil, brewer's yeast, vitamin C, and digestive enzymes (pancreatin with bile and betaine hydrochloric acid with pepsin). Jonathan V. Wright M.D. says, "In my experience, the use of hydrochloric acid supplements in adequate doses is extremely effective in reducing the severity of (acne), and, in some cases, nearly eliminating it. . . ."[20] Adding Lactobacillus acidophilus appears even more helpful than hydrochloric acid and pepsin supplements alone. Acne rosacea is often associated with low stomach acidity. Make sure there is no constipation (at least one to two movements a day) as this can be a major cause.

Dandruff. We all know about those little white flakes that appear on the hair with itching, scaling, and redness of scalp. The only symptom that has been tied absolutely to a selenium deficiency is dandruff.[21] So take the trace mineral, selenium, and a variety of nutrients, such as extra vitamin B6, vitamin A, vitamin B-complex, vitamins C and E, plus the essential fatty acids, and zinc.

Shingles. Shingles, a type of herpes, comes from the chicken pox virus, a virus which never leaves the body. Shingles often start after a period of major stress or illness. According to Adelle Davis, the diet for anyone with boils, abscesses, carbuncles, impetigo, or virus infection such as shingles should be the same as for other infections. Vitamin A and E should be particularly emphasized while infection symptoms persist, and for three or four months afterward. Be sure to take a complete vitamin and mineral formula to rebuild your entire system, especially the adrenals.[22]

The amino acid L-lysine has been effective in some studies. A Mayo Clinic study utilized 1,248 mg of lysine daily and was conducted double-blind and placebo-controlled. This dose was consistently and significantly effective in reducing the recurrence rate of herpes outbreaks. Administering lysine did not, however, reduce the duration or severity of attacks once underway. Given lysine's low toxicity there is little to lose and potentially much to gain in taking lysine according to Sheldon Saul Hendler, M.D., Ph.D.[23]

Lendon Smith, M.D., says to "try a daily dose of B12 (1,000 mcg) intramuscularly for five to ten days. Use vitamin C, perhaps up to bowel tolerance—somewhere at 1,000 mg level every waking hour or two. Continue for two weeks then taper off. Vitamin E locally and orally is soothing and might cut down the chance of scarring."[24]

If you are suffering from distressing skin pain from shingles, there is also a natural, safe product for you to use. It is from the red-hot cayenne pepper, the same hot pepper you use to spice up your chili. According to *Alternative Medicine*, the active ingredient in this pepper is *capsaicin*, and when used properly, it may relieve skin pain. When this natural capsaicin cream or ointment is applied to the skin, it creates a sensation of warmth. Generally you can expect to experience pain relief after about two weeks of therapy, or a little longer. Many doctors prefer to use capsaicin for skin pain relief rather than drugs as it has fewer drug interaction problems.[25]

Recognizing Deficiencies

Recognizing minor abnormalities to good health and taking steps to correct them is preventive medicine at its best. On the following pages are just a few signs that deficiencies may be experienced. Throughout this book you will recognize other deficiency symptoms.

I want to restate my long-standing belief that all vitamins and minerals work together. For example, if you are deficient in riboflavin (vitamin B2), you can almost bet that you also are deficient in vitamins B6, B3, and so forth. The B vitamins work together and a deficiency in one nearly always signals deficiencies in the others. That is why we recommend complete vitamin and mineral formulas in sufficient potencies.

Recognizing Deficiencies
Related to Your Hair, Skin and Nails[26]

PROTEIN DEFICIENCIES

- Puffy bags under the eyes, especially in the morning, may indicate a lack of protein.
- Water retention. General puffiness around the eyes, as well as swollen ankles, face, and hands, can result from a protein deficiency.
- Nails are made of protein, not calcium as some think. A protein deficiency can be marked by split, extremely thin nails. Nails that fail to grow quickly lack protein.
- The structure of the hair follicle is protein. There are eight amino acids that the body does not produce and which therefore must come from complete protein foods such as eggs, meat, fish, and fowl. Eat small meals often with protein at each meal.
- **L-Cysteine and L-Methionine** are the amino acids that form "keratin," which is the protein structure of hair. Studies have shown that supplementing with L-cysteine may prevent hair from falling out, as well as increase the diameter of the hair shaft. These amino acids have been found to increase hair growth by as much as 100 percent. Egg yolk contains the highest amount of these two amino acids.[27]

VITAMIN DEFICIENCIES

These deficiency symptoms are only related to the skin, eyes, nose and mouth.

Vitamin A

- Drying out of the skin may signal deficiency—also rough, horny skin especially on upper arms and on thighs. The skin starts to look like goose bumps that don't go away.
- The skin has four layers of cells. Lack of vitamin A

on the bottom layer causes the cells to die too quickly. The body sends white blood cells to bring these dead cells to the surface—the manifestation may be a pimple, sty in the eye, a carbuncle, or a boil. Dead cells behind the ear drum create a fertile environment for infection and may be a primary cause of ear infection.

- A vitamin A deficiency may result in bits of mucous accumulating on the eyelashes at night and the eyelids may feel stuck together in the morning. Also results in a sensitivity to bright lights and glare.
- Vitamin A helps prevent and cure night blindness and day blindness, because it restores visual purple to the eye.
- Vitamin A supplementation is helpful with dry eye disease, in which the tear ducts dry up. It is also helpful to those whose eyes become "tired" quickly, and those who experience red "rims" around their eye lids.
- A severe deficiency can cause retinitis pigmentosa, a slow but eventual degeneration of the retina. This condition causes blindness in thousands of Americans each year, and is usually preceded by years of night blindness and other symptoms of vitamin A deficiency.
- This vitamin is essential to the normal structure and behavior of the tissues lining the mouth, nasal, sinus, and respiratory tract.
- There is available a fish oil-based, but emulsified (water-soluble) vitamin A, since some people may not be able to absorb oil-soluble vitamin A.

Vitamin B2 (Riboflavin)

- This is a widespread deficiency in America. It may take a long time to correct.
- Deficiency can cause sensitivity to light, so that you feel you must wear dark sunglasses. It can also cause faulty vision in dim illumination, burning or itching eyelids, and eyes that water easily and become bloodshot when they are strained.
- Deficiency is often marked by magenta or purplish

tongue, and lips that tend to crack and become rough, often feeling chapped. Tiny flakes of skin may peel from lips, and whistle lines or wrinkles from the lips toward the nose may appear.

- The nose, chin, and forehead take on an oily appearance, and fatty deposits accumulate under the skin, when vitamin B2 is deficient.
- A severe deficiency can cause the skin at the corners of the eye to split, and the eyes burn and become fiery red.
- B2 is helpful in preventing cataracts and glaucoma.

Vitamin B3 (Niacin or Niacinamide)

- Deficiency marked by brilliant red, coated tongue, and mouth, throat, and esophagus may become inflamed—it may be difficult for older people to eat.
- Canker sores may indicate a vitamin B3 deficiency.

Pantothenic Acid (Vitamin B5)

- Pantothenic acid has been found to be a factor in restoring gray hair to its normal color in experimental animals, although this finding has not as yet been confirmed in humans. Rats deficient in pantothenic acid had hair which turned course and gray prematurely, and they seemed to age faster.
- Helpful with dermatitis and eczema.
- An enlarged, "beefy," furrowed tongue may signal a pantothenic acid deficiency.

Vitamin B6 (Pyridoxine)

- Most recognized deficiency is greasy, scaly dermatitis —even between eyebrows, sides of nose, around mouth, and behind the ears. The skin may be red and inflamed and scaly with dandruff.
- Babies get "cradle cap" when their mothers are deficient in B6 during pregnancy.
- Slight B6 deficiency is dry skin with oily T-zone (forehead, nose, and chin).
- Outbreaks of acne just before menstrual period may also be a B6 deficiency. In one experiment, 72 percent of women taking 50 mg of B6 daily for one week before and during their periods had no more acne.

Vitamin B12 (Cobalamin)

- A deficiency can result in pernicious anemia, which is characterized by extreme pallor (paleness), plus other symptoms.

PABA (Para-Amino-Benzoic Acid)

- PABA has been shown to help the skin condition "vitiligo," in which the skin loses its pigment and turns white. This condition may also be linked to low adrenal function.
- Supplementation can help block the harmful effects of ultraviolet light that cause sunburn and skin cancer.
- PABA has helped reverse gray hair in rats. Deficiencies in pantothenic acid, biotin, and folic acid are also related to gray hair.

Folic Acid (Folacin or Folate)

- Folic acid restored gray hair to natural color.
- The deficiencies are much the same as for vitamin B12. An inflamed and sore tongue may occur.

Biotin

- Helps with hair growth.
- The first symptom of deficiency is usually scaly dermatitis.
- A deficiency can result in an increased sensitivity of the skin, even burning or a prickling sensation. Pallor, or an extreme or unnatural paleness, may also occur.

Inositol

- May help prevent thinning hair and baldness. It is also a lipotropic factor (a fat emulsifier), which helps fats to move normally, without getting deposited in the lining of the arteries. Also used for weight loss. Its highest concentration is found in the heart and brain.

Vitamin C (Ascorbic Acid)

- Deficiency marked by bruising (hemorrhaging under the skin). Older people are most susceptible because the medication they often take destroys vitamin C in their body.

- Vitamin C forms collagen in the skin, which is the "cement" that supports and holds the tissues and organs together. It keeps the youthful skin tissues soft, firm, supple, and wrinkle-free. Collagen helps keep your skin from sagging.

Bioflavonoids

- Helps prevent bruising since bruises are broken or damaged capillaries.
- Bioflavonoids have been shown to relieve the painful throbbing and swelling of mild cases of varicose veins, and to help eliminate the small veins that can appear on the face.

Vitamin D

- When ultraviolet rays from sunlight hit the skin, a form of cholesterol in the body is converted into vitamin D. Dark skinned people do not produce their own vitamin D as efficiently, since their dark pigment screens out much of the ultraviolet rays. If you are indoors for several months of the year, make sure to supplement with vitamin D.

Vitamin E

- Experiments with premature aging found that wrinkles could be prevented by giving large amounts of vitamin E.
- Pregnancy Mask—the brown pigmentation that appears on the faces of some pregnant women may be caused by a vitamin E deficiency, or it may indicate low adrenal function. A woman with this condition may also need extra pantothenic acid.
- Liver spots—brown pigmentation on the back of the hands caused by oxidation of fats—are linked to a lack of vitamin E. It is essential that a person take all the antioxidants—beta-carotene, vitamin C, selenium—for healthy skin.

MINERAL DEFICIENCIES

These deficiency symptoms are only related to the skin, eyes, nose and mouth.

Calcium
- In many cases, a calcium deficiency is responsible for dark circles under the eyes. Allergies may also cause this.

Iodine
- A deficiency may cause goiter, which is characterized by an enlarged thyroid gland that can cause bulging of the eyes, plus other symptoms. If your eyes seem too large and protruding, read more about the thyroid in Chapter 8.

Iron
- An iron deficiency results in nails being concave or spoon like in shape—both fingernails and toenails. The nails may also lack their normal half moon shape at the base of the nail.
- Vertical ridges in the nail may be a sign that anemia is present. This may also be a sign of a deficiency in zinc or calcium.
- Skin lesions such as pimples, boils, and the like are far more likely to occur in individuals low in iron.

Potassium
- A deficiency in young people may result in acne, while in adults a deficiency can cause dry skin.

Sulfur
- Sulfur is found in every cell of the body and is particularly necessary for beautiful hair, skin, and nails.
- Protein foods, such as egg yolks, are the richest natural source of sulfur.

Selenium
- The only symptom tied to a selenium deficiency is dandruff. This trace mineral is sometimes added to shampoos to treat seborrhea dermatitis (dandruff).

Silica or Silicon (trace mineral)
- This has been found to help with the hair, skin, and nails. It helps build connective tissues in the body.

Zinc
- White spots on the nails, or nails with an opaquely white appearance, can signal a zinc deficiency.

OTHER CONSIDERATIONS

Low Thyroid
- A low thyroid output can cause hair to become course, dry, and brittle. Hair loss can be quite severe.
- The nails become thin and brittle and typically show transverse grooves in those with low thyroid production.
- Protruding or bulging eyes may be an indication of low thyroid.
- Skin cold to the touch, especially hands and feet.

What Should You Apply to Your Skin?

Your skin is the largest organ of your body. It breathes and releases toxins if necessary through perspiration. What most people don't realize is that *whatever you put on your skin absorbs into your bloodstream!* So be aware of the chemicals, make-ups, creams, and cleansers that you use daily.

Your nutrition store has a wide variety of natural skin and hair-care products, most of which do not have the high price tag of cosmetic counters. These natural cosmetics use the least toxic preservatives and substances to preserve their product.

Along with suggesting that a person eat a healthy diet, and take vitamins, minerals, and fatty acids, most leading nutritionists frequently recommend certain skin-care products that have a long history of documented beneficial effects. Some of these substances have been used successfully for thousands of years.

Aloe Vera Has Been Used Since Biblical Times

Aloe vera is a plant that everyone should have in the home for skin emergencies. Aloe vera has remarkable healing abilities. It has properties for promoting the removal of dead skin and stimulating the normal growth of living cells. Its enzymes dissolve dead surface-layer cells, tighten pores, and have anti-bacterial qualities that fight infection. Aloe can also stop pain and reduce the chances of scarring while helping the healing process. It is valuable for burning, itching, minor cuts and first and second degree thermal burns.[28]

Interestingly, aloe has a composition similar to that of human blood plasma and sea water. Its pH is the same as human skin.[29]

To use fresh aloe, simply cut off part of an aloe vera leaf, split it open, and spread the gel over a burn, cut, scrape, or infection. Aloe can also be used as an after-shave lotion or moisturizer. There are many aloe vera products from cosmetics, to pure juice and gels.

Vitamin E Oil Is a Cellular Healer

Vitamin E is a fantastic antioxidant and cellular healer that the skin can absorb. The pure oil is wonderful for treating scars, burns, and other skin rashes, as it both moisturizes and heals wounds. Dr. Shute did this original research using vitamin E for scars and burns. For more detail, read Chapter 3 on antioxidants. There are various potencies of this oil available, some with 5,000 IU per one-ounce container, or others with as much as 32,000 IU—a very heavy and sticky consistency.

You can add an ounce of 32,000 IU pure vitamin E oil to four ounces of 100 percent pure cold-pressed jojoba oil, or a moisturizing lotion or cream. Or you may squeeze 10–20 softgels of vitamin E (400 IU) into your favorite hand and body lotion. This way, the vitamin E oil goes on easier. In the evening after your face is cleansed, spread this combination oil over your entire face, neck, and arms. It is oily, but absorbs quickly. In the morning, your face will be soft and moist. Ladies, rub this mixture on your legs after you have shaved.

Vitamins A & E—One of Mother's Beauty Secrets

Natural vitamin A from fish oil—not synthetic forms—is also excellent to add to the lotion just described. Vitamin A mixed with lotion is one of the most important skin care ingredients you can use, and it will cost you very little. Vitamin A is a key vitamin related to skin health, and is a potent free-radical scavenger. Don't use cod liver oil, it smells too fishy.

Vitamins A and E were one of Mother's beauty secrets, although she freely told everyone about them. She always added 10–20 vitamin A softgels (25,000 IU) to her night-time moisturizing cream, along with vitamin E. She felt the moisturizing cream helped her skin assimilate the oil vitamins. If you don't mind a little fish oil smell of the vitamin A, the more the better. You will not believe how great your skin will look and feel! My husband uses this instead of after shave lotion.

Vitamin C Is Now Added to Creams

Information has been in the news lately about vitamin C in various skin products, and how it helps with wrinkles and fine lines. Look for creams that contain vitamins A, E, and C. I am always slightly amused when I hear that some vitamin added to a cream is called a new "miracle ingredient" for the skin. The skin soaks in these nutrients and benefits from them both internally and externally!

Royal Jelly Softens Skin and Reduces Wrinkles

A number of new products on the market contain the ingredient royal jelly. In a paper titled *"Royal Jelly in Dermatological Cosmetics,"* Hans Weitgasser, M.D., a German dermatologist, has written, "Through local application as an ingredient in face masks, creams, and lotions, royal jelly has tremendous effects at the cellular level. With regular use, the skin becomes soft and wrinkles disappear." [30]

Royal jelly apparently works by stimulating the circulatory system, delivering more food and oxygen-laden blood to nourish the skin and remove waste from it, according to Elfried Kirschbaumer, M.D., also a German dermatologist. Ninety percent of his patients showed a tightening of sagging skin in the face, muscles, and breasts.[31]

If you truly want to embellish the cream I described above, you might also pierce a few royal jelly softgels and squeeze them into your moisturizer cream along with gels of vitamin A and E. You'll have a nutrient-packed face cream!

Jojoba Oil Is for Topical Use Only

Jojoba oil is another fantastic oil for skin and hair, but it is only for external, topical use. This oil is a pure and natural plant extract that penetrates and moisturizes the skin without leaving an oily residue. It can be used to remove make-up and cleanse clogged pores, leaving the skin clean and blemish free. It is excellent for inflamed skin, psoriasis, eczema, acne, and as an aftershave moisturizer.

Use this luxurious oil to soften your hands and feet. Rub the oil into your skin after bathing. It is very similar to human sebum, which oils the hair and skin, and it helps your body retain body heat and prevent sweat evaporation.

Jojoba oil rarely goes rancid because of its natural antioxidant properties. The vitamins A and E can be added to this natural oil, as I discussed.

Every few weeks, use jojoba oil for moisturizing the scalp to prevent dandruff. It is also good for split ends. After the oil is massaged into your scalp and hair, wrap your hair in a scarf and go to sleep. In the morning when you wash your hair, you'll find it vital again, with lots of body and shine.

Alpha Hydroxy Acids Are a Natural "Peel"

Everyone who is interested in skin care has no doubt heard about the Alpha Hydroxy Acid (AHA) products that have flooded the market in recent years. They appear to work as 'natural' chemical peels.

Strong chemical peels, which many dermatologists use, destroy the upper layer of skin cells and trigger new collagen production at a deeper level. The new collagen helps preserve the skin's elasticity and makes it look more youthful. Fruit acids work in a similar way, but they're more natural and gentler. There is also less irritation, and they do not result in extreme sun sensitivity, which often occurs with the use of standard chemical peels and certain skin drugs.

The fruit acids are a gentle, effective way to treat wrinkles and fine lines. Alpha hydroxy acids remove dead skin by loosening the intracellular cement between the old and new epidermal cells and dissolving the dead surface cells. This improves the skin's texture and causes discolored patches to slough off and disappear.

There are several kinds of AHA's available: *glycolic acid* from sugar cane, *malic acid* from apples, *citric acid* from oranges, lemons and limes, *tartaric acid* from wine grapes, and *lactic acid* from milk. *Glycolic acid* has the smallest molecules and is more effective at exfoliating (sloughing off dead cells to renew skin) while those made with lactic acid are more moisturizing.[32]

If you have sensitive or fair skin, take special care. AHAs may irritate your skin. Start with a product that has a lower percentage of AHAs (2 to 4 percent), and work up to higher, more effective percentage levels.

Na-PCA Gives Skin Its Youthful Glow

Na-PCA is the abbreviated name of the *sodium pyrollidone carboxylic acid.* This substance is abundant in young skin, but sparse in aged skin. In fact, old skin contains only about half the amount of that found in young skin. Na-PCA is the most important of the natural moisturizing factors found in human skin. It is synthesized from glutamic acid, a nonessential amino acid. The ability of skin to hold moisture is directly related to its Na-PCA content.

Keep in mind always that it is water that keeps skin soft and supple. Na-PCA pulls water out of the air, moisturizing the skin, improving its appearance, and giving it a moist and youthful glow. It is not a cosmetic cover up—it is a physiological correction of an age-related deficiency. It provides quick relief from dry and cracked skin.[33] You'll probably find Na-PCA combined with aloe vera products in your nutrition store.

Chamomile Is More than Tea

Chamomile is an anti-inflammatory herb that is finding increased application for topical treatments of skin disorders such as psoriasis and eczema. Chamomile's primary active component *levomenol,* may help reduce lines and wrinkles caused by the sun and environmental factors. This key therapeutic component in chamomile promotes the skin's ability to heal itself.

Doctors at the Dermatological Clinic in Bonn-Venusberg, Germany, found that levomenol can inhibit the release of histamines, which are a major contributing factor in psoriasis, eczema and contact dermatitis.

According to Rob McCaleb, President of Herb Research Foundation in Boulder, Colorado, levomenol supports skin metabolism and contributes to the acceleration of cell and tissue regeneration, at the same time inhibiting inflammation. By stimulating the skin to repair itself, levomenol re-establishes "normal structure to damaged skin."

Tea Tree Oil Is "Oil of Melaleuca"

Tea tree oil is a topical oil known as "oil of Melaleuca." This is an incredible germicide, bactericide, and fungicide that doesn't damage healthy skin. It cleans an affected area and lets the body heal itself. For centuries, the aborigines of Australia have used the leaves as poultices for infected wounds and skin problems.

Tea tree is effective in treating all sorts of skin conditions, including psoriasis, without irritating the skin. It also relieves a variety of skin conditions such as burns, acne, cuts, insect bites, stings, rashes, athlete's foot, sores, and can be used as a flea repellent, and as a product to combat nail fungus! This is one product everyone should have in their medicine cabinets. It is a totally safe and natural product, but again, only for external use. Some medical journals recommend "Oil of Melaleuca" as a vaginal douche for yeast problems (*candida albicans*).[34]

Wild Mexican Yam Cream

The Mexican Yam (*Dioscorea villosa*), was first mentioned for its miraculous healing uses in 25 B.C. in the Pen Tsao Ching by the Chinese, who highly valued the herb. It has played a prominent role in folk medicine for several centuries, but it was not until 1936 that Japanese researchers extracted a chemical called *diosgenin* from the dioscorea yam, and discovered that the extract was remarkably similar to some of the adrenal hormones in the human body, including progesterone.

Now it is being used for women with menopausal symptoms to naturally balance their hormones. It is used as a topical cream, and also vaginally.

Most evidence shows wild yam extract does not raise DHEA blood levels. But some authorities feel the wild yam extract is still effective, even though the blood levels stay the same. Wild yam extract is usually used as a transdermal cream (absorbed through the skin). Some find it effective for women with menopausal hot flashes. You can find these yam creams in your nutrition store.

Oil Baths Are a Great Home Remedy— Avoid Strong Soaps

When you bathe, avoid using strong detergent soaps. These soaps strip away natural oils and moisture from your skin. Instead, try mild, unperfumed soaps. Excessive bathing or showering robs your body of natural moisturizing oils as the water is usually very alkaline.

Here is a Great Home Remedy for People with Itching Skin, Eczema, or Very Dry, Flaky Skin:

Put about 6 inches of warm water in your bath tub. Then add 1-2 cups of inexpensive white vinegar to help turn the alkaline water into a more neutral pH. Your skin has a slight acid mantel to it and city tap water is very alkaline.

To this, add 3-4 tablespoons of oil (canola, soy, safflower oil—the type of oil you normally would use in cooking). Stir it up in the water. Olive oil is great but it smells too strong for my liking. Soak in this water for about 10 minutes. This allows your skin to pull in the oil, much like a sponge.

This is an excellent treatment for children who have eczema and itch all over. Just let them play in the water for awhile.

Blot your skin dry with a soft towel; you don't want to wipe off all the oil.

You may want to apply a thin layer of jojoba oil mixed with vitamins A and E to your body before you go to bed. This will really feel great!

May you always have beautiful, healthy skin, hair and nails!

Chapter 5

Our Windows

To The World

Preventing Glaucoma, Cataracts and Other Eye Conditions

"The health of the eye is largely dependent on a variety of nutrients, especially oxygen. The amount of blood which flows through the eye highlights the essential need of proper nutrition for optimal eye health and function."
—Gladys Lindberg

Sight is our richest sense, our link to the world and its wealth of imagery. It's always amazing to me when I study the eye to think of all the processes that must take place in order for us to be able to see. Each waking second the eyes send about a billion pieces of fresh information to the brain. The eye can sense about 10,000,000 gradations of light and 7,000,000 gradations of color. We see in such detail because the eye is almost an extension of our brain.[1]

The health of the eye is largely dependent on a variety of nutrients, the foremost of which is oxygen. When the normal functions that deliver nutrition and oxygen to the eye begin to fail, many disorders soon follow. Most of these disorders are associated with aging—cataracts, glaucoma, and macular degeneration. But are they *truly* linked to *aging*? They may not be!

Signs of Aging?

Although cataracts, glaucoma, and macular degeneration have been called "signs of aging" for years, these health problems may also be averted or lessened with proper diet and nutritional supplements. In both human and animal studies, antioxidants seem to offer the greatest protection against age-related degeneration of the eyes.

Cataracts

The lens of the eye is the only transparent organ in the body. A cataract is a loss of this transparency which eventually interferes with vision. It never causes complete blindness, because even a densely opalescent lens will still transmit light. However, with increasing loss of transparency, the clarity and detail of the image is progressively lost. Even at a fairly advanced stage, a cataract may not be apparent to a casual observer. Cataracts usually occur in both eyes, but in most cases, one eye is more severely affected than the other.

Worldwide, some fifty million people are afflicted with cataracts, including about half of the worldwide population over the age of 75. At present, about 30 percent of all Americans age 75 and older have cataracts. In fact, almost everyone over the age of 65 has some degree of cataract, but usually to a minor degree and often confined to the edge of the lens where it does not interfere with vision. More than 1.2 million cataract surgeries are performed each year in America. The condition is so common that cataracts are almost considered "normal" in the elderly.[2]

Cataract Patients Deficient in Vitamin C.

Many investigators, beginning as early as 1935, have reported that cataract patients have very little vitamin C in the aqueous humor (the fluid held between the lens and the tissue at the front of the eye). According to the late Linus Pauling, Ph.D., in a normal person there is twenty-five times more vitamin C in the aqueous humor of the eye than in blood plasma.[3]

Supplementation with vitamin C has caused early cataracts to regress or even disappear. The vision of 60 to 90 percent of patients with early cataracts improved in one study, with some cases of improvement labeled "dramatic."[4]

Low vitamin C has actually been labeled by researchers as the cause, not the consequence, of cataract formation.

What I want to know is why, after sixty years of research, this information hasn't been told to every senior citizen as part of their health care program? Now you know!!

Cataracts Can Regress, Reverse, or Disappear.

Dr. Morgan Raiforth, a pioneering ophthalmologist, showed in a series of published photos that arteriosclerotic damage in the retinal vessels could be *reversed* by using 1,200 IU of vitamin E and three to five grams (3,000 to 5,000 mg) of vitamin C. The vessels in the retina of the eye are readily visible through the dilated pupil since they are covered by only a single layer of cells. As a result, all the pathological changes such as hemorrhages, exudates (oozing of fluid from vessels), scars, and other types of damage in the arteries, veins, and capillaries—can be seen and photographed. The changes with vitamin E and vitamin C therapy are visible, and dramatic in his report.[5]

An extensive review of nutrition and eye disorders appeared in the February 1994 issue of the *Journal of Nutritional Biochemistry*. In one U.S. study, high blood levels of vitamin E and iron were linked to a reduced risk of developing cataracts. High levels of glycine and aspartic acid, two amino acids, also decreased cataract risk, according to researcher G. E. Bunce.[6]

In another large-scale study, researchers reported that volunteers who had high levels of vitamin E in their blood had only half the risk of developing nuclear cataracts, which involve the central part of the lens of the eye, compared to those with low levels of vitamin E in their plasma. Vitamin E also offered protection against cortical cataracts, which involve the periphery of the lens.[7]

Researchers have estimated that if a person is able to delay cataract formation by only ten years, they lower their need for an operation by 50 percent. Just think of the impact in savings on our national health-care cost![8]

Vitamins E and C are Both Valuable. Many other studies have concluded that vitamins C and E are important for the prevention of senile cataracts.[9] In one study, individuals who took only moderate amounts of vitamin E (400 IU) and vitamin C (500 mg) for five years were cataract free.[10]

Ophthalmologist Robert Azar used a combined nutritional plan to reverse cataracts in his clinic, which treats 25,000 patients annually. He places cataract patients on a low fat, complex carbohydrate diet that stresses fish, fowl, and fresh produce. Patients are supplemented with vitamin C, water-soluble vitamin E, and zinc for two months. If improvement is noted, surgery is delayed. He reports that many people on the program improve enough to make surgery unnecessary.[11]

Other nutrients that should be included are vitamin A (from fish oil), the bioflavonoids (grape seed extract and pine bark extract—Pycnogenol®), bilberry and the complete vitamin B-complex. Research indicates that the elderly should also consider taking a complete mineral complex that includes: selenium, zinc, calcium, magnesium, and manganese—all of which have been linked in the scientific research journals to eye health.

Glaucoma

Glaucoma is a painful affliction in which there is increased pressure within the eyeball, often resulting in blindness. Glaucoma sometimes has a hereditary cause, or it may result from an eye infection, injury, or emotional stress. It can often be controlled by medication. If you have glaucoma, I suggest you follow your physician's advice, as well as the nutritional plan for cataracts described above.

Dr. Cheraskin studied sixty glaucoma patients, ages 26 to 74, and found that when vitamin C intake was increased to 1,200 mg, the pressure on the eyes was decreased.[12] Other investigators have reported similar results.

Perhaps most striking was a report in which glaucoma patients were given very high doses of vitamin C (30 to 40 grams a day, which was .5 grams per kilogram of body weight) for a period of seven months. I am sure this was a buffered powder (neutral pH) so it wouldn't upset the stomach. The pressure in the eye decreased to about one half! This high dosage controlled the glaucoma for some patients, while others had a decrease in the amount of medication they needed to control the condition.[13]

Macular Degeneration

While cataracts are thought by many to be the primary cause of vision loss in the elderly, a little-known eye condition called age-related macular degeneration actually ranks as the leading cause of irreversible blindness among older Americans. The disease afflicts one out of three people over age 75.

Macular degeneration is a progressive but painless disorder that affects the central part of the retina, causing gradual loss of vision. It usually affects both eyes, either simultaneously or one shortly after the other.

The macula is the part of the retina that distinguishes fine detail at the center of the field of vision. Degeneration begins with partial breakdown of an insulating layer between the retina and the choroid (layer of blood vessels behind the retina). Fluid leakage occurs, and new blood vessels growing from the choroid destroy the retinal nerve tissue and replace it with scar tissue. The effect is roughly a circular area of blindness, increasing in size until it is large enough to obliterate two or three words at normal reading distance.

With early diagnosis, it sometimes is possible to seal off the leakage with laser surgery. The disorder is untreatable once it has resulted in blindness.[14] The condition, however, can be helped in both early and late stages to stop or slow the degeneration, and much can be done to help prevent it. All the nutritional supplements for cataracts and glaucoma are also important to take for macular degeneration, especially for the preventive stage and early diagnosis.

Retinopathy

This is a disease or visual disorder of the retina, characterized by hemorrhages of the retinal blood vessels. It is usually associated with either hypertension or diabetes, and it is a major cause of blindness among diabetics.

Dr. Melvyn Werbach M.D., explains that platelets are small disk-shaped particles in the blood that are the building blocks of blood clots. Diabetics' platelets are prone to clump together. This is believed to contribute to the tendency for diabetics to develop diseases of both small and large blood vessels. Supplementation with vitamin E has been shown to reduce this abnormal clumping tendency and to reduce elevated blood fats. Vitamin E may therefore help to prevent the development of such complications.[15]

Of course all the antioxidants I have mentioned should be added to a diabetics program. Chromium and selenium would also be valuable in addition to the complete vitamin and mineral formula.

Pharmaceutical Drugs. Leonard Levine, Ph.D., reports certain prescription drugs can "impair the biological health of the visual system."[16] People who experience unexpected visual disturbances when they are taking medications can't determine for themselves whether the drugs are the cause. The best course is to consult your physician.[17] *The Physician's Desk Reference* lists 94 medications that can cause glaucoma, including steroids, antihypertensives and antidepressants. Be sure to check the side effects of the medications you are taking if you are having problems with your eyes.

Nutritional Suggestions for Various Eye Conditions

Bilberry

Interest in bilberry (*Vaccinium myrtillus*) was first aroused when the British Royal Air Force pilots reported improved night vision on bombing raids during World War II after they were given bilberries and bilberry jam. Subsequent studies showed that giving bilberry extract to healthy subjects resulted in improved night-time visual acuity, especially after exposure to glare. "It helped against fatigue, reduced eye irritation, nearsightedness and nightblindness, extended the range and sharpness of vision, aided in the adaptation to darkness by accelerating regeneration of the retina and helped to restrain the development of conditions such as glaucoma cataracts."[18]

Ginkgo Biloba

Ginkgo biloba extract has antioxidant activity, improves arterial blood flow, and enhances cellular metabolism. It is known for its anti-aging properties and has been used in some cultures for centuries to help prevent degenerative changes in the eye. Ginkgo improves blood circulation in the eye and related eye structures such as the retina which helps prevent macular degeneration.[19] More information on ginkgo is found in Chapter 6.

Bilberry and Ginkgo. Clinical studies in humans have demonstrated that bilberry extract (25 percent *anthocyanidin* content), ginkgo biloba extract (24 percent *ginkgo heteroside* content) and zinc sulfate are capable of halting progressive vision loss. Bilberry and ginkgo are potent in their antioxidant and free-radical scavenging activity, and the anthocyanidins and ginkgo heterosides appear to have some degree of specificity for the eye.[20]

Importance of Carotenoids

A study reports that a higher intake of carotenoids (for example, beta-carotene) was associated with a lower risk for macular degeneration. Writing in the *Journal of the American Medical Association*, Johanna M. Seddon, M.D., evaluated 356 cases of advanced stage macular degeneration for one year, with ages from 55 to 80 years against 520 control subjects. After adjusting for variables, she found that the highest intake of carotenoids, for example beta-carotene, was associated with 43 percent lower risk of macular degeneration compared to the lowest one-fifth. "A regular intake of spinach and collard greens was especially protective," she said.[21]

Carotenoids—Lutein and Zeaxanthin

Two particular compounds contained in green leafy vegetables—lutein and zeaxanthin—are carotenoids, members of the family of red and yellow pigments that include beta-carotene. Scientists speculate that by accumulating in the retina and filtering out certain types of light rays that may cause damage, these compounds may leave both the retina and the macula less vulnerable to degeneration.[22]

Flavonoids and OPCs from Grape Seed and Pine Bark

A group of compounds found in plants, like grape seeds and pine bark, contain *flavonoids* which have antioxidant and anti-inflammatory effects for the eye. They are also found in high concentrations in blueberries, grapes, and other dark berries. These flavonoids improve night vision and adaptation to the dark. They help regenerate collagen and shield it from free-radical attack.[23] They help strengthen and restore permeability of capillaries to allow more oxygen, nutrients, enzymes and hormones to pass through cell membranes to replenish all the trillions of cells in the body.[24] This promotes smoothness and elasticity of the skin, improving circulation in the eyes and limbs. They also increase memory capacity since these compounds pass the blood-brain barrier.[25] They also improve visual acuity and improve capillary integrity to reduce hemorrhage in diabetic retinopathy.[26] More information on OPCs is found in Chapter 3.

All the Antioxidants

The *Journal of Nutritional Biochemistry* has also reported that antioxidants, such as vitamins E, C, and the carotenoids, can directly intercept and reduce the free-radicals that damage the eyes.

G. E. Bunce, Ph.D., of the Virginia Polytechnic Institute in Blacksburg, has suggested that these substances are able to diminish, but not necessarily prevent, oxidant and photochemical damage to the lens and retina. Dr. Bunce recommends vitamin E 200 to 400 IU a day, vitamin C 250 mg a day, and beta-carotene 25 mg a day as supplements to reduce the oxidant burden. He also adds that the oxycarotenoids (lutein and zeaxanthin) are important antioxidants and serve as light-absorbing pigments in the retina.[27]

Wolfgang Schalch in *Free-Radicals and Aging* explains that of the approximately 600 naturally occurring carotenoids, lutein and zeaxanthin are crucial constituents of the macula lutea (the yellow spot in the macula). Researchers believe they may prevent damage to the eye by filtering out visible blue light.

Most of the researchers are in agreement that if you are concerned about eye health, you need to have a high daily intake of all the antioxidants to prevent free-radical damage. This includes vitamins A, E, C, B-complex, plus the minerals zinc and selenium. There is no cure for many eye problems after they have taken hold, except surgery for cataracts. Prevention is the best solution!

Addition of Selenium and Increased Vitamin C

Wolfgang Schalch recommends a similar vitamin program as Dr. Bunce but adds the additional antioxidant selenium in a dose of 250 mcg a day, and he increases the vitamin C dose to 500 mg a day. In one study of 102 patients having acute macular degeneration for seven to twelve years, some 60 percent of those patients treated with this program reported improved or halted degenerative macular changes.[28] If the study was conducted with a higher potency of C, would the results had been even more impressive?

Several of the new products especially formulated for the eyes contain a variety of antioxidant vitamins and minerals and lutein. These special "eye" formulas are available in nutrition stores.

Vitamin B2—Riboflavin

This is one of the most widespread deficiencies in America. It can make the eye highly sensitive to light, so that a person must wear dark sunglasses much of the time. A deficiency is also marked by faulty vision in dim light; eyelids that burn and itch; eyes that water easily—and which become bloodshot if strained; and a feeling of sand or grit inside the eyelid resulting in a person constantly rubbing or wiping his or her eyes.

A person who has an increased twitching of the eyelids may have a B2 deficiency (as well as a magnesium and B6 deficiency). A severe deficiency is often manifested by the skin at the corners of the eye splitting and the eyes burning and becoming fiery red.[29]

Vitamin B2 helps with the prevention of both cataracts and glaucoma, according to numerous research reports. It is a necessary cofactor for the antioxidant enzyme, glutathione reductase. A deficiency in animals leads to cataracts.

Vitamin B6—Pyridoxine

If you wear contact lenses and have a problem with "dry eye disease," take note. A number of cases in Canada reported that daily supplementation with 500 mg of vitamin B6 increased tearing sufficiently to allow the wearing of contact lenses. Other supplements needed were niacinamide, vitamin C, zinc and magnesium.[30]

Vitamin A

Vitamin A deficiency has been linked to night blindness, a quick tiring of the eyes, sensitivity to bright lights and glare, less accurate day vision, dry eye disease (the tear duct dries up), red rims around the eye lids, and mucous on the eyes at night (sometimes to the point where the eye and eyelid feel stuck together in the morning).[31]

A severe deficiency results in retinitis pigmentosa, a slow but eventual degeneration of the retina. This causes blindness in thousands of Americans each year. It is usually preceded by years of night blindness and other vitamin A deficiencies.

The Medical Tribune, August 22, 1991, reported that lack of just this one vitamin leads to blindness in India and says that vitamin A deficiency affects 10 to 40 million children worldwide, about half of whom live in India. In addition to blindness, such children are more likely to have respiratory or gastrointestinal problems.

Zinc

Investigators feel that a zinc deficiency may play a role in preventing macular degeneration. Zinc affects parts of the eye in which zinc is known to have an important impact on the metabolic function of enzymes crucial in vision. A double-blind, placebo-controlled trial was set up to explore this possibility. In a twelve to twenty-four month follow-up, they found that patients given zinc supplements had significantly less visual loss than the group that received placebos. The zinc was given in 100 mg tablet form, twice a day with meals. The side effects were minimal.[32]

The Tufts University Diet & Nutrition Letter reports that it now appears as though simply eating a diet rich in spinach, collards, kale, and other dark greens may help stave off macular degeneration. The connection, judging by new research, seems to be that certain substances in leafy vegetables and other produce are found in the portion of the eye subject to damage from age-related macular degeneration.

The Essential Amino Acids—Protein

As cells deteriorate, people age. As cells malfunction, people get sick. When you have cells that are missing the essential amino acids, the body will "cement" you together with scar tissue. When that scar tissue appears in your eyes, you have cataracts. Protein is what every living cell of your body is made of. So get enough protein![33] Review Chapter 4 on the value of protein.

Glutathione an Amino Acid

The main function of glutathione is to break down and dispose of potentially dangerous toxins that invade the body. Glutathione is an antioxidant that protects every cell, tissue, and organ in the body. In addition to rejuvenating old and weak immune systems, it may also help prevent macular degeneration. Read more about this amazing antioxidant in Chapters 3 and 6.

Taurine

Taurine is a sulfur-containing amino acid which may protect cells from the harmful effects of ultraviolet light. Some taurine is made in the body from methionine and cysteine, but eventually these sources may prove inadequate and retinal degeneration is one of the consequences. Very large quantities of taurine are found in the retina of the eye of many mammals. Taurine is present in meats and animal products but not in plant products.[34]

Exercise for the Eye

Eye exercises are important for visual health. Dr. W. H. Bates developed "The Bates Method" which is a set of eye exercises to reduce eye stress and correct eye and vision related disorders. He said, "perfect sight is a product of perfectly relaxed organs, unconsciously controlled," and that, "vision improves naturally when people stop interfering with it. Under relaxed conditions, refractive errors tend to be self-correcting." Check into this method for some exercise and you may want to read his classic book *Better Eyesight Without Glasses*.[35]

Chapter 6

Anti-Aging

Nutrients For Our Brain

What We Can Do
to Enhance Thinking,
Elevate Mood, Boost Memory
and Prevent Alzheimer's Disease

"The health of our brain and body go hand in hand.
One can not proceed without the other. Like the
other organs of our body, the brain requires fuel,
special nutrients, and even exercise, to keep our
mind functioning properly."
—**Gladys Lindberg**

Scientists have been trying to unravel the complexities of the brain for centuries, but they still do not fully understand the mysteries of our body's most complex organ. Since we are all unique, I doubt that researchers will ever learn all the answers.

Still, there is now evidence that age-related changes in the brain physiology are influenced by the biochemical environment of the brain. There are numerous compounds in common foods and natural substances that can have a favorable impact on that biochemical environment. I hope to bring you some of the scientific research on these nutrients and natural products in relation to brain function.

Of all the organs in the body, the brain may be the most sensitive. In addition to the healthful benefits of thinking, learning, and reasoning, the brain is subject to many life threatening disorders, such as stroke, meningitis (an inflammation of the membranes covering the brain), senile dementia, Alzheimer's disease, and others.

Basic Brain Function

Weighing less than three pounds, the brain is one of the busiest, most metabolically active organs in the body. Although it represents less than 2 percent of the body's total weight, the brain is involved in 15 percent of the body's total blood flow, 25 percent of its oxygen utilization, and at least 70 percent of its glucose (sugar) consumption.[1]

Unlike other organs, the brain—which is composed of a compact network of more than ten billion nerve cells—is not capable of storing its own supply of energy. It depends, rather, on a constant flow of blood to keep it supplied with nutrients. While other organs in the body can metabolize fat and protein for energy, the brain must depend primarily on glucose from the blood for energy. Without the proper nutrients, proteins used by nerve cells in the brain cannot be manufactured, which can lead to impairment of mental functions such as memory. Finally, unlike other tissues in the body that can heal after an injury, brain cells are incapable of regenerating themselves.[2] This makes the brain especially vulnerable to illness and injury. In sum, the brain is highly dependent upon the nutrients carried to it in the bloodstream. It must have a continual supply of glucose, oxygen, and other essential nutrients.

Blood-Brain Barrier

Since the brain depends primarily on glucose for most of its metabolic activities, it has a special apparatus to pump glucose from the blood into the brain cells across a special blood-brain barrier. This barrier also prevents most large molecules and toxins in the blood from migrating into brain tissue, keeping many potentially damaging substances out of the brain. The barrier allows small molecules—such as oxygen, glutamine, anesthetics, alcohol, and certain toxins to cross the barrier easily. This protective mechanism, of course, can be compromised by disease, such as infection.[3]

The quality of nutrients fed to each of these areas of the brain directly impacts a person's ability to think and remember, as well as the person's mood.

Both Physical and Emotional Involvement

Age-related decline in brain function is extremely common and sometimes a serious problem. The condition is often referred to as senile dementia, mental deterioration, memory impairment, and cognitive decline.

Elderly individuals often are taking a wide variety of prescription and over-the-counter medications, which can adversely affect mental function. These medications can also cause mood swings and depression.

People come to me with many types of nutritional problems, and some are related to emotional ones. When a person is physically stronger and in better health, he or she very often is *better equipped* to cope with emotional problems or to face the difficult circumstances of their lives.

Loss of Cognitive Capacities. Let's define *cognition*. Cognition is our ability to think, reason, recognize, remember and perceive.

The progressive loss of mental agility with age has become a major focus of clinical research efforts. Beginning around mid-life, the brain's higher functions of memory, learning and concentration begin to fade. According to Paris Kidd, Ph.D., "Over the adult life span, individuals who are otherwise healthy can lose as much as half (50%) of their cognitive capacities, as measured from tests related to everyday tasks that rely on cognitive skills. Such progressive and insidious loss of the brain's higher functions can have a telling effect on personal productivity, can damage self-esteem, and bring considerable distress to many aging adults." [4]

Aging is Stress

Aging itself is a form of stress which we will all inevitably encounter. Stress increases our need for many nutrients, and when these needs are not met, deficiencies develop. These deficiencies, in effect, rob the brain of vitamins and minerals necessary to help brain enzymes produce enough brain chemicals to keep a person functioning at a normal level. A downward spiral can result. The greater the impact of stress, the greater the deficiency, and the lower the brain function.

Positive Mental Attitude

I want to mention here the importance of a strong will and mental attitude of "I am going to make it," or "I am going to get well," or "thank you Lord for my healing." Researchers have finally proven there is a link between the immune system and the brain.

Of course the Bible refers to this several times. The book of Proverbs says, "For as a man thinketh in his heart, so is he." There is another scripture in Philippians that says, "Finally, brethren, whatsoever things are true, whatsoever things are honest, whatsoever things are just, ... pure, ... lovely, are of good report; if there be any virtue, and if there be any praise, think on these things." (Phil 4:8)

We also need to program our mind and see ourselves living

a healthy, active life, free of disease, into a ripe old age. This is anti-aging at its best!

Hypoglycemia:
Major Emotional Symptoms

Mood swings may be directly associated with an inadequate diet. Some of the major symptoms of hypoglycemia or low blood sugar are irritability, depression, constant worrying, unprovoked anxieties, insomnia, antisocial behavior, crying spells, lack of concentration, phobias (fears), mental confusion, and even suicidal intent. If you are experiencing depression, anxiety, panic attacks, and other emotional problems, eliminate the possibility that your problem may be the result of low blood sugar. We need to *eat* small feedings *often*, and *eliminate sugar and refined carbohydrates* from the diet and include a vitamin and mineral formula to your own health-building program. Read more on hypoglycemia and a complete nutrition program in Chapter 13.

Ruling Out Food Factors

Foods have been known to induce depressions through a variety of mechanisms, including cerebral allergy, food addiction, hypersensitivity to chemical food additives, reactions to molds, and so forth. Sugar, refined and processed foods, and alcohol have also been related to mood swings. Watch a child have an allergic response to a chocolate dessert and you will see their personality change before your eyes. Allergic disorders are common among those who are depressed.

Depression may also be associated with levels of caffeine consumption greater than four cups of coffee a day. Eliminating caffeine and sugar has been shown to lift depression within a week![5]

Vitamin and Mineral Deficiencies
and Depression

A number of vitamin deficiencies have been linked to depression, especially deficiencies in biotin, folic acid, pyridoxine (B6), riboflavin (B2), thiamin (B1), vitamin B12, and vitamin C. Folic acid, in particular, has been associated with depression. The worse the depression, the lower the level of folic acid in the blood, a fact that is often a consequence of poor diet or the use of alcohol and drugs.[6]

Mineral deficiencies of calcium, iron, magnesium, and potassium have been associated with depression. Excess or toxic amounts of vanadium have also been linked to it.

Be Sure to Check Thyroid Function

A person who is suffering from depression should also check his or her thyroid function. If you have a history of cold hands and feet, weight gain, and generalized fatigue, thyroid malfunction may be the root cause of your depression. The work of Dr. Broda Barnes has documented this connection. Read more about the thyroid in Chapter 8.

Physical Exercise Helps in Depression

We all feel better after taking a brisk walk or engaging in vigorous activity. Exercise increases dopamine levels in the brain and also the level of endorphins. We now know that endorphins create a sense of well being and even relieve pain.

Physical activity tends to decrease anxiety, hostility, and other stress-related disorders. Aerobic exercises, slow jogging, stationary bike riding, or any physical exercise undertaken for at least thirty minutes to an hour is excellent. Ideally, such exercise should be part of a fitness program for everyone at least four times a week. Many authorities feel one of the main causes of depression in the elderly may be a lack of physical exercise.

Understanding Neurotransmitters

Communication within the brain, and between the brain and the rest of the nervous system occurs through many different chemicals and electrical impulses. We think of nerve impulses throughout the body as being electrical, but the transmission of these impulses from one neuron to the next is achieved both chemically and electrically. Different parts of the brain contain different concentrations of these brain chemicals, and when these balances are disrupted, a variety of neurologic and psychiatric diseases may occur. The majority of these chemicals, known as neurotransmitters, are made up of amino acids.[8]

Eight essential amino acids are found together in adequate amounts in all animal products such as cheese, milk, chicken, beef, and certain vegetable proteins such as soy.

Certain amino acids are known to be involved in the synthesis of important neurotransmitters. Here are a few of the most important:

A Simple Amino Acid—DLPA

In Dr. Andrew Weil's *Self-Healing: Relieving Depression Simply,* he states that people with mild to moderate depression can benefit by combining regular aerobic exercise with a simple amino acid and vitamin formula. Dr. Weil prescribes a waking dose of 1,500 mg of DL-phenylalanine (DLPA). This amino acid mood elevator taken on an empty stomach is absorbed into the blood and brain, which use it to synthesize more of the excitatory neurotransmitters that increase wakefulness and energy. Along with DLPA, Dr. Weil suggests 500 mg of vitamin C, 100 mg of vitamin B6, and a small piece of fruit or small glass of fruit juice, followed by at least a 45-minute wait before eating breakfast. In the evening you should follow the same routine. Along with the DLPA, take with the vitamin C and B6. If on medications, the recommendation is usually safe, but consult your physician.[7]

Tryptophan

Tryptophan is an essential amino acid, which means we are unable to make it within our bodies and therefore must depend upon our food supply for it. Until 1989, it could be purchased over-the-counter as a supplement, but it is now only available by prescription. It has been found to be directly linked with the neurotransmitter serotonin. Serotonin is thought to be an inducer and regulator of sleep. It also controls states of consciousness, mood, and may reduce sensitivity to pain and have tranquilizing effects.[8,9]

The newest antidepressant medications attempt to change the serotonin balance in the brain to elevate a person's mood, but they have many side effects. Researchers at the Massachusetts Institute of Technology discovered that the serotonin concentration in the brain is directly proportional to the concentration of brain and plasma tryptophan. This was the first accepted demonstration of the direct dietary control of a brain neurotransmitter by tryptophan, a single amino acid.[10]

Tryptophan is not an easy amino acid to get from your diet, but good sources are milk and turkey. It is also found in soy protein, and small amounts in brown rice, peanuts, pumpkin, lentils and sesame seeds. Tryptophan is regarded by some as nature's weapon against depression and insomnia. A warm glass of milk before bed to help you sleep may not be just an old wives tale, but may be an effect of tryptophan!

Tyrosine

The amino acids phenylalanine (DLPA) and tyrosine are precursors of the catecholamines, which are adrenaline-like neurotransmitters. Norepinephrine and epinephrine are the neurotransmitters that are released in the "fight or flight" response. When confronted with a stress, these chemicals increase your heart rate, blood pressure and level of arousal. Tyrosine is a precursor to another important neurotransmitter called dopamine, which is vital for normal muscle tone. Abnormalities in dopamine concentration in parts of the brain lead to Parkinson's disease. Tyrosine is also essential for normal thyroid hormone production. It has been determined to be a safe and lasting therapy for depression, mood, hypertension, Parkinson's disease, low sex drive, appetite suppression, and therapy for cocaine addicts. It is also felt to be useful for those of us living high stress lives.[11] Very little tyrosine is found in cereals, vegetables, fruit or oils. The best dietary sources are meats, wheat germ, soy and other animal proteins.

Glutamine, Glutamic Acid, Gamma-Amino-Butyric Acid (GABA)

These three amino acids are relatives of each other, and each one affects the metabolism of the others. All three have been shown to be effective in treating decreased mental performance from various causes.

Glutamine performs a number of functions related to brain metabolism. It serves as a major fuel source for the brain as well as the rest of the body. See the later pages for more information on this valuable amino acid.

Glutamic Acid is considered a stimulant neurotransmitter. It is one of the most highly concentrated amino acids in the brain, and has been found in particularly high quantities in the hippocampus, or memory center of the brain.

GABA is a calming neurotransmitter and actually affects brain cells the same way as alcohol or many popular sedatives, but obviously without the side effects or addictions.

All three amino acids have documented therapeutic value in the treatment of hypertension, schizophrenia, aging, dyskinesia, Parkinson's disease, epilepsy, alcoholism and other diseases.[12] Dr. Carlton Fredericks reported that supplements of glutamic acid or of glutamine have brought behavior improvement in elderly patients with psychiatric illness. He has also seen rises in the IQs of children given glutamic acid. They don't all respond, and responses differ in degree, but sometimes 9 or 10 grams of glutamic acid, or a gram of glutamine daily, will produce impressive improvements in the ability to learn, to retain and to recall.[11]

The bottom line is this: you must have adequate protein intake on a regular basis in order for you to have sufficient amino acids in your system for optimum brain function!

Essential Nutrients for Healthy Brain Function

Scientific evidence is currently stimulating a resurgence of interest in the link between nutrition and cognition. Interest is focused on what is called "subclinical" malnutrition—which is a nutritional deficiency that is relatively mild. These subclinical deficiencies manifest themselves with very subtle symptoms, generally ones related to brain functions such as intelligence and memory.

Numerous studies have confirmed that a selective vitamin deficiency can cause mental problems at any age. Dr. Carl Pfeiffer was just one of several who studied the aged and found that when people of the same age are compared, those with senility are more likely to be deficient nutritionally. Malnutrition is one cause of reversible senility, as long as the senility has not progressed too far.

The Vital Vitamin B-Complex and our Brain

We know the B-complex vitamins are essential for all aspects of the nervous system, including brain function. The B vitamins need to be taken together in adequate amounts throughout one's life.

In a study of 228 individuals between 73 and 102 years of age, 30 percent had low blood levels of one or more B vitamins. These deficiencies occurred even though food intake was adequate and all were taking a daily vitamin supplement. This study suggests that absorption of B vitamins is impaired in a large portion of the geriatric population.[13]

All of the B vitamins help with brain function:

- **Thiamin (B1)**—the brain and nerves are the first areas of the body to show signs of a deficiency. Symptoms may include mental confusion, subjectively poor memory, difficulty in concentration, and even mental illness.
- **Riboflavin (B2)** helps with cognitive impairment and mental deficit.
- **Niacin (B3)** is considered a memory enhancer and a method of treatment for senility.
- **Pantothenic acid (B5)** is essential to support the adrenal glands when a person comes under stress.
- **Pyridoxine (B6)** is necessary for the manufacturing of valuable neurotransmitters essential for mental functions.
- **Cobalamin (B12)** increases the rate at which new material can be learned.
- **Folic Acid** has been shown to prevent senility or dementia.

I want to explain a few of these in more detail for you...

The Importance of Niacin in Aging

As a person ages, the importance of the B vitamins increases, according to Abram Hoffer, M.D., Ph.D., author of *Orthomolecular Medicine for Physicians*.[14] Hoffer sites vitamin B3—niacin and niacinamide—as being especially important in preventing or treating senility. As a Canadian psychiatrist, Hoffer has found vitamin B3 very effective in restoring memory, improving energy levels, lessening the need for sleep, and increasing alertness.[15]

Dr. Humphry Osmond M.D., at the New Jersey Psychiatric Institute reported that a form of niacin was effective in treating

1,000 patients with schizophrenia. Hoffer and Osmond have been reporting in medical journals for almost forty years their almost miraculous results with schizophrenic patients (which is the most serious mental disorder). They found that 75 percent of their patients were cured with niacin treatment." 'Cured' is quite a significant word, one not often used with regard to this terrible mental illness that afflicts most of the patients in our mental hospitals."[16]

Dr. Hoffer reported as early as 1962 in the Lancet:

"Niacin has some, though not all, the qualities of an ideal treatment: it is safe, cheap and easy to administer and it uses a known pharmaceutical substance which can be taken for years on end if necessary. . . . Why, then have these benefits passed almost unheeded? One reason may be the extraordinary proliferation of the phenothiazine derivatives since 1954. These are tranquilizers.

Unlike these, niacin is a simple, well-known vitamin which can be bought cheaply in bulk and cannot be patented, and there has been no campaign to persuade doctors of its usefulness."[17]

There are several forms of niacin available; plain niacin which can cause a flush to the skin, or "no-flush" niacin which is combined with inositol. Niacinamide does not cause a flush and is also effective.

Folic Acid Therapy

Surveys have found repeatedly that older people are often deficient in two B vitamins—folic acid and B12. Several investigators have reported that patients with symptoms of senility or dementia (the terms are synonymous) and who had low folic acid blood levels, showed improvement after therapy with folic acid.[18] Scientists in England found that supplementing the diets of patients with folic acid resulted in shorter stays at their mental hospital. Fortunately for the patients but unfortunately for acceptance within the medical community, this study was not a controlled study (which meant that it had no control group compared to an experimental group).[19]

Residents of nursing homes and chronic wards of mental hospitals are at considerable risk for folic acid deficiency.[20] These institutions, if they serve folate-rich green vegetables at all, are likely to do so in fairly unpalatable fashion. To compound the problem, many older people have chewing and digestive difficulties. Research shows a folic acid deficiency is often unrecognized in some elderly patients. Therefore, supplementation with B-complex vitamins, including folic acid, may be helpful to those in nursing homes, suffering from senility or dementia.

Vitamin B12 Therapy

Deficiency of vitamin B12, which results in pernicious anemia, is a common vitamin deficiency. In the vast majority of cases, a person may be getting adequate B12 in his or her diet, but lacks a stomach-produced substance called the "intrinsic factor" which is necessary for absorption of the vitamin. B12 is difficult to absorb, which is why people are often given B12 injections.

A deficiency of hydrochloric acid (HCl) production in the stomach is known to impair vitamin B12 and folic acid absorption. Up to 50 percent of people age 60 and older, experience seriously diminished hydrochloric acid production. Adding hydrochloric acid to the diets of the elderly normalizes vitamin B12 and folic acid absorption, according to Jonathan Wright, M.D.[21]

A vitamin B12 deficiency is related to some cases of mood disorders. Most elderly have symptoms of intellectual impairment, manifested as poor memory for recent events, difficulty in concentrating and difficulty at work. Some will have symptoms of a burning sensation, unsteadiness, fatigue, and sometimes urinary incontinence. A broad spectrum of psychiatric symptoms, from irritability to apathy to psychosis with hallucinations, may also occur.[22]

A Widespread B12 Deficiency? A deficiency in this vitamin may be more widespread than is generally recognized by the medical profession, because the range considered "normal" for serum cobalamin (B12) is probably lower than it should be. In many cases, senile dementia of the Alzheimer's type and "chronic fatigue syndrome," which may very well be linked to a B12 deficiency, could be reversed through B12 therapy, if diagnosed early enough.[23]

It may be that a high serum maintenance level is preferable to a merely adequate one, especially since the B-vitamins are water-soluble and any excess is excreted by our bodies through the urine.

Nursing Homes. Recent studies suggest that a small but significant percentage of patients who are presently institutionalized in nursing homes or state hospitals for psychosis or senility actually have B12 deficiencies, a treatable condition.[24]

For many years, the medical profession held to the opinion that mental symptoms did not occur in the absence of anemic changes in the red blood cells. Thus, many physicians discounted the possibility of B12 deficiency as the cause of memory problems if the complete blood count was normal. We now know that the mental symptoms can occur before any changes are evident in red cells.[25]

Vitamin B12 Injections. Vitamin B12 is a completely safe and inexpensive treatment. Dr. Alan Gaby says, "We usually forego the test in favor of a therapeutic trial of vitamin B12 injections. If the patient improves after a series of four to eight injections, we recommend continuing them on an as-needed basis."[26-27]

The usual recommendation is that a person take oral doses of B12 in the range of 1,000 to 2,500 micrograms a day. It is also available sublingually (under the tongue) which can deliver more of the B12 to the blood stream. Or as Dr. Gaby suggests, ask your physician about regular B12 injections for a few months.

Good dietary sources for vitamin B12 are fish, dairy products, organ meats (especially kidney and liver), eggs, beef, and pork. Vegetarians are often deficient in B12 and need to take it in supplement form since it is primarily found in animal products.

L- Glutamine Is a "Brain Fuel"

When I was in high school, we already knew that glutamic acid, a nonessential amino acid, improved memory. My brother and I always took it while we were studying for tests and had great hope it would work. Research showed it could improve intelligence, give a lift when a person was fatigued, and help control alcoholism, schizophrenia, and a craving for sweets.

Since then, we have learned that the brain has a protective barrier that lets in very few chemicals. Glutamic acid is one substance that is "poorly" carried across the protective blood barrier, which is why so much of it has to be consumed for an effect to be registered.

Dr. Roger Williams has shown that another amino acid, the *amide* form of glutamic acid called *L-glutamine*, can cross the blood-brain barrier more readily, and once it has crossed the barrier, it is quickly converted into glutamic acid. The L indicates a natural form of the amino acid which is used in this discussion.

Glutamine's major function is that it serves as "fuel" for the brain. It is the only other compound besides glucose (blood sugar) which can be used by the brain for energy. It has also been shown to improve the IQs of mentally deficient children.[28]

Dr. Williams observed that glutamine protected rats against the poisonous effects of alcohol, but more importantly, it stopped their craving for alcohol. He found that experimental rats fed glutamine consistently decreased alcohol consumption.[29]

Not only rats, but nine out of ten alcoholics reported that after taking glutamine supplements, they had less desire to drink, less anxiety, and slept better. Relatives and friends observing them agreed. They did not do well on a placebo.[30]

One anecdotal report in the medical literature tells about an alcoholic who stopped drinking when glutamine was administered to him daily without his knowledge. The substance is tasteless and can be mixed with food or water without a person knowing it, which is apparently what happened in this case. Two years after the glutamine treatment began, he is still free from his craving for alcohol.[31]

Dr. Roger Williams recommends one to four grams (1,000 to 4,000 mg) a day. Glutamine is a natural and harmless food substance without side effects. It is available in capsules and a high potency, tasteless powder.

There are reports that doses as high as 4,000 mg have been given to bone marrow transplant patients. All of the patients who received glutamine were statistically more "vigorous" and showed improvement in other areas as well. They felt less angry and less fatigued.[32] When you consider the sense of depression that accompanies most illness, you might ask whether depression could be diminished through the use of glutamine.

The most convenient and economical way to consume

glutamine is to eat protein foods. For every 10 grams of protein from a quality protein powder, about 1 gram (1,000 mg) of it is glutamine. There is more information on glutamine in Chapter 3.

Ginkgo Biloba:
The Chinese Herb for the Brain

Perhaps the most remarkable nutrient for potentially improving memory and warding off senility is the Chinese herb *Ginkgo biloba*, derived from one of the most ancient trees known to mankind. The single Ginkgo tree can live for 1,000 years. Research shows that the leaves of this tree, taken in supplement form, provide remarkable pharmacological action to the circulatory and nervous systems.

Ginkgo may very well be the most effective remedy available for short-term memory loss, slow thinking and reasoning, dizziness, ringing in the ears (tinnitus), and problems with vertigo and equilibrium. It is also being used to treat all types of dementia, cognitive disorders related to depression, absent-mindedness, confusion, lack of energy, Alzheimer's disease, and senility.[33]

Ginkgo is the most widely used prescription medicine in Europe. More than ten million prescriptions are written for it each year for a variety of conditions, especially those related to the circulatory system.

Ginkgo specifically enhances circulation to the small blood vessels that are the farthest from the heart, and to arteries, veins and capillaries. Ginkgo actually stimulates the release of a substance that relaxes the microcapillaries, thus increasing blood flow.[34] It also reduces leg pain from low blood flow to the limbs and is important for male impotence. Read more in Chapter 12.

A small double-blind study showed that ginkgo produced a significant improvement in long-distance vision for patients with macular degeneration, which is a frequent cause of blindness in the aged. It inhibits deteriorating vision due to oxygen deprivation to the retina.

Ginkgo affects mental alertness by changing the frequency of brain waves. Research has shown that ginkgo increases brain alpha rhythms, which are the brain wave frequencies associated with mental alertness. Increased mental alertness among volunteer subjects was evident after only three weeks of ginkgo therapy, and alertness continued to increase during the remaining three months of the study.[35]

Deterioration of Cognitive Function. Ginkgo seems to be particularly beneficial for those people who are just beginning to experience deterioration of cognitive function. A German researcher, Dr. E.W. Fungfeld, and his colleagues have concluded that *Ginkgo biloba* extract has promise in the treatment of Alzheimer's, as it appears to delay mental deterioration during the early stages of the disease. In fact, they contend that ginkgo may be able to reverse some of the disabilities associated with the disease and help the patient to maintain a normal life without hospitalization.[36]

Many studies using ginkgo have found that the leaves of the plant produce unique substances called *flavone glycosides*, which are powerful antioxidants. Scientific research regarding the therapeutic uses of the ginkgo extract are in full swing. A great deal of research has already been done in Europe, especially in France and Germany, to find more applications for ginkgo biloba in treating diseases that occur more frequently as we age.

Combats Symptoms of Aging. There are very few substances that combat the symptoms and signs of aging as well as this herb. *Ginkgo biloba* extract appears to fulfill all conditions laid down by the World Health Organization concerning the development of drugs effective against cerebral aging.[37-38]

Several forms of Ginkgo are available:
- Powdered leaves in capsules or tablets.
- Liquid extracts, also called tinctures.
- Powdered extracts (usually 6:1 or 8:1, which are unstandardized).
- Standardized extracts, 24% flavone glycosides.[39]

It is important to note that only the highly concentrated, extract form of ginkgo has been used in research studies: One kilo of extract being produced from fifty kilos of leaves (50:1). If you desire to purchase ginkgo biloba, find an extract which is standardized with 24 percent flavonoid glycosides, which is the active ingredient. Other less concentrated extracts are also available, but these have a much weaker action than that which has been tested conclusively. Most authorities recommend a dosage of 120 mg a day, which is 40 mg three times a day, or follow product label instructions.

Acetylcholine: A Major Neurotransmitter

Years ago Carlton Fredericks Ph.D., recommended giving choline, the vitamin B cousin, to increase the amount of acetylcholine in the nervous system. Acetylcholine is a major neurotransmitter that mediates our emotions and behavior and provides an important chemical bridge between nerve cells. Lecithin is the richest source of choline, which the brain converts to acetylcholine.

Lecithin. As a "purifier" of brain or central-nervous system functions, pure lecithin—phosphatidylcholine—certainly has few, if any, equals in the opinion of Dr. Sheldon Hendler. Phosphatidylcholine, the precursor of acetylcholine, has been given to patients to correct an acetylcholine deficiency. Short-term memory was improved in some patients who took daily doses of phosphatidylcholine (lecithin) for four months. Supplemental choline also enhanced short-term memory.[40]

Psychological Disorders. Lecithin also has been useful in detoxifying some of the severe side effects of the neuroleptic drugs and major tranquilizers used in the management of psychological disorders such as psychosis, according to Hendler. One of the worst side effects of these drugs is *tardive dyskinesia*, which is characterized by involuntary movement of the neck, head, and tongue. When used for six months or longer, these drugs deplete the brain of choline and acetylcholine, resulting in deficiencies that can last even after the neuroleptic drugs are no longer taken. Supplemental phosphatidylcholine can often arrest the involuntary movements of tardive dyskinesia, and it has been used with some success in patients with other neurological diseases such as *Gilles de la Tourette's* syndrome, *Friedreich's* *ataxia*, and a form of dyskinesia caused by the anti-Parkinson's disease drug, *Levodopa*.[41]

When Lithium has Failed. Choline and phosphatidyl-choline have also been employed in managing some forms of mania. In fact, these nutrients have been successful in cases where the mineral lithium has failed. In one study, the combination of lecithin and lithium significantly reduced the severity of manic episodes. However, when lecithin was discontinued and the patients were getting only lithium, 75 percent had a worsening of their problem.[42]

Improves Memory. Increasing the amount of acetyl-choline in the brain may open the way to improving mental function, particularly memory. Researchers at Ohio State University found that mice fed a diet laced with choline-rich lecithin or phosphatidylcholine had much better memory retention than animals given regular diets. When their brains were examined under a microscope, the lecithin-fed mice showed fewer signs of aging.[43] Specifically, the lecithin-fed mice had brain cell membranes that were less rigid and with fewer fatty deposits in them. As the brain ages, its cell membranes become more rigid with fatty deposits and they lose their ability to take in and release brain chemicals and to relay messages. This can cause memory loss and confused thinking.

As we age, brain cells also tend to lose parts of the nerve cells (*dendritic spines*) that convey impulses to the nerve cells in the body. These chemical receptor areas are very important in transmitting information. This loss in nerve cells results in a condition that may be analogous to a bad phone connection—messages tend to get distorted or lost. However, lecithin-fed mice in the study above had the same number of dendritic spines as younger mice.

Lecithin granules contain approximately 25 percent phosphatidylcholine. There are other forms that contain approximately 55 percent phosphatides but they are more expensive. The easiest way to consume lecithin is to mix it into juice, a breakfast drink or use on dry or cooked cereal. Granules are much more economical and potent as it takes approximately 10 large lecithin capsules to equal one tablespoon of granulated lecithin. All forms should be available at your nutrition store.

Phosphatidylserine:
A Remarkable Brain Cell Nutrient

Phosphatidylserine (PS) is a naturally-occurring phospholipid and is similar to other phospholipids that include phosphatidylcholine and phosphatidylinositol. Until recently, commercial lecithin contained only trace amounts, but new products include enriched powdered compounds, softgel capsules, and even liquid blends. Recent breakthroughs in technology have made phosphatidylserine (derived from soy) available commercially in a concentrated form, albeit quite expensive. It is considered an important dietary supplement for the support of brain function.

Essential to Functioning of all the Cells of the Body. The concentrated phosphatidylserine is derived from soy phospholipids and clinical studies have shown that when it is taken on a regular basis, it can help adults maintain and improve learning and memory. Phosphatidylserine is essential to the functioning of all the cells of the body, but it is most concentrated in the brain. Human research studies dating back to the 1970s indicate that phosphatidylserine tends to decline with age and that supplementation can benefit many cognitive functions (the capacity to think and reason). Some 35 human studies span almost three decades, according to Paris M. Kidd, Ph.D.

Numerous other studies involved subjects with existing, measurable losses in memory, judgment, loss of abstract thought, and loss of other higher mental functions, and in some cases, changes in personality and behavior. The results of the studies showed conclusively that, in mature adults, phosphatidylserine helped maintain cognition, concentration, and related mental functions. The dosages of these studies ranged from 200 mg to 300 mg a day.[44]

Subjects Showed Significant Improvement. In two of the studies conducted in 1991, Thomas Crook, Ph.D., of the Memory Assessment Clinics, Bethesda, Maryland, studied 149 subjects between the ages of 50 and 75. The patients received either a placebo or 300 mg of phosphatidylserine (100 mg three times a day) in a double-blind study, for twelve weeks. The subjects showed significant improvement with the following functions:

- **Name-Face Recall.** Learning and matching of names with faces.
- **First-Last Names.** First and last names presented, then last names given for pairing with the first names. Also assesses verbal memory.
- **Face Recognition.** A test of visual memory.
- **Grocery List.** To help assess verbal learning and memory.
- **Telephone Dialing.** Memorize and retain a telephone number, under different conditions of delay and distraction.
- **Misplaced Objects.** Placement and recall of keys, glasses, other common household objects—"verbal-visual associative memory."
- **Divided Attention.** Simulates driving a car, also recall of radio reports while driving. Reaction time and verbal vocabulary memory.[45]

Reduced Cognitive Age. The benefits were greatest in those with the most impaired memories. The benefits persisted at least four weeks after the supplementation was discontinued. The researchers noted that phosphatidylserine reduced the "cognitive age" of 64 to the cognitive age of 52—roughly 12 years of improvement! This was a win in the case of name-face recognition.[46]

I met with Parris M. Kidd, Ph.D., in 1996 at the Natural Products Expo West convention in Anaheim, CA and again at a convention in Nashville where he spoke. He said that when phosphatidylserine is taken orally, it is rapidly absorbed and readily crosses the blood-brain barrier. Normal aging can bring about neurotransmitter disturbances, metabolic decline, and nerve connection dropout.

Dr. Kidd believes phosphatidylserine makes clinically measurable contributions to all of these brain functions, and furthermore, toxicological studies have shown it to be completely safe without side effects.[47]

Memory and Learning Improved. Dr. Kidd pointed out a study in 1993 by an Italian doctor who carried out a major, randomized, double-blind, placebo-controlled study of 125 subjects aged 65 to 93. They came from 23 institutions in northern Italy and all suffered from moderate to severe cognitive decline.

Following six months of phosphatidylserine supplementation, scores on memory and learning improved significantly. In addition, scores on standardized neuropsychological tests for withdrawal and apathy also improved. The investigator concluded, "These observations are remarkable, particularly since . . . the large number of subjects enrolled . . . represents the geriatric population commonly encountered in clinical practice."[48]

At the conclusion of another Italian study the author stated, "Phosphatidylserine appears to exert an action in two distinct contexts: one relating to the cognitive effects of vigilance, attention and short-term memory, and the other relating to behavioral aspects such as apathy, withdrawal, and daily living."[49]

Supplements Are Necessary. Since phosphatidylserine is not found readily in common foods, supplementation with the concentrated product may prove to be highly desirable, particularly to mature adults experiencing a decline in mental ability. Phosphatidylserine may be taken in combination with a healthy diet, vitamins, minerals, antioxidants, and other appropriate nutrients, as part of an integrated total nutrition program that includes exercise.

According to Dr. Kidd, to prevent or even reverse the symptoms of brain aging, it is a good idea to take this product for a period of time to see if you can obtain results. There are new "brain formulas" in your nutrition store that contain this product, or it can be purchased as pure phosphatidylserine (PS).

Acetyl-L-Carnitine:
Age Associated Memory Impairment

Acetyl-L-carnitine (ALC) occurs naturally in the body, where it transports fats across a membrane into the energy burning mitochondria of each cell. Acetyl-L-carnitine is a close relative of carnitine, a naturally occurring nonessential amino acid.

A Cognitive Enhancer. Researchers noted that elderly heart patients treated with carnitine demonstrated improved mood. This led to many studies on the effects of acetyl-L-carnitine on cognitive disorders. Acetyl-L-carnitine appears promising as a cognition enhancer for normal, healthy people, as well as a form of treatment for age-associated memory impairment and even Alzheimer's disease.

Recently Italian researchers published a landmark study which confirmed that acetyl-L-carnitine improved performance in young, healthy people. The research was conducted on 17 subjects who were given either 1,500 mg of acetyl-L-carnitine a day or a placebo for thirty days. They were tested before and after treatment using video game style devices designed to evaluate attention levels and hand-eye coordination and reflexes. The reflex speed was markedly increased among those who received acetyl-L-carnitine, and their error rate and task completion times were reduced three to four times, compared to the control subjects. Those receiving ALC showed no adverse effects.[50]

For the Elderly. Two other Italian researchers evaluated 236 mentally-impaired elderly people being treated with acetyl-L-carnitine in a large multicenter study. The treatment lasted more than five months, with subjects given either a placebo or 1,500 mg of acetyl-L-carnitine a day. All were tested for cognitive function, emotional state, and social behavior. Those who took acetyl-L-carnitine improved significantly, especially in memory, constructional thinking, and emotional state.[51] In several other studies, especially one at the University of Modena in Italy, the effects of acetyl-L-carnitine supplementation persisted long after the treatment ended.

Depression. Researchers in Italy studied the effects of acetyl-L-carnitine on 60 depressed people between the ages of 60 and 80. They were given either 3,000 mg of acetyl-L-carnitine or a placebo for sixty days and were tested repeatedly for depression and general well-being. Acetyl-L-carnitine reduced the severity of depression and improved the quality of life significantly.[52]

Sleep. Researchers also found that acetyl-L-carnitine helped with sleep disturbances. Sleep disturbances can disrupt the *circadian rhythm* (our biological "clock" or natural sleep/wake cycle) which can result in clinical depression. Circadian disturbances also can have a profound adverse effect on memory. Acetyl-L-carnitine appears to reduce sleep requirements while improving the quality of sleep.[53]

Many other studies have shown similar results with people with senile depression who were given acetyl-L-carnitine in doses ranging from 500 to 3,000 mg a day.[54]

Senility. Studies have also shown significant improvement and effectiveness of acetyl-L-carnitine on people with senility.[55]

Acetyl-L-carnitine is an effective treatment for mental impairment resulting from senile dementia. A study with 60 elderly patients concluded that subjects given 2,000 mg of acetyl-L-carnitine a day showed statistically significant improvement in the behavioral scales, memory tests, the attention barrage test, and a verbal fluency test.[56]

Alzheimer's Disease. Acetyl-L-carnitine is regarded by scientists and pharmaceutical companies as one of the most promising substances for the treatment of Alzheimer's disease.

Several studies showed acetyl-L-carnitine may retard deterioration in some cognitive areas in patients with Alzheimer's disease, significantly reduce the progression of the disease, or have a beneficial effect on some clinical features of Alzheimer-type dementia, particularly those related to short-term memory.[57] The only side effect noted was nausea in a few patients, particularly when acetyl-L-carnitine was taken on an empty stomach. Several other studies have confirmed that it improves memory, attention span, and alertness in Alzheimer's patients.[58]

How Much to Take? I recently came across the book *Smart Drugs II* by Ward Dean, M.D., and then met him at a convention and attended his lecture. I was glad to learn more information on acetyl-L-carnitine, as he is an expert in the field. Dr. Dean recommends a dose of 1,000 to 2,000 mg a day in two divided doses. You can find this product in your nutrition store in a 500 mg potency. This product is not recommended for those who are pregnant, lactating, or are hypersensitive to acetyl-L-carnitine.[59]

Pregnenolone:
A "New" Hormone for our Brain

Pregnenolone is a hormone that is key to keeping your brain functioning at peak capacity. Some scientists believe it is the most potent memory enhancer of all time. It appears to make us not only smarter, but happier along with a heightened sense of well-being.

Like the other steroid hormones—estrogen, progesterone, DHEA, testosterone—pregnenolone is synthesized (made) from cholesterol. Cholesterol is first made into pregnenolone and used in the body in that form. What the body does not use undergoes a chemical change which "repackages" into DHEA. DHEA is also broken down into estrogen and testosterone. Because pregnenolone gives birth to the other hormones, it is sometimes called the "parent hormone". Pregnenolone provides the raw material for these other hormones. As the level of pregnenolone declines, so will the levels of the other hormones that are made from it.[60] William Regelson, M.D., has shown that pregnenolone is produced both in the brain and in the adrenal cortex. Like the other hormones, pregnenolone production declines with age. By the time you are 65, you're making approximately 60 percent less pregnenolone than you did in your 30s.

Pregnenolone was one of the first hormones studied and was proven safe and effective. Back in the mid-1940s it was tested on students and workers and markedly improved their ability to learn and remember difficult tasks. It has been rediscovered in both animal and human studies which indicate that pregnenolone may be the ideal memory-enhancing drug and also the most memory-enhancing substance known, according to Dr. Regelson. This exciting research on pregnenolone and memory is being conducted jointly at two distinguished institutions, the Beekman Research Institute at the City of Hope Hospital and at St. Louis University School of Medicine.

In a 1992 animal study, Eugene Roberts, Ph.D., at the City of Hope, showed that pregnenolone was 100 times more potent than any other agent in improving memory. John E. Morley, M.D., from the University of St. Louis, involved in this study said, "It is clearly by far the most potent of the neurosteroids for improving memory by light-years, and it has a much broader memory response than any of the other neurosteroids. This makes it almost an ideal agent for looking at memory and the consequences of the age-related deterioration of memory."[61]

Due to recent legislation, pregnenolone, like DHEA, is now

being sold over the counter and is available in some nutrition stores. Pregnenolone is effective, well tolerated, and causes no known side effects. Human studies of this hormone have shown improvements in concentration, reduction of mental fatigue, and elevation in mood. Dr. Regelson feels the right approach is to take pregnenolone with DHEA because hormones work best when they work in tandem. Make sure you read about DHEA in Chapter 11.

Magnesium and Brain Function

Low magnesium levels have been implicated in some cases of brain disease. One report in the scientific literature describes three patients who were suffering from brain disease and low magnesium stores, and eventually lapsed into a coma. They responded immediately, however, to magnesium therapy, which brought about "prompt reversal of encephalopathy (brain dysfunction) and coma."[62]

Essential Fatty Acids and the Brain

A number of seemingly unrelated mental and psychiatric disorders, ranging from depression and hyperactivity to schizophrenia and alcoholism, often respond to essential fatty acid therapy.

Essential fatty acids are found in abundance in the lipids in our nervous system. They provide a source of the production of prostaglandins and the toughening of nerve-cell membranes. A deficiency of essential fatty acids has been apparent in many of the brain disorders studied. It seems logical to assume, therefore, that supplementary GLA (gamma linolenic acid) and EPA (eicosapentaenoic acid), might be effective in treating these disorders.[63]

GLA (Omega-6) is found mainly in evening primrose oil, black currant oil, and borage oil. EPA (Omega-3) is found in cold-water fish as well as in salmon, herring, mackerel, sardines, and sea bass. Flax seed oil is another wonderful vegetable source of the essential fatty acids. All can be found in either capsule or liquid form.

DMAE and Brain Stimulation

DMAE (Dimethylaminoethanol), also known as *Deanol*, has become popular among brain stimulants. It is found in "brain foods" such as anchovies and sardines. Small amounts of DMAE occur naturally in the brain. It apparently stimulates the production of choline, which in turn alters the levels of acetylcholine (an important neurotransmitter we discussed). Research has shown that DMAE elevates mood, improves memory and learning, increases intelligence, and extends life span.

In one clinical trial by Dr. Carl Pfeiffer, patients received DMAE for chronic fatigue and mild to moderate depression. DMAE produced an increase in physical energy, personality improvements, and better sleep for those with insomnia.[64]

Another study reported in *Clinical Pharmacology and Therapeutics* showed that DMAE subjects had an increase in mental concentration and muscle tone after six weeks of taking the substance. The subjects reported more daytime energy, greater attentiveness at lectures, sounder sleep, and better ability to concentrate on writing papers or studying.[65]

DMAE is available in liquid or capsule form. No serious side effects have been reported. Those who take initial high doses may experience dull headaches, insomnia, tenseness in the muscles, but these symptoms subside when the dose is lowered.[66]

Insights into Alzheimer's Disease

Alzheimer's disease affects an estimated four million American adults, about 10 percent of all people over age sixty-five.[67] It is a progressive, degenerative disease that attacks the brain and impairs memory, thinking, and behavior. Alzheimer's disease is the most common and feared form of dementing illness, resulting in more than 100,000 deaths a year in the United States. That makes it the fourth leading cause of death in adults following heart disease, cancer and strokes. The disease is named after Dr. Alois Alzheimer (1864-1915), a German neurologist who observed the disease in his patients and initially reported it to the medical community in 1907.

Those affected with Alzheimer's disease become forgetful and confused. Although the progression is gradual and varies from person to person, the life span of a patient can be as much as twenty years after initial symptoms are observed. In addition to memory loss, there are other typical signs of the disease:
- language problems, such as trouble thinking of words
- problems with abstract thinking

- poor or decreased judgment
- disorientation in place and time
- changes in mood and behavior
- changes in personality

There is no diagnostic test for Alzheimer's disease. Physicians generally use a detailed medical history, conduct a thorough physical and neurologic exam, do mental status tests and psychiatric assessments, and other routine laboratory and neuropsychological tests.

The reason doctors find it so difficult to diagnose Alzheimer's disease is because not all patients follow the same pattern. Some people have a very rapid progression of dementia, others a much slower rate of decline. For this reason, some researchers believe the disease is actually several diseases. Part of the difficulty in conducting research for a cure lies in the fact that this disorder seems to be unique to human beings. Typical animal studies do not seem to be appropriate or applicable.

Over 30 percent of the elderly with Alzheimer's use eight or more prescription drugs daily.[68] Drug interactions probably play a greater role in dementia and confusional states than is currently realized.[69]

The disease can occur at any age, but most commonly after the age of 50. Many cases of dementia are entirely reversible.[70]

Every effort should be made to rule out these reversible factors. Over 80 percent of the elderly are deficient in one or more vitamins or minerals, which, if levels get too low, may induce dementia as we saw with vitamin B12, folic acid and niacin.

Various research studies have shown positive benefits to supplementation with vitamin E and choline, although much more research needs to be done in this area. It seems to me we should try the nutrients we have just discussed at the first signs of trouble.

Aluminum and the Alzheimer's Connection

In studying the brains of Alzheimer's patients who had died, researchers found one common denominator: *all had high concentrations of aluminum!!* Neurons of the brain cells had four to six times the levels of aluminum found in normal brain cells. Changes in the nerve cells of the cerebral cortex made these cells look like tangles of filaments—such degenerated nerve cells could not possibly transmit nerve signals properly. Some researchers believe aluminum accumulations in the body may lead to many of the health complications and debilities of old age, not only Alzheimer's disease.

A great deal of aluminum pollution can be avoided by making wise decisions about products we tend to use as a part of our normal daily living. Aluminum is found in cookware, baking powder, buffered aspirin, antacids, aluminum cans and foil, and even underarm anti-perspirants. When we apply anti-perspirants to our under arms, we are rubbing aluminum right into our lymph glands. Your nutrition store carries deodorants that do not contain aluminum. They stop odor although they do not stop all perspiration.

I recall Adelle Davis teaching against aluminum cooking utensils back in the 1960s, which is when we changed to stainless steel or iron cookware. Information about aluminum has been out for a long time, and yet our stores are still filled with beautiful, expensive aluminum cooking sets.

There is no "proof" that aluminum contributes to the cause of Alzheimer's, but it has been hotly debated in the scientific field. Aluminum leads to a decreased synthesis of other neurotransmitters (dopamine, serotonin, epinephrine, norepinephrine) as well.[71]

Neuroscientists have tried to reassure us that this accumulation is the result of the disease rather than a cause. Still, when aluminum has been injected into the brains of animals, it produces tangled brain cells that are similar to the changes seen in human brain cells.[72]

The Need for Antioxidants

Some have speculated that aluminum is an oxidant (a bad guy) stimulant. If so, then aluminum increases the activity of oxygen free-radicals. Should that be the case, then vitamin A, beta-carotene, grape seed extract, Pycnogenols®, vitamin C, vitamin E, selenium and other antioxidants may be instrumental in deactivating these potentially dangerous free-radicals.

All neurological diseases are now known to have environmental or nutritional links, according to a report in *Medical Nutrition.* The brain is much more susceptible to nutritional deficit and environmental insult than was previously understood. It is possible that long-term minor deficiency of one or more nutrients may lead to this disease.[73]

DHEA—An Important Hormone. Dr. Owen M. Wolkowitz of the Department of Psychiatry at the University of California at San Francisco has reported some small studies on depression accompanied by memory problems. Because of their positive results, they are now studying Alzheimer's disease with other researchers. Dr. Wolkowitz believes that DHEA may play a role in helping to prevent the inception or even the progression of Alzheimer's, but that it cannot reverse the disease once it has taken hold. "I think that it has more of a permissive effect; that is, if there is a neuro toxic degenerative process going on for whatever other reasons, having low DHEA levels could impair the body's natural ability to repair the damage. In other words, if there is some damage going on in the brain, having youthful levels of DHEA could facilitate recovery from the damage or hold the damage in check."[74] More information on DHEA is located in Chapter 11.

Chelation Therapy May Be Beneficial. Chelation therapy helps remove heavy metals such as lead, calcium, and aluminum from the body. If started early, chelation therapy has shown very encouraging results, almost without exception, in treating patients who are exhibiting mild forms of dementia. As Richard Casdorph, M.D., Ph.D., told me personally, "We must see the patient before there is permanent damage to the brain. If dementia or Alzheimer's disease reaches an advanced stage, then the amount of improvement is limited. What we do see in our patients with early stages of dementia is that deterioration stops once they are started on treatment, and most patients bounce back and show some improvement in their intellectual ability." You can read more on chelation in Chapter 11.

Impact of Smoking on Alzheimer's. It should come as no surprise to anyone that hundreds and hundreds of the chemicals found in tobacco and tobacco smoke may be related to Alzheimer's disease. This conclusion was made in a one-year study involving military veterans in Massachusetts. Those who smoked more than one pack of cigarettes a day were 4.3 times more likely to develop Alzheimer's disease than non-smokers. Those who smoke less than a pack a day were 1.6 times more likely to develop the disease.[75]

Physical and Mental Exercise

Finally, two of the most important things to consider in maintaining active brain function throughout our life is physical and mental exercise.

Exercise increases the endorphins and dopamine levels in the brain. It is now known that endorphins are the neurotransmitters that are stimulated by morphine; they create a sense of well being and even relieve pain.

Physical activity tends to decrease anxiety, hostility, and other stress-related disorders. Aerobic exercise, slow jogging, stationary bike riding, or any physical exercise for at least thirty minutes is beneficial. But an optimal schedule would be an hour, four times a week. It is our endorphins that make us feel better after a brisk walk or other physical activity.

Mental Exercise. Several scientific and anecdotal research studies in recent months have reported that those who continue to "learn something new" or who "exercise" their brains daily by doing puzzles, engaging in problem-solving exercises, playing chess, and doing work that requires mental activity appear to function much better, for much longer in life.

Stay Involved in Life. Passive mental activities, such as watching television, are no substitute for active mental activities. Volunteer your time to a hospital, school, nursing home, or get involved in something that interests you.

Consider taking a course at a local junior college or adult continuing education center. Learn to use a computer. You may even find such a course at your computer store or at your neighborhood YMCA. Attend seminars that put you in touch with new information. Read, not only for fun, but to "learn." Choose to keep your brain active mentally, even as you choose to stay healthy and physically active.

Chapter 7

You Gotta

Have Heart

Protecting Your Heart
and Keeping It Healthy

"Our ancestors have been eating eggs, meat, and
other good foods for thousands of years and
the first mention of heart attacks in scientific
literature was in the early 1900s. To blame heart
disease on something that had always been a part of
our diet doesn't make sense to me. It has to be something
of more recent origin, such as the refining of
flour and the introduction into the diet of processed,
devitalized foods, sugar, and hydrogenated fats."
—Gladys Lindberg

Heart disease has reached epidemic proportions in our nation, in spite of our medical sophistication. Every year, millions of people succumb to the ravages of heart attacks and strokes, and millions more are left disabled. According to the World Health Organization, more than twelve million people die every year from cardiovascular diseases. In most nations of the world, every other death is caused by cardiovascular disease, both in men and women. In the United States, one and a half million people will suffer a heart attack this year, and 300,000 of them will die suddenly before they reach a hospital or receive medical attention.[1]

The old adage "an ounce of prevention is worth a pound of cure" has never been so true as it is in heart disease.

Key Lifestyle Factors
Lifestyle factors can impact heart health in a positive way:
- normal weight
- reduced stress
- proper diet
- vitamin and mineral intake
- adequate antioxidants
- regular exercise
- smoke-free environment
- elimination of hydrogenated or hardened fats
- low sugar consumption

If you smoke, are carrying more than 20 percent additional body weight (above the normal range for your height and age), or are under heavy stress, you will need to make changes in your lifestyle if you want to have a healthy heart. There is a great deal we can do nutritionally and naturally to enhance the health of the heart, and to prevent instances of heart disease. These measures are all well documented in the medical and nutritional research literature. Only a summary of key conclusions will be included here.

Cholesterol

Cholesterol is a waxy, fat-like substance that is absolutely essential to our good health, but there are two sides to this story. On the beneficial side, cholesterol is used in the body as a building block for many complex chemicals. It is produced in many types of cells and is necessary for our bodies to function normally.

Here are some facts about cholesterol:

- Human beings synthesize about 3,000 to 4,000 milligrams (mg) of cholesterol per day and receive a somewhat smaller amount in their food, mainly from eggs and animal fat.[2]
- The adrenal glands contain the highest concentration of cholesterol of any tissue in the body. Cholesterol is the starting material for the synthesis of adrenal hormones.
- The body must have cholesterol in order to function properly, and to manufacture vital hormones, including pituitary hormones, adrenal hormones, DHEA, pregnenolone and our sex hormones which include estrogen—female hormones, and testosterone—male hormones. This is important to remember so you don't improperly "cholesterol-proof" your children. Will they have enough of these necessary hormones to develop properly?
- All tissues synthesize cholesterol but only that produced in the liver reaches the blood.
- The brain and spinal cord account for only two percent of total body weight, and yet they contain almost one-fourth of the total cholesterol in the body. The brain uses cholesterol to make neurotransmitters which conduct nerve impulses throughout the body. Cholesterol is

also an important building block of the insula
tion around nerves, which ensures nerve
impulses are conducted appropriately.

- Your skin excretes excessive cholesterol by the
normal, daily sloughing off of cells. The ultraviolet rays of the sun on exposed skin converts
this cholesterol to vitamin D-3. Cholesterol is
also the protective, insoluble skin molecule that
resists water and prevents maceration (the softening and wearing away of skin in water).

- The body makes 80 percent of its cholesterol
from fats, protein, and certain carbohydrates
within the liver and intestines. The remaining
20 percent comes from dietary sources. If
blood cholesterol rises above a certain level, the
excess is converted into bile and excreted in the
stool.

- Cholesterol is also found in the marrow within
the bones where blood cells are formed.[3]

Cholesterol: The Good and The Bad

Since 1950, a number of researchers have reported that
people with high blood levels of a certain kind of fat did not get
heart attacks. In fact, this fat, a kind of cholesterol, is so good for
you that it greatly diminishes your chances of having a heart attack.
It is a fat-protein combination referred to as high-density lipoproteins (HDLs).

In contrast, research reveals that people with high levels of
another fat-protein combination called low-density lipoproteins
(LDLs) were almost certain to have heart attacks. It is postulated
that HDLs help protect against heart attack in two ways. They
appear to interfere with the cells' ability to take in unwanted LDLs,
thus stopping the buildup of fatty deposits that can cause atherosclerosis and heart attacks. And the necessary HDLs aid the body in
excreting excess cholesterol.[4]

H. Loomis, writing in *Science,* described the HDLs as a
garbage collector that sweeps up arterial cholesterol and takes it to
the liver where it can be cleared from the body in the form of bile,
which is lost in the feces.[5]

Although cholesterol is essential for the normal functioning of our bodies, we need to make sure we have adequate levels of the valuable HDLs. The next time you have a blood test, ask the doctor to measure not just your cholesterol level, but the ratio of HDLs to LDLs. Women generally have higher levels of the beneficial HDLs than men, and this may account for the lower incidence of heart attacks among women. Information on how to naturally lower LDLs and raise HDLs is found later in this chapter.

Proper Blood Cholesterol Levels

The current magic number regarding blood cholesterol levels seem to be 200 mg/dl or less. This number may change, however, according to a person's age and according to the opinions of medical researchers and physicians. (These numbers measure milligrams of cholesterol per one hundred deciliters of blood.) Total levels of 200–239 mg/dl are considered to have borderline risk of heart disease, while levels of 240 mg/dl and higher are considered higher risk.

Stress Causes Variance

People under stress have shown normal variances in their cholesterol of 10 to 20 percent. Other factors that impact cholesterol may be the time of day the blood is taken, whether the person has been resting or rushing prior to coming to the doctor's office, whether the person was lying down, sitting, or standing. All of these factors can impact a reading. A British study showed blood cholesterol levels will rise almost instantaneously if an individual is frightened, under anxiety, in pain, or exposed to an uncomfortably loud noise.[6]

As you may have concluded by now, there is a great need to standardize the cholesterol test so there is not as much room for variance. My advice is to have several readings over a period of several weeks before you draw major conclusions about what to do regarding your cholesterol levels.

Truth About Cholesterol From Food Sources

On the basis of research related only to lipoproteins, blood cholesterol levels and atherosclerosis, many authorities have recommended that certain foods be removed from our diet because they "have cholesterol." How many foods do we see on the market today that claim they have no cholesterol!

It's the Kind of Fat. I certainly am not advocating that you ignore the dietary warnings you hear in the media. Rather, you need to monitor closely the types of fat you consume. You should eliminate hardened, heated, processed, man-made fat from your diet. What you don't necessarily need to eliminate from your diet are foods such as eggs, low-fat dairy products, and lean meat. Edward Ahrens, M.D., a longtime cholesterol researcher at Rockefeller University, has summed up the case very well in my opinion. He said, "to deny everyone red meat, eggs, and dairy products when only a minute fraction of the population has a problem with high cholesterol reduces the joy of life unnecessarily." [7]

After conducting dozens of major epidemiological studies with thousands of animals, the renowned biochemist and researcher Richard Passwater, Ph.D., stated that no clinical study has conclusively shown that dietary cholesterol causes heart disease. He wrote in his book, *The New Supernutrition*, "Although people insist on examining all the diets of the world looking for one component, such as cholesterol, to blame as a cause of heart disease, they would be doing better to look for the absence of one component, such as vitamin E. It is total nutrition, in fact supernutrition, that should be our main concern." [8]

The Famous Framingham Study

One of the most important studies regarding heart disease was one conducted by a team of Boston University Medical School physicians. It was called the Framingham Study because the physicians picked Framingham, Massachusetts, for the project. This was the first large-scale project to study human heart disease that involved an entire town. The project began in 1948 and continues today.

Thousands of adults have participated in the study, which primarily is aimed at gathering information about the relationship between diet and heart disease. One of the study's directors, William Kannel, M.D., reported that there was no discernible association between the amount of cholesterol in the diet and the level of cholesterol *in the blood*. Half of the people who died of heart attacks in the time frame of his particular research *did not* have high blood cholesterol levels.[9]

In fact, over a fifty-year period, thousands of adults in Framingham died without having elevated dietary cholesterol levels. No correlation was found between heart disease and eggs or meat. This is an important point. Cholesterol in the diet simply does not translate automatically into cholesterol in the blood! Our bodies have a feedback mechanism that decreases the amount of cholesterol we manufacture if we don't need as much.[10]

The Much-Maligned Egg. It seems almost incredible to me that eggs, the most perfect food that God put upon this earth, the food for the embryo, the food associated with new life, has taken the brunt of the cholesterol scare.

Carlton Fredericks, Ph.D., wrote, "Despite all the hue and cry, the case against eggs, which is the case against cholesterol, is in no way proved." [11]

He also observed that eggs are rich in the very substance, lecithin, that prevents cholesterol from working much of the mischief it is supposed to create in the arteries. Eggs are also rich in the B-complex vitamins choline, inositol, pyridoxine (B6), and the amino acid cysteine. These nutrients have all been used successfully in experimental medical treatments for hardening of the arteries.

Very Low Cholesterol. Low cholesterol is often associated with malignant and other "wasting" diseases. The British medical journal, the *Lancet,* reported in March 21, 1992 that low serum cholesterol may be linked to increased suicide risk. The abstract states that middle-aged people who lower their blood cholesterol concentration may be at risk for suicide and other types of violent death, although they are less likely to have coronary heart disease.

The *Lancet* also reported a study in which low cholesterol levels were associated with depression in a group of 1,020 white men aged 50 to 89. Those with cholesterol levels below 160 mg/dl were three times more likely to be depressed than men whose cholesterol levels were 200 mg/dl or higher. The researchers speculated that depression, suicide, and violent deaths in people with low cholesterol could be the result of low levels of serotonin, a chemical found in the blood that enables the blood vessels to constrict and contract. Serotonin, a chemical occurring naturally in the brain, sup presses harmful impulses such as suicidal or aggressive behavior. Fewer serotonin receptors decrease the amount of serotonin in the brain and may increase the likelihood of violent behavior.[12]

Understanding Triglycerides

Whenever cholesterol is discussed, knowledgeable people also talk about triglycerides. Triglycerides are chemicals produced in the process of converting excess carbohydrates into stored body fat and are linked to heart disease.

Blood triglyceride levels increase when you eat refined carbohydrates, products made with white sugar, such as cookies, cake, candy, anything made with white flour and even sweetened fruit juices. Serum triglyceride levels from 70 to 150 mg/dl blood are considered optimal by many health oriented physicians.

Excess sugar is converted in the body to nonessential fatty acids (glycogen stores) and cholesterol. Individuals who consumed 30 percent of their calories from sugar—which is a little more than the average in the American diet—developed significantly higher levels of cholesterol and triglycerides in their blood than the control subjects in the experiment.[13]

Sweet and Dangerous. Many authorities, including the biochemist and researcher John Yudkin, M.D., Ph.D., author of five books including *Sweet and Dangerous*, states that triglyceride levels are an important factor in predicting the likelihood of an individual developing a heart attack. Both triglycerides and LDL cholesterol contribute to heart disease potential.[14]

Dr. Yudkin blames sugar consumption for increased heart disease in the industrialized nations, and has a great deal of research to back up his claim. He contends that sugar is not only a cause, but the main cause. An article in The *American Journal of Clinical Nutrition* reported that the most consistent data dealing with diet and high triglyceride levels concerns sugar. When sugar is withheld, triglyceride levels fall. Diets high in complex carbohydrates such as cereals, breads, vegetables, and seeds do not have the same effect.[15]

Obesity is probably the major cause of *mild* elevated triglycerides. However, other situations that can lead to high triglyceride levels include alcohol abuse and the use of certain drugs, some diuretics, oral contraceptives, products containing female hormones, Acutane® (an acne drug), and some drugs used for treating heart conditions.[16]

All of these factors dealing with cholesterol seem to be related, in my opinion. We know that sugar raises our insulin level and is related to diabetes. It is estimated that half of those with coronary artery disease and three quarters of stroke victims develop their circulatory problems prematurely as a result of diabetes.

Vitamin C Decreases Total Cholesterol. We need to increase our vitamin C intake since it is so beneficial to the cardiovascular system. Two to three grams of vitamin C per day, given over several months lowered triglyceride levels an average of 50 to 75 percent. This is only observed in patients with initially high levels of triglycerides. This fact shows that vitamins have primarily a regulatory effect, they lower blood factors only when necessary. Vitamin C decreases total cholesterol, harmful LDL cholesterol, and triglycerides, and it increases good HDL cholesterol.[17]

Hardened fats increase the amount of oxidation in the body, resulting in greater amounts of free-radicals roving around in your body. To fight these free-radicals, consume antioxidants such as vitamins E, C, A, beta-carotene, selenium, grape seed extract and/or pine bark extract (Pycnogenol®). We need better overall nutrition, and must eliminate white sugar, overly processed foods, chemical preservatives, white fat on meats and hydrogenated, hardened fats like margarine. These principles are much more important than eliminating all red meat, eggs, and dairy products from our diet!

Heart-Smart Nutrients

Among the foremost nutrients that help strengthen and revitalize the heart muscle are the antioxidants. Several of the antioxidants also have great benefit in lowering cholesterol, lowering blood pressure and protecting the heart from damage.

Vitamin E—The Great Protector

Vitamin E is the oldest recognized biologic antioxidant. It may have even a more basic function, however—the production of energy. In these two capacities, vitamin E is of the utmost importance in maintaining good health at the most basic of levels. Vitamin E also appears to help slow the aging process and prevent premature aging. In fact, it has been called the "anti-aging vitamin."[18]

Vitamin E also decreases the need for oxygen in the tissues and organs of the body. Mega vitamin levels of vitamin C and trace levels of selenium also share this function. Additionally, vitamin E improves the transportation of oxygen by the red blood cells.

Much of the early research relating vitamin E and the heart has been done by Drs. Wilfrid and Evan Shute. I talked about their work in the opening chapter. Together, they operated a clinic in Canada.

Wilfrid Shute, M.D., reported a study he conducted at his clinic where he found that vitamin E in 300 to 3,200 IU doses a day was quite successful in helping both individual cells and tissues in general to function normally.

Fantastic Color Slides. A number of years ago, my mother and I had the privilege of hearing Dr. Wilfrid Shute discuss his work with 38,000 cardiac patients at a National Nutritional Foods Association convention. During his lecture he showed slides which I will never forget. Among them were pictures of patients with ulcerated amputated stubs, diabetic gangrene, terrible ulceration, and severe burns, all of which refused to heal. But, after vitamin E, usually 600 IUs daily, had been given to the patients, and vitamin E ointment had been used, all the patients were restored. Ulcerated and naked wounds healed more rapidly with vitamin E therapy, and the scar tissue did not contract and was not tender. Vitamin E was even shown to prevent disfiguring scars and to help heal old scars. Remember this if you need a scar to heal after an operation.

I find it exciting to now see research confirming the benefits of natural vitamin E to the heart. Their research has been duplicated and added to by a number of outstanding researchers throughout the years.

"Your Heart and Vitamin E" is the classic book by Dr. Evan Shute. He and other researchers have found that vitamin E provides these direct benefits to the heart: [19]

- **An Antithrombin.** It helps dissolve fresh clots and prevents their formation in arteries and veins. It is useful in treating and preventing phlebitis (inflammation of the walls of the vein). As a preventive measure against strokes, vitamin E helps prevent arterial and venous thrombosis or clots in the circulatory system of the brain.

- **Restores Capillary Permeability.** It helps dilate the capillaries and thus helps circulation of blood throughout the body. This effect is of great value in conditions where there is a spasm in a vessel wall or a significant degree of vessel damage, either acute or chronic.

- **Increases Collateral Circulation.** Vitamin E steps up collateral circulation (alternative blood pathways), a process in which smaller vessels dilate to carry a larger volume of blood around a blocked vessel.

- **Decreases Amount of Heart Muscle Death.** In cases of heart attack, vitamin E in high doses appears to decrease the amount of heart muscle death. [20]

- **Lowers Heart Disease Instances.** Dr. Richard Passwater, one of my favorite authorities, describes a study involving 17,894 participants who had taken various amounts of vitamin E for different periods of time. The heart disease rate of these participants was compared to that of the general population having identical ages. In all instances, where persons consumed 400 IU or more of vitamin E daily for more than two years, their rate of heart disease was significantly lower than normal (3 per 100 compared to 32 per 100). The amount of heart disease in any age group decreased proportionally with the length of time vitamin E had been taken. In fact, Dr. Passwater noted the length of time was more important than the dosage beyond the minimum of 400 IU taken daily.[21]

- **Reverses Arteriosclerotic Damage.** Dr. Morgan Raiforth, a pioneering ophthalmologist, has shown with a series of published photos, that arteriosclerotic damage in the retinal vessels can be reversed by using 1,200 IUs of vitamin E, and three to five grams (3,000 to 5,000 mg) of vitamin C on a daily basis.[22]

Protective Benefit After Bypass Surgery. The School of Medicine at USC recently reported a study in which all patients who had undergone bypass surgery were carefully monitored for new fatty deposits in their arteries by angiograms—a type of heart X-ray. The angiograms revealed that patients taking the most vitamin E had much smaller lesions on their arteries than did those taking less vitamin E or none at all. The benefits were particularly noteworthy because the men taking larger amounts of vitamin E began the study with higher blood levels of cholesterol. Many researchers believe that cholesterol becomes dangerous only when oxidized in the absence of vitamin E.[23]

Since Vitamin E Has No Known Side Effects, a number of physicians are apparently beginning to prescribe vitamin E to their patients. I applaud their decision! Mother began recommending vitamin E to all her clients in 1949 after she had read Dr. Shute's original work.

Dr. Shute also recommended 400 IUs of vitamin E as a preventive measure. He would increase this dosage to 800 to 1200 IUs daily. If you have extreme high blood pressure, increase your vitamin E very slowly, due to its blood thinning effect at higher doses and be under the care of an orthomolecular doctor (one who understands nutrition).

Protection from Heart Attack

A study reported by the World Health Organization in Geneva, Switzerland, reported that low blood levels of vitamin E were a more important risk factor than either high cholesterol or high blood pressure in deaths due to ischemic heart disease (heart attacks). Many people assume that lowering cholesterol is the most important thing they can do to decrease their risk of heart attack. This study provides documented evidence that increasing important vitamins seems to be *more than twice as important* in protecting a person from heart attack.[24] Our vitamin E levels need to be maintained!

Heart Association Study. The American Heart Association's annual science writer's meeting showed that vitamin E blocked negative changes in the bloodstream of men given 800 IU daily for three months.

The Heart Association president, Dr. W. Virgil Brown of Emory University in Atlanta, admitted, "Most of us in medicine have pooh-poohed megadoses of vitamins, but Dr. Ishwarlal Jialal's work has a good ring to it."[25]

Dr. Jialal's work proposed in his study that "fats in the bloodstream become lodged in the blood vessel walls and begin to clog arteries only when they have chemically combined with oxygen to turn rancid, the way butter does after being left out too long."[26]

Dr. Jialal supports the theory that heart disease begins when the dangerous low-density lipoprotein (LDL), the major cholesterol carrier, is oxidized by particles in the bloodstream called free-radicals. Oxidized LDLs appear to begin the formation of blood vessel clogging plaque that leads to atherosclerosis (plaque in the inner artery wall) or hardening of the arteries.

Reducing the Risk with Antioxidants. He further suggested that antioxidant nutrients may be instrumental in preventing LDL oxidation and reducing the risk of atherosclerosis. "We found that vitamin C, vitamin E, and beta-carotene all inhibited the unwanted LDL oxidation and the early stages of plaque formation in our laboratory studies," he said. "Vitamin C and beta-carotene almost completely prevented LDL oxidation (95 percent and 90 percent respectively), while vitamin E inhibited oxidation by 45 percent." He compared vitamin C to *probucol*, a cholesterol-lowering drug. Jialal concluded that both have antioxidant properties, but probucol is a drug and not free from serious side effects.[27]

Vitamin E Prevents Stickiness. Along with its antioxidant properties, vitamin E acts as a surfactant (makes things slippery) so it minimizes the tendency of blood platelets to stick together and form clots. A significant decrease in adhesiveness (stickiness) of platelets was noted after only two weeks of daily supplementation with 400 IU of vitamin E. This has important implications for coronary artery disease. If platelets can be kept from sticking together to form clots, and also kept from adhering to vessel walls, the blood flow remains much more unobstructed and even.[28]

The Cambridge Heart Antioxidant Study, published in the *Lancet*, March 23, 1996, evaluated approximately 2,000 patients with a history of heart disease in a randomized, controlled trial. Half received 400 or 800 IUs of vitamin E daily, the others received a placebo. They were followed for a total of 510 days and the researchers noted a 75 percent reduction in heart attacks in the vitamin E group, compared to the placebo group. These research studies go on to explain the benefits of vitamin E, which was from supplements, not food sources.

Beta-Carotene Cuts Heart Disease

Beta-carotene (the precursor of vitamin A) benefits the heart for many of the same antioxidant reasons as vitamin E. We once may have laughed at nutritional enthusiasts who insisted, "Eat your dark green vegetables" or "drink your carrot juice," but no more! These dark green and yellow vegetables are the richest sources of beta-carotene.

Harvard Study. A Harvard researcher, Charles H. Hennekens, M.D., examined the relationship between dietary beta-carotene and vitamin E, and risk factors for heart disease. He studied a group of 333 participants in the U.S. Physician's Health Study who had stable angina (chest pain) and who had not had a previous heart attack or stroke. Dr. Hennekens concluded, "Those physicians who took 50 mg of beta-carotene as a supplement every other day had [not quite] half as many heart attacks, strokes and deaths related to heart disease as those who did not."[29]

A Much Lower Risk. In Dr. Hennekens' presentation before The New York Academy of Sciences in 1992, he also reported on a study that followed 87,245 female nurses over an eight-year period. "Those nurses who consumed higher amounts of beta-carotene and vitamin E were less likely to develop heart disease. When we compared women in the top 20 percent of vitamin intake to women in the bottom 20 percent, we found the high vitamin group had a much *lower risk* of developing heart disease." [30]

The *Lancet* reported on July 8, 1995, that dark-green leafy vegetables are a rich source of micronutrients, but some people have trouble converting beta-carotene into vitamin A (retinol). The researchers cited the need in the diet for other foods that help overcome a vitamin A deficiency, such as the foods naturally rich in retinol (eggs, cod liver oil, whole fish, and liver) and fortified foods. [31]

Vitamin C and Lipoprotein(a)

Linus Pauling, Ph.D., and Matthias Rath, M.D., along with other researchers at the Linus Pauling Institute of Science and Medicine now at the University of Oregon, evaluated the prevention and treatment of heart disease for a number of years. In 1989, Dr. Rath made a significant discovery. At the time, researchers assumed that cholesterol deposited in the arteries in atherosclerotic plaques was the dangerous LDL cholesterol, and that the amount of LDL in blood serum was the major risk factor for heart disease.

Dr. Rath found, however, that the real culprit was not LDL but another lipoprotein, called **lipoprotein(a)**—a substance usually ignored in blood analysis. He concluded that lipoprotein(a) is the substance that is present in abnormally large amounts in patients with heart disease and that it is the greatest risk factor, not the bad LDL or total cholesterol level. [32]

In later studies, Drs. Pauling and Rath discovered that lipoprotein(a) and vitamin C are connected. They concluded that a low intake of vitamin C allows lipoprotein(a) to lay down these plaques and thus, a low intake of vitamin C may be the primary cause of heart disease! [33]

They suggested that vitamin C and other orthomolecular substances might prevent or even reverse plaque formation and angina pectoris. [34]

Vitamin C and Collagen. In making their argument, Drs. Pauling and Rath pointed out that stores of vitamin C in the body directly determine the stability of the body's structural tissues, especially collagen, which functions in the body somewhat like steel reinforcement in a skyscraper. When there is an acute vitamin C deficiency, the collagen dissolves and the body literally breaks apart at the cellular level. Although acute and complete vitamin C deficiency is virtually unknown in America today, chronic dietary vitamin C deficiency is widespread. The consequences of insufficient vitamin C intakes over decades can have a disastrous effect on the body, and especially upon the walls of the blood vessels.[35]

Deposits of Plaque and Vitamin C. These two researchers believe that the deposit of plaque on the arterial walls is something of a desperate defense reaction on the part of the body. The arterial wall, having become fragile because of vitamin C deficiency, needs to be repaired from the inside. In depositing plaque and other clotting factors, the body is attempting to strengthen or build up the walls that have been weakened. They theorize that heart disease is actually an early stage of scurvy, which is a chronic vitamin C deficiency.

Dr. Pauling—"They are betting on the wrong horse."

"Hundreds of millions of dollars have been spent by the National Institutes of Health, the American Heart Association and other agencies in support of studies of cardiovascular disease in relation to LDL and HDL cholesterol, triglycerides, saturated fats and unsaturated fats. Very little attention has been paid to vitamin C and other vitamins.

I think that these agencies have been betting on the wrong horse. It is fortunate that vitamin C is not a drug—it is an orthomolecular substance, normally present in the human body and required for life, and it has extremely low toxicity. You do not need to have a physicians' prescription or the approval of the medical establishment to use it in the best way to improve your health and to prevent heart disease. Your knowledge may even be greater and your judgment better than theirs." [36]

Matthias Rath, M.D., states that the main risk factor of human atherosclerosis is the instability of the vessel wall as a consequence of vitamin C deficiency. High cholesterol levels or other risk factors in the blood are a risk for heart disease only if the wall of the arteries is weakened by vitamin C deficiency. [37]

Blood Platelet Adhesions. Impressive research from around the world shows that vitamin C and E reduce blood platelet adhesion—a very important discovery since blood clotting is one of the causes of many heart attacks. British and Swedish scientists have reported that vitamin C does this by reducing the stickiness of the blood. [38] You also read earlier that vitamin E decreased blood platelets from sticking together.

Researchers in Berlin, Germany, found that one gram (1,000 mg) of vitamin C daily normalized blood platelet adhesion and reduced the interaction of platelets within the arterial walls. [39] Yet another study showed that a group of patients with coronary artery disease who took one gram of vitamin C every eight hours for ten days significantly decreased platelet adhesiveness and platelet aggregation. [40]

Heart Disease a Vitamin Deficiency? Just when we thought cholesterol was the main culprit in heart disease, we are seeing research that indicates that the true culprit may be a vitamin deficiency!

Coenzyme Q 10 and the Heart

Coenzyme Q 10—also called CoQ10, ubiquinol 10 or vitamin Q—is now being called a "miracle nutrient" by many. It is an essential component of the metabolic process involved in energy (ATP) production.

Dr. Karl Folkers, who was professor and director of the Institute for Biomedical Research at the University of Texas in Austin, has been recognized for years as the world's leading researcher in CoQ10. I had the honor of hearing Dr. Folkers lecture at an Anti-Aging conference in 1996. When I told him about this book and that I'd quoted him, with a twinkle in his eye he said, "Oh, don't believe a thing I've said." He is over 90 years old and charming! During his lecture Dr. Folkers said, "I don't use the word "cure" lightly but CoQ10 is the 'cure' for heart disease."

He has conducted biochemical, biomedical, and clinical research on CoQ10 for some thirty-five years and has succeeded in establishing its structure and in isolating CoQ10 in human hearts. The highest concentration of the enzyme is in the heart muscle. His research shows a definite link between CoQ10 deficiency and human heart disease.[41]

Progress in Cardiology. At the conclusion of the 1986 conference where Nobel Prize winners reported on their research with CoQ10, Dr. Folkers made the following remarks as he accepted the Priestley Medal, the highest award given by the American Chemical Society:

> "We have heard that patients in advanced cardiac failure, who had only a few months to live, under close medical care, have revealed almost miraculous improvement after treatment with CoQ10, and such is a step of progress in cardiology. Proof of effectiveness of CoQ10 in cardiology is now known to medical science. . . . Proof of the safety of CoQ10 is known."[42]

Dr. Folkers reported dramatic effects of CoQ10 therapy for advanced cardiac patients—"those who frequently experience discomfort with any physical exertion, and often have pain even when they are at rest. Such patients invariably do not survive long on conventional therapy."[43]

Clinical Studies Using CoQ10

The use of CoQ10 to treat heart disease has become well established in Japan, where researchers began testing CoQ10 for heart disease in the 1960s, completing twenty-five studies, including two large double-blind trials by 1976. The results showed about a 70 percent improvement of the patients. By 1987, more than ten million Japanese were estimated to be taking CoQ10 as a prescription drug for cardiac problems.[44] Here in the United States,

CoQ10 is not a prescription drug and is available at your nutrition store.

Congestive Heart Disease. The newsletter of the Linus Pauling Institute of Science and Medicine reported some of the many clinical studies on the treatment of congestive heart disease with CoQ10, which support the following conclusions:

- The high correlation between occurrence and severity of congestive heart disease and the level of CoQ10 in the heart indicates that a deficiency of CoQ10 may be a causative factor of congestive heart disease. Cardiomyopathy (disease of the muscle of the heart) can be substantially, but not solely, a consequence of a deficiency of CoQ10.
- This deficiency can be corrected by taking oral supplements of CoQ10. An oral intake of 30 to 120 mg per day of CoQ10 has been shown to improve cardiac function, extend life span, and increase the well-being of about 75 percent of patients with congestive heart disease. Therapy with CoQ10 can result in profound increase both in cardiac function and in the quality of life of a failing cardiac patient.
- The response to CoQ10 may take weeks or months. CoQ10 acts as a vitamin, rather than a drug. Thus, the therapy must be continued for weeks, sometimes months, before the positive benefits are realized. However, if the deficiency is large, the effects of CoQ10 may be seen in a few days. In many instances, the therapy may need to be continued indefinitely. If the CoQ10 therapy is discontinued, the improvement may cease and the condition revert to its prior status.
- CoQ10 therapy improves cardiac function only when the CoQ10 level of the heart is low. There is little benefit in taking supplemental CoQ10 unless the heart has low amounts of this enzyme. However, maintenance of normal CoQ10 levels appears to be less likely as a person ages. Morbidity

(death) tends to occur if the CoQ10 level of the heart is less than 75 percent of normal and survival is rare at 25 percent of normal.[45]

A Stronger Pumping Action

Researchers have treated heart failure patients with CoQ10 with considerable success. CoQ10 is said by these researchers to enhance the pumping capacity of the heart and to eliminate the major side effects associated with conventional heart failure drugs. Patients with very severe forms of heart failure seem to benefit the most, showing an increase in pumping action of more than 200 percent after taking CoQ10. In general, the more severe the heart failure condition, the greater the benefit.[46]

Another study reported an increase in the production of energy in heart-muscle cells. In this study, some 91 percent of the patients showed improvement within thirty days after beginning CoQ10 supplementation.[47] What exciting news this is! We should all be taking CoQ10 to support the integrity of our hearts.

Effective in Many Other Areas. CoQ10 is also effective in many other areas such as periodontal (gum) disease, hypertension or high blood pressure, muscular dystrophy, cancer, athletic performance, weight loss, anti-aging, and thyroid and thymus gland function. Dr. Folkers has shown that CoQ10 strengthens the immune system.[48]

Even Anti-Aging Benefits. The new promise for CoQ10 is its anti-aging benefit. CoQ10 supplements have been shown to re-energize aging tissues and to alleviate the effects of many aging related processes and age associated diseases.[49]

This vitamin-like nutrient appears to have great benefit to all of us. Many people find 30 to 60 mg to be effective, and other authorities recommend 90 to 120 mg a day. This is an investment in the future, like an "insurance policy of good health" that will pay off in our later years.

The Value of L-Carnitine

L-Carnitine is an amino acid-like compound found in all animal and human tissues, with the highest concentrations found in the adrenal glands and heart muscle. It is synthesized in the liver, where it is converted rapidly from the amino acids lysine and methionine. The process of conversion requires adequate vitamin C to be present.[50]

L-carnitine is critical for a strong heart because it helps to expand the blood vessels, making the heart's job easier. No other organ in the body has more L-carnitine in it than the heart. In fact, L-carnitine levels in the heart are approximately 100 times that of the L-carnitine levels in the blood.

Studies have shown that L-carnitine is an effective nutritional agent in managing ischemic heart disease (heart attack), abnormal heartbeat rhythm (cardiac arrhythmias), and elevated triglyceride levels. This safe and effective nutrient also raises serum HDL levels (the beneficial cholesterol). This can be important to patients who are unable to exercise.[51]

A minimum daily dose of 900 mg of L-carnitine is required for therapeutic benefits. This nutrient works so rapidly that triglyceride levels dropped to within normal limits in fifteen days for 73 percent of the patients of one study.[52]

May Reduce Risk of Death by 90 percent. In another study, 160 patients who had recently suffered a heart attack were divided into two groups. One group received standard care, while the others received standard care plus 4 grams (4,000 mg) a day of L-carnitine. After twelve months, 12.5 percent of those in the standard care group had died, compared to only 1.2 percent in the L-carnitine group. L-carnitine treatment following a heart attack may reduce the risk of death by as much as 90 percent! No other treatment so far has produced such dramatic results.[53]

L-carnitine has also been shown to be helpful to those who experience angina, symptoms related to mitral valve prolapse, and those who have hardening of the arteries in their legs.[54]

Dosage. The usual dosage is 500 to 4,000 mg a day in divided doses. The recommended amount varies according to the severity of the condition being treated. There seems to be a synergistic effect with magnesium and CoQ10.

As people age, they tend to produce less L-carnitine, so older people may be wise to add this to their nutritional program.

L-Carnitine with CoQ10. According to Dr. Whitaker, "No studies have looked at what happens when both L-carnitine and CoQ10 are used together. Because of their overlapping mechanisms of action, I believe that combining them would produce much better results than using either separately. Both L-carnitine and CoQ 10 have been shown to produce as good a result as standard drug therapy for angina." [55]

Dr. Whitaker recommends taking 500 mg of L-carnitine, twice daily, and 30 to 100 mg of CoQ 10, three times daily. [56]

Magnesium—Essential for Life

Magnesium is a major mineral component in our bodies. It is absolutely essential for life, and is required for every major biological process, including the electrical stability of cells in the heart, the maintenance of membrane integrity, muscle contraction, nerve conduction, and the regulation of vascular tone—all of which have direct bearing on the health of the heart muscle.

Magnesium appears to regulate the "gate" through which calcium enters the cells to "switch on" vital functions such as the heartbeat. [57] It is vitally important that magnesium and calcium be in balance for the heart to beat regularly.

Magnesium has been shown to improve different forms of irregular heartbeats and arrhythmias, including:

- rapid beating of the heart chambers
  (*ventricular tachycardia*)
- fibrillation of the heart chamber
  (*ventricular fibrillation*)
- irregular heartbeat originated in the smaller
  chambers of the heart situated above the main
  chambers (*supraventricular arrhythmia*)[58]

One of the causes of ischemic heart disease (heart attack) is that the coronary arteries fail to provide all of the oxygen the heart demands. The result is a spasm in the smooth muscles of the artery walls. Inadequate magnesium has been related to greater susceptibility to muscle spasm. Thus, an increase in magnesium can be beneficial in heart disease to counteract vessel spasm.

Calcium-Magnesium Imbalance. This same principle applies to the overall heart muscle. Calcium is crucial for the heart muscle to work properly. If too many calcium ions enter the heart cells because magnesium is in short supply, then the effect can be disruptive, introducing toxic, killing forms of oxygen. Some researchers suggest that this may be the very root of heart-tissue death, and thus, of myocardial infarction (heart attack).

Sheldon Hendler, M.D., Ph.D., holds to this position, and also believes that the resulting magnesium-calcium imbalance may also be the main obstacle to overcome in helping the heart to heal after a heart attack. Once calcium has the upper hand, it is all the more difficult for magnesium to promote the nucleic acid and protein synthesis necessary for the mending process in the heart muscle. Dr. Hendler says, "We do know that magnesium deficiency predisposes humans to potentially fatal disruptions of normal cardiac rhythm (cardiac dysrhythmia). Investigators have successfully treated ventricular dysrhythmias with magnesium. These disorders had not been improved by conventional drug therapy." [59]

Diuretics and Digitalis are known to diminish magnesium levels. Many times blood tests do not reflect a total body magnesium deficit. Cellular levels have often been found to be low even when blood levels of magnesium were within normal range. The cellular measure is a far more accurate gauge and should be employed more often, especially if a person is taking diuretics and digitalis. The problem is that there is no easy way to measure cellular levels. So if you are on these medications, discuss with your doctor whether you can add the minerals potassium and magnesium to your program.

Heart Attacks and Intravenous Magnesium. Recent studies in the *Lancet* have shown that those who have acute heart attacks have a much higher survival rate, or fewer life threatening dysrhythmia incidents, if magnesium is given to them right after the attack. I recently saw a very interesting television program on the Public Broadcasting System (PBS) in which a patient was rushed to an emergency room after a heart attack and a doctor immediately began to administer magnesium intravenously. This stopped the attack and prevented further damage to the heart, according to the experts on the program. This is important since 300,000 heart attack victims die before they reach the hospital.[60]

Stephen Gottlieb, M.D., is quoted in *Emergency Medicine* as saying, "It's so safe and inexpensive that I can't think of a reason not to give it."

Vitamin B6 Has Preventive Value

Many researchers have shown, through carefully controlled experiments, that the B-complex vitamins are critical in avoiding heart disease. Pyridoxine (B6) has been shown to:

- combat the development of atherosclerosis
- reduce the risk of blood clots in coronary arteries
- normalize blood lipids (fats)
- reduce elevated homocysteine levels
- reduces the risk factor for heart attacks and strokes [61]

Vitamin B6 is a vital part of the coenzyme that helps form lecithin in our bodies, and lecithin is a known fat metabolizer with great benefit in helping lower cholesterol.

In one experiment, rhesus monkeys were fed high cholesterol diets. The monkeys developed human-like arterial plaques when they were deficient in B6, but not when they were well-supplied with the vitamin. Even though the cholesterol level of some of the monkeys was elevated to four times that of others, they didn't develop cholesterol plaques if they had adequate B6 levels. In fact, they had fewer plaques than monkeys fed far lower cholesterol diets, but which were deficient in B6. These experiments with monkeys were later confirmed by other researchers, and also were replicated using dogs and chickens with similar results.[62]

Are You Deficient? Vitamin B6 is indispensable for the manufacturing of Coenzyme Q 10, a vital enzyme for the heart. Since a widespread deficiency of vitamin B6 among Americans has been well documented, it follows logically that a widespread deficiency of CoQ10 is very probable in the American population, especially among the elderly. If you are concerned about your heart, consider taking a complete B-complex vitamin that contains at least 50 to 75 mg of vitamin B6.[63]

Folic Acid and Heart Disease

A deficiency of another of the B-vitamins, folic acid, is now being linked to heart disease. In 1995, the *Journal of the American Medical Association* (Vol 274) reported that folic acid may also help protect against heart disease, and after thorough investigation of existing data, the researchers concluded that between 13,500 and 50,000 coronary artery disease deaths a year could be avoided.

As long ago as 1969, Kilmer McCully, M.D., suggested that many Americans might have high levels of homocysteine, an intermediate metabolic amino acid, in their blood, either from their diet or because they inherited a genetic defect that required they consume sufficient amounts of the B-vitamin to keep homocysteine levels down.[64] One of folic acid's several functions in the body is to reduce the amount of homocysteine in the blood.

Recently, researchers have found that a high level of homocysteine in the blood is related to injured blood vessels, causing hardening of the arteries and thus, contributing to heart attacks and strokes. Folic acid supplements apparently can reduce blood levels of this amino acid combination to a safe range.[65]

The good news is that just about everyone's homocysteine levels will fall when they consume sufficient amounts of folic acid, which means that this condition is fairly easy to treat.

Vitamin B12 works in tandem with folic acid in the body. Vitamin B6 also has a homocysteine-lowering effect, so be sure to take the entire B-complex in sufficient quantity.

Copper—An Essential Trace Mineral for the Heart

Copper, an essential trace mineral for human beings, plays a role in many biochemical reactions in the body, including the production of hemoglobin, collagen, and neurotransmitters. It has been shown to be protective against cardiovascular disease.

Copper and zinc work in balance in the body. If a person is copper deficient, it is usually from excessive zinc intake. An imbalance in the zinc:copper ratio has been shown to increase the risk of coronary artery disease by lowering the levels of beneficial HDL in the blood.[66]

Copper Deficiency. Researchers at the U.S. Department of Agriculture (USDA) have found that a copper deficiency seems to be related to:

- a decreased effectiveness of the relaxing factor in the aorta, the largest artery in the human body.
- a longer time required to dissolve blood clots (in one study, mice that were copper-deficient took two and a half times longer to dissolve blood clots than animals that were given adequate amounts of copper).[67]
- high blood pressure.

These studies confirm a long held nutritional theory that coronary heart disease may be linked to inadequate copper intake in the United States and other industrialized nations. The studies also confirm that tiny blood clots are part of the plaque-forming debris that accumulates in arteries. This accumulation, of course, gradually narrows the vessels and restricts blood flow.

If clot-dissolving ability is reduced, the clot thickens, as does the plaque. The researchers noted in their study that their finding is in keeping with some sixty other studies which noted similarities between animals deficient in copper and people who have heart disease.[68]

Check your mineral supplements for the zinc:copper ratio. It should range from 10:1 to 15:1. For example, if you take 30 mg of zinc per day, and 2 mg of copper a day, your zinc:copper ratio would be 15:1.

The best food sources of copper are liver, oysters, black-strap molasses, bran, nuts (especially Brazil nuts), and seeds.

Natural Ways to Lower Cholesterol

A number of natural substances have been found to help a person lower cholesterol. The foremost are niacin, lecithin, chromium, fiber, and the aforementioned vitamins C and E.

Niacin and Cholesterol

Niacin or nicotinic acid—vitamin B3—has finally been regarded as one of the substances of choice for lowering blood levels of cholesterol. A Coronary Drug Project study published in the *Journal of the American College of Cardiology,* demonstrated that niacin was the only lipid-lowering agent to actually reduce overall mortality. The study on 8,000 men showed that niacin resulted in about 27 fewer non-fatal heart attacks. Its long-lasting effects were demonstrated in a 15 year follow-up study of the original men, which showed the long-term death rate of patients treated with niacin was actually 11 percent lower than the group receiving a placebo, even though the treatment had been discontinued many years earlier. It took several years for the lifesaving results to show up in all of the statistics.[69]

In a Harvard University Medical School study, cholesterol was lowered 18 percent in over 100 heart patients taking a gram (1,000) of niacin daily. Niacin also improved the beneficial HDL. A dosage of 1,500 mg (1.5 grams) daily can result in a lowering of the dangerous LDL by 30 percent. Dosages up to 7,500 mg daily have been used to lower blood cholesterol levels an average of 45 percent. This is two drastic a dose to be unsupervised and should only be done under the guidance of a physician.[70] Researchers showed that 800 mg was found to be ineffective. But in some, a dose as little as 1,200 mg per day was found to be effective.

In an article in the *Journal of Lipid Research*, Scott Grundy and his co-researchers reported that a niacin treatment resulted in a 52 percent reduction in cholesterol and an amazing 52 percent reduction in triglycerides. Grundy concluded, "To our knowledge, no other single agent has such potential for lowering both cholesterol and triglycerides." These results were found even in spite of the terrible diet the patients were asked to eat for the study, a diet of 40 percent fat, mostly from lard! [71]

Triglycerides, HDL & LDL. Abram Hoffer, M.D., Ph.D., who uses mostly nutritional methods in treating his patients, has said, "One of niacin's most striking effects is its ability to lower dangerous blood fats, which effects the course of many serious conditions. There is a close relationship between blood vessel diseases and fat metabolism. Niacin (not niacinamide) is one of the most effective broad-spectrum hypolipidemic (fat-lowering) agents. It lowers cholesterol levels, triglyceride levels, and the most dangerous, low-density lipoproteins (LDL) and at the same time elevates the desirable high density lipoproteins (HDL)." [72]

Dr. James D. Alderman, senior fellow in cardiology at Beth Israel Hospital in Boston, has concluded that niacin in doses up to two grams a day can "offer more lipid (fat) lowering benefits than traditional medication or diet alone." [73]

Watch Out for the Flush. You may find if you start taking niacin that you experience a "niacin flush," which is caused by arteries opening and bringing blood rapidly to the head, neck, and upper part of the body, making it very warm and in some cases, hot. Various forms of "flush-free" or "no flush" niacin are now available in nutrition stores. There are some products that consist of inositol hexaniacinate, a special form of niacin composed of six nicotinic acid molecules bound to, and surrounding one molecule of inositol (a B-vitamin). Inositol hexaniacinate exerts the benefits of niacin without flushing or other side effects. Michael Murray, N.D., says, "it has been used in Europe for over 30 years not only to lower cholesterol, but also to improve blood blow in the treatment of intermittent claudication (a painful cramp in the calf muscle) and Raynaud's phenomena (a constriction of blood vessels to the hands). Although inositol hexaniacinate yields slightly better results than standard niacin, the big advantage is that it is safer and much better tolerated." [74]

The Value of Lecithin

Lecithin is a natural phosphatide, an essential constituent of all living cells of the human body. Lecithin is admired for its "soap-like" characteristics and the fact that it acts as a powerful emulsifying agent in the blood to help dissolve cholesterol. It works to rid the body of cholesterol in two ways:

- First, lecithin stimulates the transportation of cholesterol to the liver, before the cholesterol has a chance to accumulate or settle as plaque.
- Second, lecithin promotes the production of an enzyme that dissolves cholesterol that has already accumulated, and eases its transport to the liver. This process helps to prevent many

cholesterol related diseases, such as atherosclerosis. The vital organs and arteries are protected from fatty build-up when lecithin is added to the diet.[75]

My mother, Gladys Lindberg, always recommended the addition of one or two tablespoons of soy lecithin to her clients health routine. Lecithin is available primarily in three forms—granules, liquid, and soft gelatin capsules. The granules are most cost effective. It takes ten large lecithin capsules to equal just one tablespoon of granulated lecithin. The granules have a nutty taste and are practically tasteless. Mix it into your protein drink, with orange juice, milk, water, or sprinkled on breakfast cereal. One customer told me that he loved it on his salad with vinegar and oil dressing.

NOTE: *The good HDL cholesterol is manufactured partly from the body's natural emulsifier, lecithin.*

Nutrients such as polyunsaturated fatty acids, the B-complex vitamins, and the minerals magnesium and phosphorus are used by our bodies in the manufacture of lecithin. If we are deficient in any of these nutrients, our bodies will not make the right amount of the essential HDL.

Lecithin is a source of linoleic acid, as well as choline and inositol, which play a number of important roles in the body. Since linoleic acid cannot be produced by the body, lecithin's role as a source of this essential fatty acid is critical. Lecithin's primary role in cardiovascular health is its ability to lower cholesterol levels, but it also helps memory. Read more about lecithin in Chapter 6.

Chromium and Cholesterol

Richard Passwater, Ph.D., in *The New Supernutrition* said chromium, in the form of Glucose Tolerance Factor (GTF), has been shown to improve good cholesterol HDL by 18 percent, decrease bad LDL cholesterol by 18 percent, improve the HDL/LDL ratio by 44 percent, and even lower the blood cholesterol by 25 percent!

Gary Evans, Ph.D., who has been one of the original researchers of chromium, spoke at a Federation of American Societies for Experimental Biology meeting and stated that chromium picolinate reduced total blood cholesterol levels, lowered harmful LDL and apolipoprotein(b) levels, and increased the good HDL and apolipoprotein(a) levels.[76]

Dr. Abraham of the Department of Medicine in Jerusalem, reported the results of a study in which dietary chromium reversed the development of atherosclerotic plaques (cholesterol deposits) in monkeys.

He wrote, "These experiments have shown that atherosclerosis, even when established, can be reversed by treatment with chromium. After a relatively short treatment period of thirty weeks with chromium, there was a substantial regression of atherosclerotic lesions, compared to the group that did not receive chromium. The difference between the extent of aortic involvement in the chromium-treated and non-treated groups was significant by all the methods we used." [77] *GTF chromium picolinate* and *GTF chromium polynicotinate* are the best forms available.

Herbs and Other Nutrients for the Heart

Hawthorn Berry—The Heart Herb

Hawthorn (*Crataegus monogyna and oxyacantha*)—both the berry and flower-tops extract—is widely used in Europe for heart problems. The heart benefit properties of this herb have been reported for centuries. Regular use is said to strengthen the heart muscle. The extracts have a combination of effects that are of great value to those suffering from angina, as well as other heart problems.

A number of studies have also demonstrated that hawthorn extracts are effective in lowering blood pressure and serum cholesterol levels. [78]

According to the *Encyclopedia of Natural Medicine*, the beneficial effects of hawthorn extracts are the result of improvement in two basic heart functions: heart metabolism, and the dilation of coronary vessels, which increases the blood flow and thus, oxygen to the heart. Recommended dosage is hawthorn extract containing 10% procyanidins, 100-250 mg three times a day (or 1-1/2 tsp of tincture (1:5). [79]

Garlic's Benefit to the Heart

What are garlic's specific benefits to the heart? Garlic prevents platelets (blood cells responsible for clotting) from sticking to each other and to artery walls. By preventing excess clotting, it may protect against coronary thrombosis (blood clots), atherosclerosis, and strokes. [80]

In addition, there's strong evidence that garlic normalizes fats in the blood by lowering harmful fats and raising protective lipids. In numerous animal and human studies, components of garlic have lowered cholesterol, triglycerides, harmful LDL levels, and dangerous very-low-density lipoprotein cholesterol (VLDL), while raising the beneficial HDL level.[81]

Many medical authorities feel that garlic can reduce high blood pressure, perhaps by acting as a vasodilator.

Garlic preparations are available in liquid extract, oil capsules and tablet form. Many of the studies showing garlic's effectiveness in reducing cholesterol and in protecting the liver used Kyolic®, an odor-modified liquid garlic extract. Look for a high potency garlic in your nutrition store.

Heart Healthy Oils

The essential oils, the omega-3 fatty acids (EPA) and the omega-6 fatty acids, should be part of a healthy heart and cholesterol lowering program. This would include eating all types of cold water fish, such as salmon, herring, mackerel, sardines, and sea bass.

A study on men with high cholesterol examined the effects of supplementing with omega-3 oils or eating cold water fish. After five weeks, the beneficial HDL levels in all the men increased, and their triglyceride level decreased.[82]

Another way of getting the essential fatty acids is to use flax seed oil. Flax seed oil contains more than twice as much omega-3 oils as fish and is also a good source of linoleic acid. In addition, flax seed oil may offer other benefits that fish oil and GLA products do not.[83] It is also much less expensive. Make sure it is organic. The liquid can be found in black bottles in the refrigerated section of your nutrition store.

The omega-6 oil (GLA) is found in evening primrose oil, borage oil, and black currant seed oil. A Japanese study found that evening primrose oil had a greater cholesterol-lowering effect than all other unsaturated oils tested, including safflower and olive oils.[84]

Cayenne Is More Than a Hot Spice

Like many herbs, cayenne pepper (*Capsicum frutescens*), also known as capsicum, is used for medicinal as well as for culinary purposes. In recent years, more than 650 studies of *capsaicin* (the "hot" property in cayenne pepper) have been published, including more than 100 clinical studies in human beings. Capsicum is excellent for equalizing blood circulation, which helps to prevent strokes and heart attacks. It increases the heart action, effectively increasing circulation without increasing blood pressure.[85]

Exercise Your Heart

The birth of the "exercise movement" couldn't have come at a better time in our nation's history. While exercise is not the only answer to heart problems, it surely aids in the prevention of heart disease.

Doctors are now realizing that people can benefit from, and need, a varied fitness program. Dr. Kenneth Cooper says, "We used to think exercise had to be three times a week with your heart rate at 60 to 90 percent of capacity for twenty to thirty minutes to get any benefit. We used to see it as all or nothing. But now studies are showing we can get benefits from other exercise prescriptions. People seem to have a favorable impact on health even from moderate walking." [86]

Importance of Strength Training. In studies at Tufts University, researchers found that strength—not aerobic capacity—was a significant factor in fitness. Dr. Miriam Nelson, a research scientist at Tufts has said, "What we see is that if you look at twenty to forty year olds, their walking and running speed is directly related to their aerobic capacity, to their heart's ability to work. But for people in their eighties and nineties, walking speed is directly related to their strength. What aerobics can do for people under sixty, strength training can do for people in their sixties and older."[87]

She has also reported that quite simply, muscle strength has been shown to be the one factor most closely related to independence for older adults. Many people living in nursing homes are there simply because they are not strong enough to lift groceries, climb stairs, or get in and out of a bathtub.

To get started on a good exercise program, you may want to consider joining a group. Check your local YWCA or YMCA for classes or adult education. Many women I know go to the "Y" for swimming classes or water aerobics. I enjoy a program that alternates aerobics workouts with the use of exercise equipment and light weights.

If you can motivate yourself, there are great videos available to help inspire you to exercise. I suggest you rent before you buy so you can see which programs are best suited to your personality and ability.

As human beings, we were designed to move . . . so its important that we do! Finding a form of exercise that you enjoy is a must if you're going to be faithful in exercising regularly over time.

NOTE: Chelation therapy may be very important for the heart. This information is discussed in Chapter 11. In the same chapter there is information on the **hormone DHEA**, which shows positive effects in lowering cholesterol, preventing blood clot formation and its protection against both heart disease and stroke.

There is a very important connection between the **thyroid gland**, cholesterol and heart disease. Make sure you read Chapter 8. A simple temperature test is described for your information.

Chapter 8

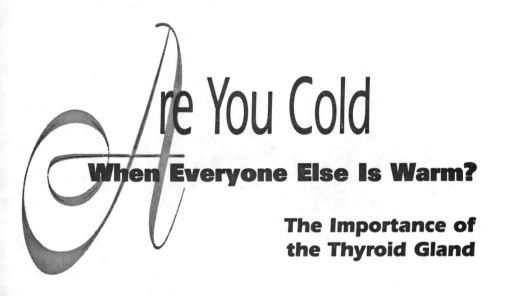

re You Cold

When Everyone Else Is Warm?

The Importance of
the Thyroid Gland

"It seems amazing that most of the people
I speak with show so many symptoms of low thyroid.
This may be the important key to unlocking
the door of abundant health."
—Gladys Lindberg

When my clients come to me with various nutritional questions, I love to shake their hand as I welcome them. Many times, much to my amazement, their hands are very cold. Then this dear person tells me how tired they are, how they have no energy, and can't get going in the morning. Not only are their hands cold, but so are their feet. This brings to mind the seminars I've attended and the lovely dinners I've shared with the charming Broda Barnes, M.D. Cold hands were one of Dr. Barnes' major symptoms of hypothyroidism, or low thyroid function.

The Need for An Optimal Thyroid Level

Thyroid problems are far more prevalent in our society than one might think. "Low thyroid" is a condition that very often masquerades as other ailments and the symptoms vary widely. The good news is that it can generally be addressed very successfully—if first you know what you are dealing with!

It may help for you to know a little about the thyroid gland, the largest endocrine gland in the human body. It controls the metabolic activity of all our cells.

The thyroid is a butterfly-shaped gland. It only weighs about two-thirds of an ounce and straddles the windpipe just below the Adam's apple. Every hour, about five quarts of blood circulate through your thyroid gland, bringing iodide (a compound of iodine with a more electropositive atom or group) to the gland, as well as hormones from the pituitary gland that stimulate the thyroid into production. Iodide is the material your thyroid gland uses to make its hormone. The thyroid gland makes, stores, and discharges thyroid hormone into the bloodstream for delivery to your cells where and when it is needed. This hormone production is normally less than 1/100,000 of an ounce.[1]

Symptoms of Low Thyroid or Hypothyroidism

Hypothyroidism is a condition in which a person has too little output from the thyroid gland. According to Broda Barnes, M.D., Ph.D., perhaps the most famous thyroid researcher and author of *Hypothyroidism: The Unsuspected Illness*, along with other authorities report that the symptoms related to low thyroid vary widely: [2]

- Sensitivity to cold—especially in hands and feet
- Fatigue—reduced energy levels, moving slowly
- Infections—especially respiratory infections
- Decreased perspiration
- Poor circulation—due to heart not pumping with sufficient force
- Coarse hair or hair loss
- Dry eyes/blurred vision
- Weight gain
- Digestion problems—irritable bowel syndrome or acid indigestion
- Constipation
- Headaches—moderate to severe
- Poor short term memory and concentration
- Low blood pressure
- Weak or dormant sex urge
- Anxiety/panic attacks
- Depression—moderate to severe
- Frequent bouts of cold or influenza
- Dry, coarse, leathery skin; pale
- Swelling or puffy eyelids
- High cholesterol and atherosclerosis
- Inability to lose weight despite constant dieting
- Wounds that heal slowly
- Menstrual problems
- Infertility
- Enlarged thyroid—goiter
- Rheumatic pain—moderate to severe
- Behavioral and emotional disorders
- Lower half of eyebrow missing
- Asthma and allergies

Each of these symptoms have been reported by people with low thyroid, as well as the feeling, "I just can't seem to get going." The effect of low thyroid is felt in each of the trillions of cells, in every organ and tissue of the body.

As early as 1957, Dr. A. S. Jackson, a nationally recognized authority on the thyroid gland published a paper in the *Journal of the American Medical Association*, declaring that low thyroid function was the most common disease entering the doctor's office and was the diagnosis most often missed.[3] The situation is much the same today.

A book written in 1960, *The Thyroid-Vitamin Approach to Cholesterol, Atheromatosis and Chronic Disease*, details a ten-year study. The author, Murray Israel, M.D., was founder of the Vascular Research Foundation in New York. In almost forty years of practice, during which time numerous studies and experiments were conducted, Dr. Israel observed that laboratory testing failed to uncover even a minute fraction of the people with low thyroid function. He found the standard tests indicated that 85 percent of his patients had normal thyroid function, yet all of them showed marked benefits from thyroid supplementation, which increased body temperature, energy, and vitality.[4]

H. Jack Baskin, M.D., vice-president of the American Association of Clinical Endocrinologists, reports eight million Americans (seven times more women than men) have some sort of thyroid problems, but only half of those have been diagnosed. A vast majority of these have an underactive thyroid. Baskin went on to discuss the diverse conditions like the ones I have listed.

"While extreme hypothyroidism is rare and is easily identified, mild cases are often not detected in routine blood tests, so subclinical hypothyroidism mostly falls through the cracks. Your doctor might try to convince you that your symptoms are 'a normal part of aging' or 'nothing to worry about.' "Don't buy it," Dr. Baskin said. "It's your quality of life that is being severely compromised, and it is your right to get to the bottom of these 'minor' ailments."[5]

So it appears, that after all these years, this information is still being ignored. But, addressing this issue may very well be the key that unlocks the door to better health for countless people.

"The Biochemical Approach to the Aging Process"

was a lecture given by Murray Israel, M.D., in New York in 1959.

He is the doctor that did the ten-year study with thyroid and vitamins for chronic diseases. He said the subject could be discussed for hours and hours and went on to say "...the one aspect which seems at this time to be the most vital and the least understood: the hormone-vitamin approach to the control of the rate of aging—a recent development which is making it possible to prolong the better years."[4]

Dr. Israel continued, "In the human being, when the thyroid gland becomes inadequate, all the metabolic processes become disturbed. The person becomes tired, nervous, irritable, depressed. The metabolic pathways become deranged—the rate of aging becomes accelerated. And this can occur at any age. There are many other factors affecting the rate of aging besides thyroid hormone inadequacy. These factors, however, are of secondary importance and can only be considered after the thyroid deficiency has first been taken care of."[5]

The Conductor of the Metabolic Symphony. "It is my opinion," Israel said, "therefore, that the thyroid hormone should be considered the conductor of the metabolic symphony. This does not mean that the thyroid hormone can conduct this symphony of all individuals and bring forth 100 percent cures or perfectly harmonious chords. If part of the members of the orchestra (such as the other glands of internal secretion which produce hormones) are not functioning, or are functioning very poorly, the resulting music will be discordant."[6]

Dr. Israel also concluded with his studies that "vitamin research has implicated a whole series of substances—chiefly members of the vitamin B-complex, for example, nicotinic acid (B3) and pyridoxine (B6), ascorbic acid (C) and lipotropic factors (choline, methionine and inositol). These need to be given in standard amounts along with thyroid extract. To put it another way, thyroid cannot be successfully or safely administered without them."[7]

A Simple Thyroid Test

The earliest studies in England show that the hypothyroid (low thyroid function) patient consistently runs temperatures below normal. The body thermostat of a thyroid deficient person generally cries for more heat, essential for the oxidation of fuel in the body. In the thyroid deficient body, the temperature falls below normal because of inadequate oxidation. In hyperthyroid (high thyroid) *too much* thyroid is circulating. So much heat is produced that the body's thermostat cannot control the body temperature precisely and the result is a low-grade fever.

Dr. Barnes studied 1,569 patients over a period of twenty years to determine the role of thyroid deficiency in heart disease. He also reviewed the medical literature, reading studies dating back to 1918 and 1925, which showed that thyroid therapy was an effective measure in preventing heart attacks.[8] How unfortunate it is that these early experiments, which clearly showed the relationship between thyroid deficiency and heart disease, were overlooked.

Dr. Broda Barnes Says, "Take Your Temperature."

He came to this conclusion as the result of studies involving more than a thousand college students, and later, thousands of soldiers during World War II. He concluded that a subnormal body temperature is a better indicator of hypothyroidism and the need of thyroid treatment than basal metabolic rate. Here is the method that Dr. Barnes has suggested as an easy test for low thyroid function:

Barnes Basal Temperature Test
for Thyroid Function

Use a mercury thermometer (not digital). Shake it down well when you go to bed. When you awaken in the morning, slip the thermometer snugly under your armpit before you get out of bed and leave it there for ten minutes. Normal temperature for this method is between 97.8 and 98.2 degrees Fahrenheit. A temperature of 97.8 or below—especially if recorded consistently over several days—may indicate thyroid deficiency. (If you have an excess of thyroid hormone, your temperature will run above normal range.)[9]

Keep in mind that a woman's temperature varies in the different phases of her menstrual cycle. If you are menstruating, take your temperature on the second, third, and fourth days of your period. Men, take your temperature for several consecutive mornings.

Thyroid Blood Tests May Not Be Dependable.
If your Barnes Basal Temperature Test reveals a consistently below-normal temperature, ask your physician for more than the usual thyroid panel of tests. Dr. Baskin stated, "For years, thyroid tests were a joke—you just about had to be dead before they showed anything. Ask for the more sensitive TSH (thyroid-stimulating hormone) test, which is a much more accurate index of thyroid function."[10-11]

The standard test to measure thyroid activity attempts to determine the amount of hormone stored in the gland, or alternatively the amount of thyroid hormone in the bloodstream. What these tests fail to do, however, is what really counts: indicate the amount of thyroid hormone available for use within the cells throughout the body.

If Your Blood Tests are Normal, Now What?

If your thyroid blood test comes back normal, but your temperature is low and you have a history of many of the low-thyroid symptoms, I suggest you read one of these books on the importance of maintaining adequate thyroid production:

- *Hypothyroidism: The Unsuspected Illness*
  by Dr. Broda Barnes and Lawrence Galton
- *Solved: The Riddle of Illness*
  by Dr. Stephen Langer and James F. Scheer

After you have read either book, I suggest you take it to your physician and ask him for his advice in the matter. Many physicians are familiar with Dr. Barnes' method of treatment and his extensive list of publications in medical journals.

I am only able to give you a brief review of this important subject, but I have seen wonderful results when my family, friends and clients used natural thyroid. The turnaround in the way they feel has been amazing. If your thyroid function is low, a doctor must prescribe thyroid tablets, as they are not available without a prescription. When thyroid therapy is indicated for low thyroid, the simple temperature test can be used to monitor the therapy.

Dr. Julian Whitaker says that in his practice, when a patient has symptoms consistent with low thyroid function, since both disease and age tend to reduce thyroid function, he starts them on a six-week therapeutic trial of desiccated bovine thyroid, regardless of what the blood test show. He uses one-half to one grain of Armour® thyroid, and carefully monitors their well-being, and follows up with increasing the dosage by one-half grain, while measuring the blood level. He says if the symptoms get better, then continue the therapy. But if there is no improvement, the treatment should be stopped. "Even though this is an extremely safe therapy, you may have difficulty with your physician . . . . the only solution to this is to shop around for a more open-minded physician," he explains.[12]

Stimulating Thyroid Production

What can be done nutritionally to stimulate a thyroid gland into producing more thyroid hormone without a prescription?

Many people have been helped by taking kelp, a natural form of iodine which stimulates the thyroid. Many fine, multi-mineral supplements include iodine as part of their formulas.

Iodine and Goiter. The thyroid needs iodine to function. A goiter may be caused by several factors. One is a lack of iodine, which causes the thyroid to swell. This can be seen on the front and side of the neck. Years ago, our government added iodine to salt to prevent the tremendous number of goiters. Now that everyone is "off salt," I see so many tired, fatigued, and exhausted people. Could their lethargy be caused by low iodine, which caused low thyroid? Iodine is also found in many seafoods. We need such a small amount: women (100 mcg), and men (120 mcg).[13]

In Japan, where residents consume about 4,000 times more iodine than Americans—mostly from large amounts of seafoods, kelp, dulse, and sea lettuce—incidences of hypothyroidism are rare.

Thyroid Glandulars. Most nutrition stores carry a natural thyroid glandular. Glandulars do not contain the thyroid hormone, but Dr. Steven Langer stated at a recent National Nutritional Foods Association convention that many people with slightly low thyroid output have been helped by taking these glandular supplements. They apparently provide just enough support to the thyroid gland to stimulate adequate hormone production for some people.

L-Tyrosine. The amino acid L-tyrosine is a precursor of the thyroid hormones thyroxin and triodothyronine. Tyrosine supplementation, when health is good and iodide intake is adequate, may increase thyroid hormone levels. There may be a relationship between dietary tyrosine and thyroid hormone synthesis under the same circumstances. A slightly increased tyrosine plasma level is found in hyperthyroidism (high); a slightly reduced level is found in hypothyroidism (low).[14]

Importance of Vitamins. Vitamin deficiencies can result in low thyroid. Make sure you are taking a balanced "stress" B-complex with meals, which improves cellular oxygenation and energy. Vitamin B12 in particular, should be taken in lozenges, under the tongue, several times a day.

The lipotropic factors that Dr. Israel discussed, choline, methionine and inositol, would be helpful. Israel said "we found that these factors, along with B6 enabled us to bring the patient to a higher maintenance dose of thyroid substance more rapidly than had been previously possible."[15]

Vitamin C can facilitate the production of the thyroid hormone. Vitamin E is also important for cellular oxygen. A person with low thyroid cannot convert beta-carotene into vitamin A, and when the body is low in vitamin A, it cannot produce the thyroid stimulating hormone (TSH). A deficiency in vitamin A (from fish oil) also reduces the ability of the thyroid to take up iodine. It becomes a vicious cycle. The bottom line is: you need all the vitamins and minerals recommended in the last chapter. Also read Chapter 3, which describes each of these vitamins in more detail.

The Natural Form of Thyroid

Alan Gaby, M.D., has reported that nutritionally-oriented doctors now prefer a natural extract from an animal's thyroid gland. Sold by prescription, this natural form of thyroid hormone is called desiccated thyroid or referred to as Armour® thyroid (from Forest Pharmaceuticals). This desiccated bovine thyroid (which more closely resembles our own thyroid hormones) contains not only T4 and T3, but other factors that we have yet to understand. This product was used long before the synthetic versions were available.

Unfortunately, many physicians routinely prescribe the synthetic form of thyroid which is sold under the name of Synthroid®. Synthroid® contains only the thyroid hormone T4, only one kind of thyroid hormone. The second most prescribed thyroid hormone is a synthetic version of T3 sold under the name of Cytomel®.

Dr. Whitaker and Dr. Gaby both use Armour® thyroid. Since Armour® seems to be hard to find at this time, the generic form is Nature-Throid®, which Dr. Whitaker also uses. These products are available from Western Research Labs (Jones Medical) in St. Louis, Missouri.

Dr. Gaby has said, "I frequently see patients who are being treated for hypothyroidism with L-thyroxine (Synthroid®), but who continue to experience typical hypothyroid symptoms, such as fatigue, depression, cold extremities, fluid retention, and dry skin. However, after switching to an equivalent (or sometimes even less equivalent) dose of Armour® thyroid, their symptoms disappear rapidly."[16]

It is heartening to find an article appearing in the *Journal of The American Medical Association,* July 24, 1996, by researchers at Johns Hopkins University who urge physicians to include testing for an underactive thyroid gland as part of routine physicals for patients after age thirty-five. The article discusses how low levels of the thyroid hormone can lead to high cholesterol levels, weight gain and depression, which often go undiagnosed. As you see, this information has been known for years and is just now beginning to be recognized and accepted.

As is true for most natural approaches, thyroid replacement therapy is never fast-acting. It might take several months for you to bring a low functioning thyroid up to normal.

Things to Avoid: There are a few herbals which cause stress to the thyroid and adrenals, such as ma-huang, guarana, and excessive caffeine, all of which should be avoided.

It is really surprising to know that there are vegetables that are goitrogenic (causes a goiter) from the cabbage family that should be limited or completely avoided by people with hypothyroidism according to Ray Peat, Ph.D. These include broccoli, cauliflower, cabbage, turnips, mustard greens, kale, spinach, Brussel sprouts, kohlrabi, rutabagas, horseradish, radish and white mustard.

These vegetables have been shown *to decrease thyroid hormone production as effectively as anti-thyroid drugs such as thiouracil.* Therefore, you need to include other varieties of vegetables and supplement with the antioxidants cod liver oil or Vitamin A, since beta-carotene is hard for hypothyroid individuals to assimilate.[17]

High Thyroid Symptoms

The other side of the thyroid coin, of course, is "high thyroid," or hyperthyroidism. If your Barnes temperature test is above 98.2, it may indicate hyperthyroid. Certain diseases such as Grave's disease or thyroid inflammation, as well as stress or worry, may cause the thyroid to produce too much thyroid hormone. This results in high thyroid output—a condition that causes the body's motor to race, the heartbeat to increase (or beat irregularly), and blood pressure to rise. A person with this condition generally feels flushed and overheated, often to the level of a mild fever. A hyperthyroid person perspires profusely, feels nervous, is sleepless, and may suffer from weight loss or diarrhea. Although this condition is rare, a person may also suffer these symptoms if they take too much thyroid supplement.

Cardiovascular Disease and the Thyroid Connection

Dr. Barnes believed what the early researchers found: they were able to prevent high levels of blood cholesterol and atherosclerosis by administering thyroid hormones. Dr. Barnes explains, "If their recommendations had been followed, cardiovascular diseases would have been conquered decades ago and much time and many lives would have been saved." Dr. Barnes noted, "by 1950, it was obvious that many cases of heart attacks were accompanied by high blood cholesterol levels. To most investigators, this suggested that the elevated cholesterol levels were causing the attacks, but to me they signaled possible thyroid deficiency." [18]

Dr. Murray Israel, in his ten-year-study, started his severely atherosclerotic patients with a history of high cholesterol intake, on a low cholesterol diet for the first few months. Also those with high cholesterol who had been on a low cholesterol diet needed to restrict cholesterol for the first few months until the thyroid was able to take effect. Israel said, "As the patient improves in his ability to utilize these lipoid elements, these restrictions become less important. The thyroxin improves his efficiency in processing lipoids and keeping them circulating, rather than deposited in tissues."[19]

(For more information on hypothyroidism contact the Broda O. Barnes, M.D., Research Foundation, Inc., at P.O. Box 98, Trumbull, CT 06611. Phone 203-261-2101)

Ruling Out Anemia

There may be reasons other than low thyroid for feeling cold. If your T3 and T4 tests return normal and you do not have a below normal temperature, you may want to have your doctor check you for anemia. Even a mild iron deficiency may result in anemia.

The general symptoms of anemia:

- pallor
- weakness
- easily fatigued
- persistent tiredness
- headache
- palpitation
- labored breathing on exertion
- restless legs syndrome [20]

Anemic preschool children's symptoms

- diminished coordination and balance
- lowered attention span
- reduction in intelligence quotient and memory

Symptoms of anemia in older children:

- difficulty reading
- poor learning and problem solving skills

A woman loses about 13.5 mg of iron through menstruation each month. For every milligram of iron lost, she needs to take at least 10 mg to replace it. This is because the body usually can absorb only about ten percent of the iron it ingests. The average American diet provides only 6 mg of iron per 1,000 calories. This means that a woman needs at least 8 mg daily (and more during pregnancy).[21]

The best dietary source of iron is red meat (especially organ meats such as liver). Other good sources are poultry, fish, ground soybean hulls, and blackstrap molasses.

Many foods considered high in iron are actually low in "iron availability"—foods such as spinach, and many green vegetables. Iron availability refers to the body's ability to absorb and use the form of iron that is in the food. Red meat is the most bioavailable form.

For those who will not eat liver, there are liquid liver capsules available that are rich not only in iron but folic acid, vitamin B12 and other natural blood building factors. Or, you may need to take supplemental iron. If so, chelated iron is the preferred form because the body more readily absorbs it. Avoid the ferrous sulfate form, although it is frequently recommended, since it destroys vitamin E and may cause constipation. The other forms often recommended are ferrous gluconate, ferrous fumarate, or ferrous citrate.

Anemia is not always a result of just an iron deficiency, but may be attributable to subtle, simultaneous deficiencies of all the vitamin B-complex, vitamins C and E, and the minerals copper and magnesium.

An article published in the medical journal *Circulation* discussed the possible relationship of elevated iron levels and the risk of heart attacks in Finnish men. The researchers demonstrated that high stored-iron levels produced by a diet of excess meat is associated with increased risk of heart attack. Michael Murray, N.D., said another way of expressing the results is that Finnish men, who eat excessive meat, have an increased risk of heart attacks, elevated LDL cholesterol (the dangerous cholesterol) and elevated iron stores. The connection between high meat consumption, LDL cholesterol and heart disease is nothing new.[22] For more on the dangers of LDL cholesterol see Chapter 7.

Chapter 9

If the Pressure
is Up–Let's Turn it Down!

Natural Ways to Lower Blood Pressure and Prevent a Stroke

"People who are healthy feel well in body and mind. Free from aches and pains, they have robust energy, a spring to their step, bright eyes, good color, and a pleasant outlook on life. That is not to say healthy people don't have their share of situations that try their patience and temper. But when circumstances are difficult, healthy people are much more likely to cope in a calm, capable manner. They are usually fit in body, soul, and spirit."
—Gladys Lindberg

Ho‍w does hypertension and stroke fit into the anti-aging puzzle?

Studies show that years of uncontrolled high blood pressure damage delicate capillaries throughout the body, and it also appears to accelerate the development of atherosclerotic plaques in the arteries. Almost one in six Americans suffer hypertension— at least 38 million Americans—and hundreds of thousands more suffer its ill effects. These include stroke, kidney disease, congestive heart failure, and eye disease.

You will not have the opportunity to enjoy your "golden years" and accomplish all you want to do in life if you allow these diseases to impair or shorten it unnecessarily.

Hypertension and Doctor's Visits

According to an article in the *Journal of the American Medical Association*, "Treatment of hypertension has become the leading reason for visits to physicians as well as for drug prescription.[1] Yearly sales of blood pressure medications are estimated to be greater than 10 billion dollars. It is estimated that approximately 80 percent of patients with high blood pressure are in the borderline to mild range."[2] If in a borderline range, many experts believe that much may be done to help these people naturally. Do not, however, discontinue any medication prescribed for you, without your doctor's recommendation.

The Silent Killer—High Blood Pressure

Hypertension has been called "The Silent Killer," because it normally has no visible symptoms.

Our blood pressure is actually the force exerted by the blood against the walls of the blood vessels. It is our blood pressure which forces oxygen or plasma—that is carrying glucose, amino acids, fatty acids, vitamins, and minerals—into the tissues through porous microscopic capillary walls. Normal blood pressure is vital to the nutrition of the cells. When the blood in the capillary beds becomes concentrated from the loss of plasma, the blood protein (albumin) attracts tissue fluids that carry waste into the vessels. This causes the quantity of blood to remain remarkably constant. Thus, by virtue of the blood pressure, all tissues are constantly bathed in fresh, nutrient-laden fluid. Also, the breakdown products from worn-out cells are removed.

When larger amounts of oxygen and nutrients are needed, the contraction of tiny muscles in the arterial walls causes the pressure to increase and supplies to be pushed more quickly to the cells. On the other hand, if few nutrients are required, these muscles relax, the pressure decreases, and food is conserved.[3]

What Are the Causes? The causes of hypertension are numerous, but any of the following may make you a candidate:

- highest risk is heredity (family history of hypertension), particularly for those of African descent
- smoking—narrows the arteries, decreases the blood's ability to deliver oxygen, and nicotine stimulates the heartbeat, increasing the need for oxygen-rich blood
- excessive drinking of alcohol
- those who are twenty pounds or more overweight—the extra pressure put on the heart to pump blood through the two extra miles of capillaries for every extra pound of fat
- too little physical exercise. Exercise relieves physical tension and, helps keep the arteries flexible and circulates the blood more widely and evenly
- unrelenting, negative stress

- eating excessive sugar—creating abnormalities of lipid, glucose, and insulin metabolism (even leading to diabetes)

Obviously, if you have mild or moderate hypertension, and if any of these factors relate to you, you should try to remedy the factors that put you at risk. A change in your lifestyle can be your most potent, positive ally in achieving better health and longer life.

Norman Kaplan, M.D., professor of internal medicine and chief of the hypertension unit at the University of Texas Health Sciences Center in Dallas has said, "I believe a non-drug approach should be the first treatment of mild hypertension, where the diastolic blood pressure (bottom figure and the reading that records the pressure of blood flow between heartbeats) is between 90 and 100 millimeters."[4]

Hypertension's Effect on the Heart

As the blood pressure goes up, the heart must work harder to push blood throughout the body. Just as with other muscles in the body, the heart can compensate for the extra work by getting bigger and stronger, but over the years, the heart basically gets worn out. Two things usually happen to the heart as a result.

First, hypertension accelerates atherosclerosis by stressing and damaging the inside lining of the arteries, promoting plaque formation. Since the heart is working harder, it requires a greater blood supply. Too much plaque can slow or stop the supply to the heart, resulting in a heart attack.

Second, hypertension damages the capillaries throughout the body, including the heart muscle. As a result, the muscle cells don't get the oxygen and nutrients they need as easily, and the heart doesn't beat as strongly. Slowly, the heart chambers begin to dilate in an attempt to maintain the blood pressure, but eventually this fails. The heart becomes enlarged, floppy and ineffective in pumping blood, and the result is congestive heart failure.

The pressure of the blood in the main arteries rises and falls as the heart and muscles of the body cope with varying demands— exercise, stress, and sleep.

Two Types of Pressure Measured:

- Systolic pressure, the high number in a blood-pressure reading, is the pressure created by the contraction of the heart muscle and the elastic recoil of the aorta (great artery) as the blood surges through it.
- Diastolic pressure, the low number in a blood-pressure reading, is the pressure when the ventricles relax between beats. It reflects the resistance of all the small arteries throughout the body and the load against which the heart must work.[5]

Blood Pressure Values

Normal..120/80 or less
Borderline...140/90–160/100
Hypertension....................................160/104

A young adult has a blood pressure reading of about 110/75 which normally rises with age to about 130/90 at age 60.

The Ideal Pressure. More and more doctors are stressing not only the importance of checking your blood pressure periodically, but also the importance of intercepting "slightly elevated" blood pressures and addressing them nutritionally. By addressing a blood pressure problem early, a person is often capable of avoiding a lifetime reliance on drugs.

Strokes—The Brain's Equivalent of a Heart Attack

A stroke results from an interruption of the brain's blood flow. It is thus a blood vessel disease, the cerebral (brain) equivalent of a heart attack.

Strokes are the third most frequent case of death in the United States among adults and the most common cause of neurological disability. Strokes and other cerebrovascular disorders affect about 500,000 Americans annually, with more than two-thirds of these patients being sixty-five or older. Because more aggressive therapies for high blood pressure and heart disease have been developed and used in the last thirty years, stroke deaths have dropped from 89 per 100,000 to 90 per 100,000. Still, the mortal ity rate for those afflicted is high. An estimated one in four stroke patients dies within a month of their brain injury. Death from stroke is 93 percent in black men and 82 percent in black women, higher than among their white counterparts.[6]

Types and Causes of Stroke

Stroke may be caused by any of three mechanisms. Thrombosis and embolism both lead to cessation of the blood supply to parts of the brain, and thus to infarction (tissue death). Rupture of a blood vessel in or near the brain may cause a hemorrhage. Any part of the brain may be affected by a stroke. Accordingly, the symptoms vary considerably.

- **Cerebral Thrombosis.** Blockage by a clot (thrombus) that has built up on the wall of a brain artery accounts for 40 to 50 percent of strokes.
- **Cerebral Embolism.** Blockage usually by a clot (embolus) swept into an artery in the brain accounts for 30 to 35 percent of cases.
- **Hemorrhage.** Rupture of a blood vessel and bleeding within or over the surface of the brain accounts for 20 to 25 percent of the cases.[7]

Symptoms of Stroke

The symptoms of a stroke usually develop over minutes or hours, but occasionally over several days. Depending on the site, cause, and extent of damage, any or all of the symptoms may be present, in any degree of severity.

There may be warning symptoms prior to strokes. These are called "transient ischemic attacks" (TIAs), because the culprit is ischemia, or lack of blood flow, and because the interruption of circulation is brief. Brain cells survive TIAs and recover full function within 24 hours in most cases.

More serious cases lead to rapid loss of consciousness, coma, and death or to severe physical or mental handicap, but some strokes cause barely noticeable symptoms. Among the more common symptoms are these:

- weakness or paralysis on one side of the body
  (*one of the more common effects of a serious stroke*)
- headache, dizziness, confusion
- visual disturbance
- slurred speech or loss of speech,
  and difficulty swallowing[8]

Nutrients that Impact
Hypertension and Strokes

A number of nutrients have been correlated with hypertension and strokes. While there is no "magic bullet" to use for either hypertension or susceptibility to strokes, there are a number of steps to take nutritionally which may help build up your health. Many important nutrients have been discussed in other chapters. The research reported in this chapter is only that which pertains directly to factors leading to high blood pressure or strokes.

Vitamins, minerals, and herbs have all been shown to have positive effects on the heart and blood vessels, with few if any side effects. Although prevention should always be our goal, these nutrients may be of benefit to those who already have heart problems.

The Relationship of Potassium and Sodium

For years, table salt (sodium chloride) has been considered a major culprit in aggravating high blood pressure, strokes, and other cardiovascular diseases. Recent studies indicate, however, that a generally low potassium intake may be one of the greater factors. Diets high in potassium appear to be protective against hypertension and stroke-related deaths.[9]

High potassium intake appears to have no effect on people with normal blood pressure, but high potassium intake does appear to lower blood pressure in many but not all with hypertension.[10]

Importance of Dietary Potassium Against Stroke.

A study by Kay-Tee Khaw, M.D., and Elizabeth Barrett-Connor, M.D., found that a high intake of dietary potassium protected people against stroke and stroke-related deaths. In fact, they found that as little as one extra serving of a potassium-rich food, such as a fruit or vegetable, may reduce the risk of stroke death by up to 40 percent.[11]

These researchers based their findings on a study of 850 men and women in an affluent community in southern California. During the twelve years covered by their study, 24 stroke-related deaths occurred. These individuals were all found to have significantly lower potassium intake than survivors and individuals who died from causes other than stroke. They also found the relationship between dietary potassium and stroke mortality was independent of blood pressure, as it also was of obesity, cholesterol level, cigarette smoking, alcohol, and blood sugar. This was an amazing finding, as we generally associate strokes with high blood pressure. Rather, they found that a lack of potassium intake was the independent risk factor in these stroke-related deaths.[12]

One does not need to take a very big leap in logic to conclude that an increased intake of potassium lowers the risk of stroke, and a decreased intake raises the risk.

Potassium to Sodium Ratio. A one-year study headed by James C. Smith, Jr., Ph.D., a chemist at the USDA's Agriculture Research service found that the 28 men and women in their study ate too much table salt (sodium chloride) and not enough potassium, exceeding the safe and adequate daily ratio recommended by the National Academy of Sciences in Washington, D.C. That ratio is 600 mg of sodium for 1,000 mg of potassium. The adults in this study were consuming 1,300 mg of sodium daily for every 1,000 mg of potassium.[13]

Recommended Range. As a matter of general information, a teaspoon of table salt contains about 2,500 mg of sodium. The recommended range of potassium is between 1,900 mg and 5,600 mg daily.[14]

Vitamin and mineral supplements, by FDA regulation, are only allowed to contain 99 mg of potassium. To take a higher amount you need a prescription. How silly this seems when a medium-sized banana contains approximately 630 mg of potassium.

When people consume a high level of potassium in their diets, they excrete more sodium in their urine. But when the opposite is true, and they consume more sodium than potassium, they may retain excess sodium in fluids surrounding cells in the body. Urinalysis can determine if your potassium and sodium intakes are out of balance, and if either is too high or low.

The Best Natural Sources of Potassium are:

One cup potato ....1,747 mg

One cup baked butternut squash............1,200 mg

One cup almonds, cashews,
    brazil nuts, or peanuts................780 to 1,000 mg

Half a cantaloupe ....885 mg

3–4 ounces of raw spinach ....780 mg

1 banana ....630 mg

1 tablespoon blackstrap molasses ....585 mg

Half cup of toasted wheat germ ....535 mg

Half an avocado ....385 mg

One cup low-fat milk ....377 mg

Medium orange ....365 mg [15]

These natural foods can provide valuable protection against strokes. Best of all, these are readily available foods, and are easy to prepare and eat.

Monitor Your Potassium Levels. If you are using diuretics (herbal or otherwise), or are on blood pressure medication, you may need a physician's prescription for extra potassium. It would be wise to have your potassium blood levels monitored regularly. Remember, when potassium is lost by a diuretic, so is magnesium. You may need to supplement this mineral also.

Calcium is Very Necessary

Research has shown that individuals with high blood pressure consume far less calcium than those with normal pressures. The diets of more than 10,000 adults were analyzed. Of the seventeen nutrients examined, low calcium was most consistently associated with high blood pressure. In the analysis of 23 studies of 38,950 people, a consistent association of high dietary calcium intake and normal blood pressure was observed.[16]

Intakes of potassium and vitamins A and C were also lower in people with higher blood pressures, while cholesterol intake was not consistently different. These researchers, who reported their study in *Science*, concluded that diets that restrict the intake of calories, sodium or cholesterol may also reduce the intake of calcium and other nutrients which may be protective against hypertension.[17]

In a well-designed study, women with high blood pressure were given either 1,500 mg of calcium or hypertensive medication for four years. The calcium-supplemented group achieved a significant drop in their systolic blood pressure. The unsupplemented group experienced a rise in their blood pressure, even though they were taking hypertensive medication.

Calcium supplementation is free of the dangerous side effects of antihypertensive drugs. As the studies indicate, calcium supplementation can be an effective non-drug means of preventing high blood pressure in high risk individuals.[18]

Calcium should be balanced with approximately half as much magnesium. (Note: Some researchers say the ratio should be equal. Watch for further studies related to this.) And, of course, potassium may also be taken for additional benefits.

Magnesium is Critical and Essential

The *Journal of the American College of Nutrition* reported that magnesium supplements are essential for helping control the blood pressure in people with hypertension. The exact mechanism is not yet completely understood, but it is thought that magnesium helps drop pressure by regulating the entry-exit process of calcium in the smooth muscle cells of the vascular network. In combination, magnesium and calcium appear to help the blood vessels contract and relax properly.

The interaction of magnesium and calcium gives the calcium the ability to get where it has to in the cells. Then, magnesium facilitates calcium in getting to the right place where it has a relaxing effect.[19] Hypertensives were shown to have significantly less magnesium in their blood cells than did normal people.[20]

The British researchers reported their findings in the *Proceedings of the National Academy of Science*. They noted that previous studies had shown magnesium supplementation to be an effective hypotensive (lowering) agent in some types of blood pressure.[21]

Vitamins A, C and Selenium Lower Mortality

The *International Journal for Vitamin and Nutrition Research* reported that high intakes of vitamin C, or fruit and green vegetables which are high in vitamin C, have been related to low-ered mortality from stroke and heart disease. The researchers suggested that ascorbic acid has a preventive effect on hypertension.[22]

In another study of adult males, higher blood levels of vitamin C and selenium were associated with lower blood pressure. This supports the hypothesis that antioxidants play a role in hypertension.[23]

A number of studies are available showing that low dietary intake of vitamin C increases the risk for high blood pressure. Dr. D.A. McCarron and his colleagues at the University of Portland analyzed the blood pressure of 10,372 persons of all ages in relation to their dietary habits. They found that the single most important factor associated with high blood pressure was a low dietary intake of vitamin C and vice versa.

Vitamin A deficiency was also found to increase the risk for high blood pressure, while the amount of cholesterol in the diet had no effect.[24]

Smokers, take note! Blood pressure increases can be measured immediately following cigarette smoking. If you are so addicted to cigarettes and can't seem to quit at this time, research shows you have some protection with at least 400 mg of vitamin C,[25] but I would recommend a minimum of 1,000 milligrams.

Coenzyme Q 10 (CoQ10)

CoQ10 is an essential component of the metabolic process involved in energy (ATP) production. Individuals with hypertension and cardiovascular disease may be deficient in CoQ10 and require increased tissue levels of CoQ10.[26]

Clinical studies have indicated that CoQ10 is of considerable benefit in the treatment of hypertension and other cardiovascular diseases.[27]

More information about CoQ10 can be found in Chapters 3 and 7.

EPA or Fish Oil Is Very Popular

Fish oils may help retard thrombosis, the deadly blood clots that cause strokes. The result can be fewer lethal blood clots. In addition, researchers at Harvard University have documented that these same fish oils reduce blood pressure, which seems to be a risk factor for both heart attack and stroke.[28]

New studies have reported that populations with high intakes of seafood, especially mackerel, salmon and other cold water fish, have a very low incidence of cardiovascular disease and hypertension. It is believed that the Omega-3 fatty acids, or EPA, can reduce not only blood pressure (systolic and diastolic), but also helps drop serum triglycerides and cholesterol. In one study, the addition of only 3 tablespoons of cod liver oil a day to the normal diet was enough to lower blood pressure.[29] Omega-3 fatty acids are also available in supplements without the added vitamin A and D (which is found in cod liver oil).

It's a great idea to start eating fish several times a week, thereby getting more essential oils in your diet. More information on oils is in Chapter 10.

Garlic—Again to the Rescue

Garlic has been known for years to stabilize blood pressure. This conclusion was even reported in the prestigious British medical journal the *Lancet*.[30] One reason may be found in garlic's high amount of selenium, a trace mineral that boosts protection against platelet adhesion.

Many cultures have used garlic to help keep blood pressure in check. Years ago, Dr. G. Piotrowski of the University of Geneva showed that garlic may dilate or open up the blood vessels and promote a free-flowing circulation that is the answer to hypertension.

Many recommend the equivalency of three to four cloves of garlic every day to lower blood pressure. Also, the enteric-coated capsules which are odor-reduced or odor-free, are also effective, especially since few people desire to eat that much fresh garlic a day. Follow the dosage recommendations on the label of the product you choose.[31]

Green Tea Also Valuable

Several studies in Japan and China have shown that green tea helps control blood pressure. A research project with 9,510 women revealed that green tea drinkers reduced their blood pressure and slashed the risk of a stroke by one-half over non-green tea drinkers.[32]

Most of the research on green tea has been focused on its

cancer-causing and cancer-preventive effects. Green tea polyphenols are flavonoids, potent antioxidant compounds.

Hawthorn Berry

The very active flavonoid compounds found in the leaves, berries and blossoms of the hawthorn plant, have an ability to increase intracellular vitamin C levels and decrease capillary permeability and fragility. Hawthorn berry and flower extracts are effective in reducing blood pressure and angina attacks as well as other functions. It is widely used in Europe for blood pressure lowering and cardiotonic activity. Hawthorn extract's effect on lowering high blood pressure appears to be a result of dilating the larger blood vessels.[33]

What About Diuretics?

Diuretics—water pills—are no longer heavily favored for lowering blood pressure. They work by removing fluid from the bloodstream, which reduces the pressure on the arterial walls. However, diuretics have a mineral depleting side effect—they cause vitally needed magnesium, calcium, potassium, sodium chloride, zinc, and iodide to be flushed away from the body along with the water! Loss of these minerals can invite greater dangers than hypertension— spasms in coronary arteries, stroke, irregular heart rhythms, and heart attack. Dr. W. J. McLennan has stated that 20 percent of the people over age sixty-five now take diuretics, and he noted that in this age group, diuretics bring on more adverse side effects than any other prescription drug.[34]

Nutritional Therapy for High Blood Pressure

David Edelberg, M.D., an internist and medical director of the American Holistic Center in Chicago, has suggested the following as a nutritional therapy to lower high blood pressure:

- cut back on sugar, salt, caffeine, and alcohol
- reduce or eliminate red meat in the diet
- 500 mg of calcium, twice a day
- 400 mg of magnesium, twice a day

- one tablespoon of flaxseed oil a day
- 400 IU of vitamin E a day
- 30 mg of coenzyme Q10, three times a day
- one hawthorn berry capsule, three times a day
- one ginseng capsule, twice a day [35]

My personal modifications to this list would be as follows. First, I do not believe we need to completely eliminate lean meat, if used in moderation. You need more than just calcium and magnesium. You should include a complete mineral formula which provides: selenium, zinc, copper, chromium, iodine, boron, manganese, and potassium. It would be important to include a complete "stress" vitamin B-complex, vitamins A and D, and at least a gram (1,000 mg) of vitamin C, two or three times a day. The additional suggestion of fish several times a week, or fish oil capsules, with high potassium fruit, vegetables and garlic would also be beneficial.

Read the last chapter on "Let's Put It All Together" and consider my suggestions for a complete nutritional program, then check the potencies of your vitamin and mineral formulas and see if they are adequate.

Low Blood Pressure

As we have shown, blood pressure means the push or force of blood against the walls of the blood vessels. Only when the tissues of the vessel walls are strong can the blood pressure be maintained at its normal level. If these tissues become flabby and weak, they exert less force against the arterial walls, and adequate supplies of all the nutrients fail to reach the cells, resulting in fatigue and lack of endurance.

Low blood pressure is also called *hypotension*. In adults the pressure is usually less than 90mm systolic (when the heart beats). In some people, their blood pressure drops when they rise from a horizontal position, which may cause light-headedness or brief loss of consciousness due to temporarily insufficient flow of blood to the brain. Severe hypotension may lead to inadequate blood circulation and shock.[36]

Since relaxation is greatest during the night, the person with low blood pressure finds that he/she is especially exhausted in the early morning, and just getting out of bed is a chore. They are usually sensitive to cold and heat, require more sleep than healthy individuals and develop a rapid pulse on exertion.

Low blood pressure is not necessarily healthy just because it isn't high. If your pressure is low, be sure you read about the thyroid in Chapter 8.

Adelle Davis, in *Let's Get Well*, recommends that the adrenal glands need to be fully supported since low adrenals play a part in both low blood pressure and low thyroid. Many of the symptoms such as feeling tired, can't get going, lack of energy, are very similar.[37] Read about pantothenic acid for adrenal support in Chapter 10.

Our adrenal glands produce a powerful steroid hormone, *aldosterone*, which is a major factor in regulating salt and water balance in our bodies, making sure that our bodies "retain" enough salt for normal function, including normal blood pressure.[38] If the adrenals are weak, less than optimum amounts of aldosterone is produced, and blood pressure falls. Sea salt, a natural salt with all the trace minerals, may be added to the diet. Make sure it's iodized.

Low blood pressure along with low adrenals may have been brought on by years of prolonged stress, which increases the need for a proper diet and supplementation of all the vitamins and minerals referred to earlier, especially pantothenic acid.

Taking Charge of Your Own Health

Nutritional supplements may aid in reversing the conditions that lead to hypertension, heart disease, heart attack, and stroke. Much can be done to prevent cardiovascular problems, which should be our primary concern. As is true for virtually all health problems, no one magic nutrient may help to correct this most serious situation. Preventive nutrition requires a multi-faceted approach; nutrients, exercise, changes in lifestyle, all working together to synergistically put this country's population back on the road to better health.

Chapter 10

When the Weather Changes, Do Your Joints Ache?

Treating Arthritis and Related Problems Naturally

"Drugs work because they 'whip' the adrenal glands
to produce cortisone, which pulls calcium out of the
bones, sugar out of the liver, and protein out of the
muscles. You feel better for a while . . . because
you are living on your own tissue. What you need to
do is help your body produce its own cortisone
and other adrenal hormones."
—**Gladys Lindberg**

One of the greatest responses I have ever had from a television appearance was after we had discussed arthritis. According to the Centers for Disease Control and Prevention, this aging, crippling disease afflicts 37 million Americans—one in seven—the vast majority of whom are middle-aged or older. One in three families is affected, at a cost of more than $8.6 billion dollars to the United States economy. Arthritis is one of the three major degenerative diseases among people in the western world as a whole. Its most common forms are rheumatoid, osteoarthritis, and gout.

Arthritis is not a single disorder, but the name given to a joint disease that has a number of causes. Arthritis may involve one joint or many in the body, and it can vary in severity from a mild ache and stiffness to severe pain and ultimately, deformity.

The word arthritis comes from the Greek word *arthron*, which means "joint" and *itis* which means "inflammation." The joint inflammation of arthritis generally manifests itself as swelling, a feeling of heat, redness of inflamed areas, and pain. Although not a direct killer such as cancer or heart disease, arthritis causes more years of pain and suffering than virtually any other disease. Its victims sometimes become virtual prisoners in their own bodies.

The Natural Approach

There is no one answer, no "magic bullet," for the treatment of arthritis. The sound approach would be for a person to do that which is necessary to build up the body as a whole. The hope, of course, is that one or more of these natural approaches will greatly benefit the person with arthritis, gout, back and disk problems, osteoporosis, carpal tunnel syndrome, or autoimmune diseases. These therapies discussed are not toxic and they may help a person build up their resistance to disease, so over time they may minimize the severity of their problem and feel better.

Dr. Roger Williams, the researcher who discovered pantothenic acid and folic acid, also advocates this approach. He has said, "Injuries, infections, allergic reactions, and psychological stresses may all play a part in the cause of arthritic disease, but the most probable underlying cause—poor nutritional environment for the cells and tissues involved—has, as usual, been neglected." [1]

Joint and Cartilage Involvement

Many difficulties associated with arthritic diseases arise from poor lubrication of the joints and all other movable structures in the body.

Joints are the areas where bones come together. Bone ends are shaped to fit together and are covered with a rubbery protective cushion called *cartilage*. The entire joint is enclosed in a capsule of dense fibers. The capsule is lined by the synovial membrane, which secretes a lubricating fluid in the spaces between the bone ends. When cartilage disintegrates, for whatever reason, bone ends rub against each other and put pressure on nerves, which causes pain.

Synovial fluid in the joints is thick, like mucous. It contains various mineral salts and mucoprotein. The mucoprotein, as other body proteins, must be produced in the body using raw materials from food and water. When any mineral, amino acid, or vitamin is deficient, or if the cells are poisoned by bacterial toxins or allergens, cells can become partially incapacitated. The result is poor mucoprotein manufacturing and in turn, poor lubrication. It is vital, therefore, that we continually feed the body the nutrients it needs to manufacture mucoprotein.

Rheumatoid Arthritis—Inflammation

Rheumatoid arthritis is the most destructive, disabling, and unpredictable form of arthritis. It is a persistent, serious disorder that begins with an inflammation of the lining that provides the lubrication of the joints. The disease then spreads to the cartilage, ligaments, muscles, and bones. The symptoms come and go, with stiff and swollen joints often more painful in cold weather. The disease can start at any age, even infancy, but usually manifests itself between the ages of thirty and fifty.

In rheumatoid arthritis, the immune system—which usually defends the body against bacteria, viruses, and cancer cells—loses its ability to distinguish between foreign invaders and the body's own tissue. It begins to attack the body, especially the joints. No one knows with certainty what deceives the immune system into attacking its own body, but several theories have been advanced and are under investigation.

Osteoarthritis—Wear and Tear Disease

Osteoarthritis is commonly called "wear and tear" arthritis. It is the most widespread form of the disease, a slow progressive disorder characterized by a breakdown of cartilage and changes in bone. It very often afflicts the fingers and weight-bearing joints: knees, hips, and spine.

When osteoarthritis sets in, the cartilage (tissue that covers the ends of the bones) becomes thin and may even disappear. This change results in decreased fluid in and around the joints. Friction increases with resulting pain and stiffness. Osteoarthritis results in pain, but rarely inflammation.

According to the Arthritis Foundation, approximately 15.8 million Americans have this form of arthritis, with nearly three times as many women as men suffering from the disease.

Injury and repeated strain can cause osteoarthritis. Poor posture, fatigue, and stress seem to hasten its onset. Obesity is by far the leading cause of osteoarthritis in large joints.

Gout—Primarily a Male Disease

Perhaps the most painful form of arthritis is gout. Fortunately, it is the form most readily controlled in most patients. Gout is primarily a male disease with about one million sufferers. For some reason, the big toe seems particularly susceptible to gout.

People once thought gout was the disease of kings—such as Henry VIII—because they associated it with foods that only kings could afford to purchase. Today, we know that gout can affect just about anybody.

Victims of gout produce too much uric acid, or fail to excrete enough uric acid. Above certain levels, uric acid forms microscopic crystals of sodium urate. These are shaped like needles and are just as sharp. When these needle-like crystals form in the joint fluid, they are "cleaned up" by special white blood cells. Unfortunately, when the white blood cells become full of crystals, they die, attracting even more white cells to clean up the debris. All these white cells cause swelling, redness, and pain.

Pantothenic Acid. The body's supply of the B-vitamin pantothenic acid is responsible for converting uric acid into urea and ammonia, both of which are excreted in the urine. The nutritional approach is to help the adrenals produce cortisone by taking pantothenic acid, probably the most important vitamin for gout. Alcohol should be omitted entirely from the diet because it increases uric acid production.[2]

Link to Vitamin E. When vitamin E is deficient, the cell nucleus from which uric acid is produced becomes damaged and uric acid is produced in excessive amounts. Rancid oils such as cooking oils, destroy vitamin E in our systems, causing an immediate imbalance of uric acid. Be sure to add vitamin E to your vitamin program.

Cherries, Hawthorn Berries, and Blueberries. These and other dark red-blue berries are rich sources of *anthocyanidins and proanthocyanidins* (flavonoid molecules that give the berries their rich color). These compounds are remarkable in their ability to strengthen collagen.[3]

Studies have shown that consuming half a pound of fresh or frozen cherries a day decreases uric acid levels and prevents attacks of gout.[4]

This doesn't sound like a very practical remedy, but the good news is that most nutrition stores carry a Black Cherry Concentrate, which is deliciously sweet and contains no added sugar. It can be added to plain yogurt or cottage cheese, or even mixed with water to make a delicious drink.

Systemic Lupus Erythematosus
An Autoimmune Disease

Lupus is one of the more common auto immune diseases that afflicts half a million Americans and 90 percent of them are women. In this disease, antibodies attack the body's own tissues and organs. Some cases are mild, with minor problems, and some are extremely severe and crippling.

Many lupus patients have arthritic joint pain, swelling, and rashes, including the most classic symptom, a rash on the cheeks. They also tend to have kidney problems and chest pain caused by inflammation in the lining of the heart and lungs and the other vital organs. Less frequently, the central nervous system is affected, but when it is, epileptic seizures, psychotic symptoms, and personality changes can result. Other symptoms may include unexplained fever, chills, hair loss, and progressive kidney disease.[5]

Autoimmune diseases are more common among older people as the immune system begins to run down and becomes less efficient. It is not known what caused the autoimmune response to occur in these people; it may be triggered by an undetected viral infection, a genetic defect, a defect in the production or metabolism of sex hormones, or a combination of all these factors.

Numerous drugs have been thought to be responsible for causing lupus, among them tetracycline and other antibiotics, procainamid, birth control pills containing estrogen, sulfasalazine and drugs used to lower blood pressure.[6]

All the nutrients that help with arthritis should help lupus patients.

DHEA is Showing Promise for Lupus

Two successful studies from the Stanford University Medical Center have shown DHEA to be an effective treatment for lupus. DHEA in large doses was given to women patients with mild to moderate lupus, and eight out of ten patients reported that they were not only feeling and doing better, but showed improvement in their immune function. The encouraging part of the study was that patients were able to reduce their dose of prednisone, a corticosteroid used to control lupus symptoms. At this time the researcher from Stanford does not fully understand how it works, but he theorizes that it works by correcting certain abnormalities in the immune system.[7]

According to Michael Murray, N.D., the adrenal hormone, DHEA at a dosage of 200 mg daily can be of benefit in some cases of lupus. Currently a large clinical trial testing DHEAs effectiveness on lupus is in progress, involving twenty-five universities and more than two hundred patients. So far the information looks promising for some of the people. Patients interested in taking DHEA should do so only under the care of a rheumatologist or trained physician, where the patients blood levels can be closely monitored.[8]

Back and Disc Problems: Let's Avoid Surgery

Dr. James Greenwood, professor of neurosurgery at Baylor University School of Medicine in Texas, reported that from a study of more than five hundred patients, "a significant number of patients with disc lesions were able to avoid surgery by the use of large doses of vitamin C."[9] Vitamin C, of course, is required for collagen production and collagen is the basic material in all connective tissue that supports muscles and bones. The minerals are also important as you will read below.

Osteoporosis: Can be Prevented and Reversed

Anyone with osteoporosis or disc problems may definitely benefit from following a good vitamin and mineral program, especially calcium, magnesium and vitamin D. Studies have shown that over a long period of time, as much as 40 percent of the calcium may be lost from the bones before the loss is diagnosed by X-ray. Chronic lower back pain is also one of the first symptoms of osteoporosis. When a person becomes immobilized by the pain of arthritis or back pain, bones quickly lose calcium and other minerals that provide strength. Calcium and magnesium are vital supplements, along with the other trace minerals, especially boron, which help us hang on to our calcium. If you want more valuable information on osteoporosis be sure to read the excellent book *Preventing and Reversing Osteoporosis* by Alan Gaby, M.D. He explains how osteoporosis can be reversed. Many people with osteoporosis have been told this is not possible. Dr. Gaby goes into great detail how to both prevent and reverse this condition.

DHEA functions as a precursor hormone which plays a role in bone loss. Preliminary results suggest DHEA is the only hormone that appears capable of both inhibiting bone loss and stimulating bone formation.[10]

Carpal Tunnel Syndrome: Hand and Wrist Disease

Carpal tunnel syndrome is a painful and crippling disease of the hands and wrists that results from compression of the principal nerve to the hand as it passes through a "tunnel" lined with synovial membrane between the tendons and ligaments in the wrist. This disorder occurs about three times as frequently in women as in men and it has a higher incidence during pregnancy and at menopause. Carpal tunnel syndrome is often associated with rheumatoid arthritis, obesity, diabetes associated with pregnancy, "tennis elbow," trigger fingers, and bursitis in the shoulder. Carpal tunnel is frequently diagnosed among those who work their wrists all day, such as computer operators, typists, postal clerks who sort mail, and so forth.

B6—Controlled Study. Vitamin B6 has been shown to shrink synovial membranes and has been used to bring relief to a number of people with carpal tunnel syndrome.

In a controlled, double-blind study of patients with carpal tunnel syndrome, those given 100 mg of B6 (fifty times the recommended dietary allowance) received great benefit, while those given a placebo had no benefit.[11]

Research published in the *Proceedings of the National Academy of Sciences* stated that patients with carpal tunnel syndrome who were given 500 mg of B6 and 50 mg of B2 supplements experienced a complete disappearance of their symptoms.[12]

Exhausted Adrenal Glands: The Impact of Physical and Emotional Stress

Studies have revealed that all forms of arthritis usually begin after years of stress, either physical or emotional. Dr. Hans Selye coined the word "stress" years ago and showed how stress exhausts the adrenal glands to the point where the adrenals no longer produce enough cortisone and other vital hormones. The adrenal hormones are essential for life. They are two glands, perched atop the kidneys that manufacture the cortical hormones, which prepares us for "fight or flight".[13] Below are some of the physical stress factors that exhaust the adrenal glands and run down our immune system:

- physical injuries
- infections
- cigarettes
- caffeine
- alcohol
- drugs of all kinds
- crash dieting
- over-exercising
- emotional trauma
- prescription medicines
- lack of vitamins and minerals
- allergies
- chemical preservatives
- antibiotics
- chemotherapy
- excess sugar
- pregnancy
- x-rays
- intense noise
- extreme heat or cold
- insecticides

These stressors tend to overstimulate, or "whip" the adrenal glands to produce cortisone. When this happens, vital calcium is pulled from the body's bones, sugar from the liver and protein from the muscles. Over time, the adrenals become exhausted to the point where no "whip" is big enough to get them going again in an adequate way.

Carl Pfeiffer, M.D., Ph.D., author of *Mental and Elemental Nutrients*, has said, "Psychiatric theory claims rheumatoid arthritis is one of the stress-induced disorders. Poor nutrition, repeated bacterial infection, and a host of other causes are more apt to be the real cause of rheumatoid arthritis."[14]

Can a person have a healthy body and a disturbed mind? It's highly unlikely. When we are physically healthy we have a greater ability to handle emotional trauma and will take better care of ourselves physically.

The elements necessary for normal adrenal hormone production are protein, vitamins A, C, and E, pantothenic acid and the entire range of B-vitamins. A diet deficient in these raw materials limits the ability of the adrenal glands to function under stress.

Whole raw adrenal glandular tablets help support the adrenal glands, allowing them to repair themselves so they can again secrete their own cortisone and other vital hormones. Glandulars have been very effective for many people.

Pantothenic Acid for Adrenal Support

It appears in the research that virtually every person suffering from an illness that is helped by cortisone—arthritis, lupus erythematosus, gout, and dozens of others—is likely to be deficient in the B-vitamin, pantothenic acid. Pantothenic acid protects the adrenal cortex from damage and stimulates the adrenal glands to increase production of cortisone and other adrenal hormones important for the body's reaction to stress.[15]

Pantothenic acid is made in several forms, among them pantothenol and calcium pantothenate. Actions are identical for all forms. Authorities recommend a range of 200 mg up to 1,000 mg in divided doses to build resistance to stress.

Dr. Agnes Faye Morgan was the first to demonstrate that a deficiency in pantothenic acid causes degeneration of adrenal gland tissue, with internal bleeding and, interestingly, premature gray hair in animals. Restoration of the vitamin to the diet caused repair of the gland and recoloration of the hair! [16]

Dr. Roger Williams, who discovered pantothenic acid, has noted in his research that pantothenic acid consistently brought relief to sufferers of rheumatoid arthritis, although the improvement was not a complete cure. My mother, having read Dr. Williams work back in 1949, added 200 mg of pantothenic acid to her vitamin and mineral formulas. She was so very far ahead of her time.

Royal Jelly—Rich in Pantothenic Acid. English

researchers studied the effects of pantothenic acid on rheumatoid arthritics. They found that large doses were helpful but they encountered what seemed to be an invisible ceiling on blood levels of this nutrient—that is, increasing the dose beyond a certain point yielded no rise in the vitamin concentration in the blood. Aware also that *royal jelly*, the food bees create for queen bees, is extraordinarily rich in pantothenic acid, they conjectured that this food source might contain factors or a factor that makes the vitamin more effective in the body. They showed that royal jelly, given along with megadoses of the vitamin, removed the invisible ceiling. Blood levels of pantothenic acid went up in proportion to the increased dosages. As the blood concentration rose, benefits to the patients increased in like manner.[17]

Vitamin C—Also Essential for the Adrenals

The adrenal glands have the richest concentrations of vitamin C in the body, and during great stress, the vitamin C content of these glands can be depleted within minutes.[18] The role of vitamin C in the chemistry of these glands is very complex, but what is vital for us to know is very simple:

- vitamin C is essential for the manufacturing of the stress hormone adrenaline.
- vitamin C not only increases the production and utilization of cortisone, but also appears to prolong its effectiveness.
- when vitamin C is depleted rapidly, restoration to an adequate level takes more time than the depletion took.[19]

Dr. Linus Pauling estimated that normal requirements for vitamin C should be between 250 and 2,500 mg per day. An arthritic is not "normal," however, and should definitely strive toward a higher amount, particularly since we know that adrenal dysfunction is part of their condition.

The cement that holds us together. Another reason to take vitamin C is that it helps in the synthesis and maintenance of collagen. Collagen is the intercellular "cement" that literally holds the cells in various organs and tissues together. Its various fibers form the connective tissue of the body. Collagen is found in skin, bones, teeth, blood vessels, eyes, heart—in fact, all parts of the body.[20]

Recent studies have also shown that when levels of vitamin C are high, the synovial (lubricating) fluid of the joints allows for greater mobility.

Vitamin C is destroyed particularly by smoking or when large doses of aspirin or cortisone is taken.

Nutritional Help
For All Forms of Arthritis

Those with arthritis seem to have an imbalance of a number of minerals, further supporting the idea that this disease is linked to a poor nutritional environment.

Dr. Carl Pfeiffer cites a number of studies showing that copper levels are high in arthritis patients while zinc and manganese levels are low. The high copper level may be the result of a lack of elemental sulfur in the diet.

He says, "Rheumatoid arthritis patients should have zinc, manganese, niacin and vitamin C, with two eggs per day for their sulfur content." Dr. Pfeiffer points out that arthritics should have a carefully balanced diet high in the B vitamins and he suggests taking ten tablets of brewer's yeast twice a day as part of his plan to help arthritics.[21]

Lead pollutants in the environment may contribute to arthritis in Dr. Pfeiffer's opinion, and he recommends vitamin C as a means of helping provide protection against this contamination.[22] Chelation also removes lead from our system and is discussed in Chapter 11.

Crippling arthritis in a five year old. When I was president of the American Nutrition Society, I asked Robert Bingham, M.D., author of *Fight Back Against Arthritis*, to present to our audience the program he has used for decades to treat arthritics at his clinic in Desert Hot Springs, California. Dr. Bingham described a five-year-old patient with hips and knees so contracted "she could only lie on her side." She could not sit in a chair. For two years she had been a patient in a well-known hospital, but she had only grown progressively worse. Her parents were told to take her home with the prognosis, "There is no hope of any improvement or cure."

She was taken to Dr. Bingham's clinic and this young girl was given fresh blended vegetable and fruit juices, eggs, and certified raw milk in five small meals a day. She received liquid vitamin supplements, including cod liver oil, vitamin C, and the B-vitamin complex "in therapeutic doses," which we would call megavitamin therapy. She was placed in a warm water pool to relieve pain and improve circulation. The therapists exercised each of her joints under the mineral waters. Within four weeks, the pain and swelling of her joints had improved so that she could sit in a chair. Within six months she was discharged, able to walk and ride a tricycle.[23]

Dr. Bingham identified the following nutrients and doses as being essential for arthritis therapy:

- vitamins A and D in capsules from fish liver oils
- the B-vitamin complex, also natural sources of B-vitamin: as nuts, grains, brewers yeast and wheat germ
- vitamin C, with a starting dose of 2,000 mg daily
- vitamin E in an initial therapeutic dose of 1,600 IU and a maintenance dose of 800 IU daily
- calcium, magnesium, phosphorus, and other trace elements such as zinc, chromium, and copper
- digestive aids such as enzymes and hydrochloric acid
- a high-protein diet
- plant extracts, especially yucca

Important Common Dietary Factors

Dr. Bingham also stated that two common dietary factors are found in nearly every arthritis patients, regardless of diagnosis. This may be the main contributing factors in the cause of all arthritis:

1) an abnormally low intake of protein
2) an abnormally high intake of refined carbohydrates.

Niacinamide (B3)—Disappearance of Joint Pain

William Kaufman, M.D., Ph.D., who taught at the University of Michigan Medical School and at Yale University, was a pioneer in the field of vitamin therapy for rheumatism and arthritis. He was inspired by the findings in the 1940s and 1950s of Dr. Tom Spies, one of Mother's favorite researchers, who worked with pellagra (characterized by dermatitis, inflammation of the tongue, diarrhea, and emotional and mental symptoms). Dr. Kaufman was impressed by the disappearance of joint pain in pellagrins treated with niacinamide. His primary interest was the response of arthritics to doses of the vitamin, and he noted that it slowed or reversed many symptoms that were ordinarily blamed on aging. When the niacinamide treatment was stopped, the abnormal state returned within a day or two.

After several published accounts, Dr. Kaufman reported to the American Geriatric Society that most of his patients improved greatly on a regimen of one to five grams (1,000 to 5,000 mg) of niacinamide per day in divided doses (6 to 16 doses per day), continuing for as long as nine years. He observed no negative reactions in several thousand patients he treated during these years of continuous use. For those with restricted mobility of joints and manifestations of a deficiency of niacinamide, he recommended treatment with four to five grams (4,000 to 5,000 mg) of niacinamide per day.[24]

Frequency of dose important. Dr. Kaufman's studies involving niacinamide repeatedly emphasized the need not only to take the right dose of this vitamin, but to take the vitamin at right intervals. The vitamin breaks down in the body in a relatively short time and any excess is excreted in the urine. For these reasons, frequency of dose is as important as the total amount taken daily.

Dr. Kaufman and other researchers have recommended 250 mg be taken every three hours, for six doses a day. A single dose of 1,500 mg of niacinamide, or three doses of 500 mg each, are not as effective in maintaining blood levels. Although the total is the same, the action within the body is different. Dr. Kaufman found this treatment to be appropriate both for those with osteoarthritis and those with rheumatoid arthritis.[25]

Many of Dr. Kaufman's patients showed striking improvement in mental health as well as physical health on this niacinamide regimen. It is important to note that Dr. Kaufman used *niacinamide*, a form of the B3 vitamin, *not niacin*, which gives a flush to the skin and is the form that works well in managing cholesterol levels.

Vitamin B6—Brings Relief

Another vitamin that brings relief for sufferers with rheumatism, menopausal arthritis and carpal tunnel syndrome is vitamin B6 (pyridoxine). This vitamin shrinks the synovial membranes that line the bearing surfaces of the joints. It thus helps to control pain and to restore mobility to the elbows, shoulders, knees, and other joints, according to Dr. John M. Ellis, a physician and researcher from Texas.[26]

The author of *Free of Pain*, Dr. Ellis, reported that vitamin B6 is effective at an intake level of 50 to 100 mg per day, and more for some people.

Motion pictures taken before and after treatment with vitamin B6 give clear proof that it reduced swelling in hands and fingers, improved hand and finger dexterity, prevented transitory nocturnal arm paralysis, and halted nighttime leg cramps and muscle spasms. Shoulder pain was reduced or eliminated and shoulder and arm function was improved in his patients.[27]

All Antioxidants are Valuable

Many studies have shown the value of all the antioxidants in the relief of arthritis. Successful antioxidant therapy for rheumatoid arthritis requires a synergistic combination of several antioxidants. In addition to the vitamins mentioned above, the minerals magnesium and calcium also supply the synovial (lubricating) fluid, as does vitamin A, C, E and beta-carotene. Be sure to read Chapter 3 for more information on antioxidants.

Selenium. Researchers have found a special benefit to selenium when combined with antioxidant vitamins A, C, and E.[28]

In a clinical trial using a formula containing selenium and these three vitamins, 64 percent of the patients, many of them very severely afflicted, reported considerable reduction in pain after only three months. One of the patients told a newspaper reporter, "I thought that I would never get rid of the pain. But now I have full movement of my hip and no pain whatsoever.[29]

Other researchers have found that the greater the selenium deficiency in patients, the more severe their rheumatoid arthritis.[30]

In another study, patients reported increased mobility and significantly less pain when given 350 mcg of selenium with 400 IU of vitamin E for a two-week period.[31]

Glucosamine Sulfate for Joint Strength

Glucosamine is an amino sugar normally formed in humans from glucose. The tissues containing these glucosamine molecules include tendons and ligaments, cartilage, synovial fluid, mucous membranes, several structures in the eye, blood vessels, and heart valves.

Glucosamine sulfate is one of the biological chemicals that forms all the major cushioning ingredients of the joint fluids and surrounding tissues. It helps to make the synovial fluid thick and elastic in joints and vertebrae.

The space between the vertebrae is where many nerves leave the spinal cord, which increases the value of the cushioning fluid. Any injury to this part of the back can cause the gelatinous cartilage to soften. When this happens, pressure may be put on the nerves, causing damage and loss of nerve function. Glucosamine sulfate helps increase the thickness of the gelatinous material, creating more support for the joints and vertebrae.

There have been numerous studies showing the beneficial effects of glucosamine sulfate and its relationship with the symptoms of osteoarthritis, the most common form of arthritis.[32] Glucosamine sulfate has been shown to exert a protective effect against joint destruction and is selectively used by joint tissues, exerting a powerful healing effect on arthritic symptoms.

Using glucosamine sulfate is a classic example of how a natural substance improves a condition by addressing the underlying cause and supporting the body's natural ability to heal itself.[33]
The standard dosage of glucosamine sulfate is 500 mg, three times per day. Some may need slightly larger amounts, especially if taking diuretics.[34]

A number of research studies have shown that glucosamine sulfate supplementation has better effects than the commonly prescribed arthritis drug, *ibuprofen*. Glucosamine sulfate is not toxic, so it can be used for prolonged treatment. When given orally, it has been shown to relieve pain, joint tenderness and swelling so that joint movement can increase.[35]

Our joints are rich in sulfur molecules, and glucosamine forms important cross-linkages with these other molecules to provide cartilage with strength, structure, and "shock-absorbing" properties.

Glucosamine is involved not only in the strength and integrity of joints, but it is involved in the formation of nails, tendons, skin, eyes, bones, ligaments, and heart valves. It plays a role in the mucous secretions of your digestive, respiratory, and urinary tracts.[36]

Shark Cartilage Combats the Pain of Arthritis

Much has been written recently about shark cartilage and its use with rheumatoid arthritis. William Lane, Ph.D., author of *Sharks Don't Get Cancer* and his new book *Sharks Still Don't Get Cancer*, who specializes in marine resources, has reported that shark cartilage has been used successfully to combat the pain of arthritis.

Shark cartilage contains large amounts of mucopolysaccharides (carbohydrates that form chemical bonds with water) which stimulate the immune system. This reduces the pain and inflammation of arthritis. Since cartilage is living tissue, oral dosages are believed to help repair damaged human cartilage, according to Dr. Lane.[37]

I met Dr. Lane at the Alternative Cancer Treatment Seminar in San Diego when he presented his work there. Shark cartilage is also used for cancer patients. Dr. Lane reported that shark cartilage administered orally before meals has been very effective in reducing pain in many arthritic patients. In fact, in one study, 80 percent of the osteoarthritis patients at Comprehensive Medical Clinic in Southern California responded very well. In another study with rheumatoid arthritis patients, 50 to 60 percent of the patients had significantly less pain.[38]

The benefit of shark cartilage supplementation tends to be gradual. This product is available in capsules or an almost tasteless powder form.

Bovine Cartilage is also Effective

Another cartilage product that is now on the market is from bovine tracheal (windpipe) cartilage. It has been used to treat cancer, rheumatism, and arthritic diseases including osteoarthritis, as well as ulcerative colitis, scleroderma, allergies, immunological skin disorders such as psoriasis, herpes infections, and to accelerate the healing of wounds.

John F. Prudden, M.D., Med. Sc.D., discovered the effectiveness of bovine cartilage while he was an associate professor of clinical surgery at Columbia Presbyterian Medical Center. He tested the effects of 9 grams of bovine cartilage taken orally on a daily basis by patients who had osteoarthritis. An astounding 59 percent of his 700 subjects reported "excellent" results and 26 percent reported "good" results, with the average length of remission being six to eight weeks. In all, 85 percent of his patients reported benefit from taking bovine cartilage in this therapeutic dose. Dr. Pudden believes that a reduction in the therapeutic dose of 9 grams per day may be possible for ongoing relief, depending on the patient's symptoms.[39]

A long-term, double-blind study conducted in 1987 at Charles University in Prague confirmed Dr. Prudden's earlier results. Among the 194 osteoarthritis patients participating in the study, pain scores dropped an average of 50 percent.[40]

In more than twenty-five years of human clinical testing, no toxicity has been reported with bovine cartilage, which is less expensive than shark cartilage.

The Value of Zinc and Copper

Several reports in the medical literature note that rheumatoid arthritics frequently have low levels of zinc in their hair (found in hair analysis) and blood, and there are confirming studies that cite improvement in arthritic conditions when zinc supplements have been administered. Zinc is a powerful stimulant to the immune system, so much so that conventional literature in cancer research is now reporting its benefits.

Zinc also has an anti-inflammatory effect. A double-blind study showed that zinc sulfate patients did better with regard to joint swelling, morning stiffness, walking time, and the patients' own impressions of their overall disease activity. The mineral's anti-inflammatory activity can impact directly on the rheumatoid process.[41]

Several researchers suggest that arthritis sufferers take a zinc supplement, perhaps 30 to 50 mg daily of zinc picolinate, gluconate or chelated zinc, and see if they have a positive response. Zinc should be balanced with the mineral copper at about a 10:1

or 15:1 ratio of zinc:copper.

Copper is also anti-inflammatory and is useful against some forms of arthritis. Copper levels are high in the synovial fluid of the joints, so it appears that copper has a protective effect. Higher levels are an indication that the body is rallying copper in an attempt to fight off the disease.[42]

Oils for Arthritis
Omega-3 Fatty Acids (EPA) and Cod Liver Oil

One of our friends was the late Dale Alexander, who was dubbed the "Cod Father" because of his belief that cod liver oil could bring relief to the sufferers of arthritis. He described these benefits in his book, *Arthritis and Common Sense*.

Fish oil contains EPA (eicosapentaenoic acid) and DHA (docosahexanoic acid) that make body compounds that control inflammation and pain. In the early years, Dale Alexander probably did not know about EPA, but he knew that cod liver oil helped thousands of arthritis sufferers. Today, a number of university laboratories are testing fish oils, rich in Omega-3 fatty acids, as a means of helping arthritics. The resulting studies are encouraging:

- Animal studies at Harvard indicate that EPA helps protect the body against attack by its own immune system in auto-immune diseases such as rheumatoid arthritis and lupus erythematosus, as reported in the *New England Journal of Medicine*.[43]
- An article in Clinical Research reported that fish oil supplements significantly improved symptoms in rheumatoid arthritis patients. Forty patients were given fifteen EPA fish oil capsules a day for fourteen weeks (approximately 1.8 grams of EPA a day). These patients reported that they were in less pain, their joints were less tender, and they made it through the day longer before fatigue set in than those who were in a control group.[44] The amount used in this study is equivalent to two tablespoons of Max-EPA liquid.
- A study published in the *Lancet* showed that patients with rheumatoid arthritis who received

EPA for twelve weeks had less morning stiffness and fewer tender joints. One to two months after stopping EPA, their condition deteriorated back to the prior levels.[45]

- An Australian study in 1988 showed that 18 grams of fish oil a day (eighteen capsules of 1,000 mg) for three months resulted in fewer sore joints and measurable improvement in grip strength in rheumatoid arthritis patients.[46]

*A number of studies have also showed
a direct benefit from EPA in lupus patients.*

Read your labels; usually one tablespoon of *emulsified* Omega-3 oil provides over 1,000 mg of EPA and over 600 mg of DHA. It would take approximately 10 large softgels of EPA/DHA to equal just one tablespoon. Emulsified means that the oil has been changed naturally to a water-soluble form. The result is that it tastes better, with no aftertaste of oil, and it is easier to digest. This form of Omega-3 oil does not, however, contain vitamins A and D.

Cod liver oil also contains the fatty acids and it supplies vitamins A and D, as well as some natural cholesterol. *Twinlab* honored Dale Alexander by using his name on their regular and emulsified cod liver oil products. The emulsified form is the best tasting, easiest to digest and most popular. The recommendation was to take at least two tablespoons a day. Dale Alexander insisted to me that the cod liver oil capsules were not effective for arthritis, it must be used in the oil form or emulsified liquid form.

Flax seed oil is an excellent "vegetable" source of Omega-3 fatty acids. Dr. Johanna Budwig, author of *Flax Oil as a True Aid Against Arthritis, Heart Infarction, Cancer and Other Diseases*, feels that mixing or blending flax seed oil into good protein (like cultured, lowfat milk) will nourish the body better. She has repeatedly observed that the flax seed oil and protein combination form special lipoprotein compounds that are easily digested, and the body will use them to build new tissues. She and other doctors in Europe use flax seed oil mixed with non-fat yogurt or cottage cheese as an essential part of their successful dietary therapies for many modern maladies. It can be used in salad dressing, poured over vegetables or cottage cheese. Do not cook with this oil! One or two tablespoons a day would be an excellent addition to the daily diet. Be sure to use only the organic flax found in dark bottles in the refrigerator at your nutrition store.

Omega-6 Fatty Acids (GLA)
Evening Primrose Oil

Gamma-Linolenic Acid (GLA), part of the Omega-6 family, is essential to good health. The body needs it to make a family of hormone-like compounds that control virtually every organ in the body. These compounds especially affect the heart and circulation, skin, immunity, and inflammation. The members of this vital family of compounds are called prostaglandins. Prostaglandins are so important to good health that the 1982 Nobel Prize in Physiology and Medicine was awarded to three researchers instrumental in the discovery of prostaglandins and their function in the body.

Evening primrose oil, borage oil, and black currant oil are the richest sources of GLA. Since both EPA and GLA act as anti-inflammatory agents, and their mechanisms are slightly different, they work well together—each making the other more effective.

According to a study reported in *Lancet*, GLA-rich evening primrose oil was found to be effective in controlling rheumatoid arthritis in a substantial number of patients. Some 90 percent of patients who took evening primrose oil felt better within two to four months, and more than 80 percent either stopped taking their anti-inflammatory drugs or were able to reduce the amount of drugs they were taking.[47]

In another study, rheumatoid arthritis patients were given 540 mg GLA and 240 mg EPA. After a year, those who received this dosage had reduced their amount of anti-inflammatory medicine significantly.[48]

Herbal Products May Help Arthritics
Alfalfa Helps Stiffness

One of the herbals that Mother always recommended was alfalfa, taken in tablet form. A number of customers have said to me, "As long as I keep taking my alfalfa tablets every day, I have no more stiffness or pain in my hands."

Alfalfa (*Medicago sativa*) belongs to the legume family, which includes beans, peas, and clover. It is not a grass as some people believe. It is an excellent source of chlorophyll, potassium, magnesium and vitamins, especially beta-carotene and vitamin E. The reason alfalfa is so rich in vitamins and minerals is that, in its early stages of growth, the young roots have been known to penetrate as far down as fifty to sixty feet into the earth. The roots naturally "mine" precious mineral resources located deep in the soil.

Alfalfa is also an excellent source of fiber. Alfalfa tablets can be as beneficial to a person as eating a big green salad every day. They are an excellent way to prevent constipation and it is essential that arthritics keep their bowels moving easily to prevent the build up of toxins in their body.

Gladys Lindberg's recommendation for taking alfalfa tablets was this: start with two or three tablets morning and night. Gradually increase that amount until you are taking as many as ten tablets, twice a day. The tablets have a mild laxative effect with some people if too many are taken. You will soon be able to determine the proper amount for your body. If your elimination is sluggish, you should also add acidophilus.

Alfalfa has a superb calcium to phosphorus ratio, and it is the richest land source of the trace elements boron and silicon, both of which are valuable for bone integrity. One biochemist has observed that an essential alkaloid in the leaves of alfalfa works on the central nervous system to relieve minor pain.[49] This may be part of the reason the plant has been helpful with arthritics.

Dr. Hans Fisher won a Nobel Prize for unraveling the chemical structure of hemoglobin, and was surprised to find that it was almost identical to chlorophyll. When Dr. Fisher separated the heme from the protein molecule to which it was attached, the main difference between it and chlorophyll was a single iron atom at its center instead of a magnesium atom, as in the chlorophyll molecule.[50]

Cat's Claw from the Rain Forest

The Peruvian herb cat's claw (*Uncaria tomentosa*), which is also known by its Spanish name *una de gato*, contains six unique alkaloids. The presence of these compounds may explain the adaptogenic, antioxidant, anti-tumor, anti-viral, properties attributed to cat's claw.[51]

Because of its anti-inflammatory properties, cat's claw has been used successfully in the treatment of joint pain and inflammation in arthritis, rheumatism and gout. Other properties, however, may also contribute to its success. It appears some of its glycosides may add protection from pain, according to Joyce McBeth, R.N., C.N.[52]

Body systems do not function independently of one another. Arthritis, joint pain, and inflammation—as well as symptoms of chronic fatigue, allergies, immune deficiency, and many other conditions have been linked to leaky bowel syndrome, intestinal micro-flora imbalance, and toxin overload.[53] As the digestive tract is healed, other symptoms throughout the body are allowed to heal.

Yucca as an Arthritis Aid

Dr. Robert Bingham started a revival of interest in yucca (*Yucca glauca*) after he reported the positive results of a one-year research program he conducted using yucca saponin (steroid compounds that are precursors to cortisone) in treating arthritis patients. Some believe that yucca saponins improve the body's ability to manufacture its own cortisone by supplying materials needed by the adrenal glands for cortisone production.

The studies involved regular doses of yucca plant extract taken in tablet form. The patients reported less or total elimination of pain, swelling, and stiffness.

Dr. Bingham cautions that a patient should not expect sudden dramatic change. "Yucca typically works over a period of time. It is not absorbed by the intestinal tract but acts indirectly on the intestinal flora, gradually eliminating or reducing harmful bacteria and encouraging the growth of favorable bacteria."[54] Diet and exercise were adjuncts to the yucca therapy.

Perhaps of greatest significance, all patients who continued on yucca extract for six months or more obtained some *permanent reduction* of abnormally high blood pressure or excessive blood triglyceride and cholesterol levels.

The reason this extract works is not yet known, but yucca has been shown to be non-toxic. It is considered a safe and effective food supplement.

Arthritics Benefit from Devil's Claw

Devil's Claw (*Harpagophytum procumbens*) is an herb that has been used to treat a variety of diseases, including gout and arthritis. Clinical research has shown it to have anti-inflammatory and analgesic effects, thus its benefit in relieving joint pain and decreasing uric acid levels.[55]

Devil's Claw is a natural cleansing agent for removing toxic impurities from the body. It has been shown to be effective in helping hardened veins and arteries become elastic again, and it has helped patients with liver and gall bladder problems.[56] It is available in tea, tincture, or capsule form.

Using Nature's Aspirin—White Willow Bark

About 2,400 years ago, Hippocrates, the Father of Modern Medicine, used white willow bark (*Salix alba*) as an effective pain killer. For centuries before chemically synthesized aspirin was produced, people used white willow bark as a "natural aspirin."

The principal natural active agent in white willow is *salicin*. Salicin is an intermediate form of salicylic acid (or aspirin). Natural salicin seems to be converted into salicylic acid once it is in the body—with the same structure and function—except that salicin is mild on the stomach. In 1955, salicin was listed as an official botanical medicine in the *National Formulary*.

Throughout history, white willow has been used as:
- a fever lowering agent
- a pain relieving (analgesic) agent, probably because it seems to depress the central nervous system
- an anti-inflammatory agent for the treatment of rheumatism and arthritis

Salicin or white willow is slower-acting than aspirin, but its action is stronger, longer-lasting, and safer than aspirin. As you may know, aspirin can cause adverse effects on the mucous membranes of the gastro-intestinal tract, including bleeding.[57] Even though white willow is more expensive than aspirin, for many people it may be a safer product.

Eliminating Nightshades

Clinical evidence exists to lead some researchers to believe that an allergic reaction triggered by the "night-shade" family of plants appears to be the cause of arthritis. These foods contain *solanine*, a toxic substance that penetrates the immune barrier and creates a painful reaction, especially when consumed over a period of months or years.

Robert Bingham, M.D., who pioneered the research with yucca, believes that food allergies are a major problem in at least half of the people who suffer from arthritis, compared to only about 5 percent of healthy people having food allergies. He has stated, "Solanine may be the only cause of arthritis in some patients; in others, a secondary cause that interferes with their recovery." [58]

Our friend Carlton Fredericks, Ph.D., lectured about this for years. In his book, *Arthritis: Don't Learn to Live with It*, he details the need to omit nightshades from the diet.

Nightshades are various flowering plants which include **eggplant, tomatoes, peppers, potatoes, and tobacco**. The substance that links these plants is *solanine*, a glycoalkaloid which inhibits cholinesterase, an enzyme that provides agility in muscles. Studies have shown that elimination of this vegetable allergen for those who are allergic to it can control arthritis pain and relieve other symptoms of arthritis.

Norman F. Childers, Ph.D., the Blake Professor of Horticulture at Rutgers University, studied nightshades for years. He organized a group of thousands of individuals with arthritis who were willing experimentally to withdraw these foods from their diets. A large number of them became partially or totally relieved of their stiffness, aches, pains, and restricted joint mobility. [59]

In some instances, people were so badly crippled by arthritis they had to be confined to bed, or use walkers and wheelchairs. On a no-nightshades diet, they reported benefits ranging from relief to total recovery!

The Four Offending Foods

You may want to eliminate these foods for a week or 10 days and see if you are "allergic" to them. If you are allergic, it would be wise to eliminate them from your diet.

White potatoes— White potatoes were first introduced into Europe by 16th century Spanish explorers and they were first shunned as food because many people thought they were poisonous.

Glycoalkaloid and solanine are found throughout the potato, with the greatest concentration in the peel. After eating white potato, some people experience a calming effect within an hour or so, but then aches tend to set in within the next day or two.

Potato products and potato starch are found in baby foods, inexpensive yogurts, gravies, and sauces. Potato chips are a special hazard for the solanine sensitive arthritic since the conversion of potatoes into chips increases the surface area of the potato exposed to light, which raises the solanine content. French fries drowned in ketchup is a particularly troublesome combination for the solanine sensitive since two offensive foods are included.

NOTE: *Sweet potatoes and yams are of a different family of potato entirely, and may be eaten.*

Eggplant—This vegetable has only been used as a food in the present century. It was originally thought to cause emotional upset if it is eaten daily.

Tomato—The tomato was considered poisonous until the early 1800s. The solanine content was found to weaken the immune system to bring on arthritic disorders. Tomatoes are found in so many foods today—many prepared food items, as well as most Italian and many Mexican food dishes. We are a nation with a high intake of foods rich in tomatoes and peppers—from pizza to pasta to salads.

Tomato vines are poisonous to livestock. Just handling tomatoes or their vines causes some people to break out with sore, inflamed hands.

Peppers—Three main varieties of peppers contain solanine: 1) sweet and bell pepper, 2) paprika and pimiento, and 3) chili and cayenne pepper.

Most of the Mexican foods on the market today include peppers of these types. Salsa with tomatoes and peppers is double trouble. Hidden sources of peppers include hot gravies and sauces, barbecue sauces, and certain medications that contain pepper oil. Chili peppers often can irritate the gastrointestinal tract or cause skin rashes. NOTE: *Black and white pepper are not of this pepper family and are acceptable.*

Tobacco—Few people are aware that tobacco has toxic solanine content. Tobacco can impact the arthritic in two ways— with respiratory and cancer disorders, as well as injury to the immune system and antibody irritation, according to Dr. Fredericks.

For more information on the nightshades, be sure to read Dr. Carlton Fredericks' book, *Arthritis, Don't Learn to Live with It.* He covers all areas of arthritis and this would be a great addition to your library.

Natural Topical Preparations That May Provide Relief

Arnica *(Arnica montana).* Rubbed on the skin, arnica is wonderful for the relief of pain due to muscle spasm or joint inflammation. Be sure to use arnica externally only, and never apply it to broken skin.

Capsaicin—Cayenne Pepper. A cream containing small amounts of capsaicin, derived from hot peppers, seems to help symptoms of osteoarthritis. It can actually block the degeneration of synovial fluid in joints according to studies reported in *Seminars in Arthritis and Rheumatism.* Chad Deal, M.D., of the Case Western Reserve University School of Medicine in Cleveland said,"Topically applied capsaicin cream is an ideal analgesic therapy for patients with localized arthritis pain, offering proven efficacy with no systemic side effects. . . . Relief occasionally occurs within a few days, but it may take a week or two to achieve full effect." [60]

Eucalyptus Oil *(Eucalyptus globulus).*When eucalyptus oil is rubbed on the skin, it may provide relief against the pain of arthritis and rheumatism. This oil increases blood flow to the area, thus producing a feeling of warmth. It also may help soothe the stiffness and swelling associated with arthritis and rheumatism. Do not use this oil, however, on broken or irritated skin, and do not take it internally.

Commercially prepared liniments may also be used for muscle soreness or arthritis. Add eucalyptus oil to your bath, sauna and steam room treatments.

Other Things to Consider

Hydrochloric Acid. Absorption of calcium in the gastrointestinal system depends partly on the presence of hydrochloric acid in the stomach. If an excessive amount of antacids or aspirin have been taken, or if there has been a shrinking of the gastrointestinal lining, a person may have a deficiency in the production of hydrochloric acid. Hydrochloric acid tablets may help not only with digestion, but also the assimilation of calcium.

Apple Cider Vinegar. The folk remedy of honey and apple cider vinegar for arthritis may be successful in part because it stimulates the formation of hydrochloric acid in the stomach. The acid in the vinegar also aids in calcium absorption. You can mix this remedy by combining one tablespoon of honey with one tablespoon of apple cider vinegar. You may want to use this as a salad dressing, or mix the honey and vinegar with vegetable juice. Some enjoy just drinking this combination in pure water every day.

Chronic Constipation. Many people with arthritis also complain of chronic constipation. They may have had trouble with their elimination for years. Consider taking alfalfa tablets and *Lactobacillus acidophilus.* There are many colon cleansing products available in your nutrition store.

Dental Problems. A number of arthritics report infections in their teeth that they have let slide for years. There are reports of arthritis clearing up after infected teeth have been pulled. Dr. Joseph Issels, a German cancer specialist, believes that root canals can be a major source of undetected infection in the body.[61] If you are experiencing arthritic symptoms, you may be wise to schedule an appointment with your dentist.

Infections. A large number and a wide variety of infections have been linked to arthritis.[62] They can be a contributing cause, or even the sole cause of arthritis symptoms or disease in many patients.

Both with infection and constipation, *Lactobacillus aci-dophilus* may provide help. It re-implants friendly bacteria into the intestinal tract which provides help with elimination. Friendly bacteria also helps remove toxins that both come from and can lead to infection.

Mother placed those who were suffering from chronic constipation or frequent bouts with infection on a complete nutrition program. The program is outlined in detail in Chapter 13.

Lack of Motion. It is very important that you keep moving! A lack of motion—even of moderate exercise—seems to make arthritis symptoms worse. Although we tend to think of running as resulting in progressive wear and tear on the cartilage of the leg joints, studies have shown that many former long-distance runners have perfectly normal hip and knee joints, while their more sedentary friends are the ones plagued with degenerating joints.

I know of one woman who continued to type long letters to friends after she had retired from an office job because she found that the continued use of her fingers helped with arthritic pain. Swimming in warm water seems to help those who suffer from stiffness and pain in the hips and knees. Discuss with your physician the types of exercise that may be best for you to pursue ... and then choose to stay active!

I pray that the above information will help you on the path to improved health, so that you may live free of stiffness and pain.

Chapter 11

Anti-Aging
Therapies
Slowing Down the Aging Process

"People have been searching for the 'Fountain
of Youth' for countless centuries. The more
nutritional research that is being done, the
closer we may actually be to finding such a 'fountain'."
—Gladys Lindberg

A number of new anti-aging therapies may prove very promising, especially when combined with more traditional methods. Conventional medicine is not generally accepting of these therapies, but remember that just a century ago, Louis Pasteur was ridiculed for suggesting that tiny organisms he called microbes could actually kill a man. And Ignaz Semmelweis in Vienna was persecuted and finally driven mad, because he said doctors should wash their hands before performing surgery.

This information is presented for your consideration. Realize that some are still in experimental stages. I am personally acquainted with a number of people, even my own family, who have benefited from many of these "anti-aging" therapies. Those who have used them are often highly appreciative and very positive about their effects.

The Importance of Our Hormones

The National Institute On Aging (NIA) conducts research with the goal of improving the quality of life and maintaining the independence and vitality of people well into their later years. In late 1992, the Institute launched a series of ambitious interventional studies to evaluate the safety and efficacy of certain hormones, especially human growth hormones and sex steroid hormones for older people.[1]

Hormone Replacement Therapy. These studies are taking place in several institutions across the United States, with additional research being conducted at the NIA Intramural Gerontology Research Center in Baltimore, Maryland. Scientists are conducting tests in order to explore the possibility that age-related disturbances can be slowed or partially reversed by the administration of these agents. Age related decline includes changes in musculoskeletal function, body composition, metabolic function, including weakening of muscles, bones, skin, nerves, and a number of organ and tissue cells. The researchers are investigating the value of combined hormone replacement therapy, with which they hope to return growth hormone and sex hormone levels to those typical of younger people.[2] They are hopeful that the additive or synergistic effects should improve both physical and psychological functions.

As we age, the production of the hormones DHEA, pregnenolone, melatonin, thyroid, estrogen, progesterone, testosterone and growth hormone declines. It is possible that hormone replacement may be an integral part of modern medicine in the not too distant future. Testosterone and growth hormones will be discussed in Chapter 12, and pregnenolone in Chapter 6.

Is DHEA the Anti-Aging Miracle of the 21st Century?

DHEA exploded onto the market in March of 1996, and there were only one or two companies manufacturing it. But by our summer trade show convention, it seemed everyone had added DHEA to their brand of products. The list of research on DHEA is impressive. The New York Academy of Sciences, the Huffington Center on Aging at Baylor College, the National Institute on Drug Abuse (a study on DHEA and Brain Development, Aging and Memory), the University of California, San Diego, the Department of Microbiology and Immunology at Temple University, the University Hospital in Belgium and many other of the world's finest medical and research facilities have conducted extensive research into the biology, metabolism and effects of DHEA use and supplementation.

Most of the interest in DHEA was generated from articles in *Newsweek, Vanity Fair, Let's Live*, even the cover of *US News and World Report* which read, *"Staying Younger Longer—How Scientists are Pushing Back the Clock on Old Age."* Even the *Wall Street Journal* and the *CBS Morning News* discussed DHEA. They have given it the title of the *"The Mother of All Hormones."* DHEA is here to stay and is an important anti-aging nutrient we should know about.

DHEA (dehydroepiandrosterone) is a naturally occurring steroid, a type of hormone distinguished from others by its unique chemical structure. A French chemist showed that DHEA is made from another hormone, pregnenolone, and that DHEA is, in turn, converted into estrogen and testosterone in both men and women.[3] DHEA is also produced by the adrenal glands (located on the kidneys) as well as by the brain and the skin. DHEA also converts to or stimulates the production of progesterone, cortisone, and the many other steroid hormones as the body needs them.[4]

We cannot ignore the rapidly expanding body of scientific research which indicates that DHEA may be helpful for preventing and treating a wide range of medical conditions. In fact, today nearly 5,000 in-depth scientific and medical studies on the use of DHEA have been conducted and completed in the laboratories of some of the top universities and medical research facilities in the world.

These studies have shown a direct relationship between blood levels of DHEA and the inhibition of many diseases. Once DHEA has been released into the bloodstream, it is used in cellular metabolism and generates a wide variety of health and longevity benefits.[5]

Leading Anti-Aging Doctor. I had the honor of meeting William Regelson, M.D. one of the nation's leading anti-aging doctors, at the American Academy of Anti-Aging Medicine convention. He is professor of medicine at the Medical College of Virginia, and author of *The Melatonin Miracle* and now *The Superhormone Promise.*

DHEA appears to protect the body in numerous ways. Here are some of the reported benefits:

- Blood levels can indicate the present and future status of cancer and degenerative disease.
- Combats colon, breast, lung and skin cancers in animals.
- Protects the immune system and thymus function to fight against infection.
- Fights obesity by rejuvenating a sluggish metabolism, reduces body fat and helps increase muscle mass.

- Helps chronic fatigue syndrome, Epstein-Barr, AIDS and shows promise with lupus.
- Lowers blood cholesterol and triglyceride levels thereby reducing the incidence of cardiovascular disease.
- Enhances memory, improves cognitive function, helps fight senility and early stages of Alzheimer's disease.
- Helps depression and learning problems.
- Stabilizes blood sugar levels and helps to prevent diabetes in adults.
- Appears capable of both inhibiting bone resorption and stimulating bone formation for osteoporosis prevention.
- Beneficial to those with Parkinson's disease and Grave's disease.[6]

Retard Aging with DHEA. The secretion of this hormone markedly declines with age. DHEA appears in the bloodstream at about age seven, and then peaks at about age 25. The secretion decreases progressively after that age and by age 70, it has diminished by 80–90 percent.[7]

Some age researchers agree that to retard aging, a person must maintain the peak serum level he or she had at about age 25.[8]

It is currently being investigated as an anti-aging hormone. In essence, DHEA seems to rejuvenate the systems required for optimal functioning of the human body. The exciting part of the action of DHEA is that it may reverse many of the aspects of aging previously thought to be irreversible.[9]

Dr. Regelson says that his patients, who are taking DHEA regularly to restore their youthful levels, report they "feel more energetic, generally healthier, and also sexier than they had since youth. They feel this way on the outside, because, inside their bodies, DHEA is actually correcting and reversing much of the deterioration to their organs and body systems—the "wear and tear" — that has been occurring since they reached middle age." [10]

Some animal experiments have shown great promise in extending life span.[11] So far, there are no long-term studies on humans that show giving DHEA supplements can extend our life span. But, I am sure these studies will take place.

Alan Gaby, M.D., reports that this age-related decline is not known to occur with any of the other adrenal steroids. It has therefore been suggested that some of the manifestations of aging may be caused by DHEA deficiency. In Dr. Gaby's experience, some elderly people who suffer from weakness, muscle wasting, trembling, and other signs of aging, experience noticeable improvements within several weeks of beginning small doses of DHEA (such as 5 to 15 mg a day).[12]

Feeling of Wellness. Samuel Yen, M.D., a reproductive endocrinologist, of the University of California at San Diego, reported that DHEA was "associated with a remarkable increase in perceived physical and psychological well-being" among the volunteer subjects in his study, age forty to seventy, 67 percent of the men and 84 percent of the women reported feeling better. Dr. Yen found that they experienced increased energy and better sleep; they felt more relaxed and able to handle stress. Those with arthritic symptoms also reported less joint pain. None of the study participants experienced any negative side effects. Dr. Yen says, "DHEA is a drug that may help people age more gracefully." [13]

It Rejuvenates the Human Body. A fall in DHEA levels seems to be related to many forms of degenerative diseases, including cancer, heart disease, diabetes, obesity, high blood pressure, and Parkinson's disease, to mention only a few. The theory, therefore, is that raising DHEA to more youthful levels through supplementation may help forestall the occurrence of these ailments.[14] It relieves stress and may prove to be the most potent anti-cancer drug of all time.

DHEA has also been shown to restore muscle mass, help with the beginning stages of Alzheimer's disease,[15] and other memory disturbances, rejuvenate immune system function including AIDS, battles chronic fatigue and creates a sense of well-being in older people. It may also be of value in preventing and treating osteoporosis.[16]

Memory Enhancer. Forgetfulness is one of the first signs of aging. Dr. Regelson feels, "several studies that have shown beyond any doubt whatsoever that DHEA has a direct and profound effect on the brain's ability to process and store information, and those results have now led some researchers to the belief that DHEA may play a major role in preventing the terrible mind and memory-robbing scourge we call Alzheimer's disease." [17]

Enhances Immune Response. DHEA may also enhance the body's immune response to viral and bacterial infections.[18] Our immune system is based upon the cooperation of several different types of cells, which learn to recognize and then attack infectious viruses and bacteria. Dr. Ronald Klatz, in *Stopping the Clock*, feels that one way DHEA may enhance immunity is by protecting the thymus gland, which regulates T-cells. These T-cells are the body's army for search and destroy missions of infectious agents. As we age, our thymus gland shrinks, which scientists have linked with reduced immunity typical of the elderly. DHEA seems to wake up elderly immune systems to youthful levels of efficiency. DHEA may very well be responsible for decreasing age-related susceptibility to immune system "invaders" that can make us ill.

Animal research has shown that DHEA prevented thymic atrophy and improved the thymus' ability to control T-cells. Many researchers believe that DHEA supplements might also stave off thymic decline in people. The immune-enhancing effects of DHEA still need further research, as aging, infection and stress are all crucial factors that may affect its production.[19]

Anti-Cancer Effects. DHEA has protected against and slowed the progression of some cancers in animal work and in human studies. Some report it can actually block carcinogenic promotion.[20]

For example, the British medical journal the *Lancet* reported a study that followed 5,000 women and found that those who developed breast cancer had lower than average levels of DHEA in their urine *as early as nine years before* the development of cancer. The amazing part of the study was that all the women in the same age group died of breast cancer if their DHEA level was 10 percent less than average, while those with higher than average levels remained cancer-free.[21]

In another fascinating experiment, Dr. Arthur Schwartz at the Fels Institute of Temple University gave rats a potent carcinogen that normally promoted tumor growth. He found, however, that when he gave the rats an injection of DHEA prior to introducing the carcinogen, they remained cancer-free. Surprisingly, it also increased the life span of these mice by an amazing 50 percent.[22] Dr. Schwartz is in the process of developing a DHEA-based drug that may prove to be the first anti-cancer pill.

Dr. Schwartz later reported on his DHEA animal studies, "Old mice regained youthful vigor and their coats resumed their former sleek and glossy texture; incipient cancers, whether naturally-occurring or induced by artificial means, disappeared; obese animals returned to normal weight, and animals with diabetes improved dramatically." [23]

The good news, Dr. Regelson reports, is that DHEA and related steroids can block initiation or promotion of cancer depending on the model selected and can be thought as a chemo-preventives. After a study of his advanced patients who had been diagnosed with terminal cancer, Regelson said, "The true leavening grace in this is that my patients were in stable condition and out of pain for most of their 'borrowed time.' Thus, although DHEA may not have 'cured' cancer, it improved the overall physical condition in patients and greatly enhanced the quality of life they had left."[24]

What exciting news as more research is continued!
NOTE: *Be sure to read about precautions on DHEA at the end of this chapter if you have cancer.*

DHEA May Fight Obesity. DHEA may prove to be the greatest weight loss boon to overweight Americans. Dr. Arthur Schwartz says, "DHEA is a very effective anti-obesity agent." DHEA induced weight loss in laboratory animals irrespective of how much food they consumed. DHEA appeared to stimulate the substance that signals us to feel full.[25]

Dr. M.P. Cleary found that even middle-aged rats lost weight when fed DHEA supplemented food. Diabetes, a typical complication of obesity, was also dramatically decreased. It appears from the most recent data that food deprivation, as dieting, is simply not necessary when using DHEA to lose weight. This sounds almost too good to be true, but I sure hope it is![26]

This dramatic result has prompted researchers to study DHEA as a weight loss therapy for humans. In a human study the doctors at the Medical College of Virginia recently gave daily doses of DHEA for a full month to men with excess body fat. A control group of overweight men were given a placebo. Their diet and lifestyles remained exactly the same as before the study. The men in the DHEA group experienced an amazing 31 percent reduction in body fat and this lost body fat appeared to give way to new muscle. There was no change at all in the weight of men on the placebo.[27]

Osteoporosis Prevention. Dr. Alan Gaby, author of *Preventing and Reversing Osteoporosis,* says that DHEA reads like the "who's who in osteoporosis prevention." His excellent book is suggested reading for those with or who want to prevent osteoporosis. DHEA functions as a precursor hormone, and can be converted by the body into other hormones including estrogen and testosterone, both of which play a role in the prevention of bone loss. In a study of postmenopausal women, administering DHEA increased serum levels of both testosterone and estrogens (estradiol and estrone).[28]

Bone-Building Effects. Also, DHEA may be capable of raising the levels of *progesterone* (a hormone manufactured by the ovaries). Dr. Gaby reports, "Although DHEA is not converted directly into *progesterone*, it may, through a feedback mechanism, indirectly increase the production of progesterone. Both DHEA and progesterone are produced from the same precursor hormone, pregnenolone. If enough DHEA is present, then pregnenolone will be converted primarily to progesterone, rather than to DHEA."[29] DHEA might, therefore, augment the bone-building effect of progesterone. Preliminary results suggest that progesterone is at least as important as, and possibly even more important than, estrogen, in preventing and treating postmenopausal osteoporosis. And as far as Dr. Gaby can tell, DHEA is the only hormone that appears capable of both inhibiting bone resorption and stimulating bone formation.[30]

Rheumatoid Arthritis. In a study of forty-nine postmenopausal women with rheumatoid arthritis, DHEA levels (measured as DHEA's—the "S" stands for sulfate) were significantly lower than in healthy controls. DHEA levels correlated significantly with bone mineral density of the neck of the femur (a bone in the hip) and the spine. The serum level of DHEA was able to predict bone mineral density, even after corticosteroid therapy was taken into account.[31]

Dr. Davis Lamson, a private practitioner in Kent, Washington, gave DHEA to several arthritic patients with low serum levels of DHEA. This treatment often relieved pain and morning stiffness, increased strength, and reduced the need for anti-inflammatory medication.[32]

In another study, Dr. Alan Gaby reported that forty-five post-menopausal women being treated with corticosteroids, were given 20 mg of DHEA a day which resulted in an increased sense of well-being, with no side effects.[33]

May Prevent Heart Disease. A long-term study of 242 men between fifty and seventy-nine years of age found that DHEA levels decreased with age as reported in the *New England Journal of Medicine*. Those with the highest levels of DHEA in their blood were only half as likely to die of heart disease as those with relatively little of the hormone according to researcher Elizabeth Barrett-Conner at the University of California of San Diego.[34]

In a study at the Medical College of Virginia, patients who suffered from clotting problems were given DHEA. When researchers then examined the patients' blood, they found a significant decline in their propensity to form blood clots. By preventing excess blood clot formation, DHEA may protect against both heart disease and stroke, according to Dr. Regelson.

Those with histories of heart disease had particularly low levels of DHEA, and low levels, in general, were consistently associated with increased risk of death from any cause—even after adjusting for age, blood pressure, serum cholesterol level, obesity, fasting plasma glucose levels, smoking and history of heart disease. The connection between low DHEA levels and heart disease is a particularly strong one for men. According to Dr. Sheldon Saul Hendler this important study certainly suggests, but does not prove, that DHEA may confer some protection against several, and perhaps all, degenerative processes.[35]

Lowers Cholesterol. After three months of taking DHEA, postmenopausal women showed an 8 to 10 percent decline in total cholesterol levels, which is quite significant given the fact that for every 1 percent drop in cholesterol, there is a 2 percent drop in the risk of developing heart disease. Other studies have since confirmed these findings.[36]

Improves Sexual Function. DHEA seems to turn back the aging clock when it comes to remaining sexually vital with advancing years. Men, particularly, report that it has revived their sexual interest according to Dr. Regelson. Other doctors who prescribe DHEA report that many of their male patients experience an increase in libido and that many older men who did not have morning erections for years suddenly began to experience them after taking DHEA. We know that DHEA is converted into testosterone in both men and women, and that testosterone is known to enhance libido in both sexes. This would explain why those taking DHEA experience a heightened libido.

Although women also find that DHEA makes them feel better and more energetic, the heightened libido effect is not as apparent for them, possibly because women do not experience the same pronounced decline in libido that is common for men in their advancing years.[37]

Dr. Ray Sahelian, author of the book, *DHEA a Practical Guide*, states that women in their forties and fifties reported to him that DHEA gives them a powerful sex drive. He feels maybe it is even a minute increase in testosterone that may have this effect on women, whereas with men it would be hardly noticeable.[38]

DHEA for Postmenopausal Women. "It makes perfect sense that DHEA would be a useful treatment for menopause because DHEA is an estrogen precursor. This means that DHEA is converted to estrogen in the body. After menopause, when the ovaries stop making estrogen, small amounts of estrogen continue to be manufactured in the adrenal glands from hormones, including DHEA. Supplementing DHEA in postmenopausal women therefore appears to be a way of increasing estrogen levels naturally." Regelson also said that DHEA has some unique properties of its own that make it a boon for postmenopausal women.

Several clinical studies of DHEA's potential as a substitute for estrogen replacement therapy are now under way, and several that have been completed have produced positive results. Preliminary findings indicate that DHEA offers many of the same benefits of estrogen without many of the potentially harmful side effects. Although DHEA may not do everything that estrogen does, it does do a lot in terms of relieving menopausal symptoms and protecting against disease, and it may even offer a few benefits that estrogen does not.[39]

A Clinical Study: In *The Superhormone Promise* by Dr. Regelson, he discusses some valuable information for menopausal women I want to share with you. Dr. Pierre Diamond reported on a study he conducted at Le Centre Hospitalier de l'Universit's Laval, Canada. He gave DHEA replacement therapy to twenty post-menopausal women, aged sixty to seventy, for a year. None of these women were taking estrogen. DHEA was applied as a cream daily and their blood levels were measured periodically to ensure that DHEA had been restored to twenty-year-old levels. Nearly all reported an increase in energy and improvement in general well-being, but there were important physical changes:

- Dr. Diamond observed a reduction in both blood insulin and glucose (sugar) levels, reinforcing our belief that DHEA has a positive effect on insulin resistance. Since insulin resistance is a risk factor for heart disease, this suggests that DHEA shields post-menopausal women from heart disease, the number one killer in postmenopausal women.
- Although the women's weight remained the same, they did show a change in "Body Mass Index," the ratio of fat to muscle. Their levels of fat decreased, and their levels of muscle increased.
- After menopause, women begin to lose roughly 2 to 4 percent of their bone mass each year. This causes many women to suffer from hip and spinal fractures. The good news is that while the women were taking DHEA, they showed a marked increase in bone density. In fact, after a year on DHEA, the average bone mass density of the women was increased at the hip and spine, two sites that are particularly vulnerable to osteoporosis.
- DHEA produced a modest drop in blood cholesterol of 3 to 10 percent in the women. Even a modest drop can offer a significant reduction in heart disease.
- At least half the women in the study had suffered from vaginal atrophy, that is, a thinning of the vaginal wall (the endothelium), and a reduction in the production of vaginal secretions that lubricate the

vagina, which occurs commonly after menopause. These changes not only produce discomfort but they also promote vaginal infections and can make intercourse painful. It appears that DHEA may be a good remedy, and appeared to stimulate growth of the vaginal endothelium and increase vaginal secretions, thus restoring the vagina to its youthful condition.

Dr. Regelson said, "As an oncologist, what I find even more interesting was what DHEA did not do: Although DHEA did stimulate growth of the vaginal lining, it did not stimulate the growth of the uterine lining. In this regard, DHEA offers a distinct advantage over estrogen replacement therapy." [40]

DHEA is no longer a prescription drug. It has now been confirmed with the Drug Enforcement Administration that DHEA is not an anabolic steroid and is not a controlled substance because it does not promote muscle growth. DHEA is now classified as a dietary supplement according to an interpretation of the 1994 Dietary Supplement, Health & Education Act.

DHEA Dosage. Opinions differ at the present time on the optimal dose of DHEA, who should receive it, or when it should be started. Remember, we are all biologically different.

A Variety of Opinions and Recommendations:

- Dr. Alan Gaby considers a small dose, say 3 to 5 mg in the early postmenopausal period; and a larger dose, perhaps 5 to 15 mg/day, in later years when adrenal output declines; and 3 to 30 mg/day for the prevention of osteoporosis. He says much larger doses are being given to patients with cancer, AIDS, and other serious conditions.[41]
- Dr. Russe at University of California at San Francisco gave 50 mg/day for individuals over 50 with declining memory which had remarkable effects on well-being.[42]
- Dr. Julian Whitaker suggests the level of DHEA necessary to improve brain power appears to be 25 to 100

mg/day. All of the human and animal studies on DHEA have found that it is exceptionally safe. The only side effect that has been mentioned with doses greater than 90 mg/day is infrequent and mild masculinization of women. This appears as facial hair or a drop in the voice timbre. These side effects go away with cessation or reduction of dosage of DHEA.[43]

Should I Have my DHEA Level Measured Before Use? Dr. Edmund Chein, M.D., J.D., director of the Life Extension Institute in Palm Springs, says it is important that one have his or her DHEA blood level tested before beginning a DHEA replacement program. This way the physician will know how much should be replaced. A second test should be drawn one month after beginning the treatment. Dr. Chein said there is no universal standard yet developed to determine an optimal dose. It is common practice, however, for a physician to use whatever dosage will bring the serum level of DHEA sulfate to 600 mg/ml for men, and 400 mg/ml for women.

Now there are new saliva tests available where you can check your hormone levels. Many labs have these kits available and you may be able to purchase these from your physician or nutrition store. These tests do not require the drawing of blood.

Most of the anti-aging researchers I have read, Dr. William Regelson, Dr. Norman Orentreich, Dr. Samuel Yen, Dr. Ray Sahelian, and Dr. Ronald Klatz, to name a few, all agree that the DHEA levels should be monitored, to bring the levels up to "youthful age", and then checked periodically.

My friend and colleague, Marcia Zimmerman, M.Ed., C.N., who has reviewed the research on DHEA, feels that if we use the low doses, say 15 to 25 mg, it is probably not necessary to have our blood level tested. DHEA is generally well tolerated and quickly assimilated, but she does feel if we take higher doses, we should definitely have our blood levels checked.

Cautions. All of the research reports I have read say DHEA is safe in normal dosages. However, you need to know that adequate human studies have not yet been done on long term usage of DHEA. Dr. Morton Walker warns that DHEA should not be taken by those lab tested with a suspicion of prostate cancer, due to the *unproved* but much *speculated* relationship between high testosterone levels (which DHEA may stimulate) and the onset of prostate cancer.

The Life Extension Report says "patients with reproductive pre-cancerous conditions or reproductive cancer should not use DHEA, except under the strict monitoring of an experienced health care professional." [44]

This is not a product to be misused, and proper warning instructions should be followed. DHEA also should not be taken by any person who is under 40, pregnant, nursing, or taking any prescription medication, including hormone products. Persons suffering from any disease should consult a physician before using this product.

Melatonin May Reset the Aging Clock

Melatonin is a hormone produced in the pineal gland, which is situated deep behind the brain. Thirty years of laboratory research resulted in Dr. Pierpaoli's landmark studies, which demonstrated that the pineal gland is our body's natural timekeeper and is regulated by the natural ebb and flow of the hormone melatonin. We may be able to slow the process of aging, turn back the hands of time, strengthen our immune system, and thereby heighten our resistance to disease and even prolong our sexual vitality by simply restoring the melatonin levels of youth. There are thousands of animal and human studies that suggest many roles for melatonin.

Today, melatonin ranks as one of the important hormones, stimulating the release of a wide variety of other hormones from the pituitary gland. [45]

Russell J. Reiter, Ph.D., author of *Melatonin, Your Body's Natural Wonder Drug* and Professor of Neuroendocrinology at the University of Texas, has been researching melatonin for more than thirty years. He has concluded that melatonin is the most powerful antioxidant molecule yet to be discovered. He considers it a hormone that possibly can "reset the body's aging clock, turning back the ravages of time." [46] Scientists may be on the verge of discovering the real "fountain of youth" that Ponce de Leon only dreamed about.

An Interesting Study on Mice. Dr. Frank Varese of Laguna Hills, California, is the doctor that introduced me to the world of natural hormone replacement several years ago. To spur my interest in melatonin, he gave me a cassette tape by William Regelson M.D., one of the premier researchers on the product.

Here's what Dr. Regelson, co-author of *Melatonin Miracle,* wrote about on a mice study he conducted.

"In fall of 1985, I began the first of what would be many experiments testing the effect of administering melatonin supplements to older mice. I selected healthy male mice that were nineteen months old (human equivalent of about 65 years), they live to about twenty-four months. I divided the mice into two groups, one given melatonin in the evening drinking water, the other group regular tap water, everything else, diet, living conditions, was exactly the same.

At first, I could detect very little difference between the two groups of mice. Within five months, however, the difference was astonishing. The untreated mice began to display the expected signs and symptoms of old age—of senescence. They lost muscle mass, they developed bald patches, their eyes grew cloudy with cataracts, their digestion slowed down, and so, generally, did they. In sum, they seemed worn out and tired—they were winding down and becoming old.

On the other hand, the melatonin-treated mice looked, and behaved, like their grandchildren. The mice on melatonin had actually grown more fur and continued to boast thick, shiny coats. Their eyes were clear and cataract-free, their digestion had improved, and, instead of growing thin and wasted in the manner of the non-melatonin-treated mice, they maintained their strength and muscle tone. The vigor and energy with which they moved around their cage resembled the behavior of mice half their age," Dr. Regelson said.

Most importantly, they lived much longer! The untreated mice, having reached their expected life span of about twenty-four months (70 to 75 years in human terms), began to die. Yet the melatonin mice lived on and on—an astonishing six months longer, which in human terms would amount to gaining and extra 25 years of life, or living well past 100." [47]

This is exciting information. Dr. Regelson went on to determine the cause of death and found that most of the untreated mice had died of cancer, common for their breed and age. But much to his surprise, the melatonin-treated mice had remained disease-free throughout their extended lives. He said their organs had shrunk, typical of old age, but they did not suffer or die from cancer.

Dr. Regelson had succeeded in reversing the aging process in these animals, but what this experiment revealed about aging was even more remarkable. "This experiment proved that disease is not an inevitable part of aging, and that it is possible for us not only to live longer lives, but to live them in strong, disease-free, healthy bodies. Senescence, the downward spiral that we have come to associate with aging, does not have to occur. Melatonin can stop the spiral." [48] Melatonin holds several pieces to the puzzle of living longer.

The Mice Got Sexy. Scientific protocol demands they repeat the experiment several times to make sure they can duplicate the results. Each time the results were the same. But in one of Regelson's experiments, they used male and female mice, and discovered something exciting.

Both the males and females displayed the sexual prowess of much younger mice. In fact, right up until their death, these mice were sexually active. Regelson said this would be the equivalent of one-hundred-year-old men and women showing the sexual interest and stamina of people a third their age! [49] Amazing!

Prevents Heart Disease—Normalizes Blood Pressure. Melatonin can lower cholesterol, thereby preventing the formation of plaque deposits which can clog arteries and block the flow of blood. Melatonin can normalize blood pressure and inhibit the action of free-radicals, both of which are conditions that can destroy arteries and injure the heart. Melatonin can even blunt the destructive effects of corticosteroids, stress hormones that can inflict damage to the heart muscle and an otherwise healthy body, according to Drs. Pierpaoli and Regelson. [50]

Boosts Immune Function. Melatonin has also been effective in boosting immune function through increasing the size of the thymus, strengthening antibody response, and increasing cellular activity—all of which strengthen the immune system. Other studies have shown melatonin's immune-enhancing ability by knocking out viruses, moderating the effects of corticosteroid overproduction in response to stress, and rejuvenating thyroid function, which influences T-cell production. It also neutralizes some of the side effects of mammograms, X-rays, and surgery. [51]

The Cancer Connection. Recent research has shown that melatonin combats cancer in many different ways. It not only strengthens the immune system's ability to spot and destroy abnormal cells that may turn cancerous, but it prevents the age-related decline in immunity that can leave a person more vulnerable to cancer.[52] Melatonin can dampen the effect of hormones that can trigger the growth of certain types of cancer, including breast, cervical, and prostate cancer.[53] Low melatonin levels seem to accompany cancer growth in some studies.[54]

Melatonin as a Sleep Aid. This hormone controls our sleep-wake cycle, what scientists refer to as the *circadian rhythm*. Melatonin establishes the biological rhythm of every cell in the body. The presence of adequate amounts of melatonin induces sleep and may reduce anxiety, panic disorders, and migraines. A disruption of routine—such as shift work, travel across more than three times zones (jet lag), or even erratic daily schedules—can reduce melatonin levels and desynchronize (undo) the body's internal time clock. The gland secretes the hormone melatonin during times of darkness and is suppressed by bright light.

Those who have trouble sleeping may try melatonin. Drugs such as NSAIDs, sedatives, some tranquilizers, and anti-psychotic drugs can actually reduce melatonin levels. This may mean that a greater quantity of these drugs are needed over time to promote sleep. It also means that the REM phase of sleep may be interrupted. REM sleep is that which is required for a person truly to feel rested after sleeping. The use of melatonin, which is derived naturally from tryptophan and serotonin, may be the natural answer for giving you a sleep pattern that is healthy and doesn't leave you feeling drugged and unrested.[55]

Melatonin as a Sex-Enhancing Hormone. Sexual arousal occurs when your brain and endocrine glands pump out sex hormones. The activity of these glands is controlled by the pineal gland and one of its chemical messengers, melatonin. The same messenger is also involved in signaling clues that tell us to touch and cuddle.

Libido is largely regulated by hormones. In men the male hormones, *testosterone* and *dihydrotestosterone*, among others, govern arousal and erection. In women, female hormones *estrogen and progesterone* and also male hormones or androgens are involved in the sex drive. In order to feel sexy, aroused and interested, you need to produce normal levels of these hormones, and it is the duty of melatonin to make certain we do. Fluctuations in our melatonin levels stimulate the pituitary gland to release a number of hormones that regulate sexual activity. These hormones include *luteinizing hormone* (LH), which is involved in ovulation and the secretion of estrogen; *follicle-stimulating hormone* (FSH), which regulates the production of sperm in men and stimulates the maturation of the ovaries in women; and *prolactin and oxytocin*, which stimulate milk production and maternal bonding. The normal ebb and flow of hormones is essential to our ability to respond sexually.[56]

Heightens Endorphins. Melatonin can also make sex a more pleasurable experience at any age. Melatonin heightens the effect of endorphins, the natural tranquilizers produced by our bodies that can relieve pain, stress, and create a sensation of pleasure and well-being. Melatonin's endorphin enhancing ability, which increases the pleasure of lovemaking, becomes even more important with each passing decade. As we age, we often lose our ability to experience pleasure. Through its effect on endorphins, melatonin can help relieve stress, and thus, create an environment that is more conducive to lovemaking.[57] Drs. Pierpaoli and Regelson believe that taking melatonin supplements at bedtime later in life, starting at the time when natural levels begin to drop, may help restore these other hormones to more youthful levels and thus enable us to maintain our youthful levels of sexuality as well.

How Much Should I Take? The amount of melatonin a person should take is still being debated. Some researchers believe it should be taken in small amounts, such as 0.5 mg a day, while others recommend larger amounts (3 mg a day or more). Drs. Pierpaoli and Regelson recommend these dosages, which are based on a person's age:

Age	Dose of Melatonin
40–44	0.5 to 1 mg at bedtime
45–54	1–2 mg at bedtime
55–64	2.25 mg at bedtime

65 74 . . . . 3.5 5 mg at bedtime
75 plus . . . . 3.5–5 mg at bedtime

If a recommended dose leaves you groggy in the morning, the dosage is too high for you. Reduce it until you find the right level for your body. Many authorities suggest that 1 mg a day should be adequate for a long period of time.

It is important that melatonin only be taken at night, about a half hour before bed.

It is not known whether larger doses of melatonin are safe for long-term use. Hormones are extremely potent biological compounds that are usually effective in small doses. While melatonin shows great promise as an anti-aging hormone, we need to regard it with respect. Scientists will continue to explore its power. As of this writing, there are no known side effects.

Cautions: Melatonin is not recommended for people under 40 years of age as you don't want to interfere with your own production of the hormone at an early age. It should not be taken by children, pregnant or lactating women unless under a doctor's supervision. You can find this "natural anti-aging nutrient" in several potencies at your nutrition store.

Estrogen & Progesterone For Women

The *Dictionary of Medical Terms for the Nonmedical Person* defines estrogen as "a general term for the female hormones (including *estradiol, estrone, estriol*) produced in the ovaries (and in small amounts in the testes and adrenals). In women estrogen functions in the *menstrual cycle* and in the development of secondary sex characteristics (e.g., breast development in adolescence). As a synthetic preparation, sold under many trade names, estrogen drugs are used to treat menstrual irregularities, to relieve symptoms of *menopause,* to treat cancer of the prostate, and in oral contraceptives."[58]

Caution is used because estrogen has side effects, some highly debated. These include stroke, gallbladder disease, liver tumors and enlargement, fluid retention and weight gain, headaches, endometrial cancer and fibroids. Estrogen is not recommended for patients with uterine or breast cancer, a strong family history of breast cancer, obesity, phlebitis, varicose veins, diabetes, hypertension, edema, fibroids or fibrocystic breast.[59]

The above references vividly demonstrate the current paradox surrounding the use and treatment of one of the most researched hormones of this century. Are its benefits of great value to the untold numbers of women using the therapy? Yes, undoubtedly. However, more attention is now being directed towards its side effects.

Therefore, a serious, honest look at the benefits versus the downside of synthetic estrogen is in order. Indeed, new revelations about the efficacy of natural estrogen and progesterone have caused many authorities to reconsider past beliefs and introduce new thinking to this controversial subject. I've cast my vote with the "natural" side and explain why in the next few pages.

The Side Effects of Estrogen

In 1995, Emory University published, along with the National Cancer Society, a report of an 8-year study of over 240,000 women. The study found that those women who were on unopposed estrogen (estrogen without progesterone) had a 72% higher risk of fatal cancer of the ovary.[60]

According to the medical journal *Primary Care and Cancer*, from the M.D. Anderson Cancer Center, the latent period from exposure to hormones and the development of overt malignancy may be as long as 15 to 30 years. As with most substances known to cause cancer, risk is related to both intensity and duration of exposure, and these variables are hard to quantify. The journal also reported that the induction of any cancer is an unacceptable side effect for an elective therapy unless an overriding benefit can be demonstrated.[61]

There are numerous studies going back to the 1960s on estrogens involvement as a suspected cancer causing agent. The latest medical reports tell us that cancer of the breast will affect one in every nine women, which is a dramatic increase. Of course, this is just breast cancer. The American Cancer Society also reported that cancer affects one in three people in this country.[62] This statistic is startling! One person in every three is going to get cancer! What is causing this response in our bodies?

An excellent television program was presented on PBS (Public Broadcasting System—Oct 1993), on breast cancer by Dr.

Susan Love, a cancer surgeon at UCLA. She reported that more women have died of breast cancer in this country than American lives lost fighting all this country's wars. One woman dies every 12 minutes from breast cancer. Dr. Love stated that it takes 8 to 10 years before you can feel a lump, so do get several medical opinions before you make a final decision on your type of cancer treatment.

Estrogen could stimulate the growth of an already existing cancer, and women with a personal or family history of breast cancer are often advised to avoid estrogen altogether. Also, if you discover you have cancer, usually one of the first treatments to be administered is an estrogen blocking substance. Of my many friends who have passed away in recent years, death came not from a stroke, or osteoporosis or heart attack, but usually from cancer.

Natural Estrogen Replacement

Estrogen is not a single substance, it exists in the body in at least three forms. *Estrone* and *estradiol* are relatively potent estrogens in their ability to relieve menopausal symptoms such as hot flashes. Unfortunately, Dr. Alan Gaby reports, they also appear to be the forms of estrogen that promote cancer.

However, there is a third form of estrogen, called *estriol*, and it also occurs naturally in the body. In contrast to the cancer-promoting effects of the other two estrogenic compounds, estriol has actually been shown to have anti-cancer activity.

Estriol is considered a weak estrogen because more estriol is required to relieve menopausal symptoms, but if a proper dosage is given, symptoms do improve. A dose of 2 to 4 mg of estriol is considered equivalent to, and as effective as, 0.6 to 1.25 mg of conjugated estrogens or estrone.[63]

The Value of Converting Estrogen to Estriol. Our dear friend, the late Carlton Fredericks, Ph.D., in his book, *Breast Cancer: A Nutritional Approach,* stated, "the body breaks down estrogen, degrading it into a much less active, and thereby unthreatening hormone estriol. In converting estrogen into estriol, the body actually turns a carcinogenic (cancer-producing) compound into a harmless chemical and is ultimately excreted. Even better than harmless: more estriol and less estrogen means less breast cancer and a reduced tendency to clots and strokes in women overproducing or taking supplementary doses of estrogen, even in the use of

birth control pills. Thus the ratio between the two hormones, as reflected in the urine, can, if favorable, help to block the way cancer develops in the sex organs."

Dr. Fredericks writes, "this isn't theory—in population groups where the women tend toward higher estriol and lower estrogen levels, breast cancer is always less frequent."[64] The impetus for this was a series of studies in the 1930s and 1940s indicating that the liver is the essential organ necessary to convert the most active form of estrogen, estradiol, to the much less active form, estriol.

Estriol, the Forgotten Estrogen. Dr. Alvin H. Follingstad, reported in his article in the *Journal of the American Medical Association*, "Estriol, the Forgotten Estrogen," that estriol should be given to women who need estrogen therapy but who are at high risk for developing cancer. The role of estriol in post-menopausal hormone replacement therapy should, therefore, be given a closer look.

Jonathan V. Wright, M.D., of Kent, Washington, is a leading authority in nutritional medicine. I receive his informative newsletter, "Health and Healing", co-authored with Dr. Alan Gaby. Dr. Wright began working with estriol in the early 1980s, as an alternative to the conventional estrogen medications. He developed an estrogen formula designed to maximize the benefits of estrogen, while minimizing the risks. Some women he treated did not have complete remission of menopausal symptoms with just estriol, so the dose was increased. A few women did not tolerate the very large doses. He found that the appropriate proportions for a combination pill would be 80% estriol, 10% estrone, and 10% estradiol. Dr Wright named the formula *tri-estrogen* (or *three-estrogens*). He found that 2.5 mg dose of tri-estrogen is usually effective for relieving menopausal symptoms such as hot flashes and vaginal atrophy. Dr. Wright generally administers tri-estrogen in a cyclical fashion, 25 days per month, adding natural progesterone for 12 days at the end of the cycle. He hardly ever encounters withdrawal bleeding, although it does sometimes occur if large doses are given.

Progesterone Relieves Symptoms

Progesterone is a hormone that in many cases can safely and effectively relieve menopausal symptoms, protect against cancer, act as a natural tranquilizer, prevent osteoporosis and may even stimu late new bone formation. Sounds like something every menopausal woman should be taking. However, there seems to be confusion as to what progesterone really is. Progesterone was first crystallized in 1934, and today is available from plant sources. Natural micronized progesterone is an exact chemical duplicate of progesterone that is normally produced by the ovaries. Synthetic progesterone, called *progestin* (such as Provera), mimics the action of the progesterone, but the body does not respond in the same way. Studies have shown that synthetic progestin actually reduces the level of progesterone in the blood stream.[65]

Women who take synthetic progestin sometimes complain of bloating, headaches, moodiness, or other side effects. *The Physician's Desk Reference,* (PDR) 1995, lists columns of con-traindications, and some of the side effects are toxic. Women taking *natural* progesterone experience a mild tranquilizing effect and an enhanced feeling of well-being.

There are many ways progesterone is used in our bodies. Progesterone is produced in huge amounts by the placenta during pregnancy. If a woman doesn't produce enough progesterone she will have a miscarriage. Progesterone is given to women who have trouble carrying their pregnancy to term. I think it is interesting the French so-called abortion pill, RU-486, works by blocking the action of progesterone, resulting in spontaneous abortion of the preg-nancy.[66]

My physician friend, Frank Varese, M.D., encouraged me to attend a presentation by Ray Peat, Ph.D., from Oregon, who was lecturing on the subject of natural progesterone, its many roles in human health, and how the medical profession has ignored this important hormone. I was able to discuss this subject with Dr. Peat, and was impressed enough with his research that I am personally using the natural progesterone. He has ingeniously pre-mixed his progesterone in vitamin E oil for better assimilation.

Are there Side Effects with Natural Progesterone?
Natural progesterone is almost entirely free of side effects. The only disadvantage is that it is short-acting. Because it is short acting the oral route of progesterone administration has long been considered impractical because of poor absorption. Contrary to these teachings,

recent reports confirm that significant serum progesterone levels can be achieved by micronization and dissolution in oils consisting of long-chain fatty acids.[67] Consequently, progesterone is usually administered by rectal or vaginal suppository, or by transdermal cream. Some use chewable tablets, while one lab mixes the powder with oil for slower assimilation.

Natural Progesterone Cream. I appeared on "The Doctor's Night" on Trinity Broadcasting Network with several doctors, including Julian Whitaker, M.D., who discussed natural progesterone cream. He stated that if you have hot flashes, take a little of this cream and rub it on your skin. The hostess, Jan Crouch, started to giggle and said, "Where do you rub it?" We all laughed. He told how you can apply it to your stomach, arms, or other areas of your body. Dr. Whitaker explained it is absorbed transdermally into the fatty layer under the skin. With continued use, the natural progesterone is distributed throughout the body via the blood stream. The full benefits may not become apparent until after several weeks or even several cycles, if using it for PMS, or several months if using it for menopause. This time frame depends on the difference in body fat content and the relative progesterone deficiency status.

It is reported that skin areas to which progesterone cream has been applied become less dry and more youthful in texture. Skin aging may be prevented more effectively with progesterone than with estrogen creams.

William Regelson, M. D., feels that if you are taking estrogen, progesterone cream may not be strong enough to prevent the buildup of excessive uterine tissue and protect against cancer. If you are on estrogen, or if you are a "candidate" for it, discuss with your physician the use of natural progesterone from a "compounding" pharmacy.

Progesterone Contributions. What really caught my attention was when John R. Lee, M.D., sent me a list of benefits of natural progesterone. His article states, "as women approach menopause, they find themselves losing energy, retaining fluids, fighting fat, developing wrinkles and facial hairs, prone to headaches and depression, and less interested in sex. Common wisdom assigns these symptoms to simply aging."

He went on to say, "They see their doctors, take their diuretics and, occasionally, thyroid medication, and face their future with fading enthusiasm. They seek out cosmeticians for their wrinkles, see their beauticians more often for their thinning hair, and take more calcium for their thinning bones. What they are unaware of is the importance of proper hormonal balance, particularly the lack of this singularly important hormone, progesterone."[68]

Dr. Peat feels you can use natural progesterone instead of estrogen, because it is also a valuable bone builder.

Estrogen Conversion in a Healthy Liver

Dr. Carlton Fredericks reports, "regardless of the sources of the female hormone, your liver must cope with it, converting it into less active compounds, terminating in *estriol*. On the success of that conversion, your well-being, your life itself, may depend. And for that conversion, your liver requires the help of an excellent diet." It is possible to pinpoint nutritional factors critical to support this liver function. They are the vitamin B-complex, a group of vitamins that occur together in foods. Nutritional yeast (Brewer's yeast) is the greatest natural source of these B-vitamins and also protein. The degradation of estrogen was demonstrably not efficient with a diet low in B-vitamins and highly effective in the presence of an adequate supply of these nutrients. Protein also proved to be a critical nutrient to support this liver function, for the vitamins were ineffective if the diet contained too little of such foods as meat, fish, fowl, eggs, or dairy products.[69]

Fredericks continues, "It was found that 'well fed' women with estrogen dependent disorders, ranging from premenstrual tension and prolonged menstruation to excessive hemorrhaging and cystic mastitis, lost their symptoms when more generously supplied with the vitamin B-complex and protein." He also explained that an important group of nutritional compounds called the *lipotropic factors*, are choline, inositol, and the amino acid, methionine. An antioxidant formula with extra vitamin E and C, should be an important part of the daily program, along with evening primrose oil (GLA) a valuable source of prostaglandin E1.

Lipotropic Factors—Choline and Inositol. Two known vitamins, related to the B-complex, are directly involved in supporting liver degradation of estrogen. They are *choline* and *inositol*, but because the quantity required for both, and because of space limitations (the size of the tablet) in most B-complex tablets, little is added. Choline and inositol are needed in sufficient amounts to be effective as factors involved in fat metabolism, and estrogens are fat-soluble hormones; and both factors have long been known to have important beneficial effects on the liver.

That doesn't mean that the other B vitamins don't play a part in the control of estrogen, but choline and inositol are key factors. They may be purchased separately in your nutrition store under various names: *Choline-Inositol, Lipotropic Fat Metabolizers* or *Fat Burners*. Look for higher potency forms of choline and inositol with methionine and other nutrients.

For more important information: Betty Kamen, Ph.D., a long time friend from our industry has written a book, *Hormone Replacement Therapy, YES or NO?* She goes into great detail on the value of using natural progesterone.[70]

Another fine book on the subject is by John R. Lee M.D., *What Your Doctor May Not Tell You About Menopause.* I think it is interesting that Dr. Lee heard a similar presentation given by Dr. Peat, Ph.D., and this is what inspired his interest in natural progesterone. After thirty years, Dr. Lee is retired from private practice and now teaches professionals and lay audiences about the importance of hormone balance, using natural progesterone.

You must make the final decision, but at least make it from an educated position. Read more about women's special needs in Chapter 13.

Chelation Therapy for Blocked Arteries

Some on the forefront of nutrition research believe strongly in chelation therapy, and have solid evidence, research results, and statistics to back up their beliefs. Chelation therapy (key-lay-shun) is a procedure that costs about one-tenth what bypass surgery costs, has minimal risk factors associated with it, and causes very little, if any, pain. It has a growing reputation as a "treatment of preference" for blocked arteries.

Chelation therapy is aimed at stripping lead, aluminum, mercury, cadmium, and unwanted calcium deposits from the arteries and other parts of the body in a way that allows these materials to be excreted through the kidneys. To accomplish this, physicians administer an amino acid solution called ethylenediaminetetraacetic acid (EDTA) through an intravenous drip into the bloodstream, for about 3 hours, 2 to 3 days a week. The number of treatments would be suggested by the physician, but usually 20 to 30 treatments are administered.

Originated for Lead Poisoning. The therapy originated in Detroit, Michigan, in 1948 as a means of treating victims of lead poisoning. Physicians found that after the treatments, their patients showed marked improvement in their arteriosclerosis. Further experimentation resulted in the treatment we know today.

The word "chelate" comes from the Greek *chele*, which refers to the claw of a crab or lobster, implying a firm, pincer-like hold. EDTA floats past a hardened area in a blood vessel, and its strong attraction for calcium and lead causes it literally "to pick up" the offending mineral and pull it out of the area.

The treatment is given by member physicians of the American Academy of Medical Preventics (AAMP) in medical centers across the nation. Approximately six million infusions have been administered in the United States solely for the purpose of reversing degenerative diseases associated with hardening of the arteries. In the past twelve years of record keeping, not one death has occurred due specifically to chelation therapy when it has been administered by physicians who followed the standard protocol established by the American College of Advancement in Medicine.[71]

To find a physician who is trained and competent in chelation therapy, contact the American College of Advancement in Medicine (ACAM), 23121 Verdugo Drive, Suite 204, Laguna Hills, CA, or phone (714) 583-7666 or (800) 532-3688. ACAM lists more than 2,000 doctors across the nation who administer chelation therapy.

Medical Literature and Clinical Studies. The medical literature contains some 10,000 articles about chelation, of which 1,800 were clinical studies. All but one of these many studies describe favorable results![72]

H. Richard Casdorph, M.D., Ph.D., Diplomat of the American

Board of Internal Medicine, has been at the forefront of chelation therapy and uses it daily in his practice in Long Beach, CA. I discussed chelation with him and he told me that clinical studies on chelation have documented directly the effectiveness of this therapy in treating sclerotic heart valves, coronary heart disease, atherosclerosis, intermittent claudication (leg pains due to lack of circulation), gangrene, angina pectoris, heart attacks, stroke, senility, and even Alzheimer's disease. Studies have shown that the basis of most of these problems is poor circulation caused by hardening of the arteries.[73]

"Chelation Therapy: One of Medicine's Best Kept Secrets." In this article by Gary Null, it was reported that chelation has also been shown to help multiple sclerosis, arthritis, macular degeneration (a disease that causes blindness), hypertension, diabetes, and adverse reactions to environmental pollutants.[74]

Chelation has restored victims of severe angina to health, with complete freedom from pain and vastly improved tolerance for exercise. Many reported an improvement in intellectual function as chelation therapy improved the circulation to their brains.

The American Medical Association has not endorsed chelation therapy completely, ruling it is not useful because the effects are not lasting. The pharmaceutical and health insurance industries also stand in opposition to the therapy. Yet, the Food and Drug Administration has approved EDTA for use in chelating lead and digitalis intoxication.

We should perhaps keep in mind that not all bypass surgery and angioplasty patients experience lasting effects unless they make significant lifestyle adjustments, including the addition of exercise and very often, a change in dietary patterns.

Magnesium—a Key Mineral. Dr. Casdorph pointed out that magnesium is one of the key ingredients in the chelation formula, and it is added to every IV of EDTA solution. After the magnesium enters the bloodstream, it breaks away from the EDTA and serves to dilate arteries and relax smooth muscles so that the EDTA is more effective in its work of binding calcium, aluminum and other abnormal metals that should not be in the bloodstream, and then carrying them out of the body by way of the urine.

Also Used for Prevention. My mother was a great advocate of chelation therapy. She had the treatment several times as a preventive measure to keep her arteries clear.

The benefit of chelation is that it provides an alternative means of treating blocked arteries in a preventive way, prior to emergency situations for which bypass surgery may be the only solution.

A Cardiovascular Surgeons View. Ralph Lev, M.D., M.S., who is a clinical associate professor of surgery at New Jersey Medical School, has said, "As a practicing cardiovascular surgeon, I and many of my associates have patients who are not surgical candidates. These patients are then often relegated to a life of continued disability and pain. A member of my family fell into this group and was told to 'go to a nursing home and die.' He was instead treated with EDTA chelation therapy and is alive and comfortable three years later. I often observe similar benefits for patients in my own practice who have had chelation therapy. Those of us in academic medicine and surgery should put aside our blinders, open our minds, and delve further into any promise of improvement for those unfortunates who have no other hope." [75] Dr. Lev is also a vascular surgeon and chief of cardiothoracic surgery at John F. Kennedy Medical Center.

Repair Clogged Plumbing. You can repair clogged plumbing, but for truly lasting results, you need to correct the problems that created the clogged plumbing in the first place. Those who administer chelation therapy recommend to their patients certain lifestyle changes: cessation of smoking, intelligent choices of food, and proper use of vitamins and minerals. They frequently recommend an increased use of antioxidants, plus minerals, lecithin, garlic, rutin, and even kelp to help the thyroid.

More information is available in several good books: *The Chelation Way* by Dr. Morton Walker; *Toxic Metal Syndrome* by Dr. Morton Walker and Richard Casdorph, M.D.; *Bypassing Bypass, New Techniques of Chelation Therapy* by Elmer M. Cranton, M.D.

Cell Therapy Uses "Like to Treat Like"

Cell therapy has been used with growing acceptance throughout the world in recent decades. It currently is not legal in the United States, but it is available in Switzerland and most other European nations, the Bahamas, and other nations around the world.

This type of therapy is actually quite old. Skin transplants from animals to humans were mentioned by Hippocrates, and physicians have long held the opinion that incorporating human or animal organs from a young and vital body may have a therapeutic effect.

We have had the pleasure of knowing Joachim Stein, M.D., from Heidelberg, Germany, who points out that both Aristotle and one of the oldest known medical documents, the Papyrus of Ebers, mention a number of preparations made from animal or human organs. In the sixteenth century, Paraclesus offered this prescription: "Heart heals heart, kidney heals kidney." [76]

The Swiss Surgeon, Dr. Paul Niehans, is credited with having developed cell therapy as we know it today after saving a dying woman whose parathyroid glands had been damaged during thyroid surgery. He saved her life with an injection of a suspension of animal parathyroid glands.

As his research progressed, he discovered that the cells from embryonic sheep tissues, injected into the muscles of an older or exhausted person, had a rejuvenating effect. He also observed that injections of animal cells from specific embryonic organs could improve the same organ in a human being. Thus, heart diseases were treated with heart cells, liver problems with liver cells, and so forth, just as Paraclesus had suggested. [77]

Animal Embryonic Cells Not Rejected. Dr. Niehans further found that the adult human body did not reject these embryonic animal cells. Cell therapy promotes physical regeneration and is used to stimulate healing, counteract the effects of aging, and treat a variety of degenerative diseases. Cells do not actually travel whole, but are broken down to their molecular levels and incorporated in similar structures.

According to Tom Smith, M.C., Ph.D., H.M.D., D.Hom., "The main benefit of cell therapy is an overall stimulation of the body and its processes." Dr. Smith views cell therapy as an adjunct to other forms of therapy and believes it gives the body a basic support system that allows other therapeutic measures to work more successfully.

Whole Cells—to Cell Components. At his International Clinic for Biological Regeneration, which has branches in England

and the Bahamas, Dr. Smith uses injections of disease-free omnigenic (whole embryo) ultrafiltrate. He told me the process of ultrafiltration is the fine filtering of homogenized whole cells down to cell components. Ultrafiltration removes the surface coat and its antigenic material (a protein or carbohydrate substance, such as a toxin or enzyme) in order to reduce the risk of rejection. This also eliminates the risk of allergic reaction.[78] More information about the clinics is available in the references section.[79]

Glandular Therapy is Based on a Theory Similar to Cell Therapy

Glandular therapy is being called by some as "the ultimate in nutritional research." It has caused a lot of interest among health conscious people through the years. The raw glandular supplements used are specialized nutrients intended to improve the nutritional environment of the body's own glands and organs. The underlying rationale for these supplements is that *like cells help like cells*. For example, adrenal concentrate is used to support adrenal gland function.

The sources of these oral enzymes, active, whole-food tissue concentrates are healthy young animals, mostly beef or lamb. The materials are left raw, meaning that at no time during the processing or tableting are they exposed to temperatures higher than 37° centigrade (or 98.6° Fahrenheit). Thus, their intracellular components are preserved intact.

Support For Sluggish Organs. Research studies are now starting to appear in support of glandular therapies taken orally in tablet form. Although partially destroyed during digestion, the glandular components seem to find their way to the corresponding organ in the body. For example, studies with calf thymus administered orally have demonstrated impressive clinical results in a variety of infectious conditions. Orally administered spleen extracts have been shown to increase white blood cell counts.[80] These glandulars are available in capsule, tablet or tincture at your nutrition store.

My Comment: With all the information presented in this chapter, I hope you will find some answers to your health challenges. The anti-aging therapies were reviewed on the premise that many of the consequences of aging can be altered with preventive measures or alternative medical techniques.

Chapter 12

Men's Unique

Anti-Aging Therapies for Men

"There seems to be many therapies to keep aging men with a spring in their step and a twinkle in their eye. An excellent nutritional program with all the vitamins, minerals and hormones seem to be the bottom line."
—Gladys Lindberg

T his entire book contains valuable information to help build your health. However, there are certain nutritional situations exclusive to men that may need extra attention, which are included in this chapter for your consideration.

Anti-Aging Therapies for Men

As we age, production of the hormones DHEA, testosterone, and growth hormone declines. Men especially should be interested in these hormones since they help keep energy levels high and affect muscular strength and sexual stamina.

A darling couple in their mid-70s were discussing their nutritional needs with me. She was very enthusiastic and had been taking her supplements for years, but her husband was not very interested. I finally said to him, "Now you need to be able to keep up with your wife, so you can chase her around the house!" We all laughed. Later, he came up to me and whispered, "Do you have something to take in case I catch her?"

Testosterone—The Male Sex Hormone

Scientists of ancient days have known that the removal of the testicles would take away the vitality and aggression of men and beasts. Historically, castration (removal of testes) was performed on male slaves who guarded Moslem harems. It was also used on some male singers during boyhood to preserve a high-pitched voice.[1]

The testicles are male gonads, or sex glands, that produce sperm and secrete *androgens*. The production of androgens by the testes is controlled by certain pituitary hormones, called *gonadotropins*. The most important and active of the *androgen* hormones is *testosterone*, the male sex hormone. Testosterone is produced chiefly in the testes, but also in small amounts in the adrenal glands and in the ovaries of women. It stimulates bone and muscle growth and is responsible for the development of male secondary sex characteristics at puberty, including enlargement of the penis and the growth of facial and body hair.[2]

Testosterone is the hormone that makes men "feel in their prime." If testosterone is restored to youthful levels, you will feel as you did when you were at your peak of physical and mental strength. You'll feel sexier, stronger, and healthier. In a real sense, testosterone is the ultimate aphrodisiac. Testosterone is responsible for the sex drive in both men and women, and it is the hormone that stimulates our desire for sexual activity and orgasm.

Testosterone is one of the most neglected hormonal difficulties in all of medicine, according to Herbert L. Newbold, M.D., in *Mega-Nutrients for Your Nerves*. Dr. Newbold taught neurology and psychiatry at Northwestern University Medical School and authored a textbook on psychology (which is used in medical schools around the world). He now considers himself a nutritional psychiatrist, who recognizes that the results of vitamin, mineral, hormonal, and other deficiencies are generally not taught in medical schools.[3]

Dr. Newbold routinely tests serum testosterone levels of all his male patients, and he finds that a large number (20 to 30 percent) suffer from a deficiency. The lack of testosterone could be the result of emotional illnesses, testicle damage, male menopause (where they experience a gradual decline of hormonal output), or excessive alcohol or marijuana consumption. He recognized early on in his research that his patients with low testosterone levels had grossly deficient diets. Dr. Newbold said, "Recently it has also been discovered that male homosexuals, as a group, have significantly lower serum testosterone levels than heterosexual males, which must be a blow to those who contend that male homosexuality is a purely psychological disorder."[4]

Male Menopause—Importance of Testosterone. Men who are experiencing "male menopause," known as *andropause,* are now interested in testosterone and what it can do for them. Andropause does not happen as quickly in men as menopause does in women. While andropause and menopause share similarities, the rate of the fall of total plasma testosterone is much slower than the rather rapid drop in estrogen levels associated with menopause.

Edmund Chein, M.D., J.D., of the Life Extension Institute in Palm Springs, reports the testosterone drop in men is about 1.5 percent per year. While the total testosterone of a male does not drop drastically, the free testosterone, which is the biological active part of testosterone, does drop precipitously with aging. In fact, a significant drop in free testosterone can occur as early as the forties, causing impotency or libido problems.

Dr. Chein said, "Impotence is an alarming signal. All the other organs degenerate in tandem with the degeneration of the male testes. Once a man becomes impotent, he loses his drive for life, has impaired erections, his muscles become thinner, and mental acuity fades. He frequently becomes depressed and has aches, pains and stiffness, as well as decreased mobility. In some cases, there is excessive perspiration similar to menopause in women."[5]

Low testosterone can also predict susceptibility to abdominal weight gain, a pattern of obesity that is associated with heart disease, diabetes and hypertension. Testosterone, like estrogen, is a hedge against osteoporosis. It also seems to be associated with better sleep quality, and its deficiency in senior men may account for the familiar sleeplessness of older age.

Testosterone occurs naturally in adult women at a level around one-tenth of that found in men. Women's adrenals pump out other androgenic hormones like DHEA and androstenedrone, also considered longevity hormones.[6]

The Value of High Testosterone. Studies show that men with high testosterone levels live longer, healthier lives and maintain sexual potency. Testosterone goes far beyond just promoting aggression, body and facial hair, and male pattern baldness. Testosterone is anabolic, meaning that it promotes muscle growth. Loss of lean body mass is a major feature of aging in both men and women. Testosterone offsets this loss.[7,8]

The most significant study about the correlation between high levels of testosterone and reduced risks of cardiovascular disease was reported in May, 1994, when the Department of Medicine at Columbia University found that low levels of free testosterone are a risk factor and correlate directly with degree of coronary artery disease in men.

Dr. Gerald Phillips of Columbia University Medical School states, "A low testosterone level may lead to atherosclerosis, and that testosterone may protect against atherosclerosis in men through an effect in lipoprotein—HDL. Administration of testosterone to men has been reported to decrease risk factors for heart attack. Low testosterone is also correlated with hypertension, obesity and increased waist-to-hip ratio."[9]

Testosterone Can be Increased or Inhibited by Lifestyle. There are certain factors that can promote or inhibit testosterone levels. A low fat diet limits testosterone production, since the cholesterol molecule is the building block for male sex hormones. Additionally, vigorous exercise promotes testosterone, but over-training may diminish it.[10] Sexual activity also boosts testosterone, but severe stress or depression may lower it. Many older men can still sire children but sperm production may be reduced.

The History of Testosterone. Dr. Edmund Chein goes through a brief history of the research studies that show the tremendous variety of benefits of the hormone testosterone:

- In 1934 scientists isolated testosterone molecule and illustrated the structure and received the Nobel Prize in 1935.
- In 1938 the beneficial effect of testosterone on impaired glucose tolerance was discovered.
- In 1939 scientists found it can improve intermittent claudication and angina pectoris and confirmed that it can cure gangrene.
- In 1945 another scientist showed it was able to stop angina pectoris.
- In 1951 it was shown that testosterone can improve nitrogen balance and increase lean muscle mass.
- In 1960 another scientist discovered it can lower cholesterol.
- In 1962 scientists normalized the abnormal electro-cardiograms of 2,000 cardiac patients with synthetic testosterone.

- In 1963 a study showed it can improve diabetic retinopathy.
- In 1964 scientists showed testosterone can lower the insulin requirements of diabetic patients and decrease the percentage of body fat.
- In May 1994 the Department of Medicine at Columbia University reported that low levels of free testosterone are a risk factor and correlate directly with the degree of coronary artery disease in men.[11]

There are several forms of natural testosterone and growth-hormone that may be administered by a physician who is an expert in hormone replacement therapy. I suggest that your physician test your blood for levels of testosterone and growth hormone. The test should determine the level of free or unbound testosterone because this is the form of testosterone actually available for use in the body. Testosterone and growth hormone are available only by prescription.

Dr. Chein reports, "Synthetic testosterone taken orally or by injection, for the most part, causes liver toxicity (hepatotoxicity) and its use is not recommended."

Many physicians now prefer to use the pure natural testosterone rather than synthetic testosterone. Natural testosterone can be delivered transdermally either in a gel form or by a patch applied to the skin, which is released gradually into the body.

Dr. Chein, who uses only natural testosterone, states, "My goal is to maintain a total testosterone level at the ideal of about 900–1,200 ug/ml (the normal range is somewhere between 250 and 1,200). The free testosterone is the biological active part, and should be maintained at a level of about 30–40 ug/ml throughout one's lifetime.[12]

A Fifth Avenue Dermatologist, Dr. Norman Orentreich, is respected nationally for his biological and endocrinological knowledge. He invented hair transplants and formulated the therapeutic products within the Clinique line of cosmetics. Now aged 73, he has been interested in aging research since he was 13. Having thought about aging for more than half a century, he is a strong advocate of hormone replacement therapy—for both men and women. He had done studies on DHEA for the National Institute On Aging, and takes it himself. "When you get to be 25, you reach your peak. Everything drops by about one percent a year. Fifty years later—by the time you're 75—you're half of what you were before" he says. "I've been taking topical (in a gel) testosterone myself for 15 years," he says. "I was almost 60. My morning erections were down. Libido was down. My beard was getting soft. My waist developed a girdle of fat. I was feeling tired and down. When I measured my blood, my androgen levels were down around 300," he concludes. All classic symptoms of male menopause. He said, "Today, I have a vigorous beard, my sexual appetite and competency is back to where it was when I was around 40. And testosterone is an antidepressant beyond words."[13]

Remember DHEA is Converted into Testosterone.
Dr. Regelson believes that for many midlife men, whose testosterone levels are normal for their age, testosterone is not necessary if they are already taking DHEA. This is because DHEA is converted into a small amount of testosterone in the body, and this, Regelson believes, will provide enough of a testosterone boost to counteract the decline. He also believes that because DHEA is what we call a testosterone precursor, it may at least postpone the need for testosterone. Thus a man in his forties or fifties may do well on DHEA alone until he reaches his sixties or seventies, at which point he may require testosterone.[14]

Human Growth Hormone Therapy

The conservative *New England Journal of Medicine* published a landmark article, "Effects of Human Growth Hormone in Men over 60 Years Old," headed by Daniel Rudman, M.D., and his colleagues at the Medical College of Wisconsin.[15] In their study, they selected 21 healthy men aged 61 to 81, and injected twelve of them with the human growth hormone, three times a week for six months. The rest of the men were untreated and served as a control.

The amazing results of the men on the growth hormone was 8.8 percent increase in lean body mass, a nearly 15 percent decrease in fat tissue, a 7 percent increase in skin thickness, and a 1.6 percent increase in lower spine bone density.

Based on his study Dr. Rudman wrote: "The effects of six months of human growth hormone on lean body mass and adipose tissue mass were equivalent in magnitude to the changes incurred during 10 to 20 years of aging." In the study, the men's sense of well being and ability to care for themselves was markedly enhanced, along with a return of sexual interest and performance.[16]

Thanks to Dr. Rudman, many serious scientists and physicians all over the world began to think about aging in a different way, to look at the possibility of growth hormone replacement in the treatment of aging and age associated diseases—a condition that could be treated and even reversed. Since his report, more than 28,000 studies have appeared in other journals in England, Denmark, Sweden, the U.S. and other parts of the world describing the benefits of the growth hormones.

Dr. Ronald Klatz in his book *Grow Young with HGH,* gives glowing reports on the benefits of the growth hormones. In fact, he says it is the only age reversing drug that has passed placebo-controlled, double-blind clinical trials with flying colors, not once, but many times over.[17]

The National Institute On Aging has funded a multi-million dollar effort in nine medical centers to determine if growth hormone and other factors can be useful in helping the elderly remain strong and vigorous. The studies are still in progress.

Dr. Regelson says, "I have studied growth hormone extensively through the years and believe there is a place for growth hormone in the superhormone pantheon of age-reversing agents." He also said, "Growth hormone has a very special role to play, and its benefits will be most acutely felt by those who are in greatest need and who are suffering from more severe problems. For these people I think the risk of side effects is minimal compared to what they stand to gain."[18] This doctor believes it is possible to gain the same beneficial effects using the other superhormones, particularly DHEA, melatonin, estrogen and testosterone, which are inexpensive, easily available, and have no unwanted side effects.

"Growing weak, growing frail, and getting sick is not an inevitable part of the aging process, and by restoring our superhormones to their youthful levels, we should be able to prevent the diseases of aging," according to Regelson. He also reported, "There are special circumstances when we need to restore a failing organ or stave off a serious illness. Growth hormone can revive a dying heart, stave off kidney failure, and reverse severe osteoporosis. It is strong medicine indeed and not, in my opinion, something for standard use."[19]

As you can see, there are differing opinions on the value and long term safety of the growth hormone replacement therapy. Supporters say the growth hormone therapy can be safe with proper doses and proper methods of administration. They say we don't have 20 years to wait for all the research to be completed. Its effects on health and well-being are so remarkable, and its age-reversing properties are so great, they say it is well worth the $9,000 to $12,000 a year it costs at this time.[20] I am sure this price will drop as use is more widespread.

According to Dr. Chein of the Palm Spring Life Extension Institute, the results with growth hormone have been nothing short of amazing. It is the only hormone that can reverse all the parameters of aging.[21] Dr. Chein has prescribed the growth hormone for over a thousand patients, many of whom are physicians. He uses a small dose of only 1/2 cc from an insulin syringe, twice a day. The original researcher, Dr. Rudman, realized the dosage he used was too large. He found the optimum hormone dose was one quarter to one half as great as was previously believed. He felt all the beneficial effects should be maintained without any adverse side effects.[22]

In a 1994 review paper on the use of human growth hormone in hormone deficient adults, Drs.Rowen, Hohannson, and Bengtson of the University of Hospital of Goteborg, Sweden, had this to say: "When one does not abuse or overdose human growth hormone, there is simply NO evidence suggesting that human growth hormone replacement therapy causes any long term side effects."[23]

Dr. George Merriam of the University of Washington in Seattle, who is conducting one of the National Institute On Aging studies on growth hormone was quoted in the *New York Times*, July 18, 1995 as saying that the preliminary findings of his team includes "a complete absence of side effects."

Help for Impotence

It has been estimated that 10 to 20 million American men suffer from impotence. It is thought to affect 25 percent of men over the age of 50, but aging itself is not a cause of erectile dysfunction or impotence. Impotence is considered difficulty achieving or maintaining an erection. Doctors classify impotence as either organic (caused by physical factors) or as psychogenic (caused by psychological problems). In reality, many cases of impotence are a combination of both physical and emotional. Only recently have scientists uncovered the biochemistry that links many organic forms of impotence. This biochemical pathway seems to have a dietary component. This is not to say that a change in diet can cure impotence, but there is a suggestion that diet and nutritional supplements may play an important role.

From a large-scale study of male sexual behavior called *The Massachusetts Male Aging Study* of 1984–89, researchers looked at a cross-sectional random sample of 1,709 men between the ages of 40 and 70 years. Dr. Irwin Goldstein, an organizer of the study, points out that, "Organic factors contribute to impotence in up to 80 percent of men affected." Dr. Goldstein said, "diabetes, hypertension (medications used), smoking, chronic alcohol use and high cholesterol are major factors in male potency loss."

Many Drugs Can, in Some Cases, Lead to Erectile Dysfunction, including agents used to combat mental depression and high blood pressure. Among the most common drugs associated with impotence are steroids, some appetite suppressants, opiates, some cholesterol lowering drugs, some antihistamines, acid blockers like Tagamet®, antidepressants, tranquilizers and even antifungal agents. Smoking, marijuana and heroin are also associated with impotence.[24]

If you suspect a drug is responsible for your impotence, discuss it with your doctor and see if he can find an effective alternative for you.

The Value of DHEA for Male Impotency. The effects of DHEA on male sexual function was documented in the same groundbreaking Massachusetts Male Aging Study. This study demonstrated that the risk of severe or total impotency increases threefold with age. In other words, 5.1 percent of all forty-year olds compared to 15 percent of all seventy-year-olds complained of complete impotency. The researchers noted that impotency is often associated with underlying medical problems as we have just discussed. But, of the seventeen hormones measured in each of the men, only one showed a direct and consistent correlation with impotency: DHEA. As DHEA levels declined, the incidence of impotency increased. The Massachusetts researchers could not explain why DHEA levels were lower in impotent men. They speculated on many theories.

Dr. Regelson believes that DHEA has a direct effect on sexuality, saying, "We know that DHEA is converted into testosterone in both men and women, and that testosterone is known to enhance libido in both sexes. This would certainly explain why such men when they take DHEA experience a heightened libido."[25]

Testosterone and Impotence. A common symptom of low testosterone is a lack of sexual desire, and many men who experience this loss of desire assume that they are impotent. Dr. Regelson, author of *The Superhormone Promise*, says the fact that a man is low in testosterone does not mean that he is physically unable to maintain an erection and enjoy sex. The problem is that a man low in testosterone may simply not care enough to pursue it. He may feel impotent even though he is technically not.

Dr. Regelson went on to say, "Happily, restoring testosterone to youthful levels can turn this situation around, practically overnight. Once testosterone levels are replenished, a man will find that he has recaptured a healthy interest in sex —as well as the capacity to enjoy it."[26]

"Do You Have Something if I Catch Her?"

Optimal nutrition clearly plays a role in determining sexual stamina or impotence. For sex to work, things have to be right biochemically. We need to go back to the basics; first of all, what are you eating? What did you have for breakfast? It is important you have adequate protein in your daily routine as your muscles are made of protein. You need all the vitamins and minerals, in adequate potencies. Make sure you read the "Lindberg Program" in the last chapter, and note the suggestions. Extra vitamins E and C, plus the essential fatty acids and the mineral zinc are all essential for sexual function. Also include the single amino acids: histidine, tyrosine, arginine. There is "no magic bullet," but the following suggestions may be considered as an addition to your complete nutritional program.

The Single Amino Acids for Impotence and Increasing Sperm

It is possible to banish impotence, cure frigidity, and even stimulate fertility, providing real hope of conception, according to Robert Erdmann, Ph.D., in *Amino Revolution.*

Histidine. Dr. Erdmann reports that histidine needs to be present in good quantity for orgasm to take place. This amino acid is the parent of the active molecule histamine. Orgasm is triggered when histamine is released in the body from the mast cells in the genitals. These cells function as part of the immune system, but they also cause the sexual flush experienced during arousal. When there is insufficient histidine in the body, and histamine production is low, both men and women may find it difficult, sometimes even impossible, to achieve orgasm.[27]

Men and women take note, Dr. Carl Pfeiffer M.D., Ph.D., a medical researcher, examined the benefit of histidine for women and found that those women with low histamine levels were not able to experience orgasm. When they took extra histidine, they were able to experience orgasm for the first time. Without any psychotherapy, the women who had been given histidine broke the bonds of frigidity, achieving an enormous sense of liberation. They were given 500 mg of histidine before each meal. From Dr. Pfeiffer's research, Dr. Erdmann suggested a balanced nutritional program and a multiple vitamin and mineral formula which also includes: lysine and arginine with cofactors, vitamin B3 (niacin), vitamin B6 (pyridoxine) and manganese.[28]

Dr. Pfeiffer also examined the benefit of histidine for men, discovering what a two-edged sword it is. Male orgasm is a localized reflex caused by the release of histamine from a large concentration of mast cells in the head of the penis. As expected, the circulating levels of histidine played a significant role, both in the ability of a man to climax, and the time it takes him. The higher the levels, the shorted the time needed—so much so that for a few this led to another problem—premature ejaculation, according to Erdmann.

Dr. Erdmann reported how Pfeiffer's studies were then extended to those men suffering from premature ejaculation. He discovered that their high histamine levels could be lowered by methionine (an amino acid), taken with a little calcium as a cofactor. These men are now able to lead more satisfying sex lives.[29]

Tyrosine. Dr. Richard Passwater said that studies have shown that penile erection is achieved via a complicated pathway involving neurons. A deficiency in the nerve chemical messenger would prevent erection. Animal experiments confirmed that agents that would block or deplete the neurotransmitter (a chemical that affects or modifies the transmission of an impulse across a synapse between nerves or between a nerve and a muscle) did indeed cause impotence. If this is the case, then it is very likely—but to Passwater's knowledge untested—that the dietary amino acid tyrosine can circulate in the bloodstream to nourish the penile neurons so as to normalize norepinephrine (a hormone secreted by the adrenal medulla and a neurotransmitter released at nerve endings) production and restore penile erectile function. It is certainly worth a try and is a sensible alternative to the alternative, according to Dr. Passwater.[30]

Arginine and Sperm Production. The importance of the single amino acid arginine for normal sperm production in the human male is well established. There is a relationship between low sperm count and diets deficient in arginine. Human semen is particularly rich in arginine. Studies of men with low sperm counts in which they were given arginine supplements met with mixed results, more having shown benefit than not. In one study, 80 percent of the men had moderate to marked increases in sperm count and motility when given 4 grams of oral arginine daily—and with clear results. When the study was published, twenty-eight pregnancies were confirmed! Do not take arginine if you have kidney or liver disorders, unless you receive permission of your physician.[31]

These single amino acids may be purchased from your nutrition store, and they are also included in many combination amino acids products in lower potency. Remember, the richest source of all the amino acids are protein foods.

Vitamin C and Increased Sperm Count. Dr. Earl Dawson at the University of Texas Medical Branch in Galveston treated 35 men working in the petroleum industry who were found to have defective sperm—sperm unable to fertilize the female egg cells. After testing the men for vitamin C, the scientists found they were all very deficient in this nutrient. When they were given 1,000 milligrams of the vitamin every day, the condition was corrected and normal sperm appeared, after only one week of vitamin therapy.[32]

Herbal Medicine to the Rescue

Yohimbe—an Aphrodisiac? Twenty years ago a Danish fertility specialist gave his livestock yohimbe (*Corynanthe yohimbe*) and found it to be an instant aphrodisiac. The sexually sluggish bulls and stallions became more active and were able to perform their usual duties. Studies were done on laboratory rats with the same results.[33]

Yohimbine (the drug) comes from the bark of a tropical Yohimbe tree, native to Africa, and is made into a drug. Yohimbine is the only Food and Drug Administration (FDA) approved drug for the treatment of erectile dysfunction. There is disagreement if this drug should be used because of its side effects.

You can find yohimbe (*Corynanthe yohimbe*) the herb (not the drug), in your nutrition store. Some feel it is a testosterone precursor and is an effective body builder. Yohimbe is a hormone stimulant and is useful as a strong athletic formula herb where increased testosterone is needed.[34] You may find yohimbe alone or in combination with other herbs for men's needs. There needs to be more research on this interesting herb, as not all agree on its use or effectiveness.

Ginkgo Biloba. Today the ancient ginkgo has sparked renewed interest throughout the world because medical researchers have isolated chemical compounds from ginkgo that show startling effects in humans, including increased sexual energy and longevity.

Because ginkgo is effective on both brain function and blood flow to extremities, including blood to the penis, this compound might be especially useful as a treatment for impotence. Sixty men with impotence who had not responded to conventional treatments received 60 mg a day for 12 to 18 months. Improvement in blood flow to the penis, documented by sonography, was evident within six to eight weeks. After six months, 50 percent of the men had regained potency. This study was done by German researchers and reported in the well respected *Journal of Urology*.[35]

Ginkgo's effects are more apparent with long-term therapy. Herbalists recommend Ginkgo biloba extract, in a dosage of 240 mg daily (divided into two or three doses). The product label should state it is standardized to contain 24 percent ginkgo flavonglycosides.[36] You can read more information on ginkgo in Chapter 6.

Korean Ginseng—Used for Thousands of Years.

Korean ginseng (*Panax ginseng*) is an adaptogenic herb, one that has been used for centuries in traditional Chinese medicine as a tonic for impotence. There are no human, double-blind, placebo-controlled studies to prove its effectiveness. Interestingly, we attended a Christmas party at one of our Korean neighbors and the host was passing around liquid Korean ginseng to all the men, with great glee! He knew it worked, and tried to convince the men this was a potent aphrodisiac. You could never have convinced him otherwise, and after thousands of years of use in their culture, they must know!

In studies with animals, sperm formation and testosterone levels increased with ginseng administration. Testes grew and increased sexual activity and mating behavior was observed.[37]

Dr. Donald Brown recommends 100 to 200 mg twice daily (standardized extract containing 4 to 7 percent ginsenosides). Use continually for three to four weeks, with a one to two week break between rounds.[38]

Damiana's Many Functions.

Those familiar with damiana typically think of it as an aphrodisiac. Damiana (*Turnera aphrodisiaca*) is native to Mexico and the southwestern United States. It has been used as a major herbal remedy in Mexican medical folklore, for the treatment of impotence, sterility, diabetes, kidney disease, bladder infections, asthma, bronchitis, chronic fatigue, and anxiety. It is one of the herbs of choice for helping with sexual impotence and infertility with both males and females. It is a relatively safe but bitter-tasting herb.[39]

Sarsaparilla (*Smilax officinalis*).

Contains a testosterone-like substance for men. As we read earlier, low testosterone may mean low sexual desire. Remember in the old western movies the tough guy would ask for sarsaparilla at the bar? Sarsaparilla bark and root aid the body in producing greater amounts of the anabolic (without oxygen) hormones, testosterone, progesterone and cortisone.[40]

Prostate Problems
and Some Suggestions

Benign prostatic hyperplasia (BPH) is a non-malignant enlargement of the prostate. It can start in men as young as forty years of age, however symptoms usually do not develop until after the age of fifty. According to U.S. estimates, the incidence of BPH in men forty to fifty-nine years of age is 50 to 60 percent, and treatment costs about $1 billion annually.[41]

BPH can cause frequent night-time urination, an unfinished sensation or dribbling. When the prostate enlarges, it pinches the urethra and blocks the flow of urine from the bladder, sometimes even causing painful urination.

The Value of Zinc to the Prostate. The prostate gland contains the highest concentration of zinc in the body. Zinc levels are significantly lower in men with cancer of the prostate than in men with normal prostates.[42]

Dr. Julian Whitaker has shown that both zinc and vitamin B6 effect *prolactin*. Prolactin levels begin to increase when a man reaches his mid-forties. When the prolactin level rises, the body is encouraged to produce more 5-alpha-reductase. That is when the testosterone production begins turning into dihydrotestosterone (DHT), and that is when zinc and vitamin B6 are most needed. Both are effective in reducing prolactin levels, with no side effects. Some researchers believe deficiencies in either zinc or B6 may be a critical factor leading to prostate enlargement.[43]

In his work at Cook County Hospital in Chicago, Dr. Irving M. Bush found that a zinc deficiency was related to prostate disorders in men. He gave nineteen male volunteers 150 mg of zinc daily for two months, followed by 50 to 100 mg a day. This regimen relieved urinary frequency, irritation, and other non-bacterial inflammatory conditions. Fourteen of the nineteen men with benign hypertrophy (enlarged prostate) experienced shrinkage of the prostate to normal size, as determined by rectal probing, X-ray, and endoscopy.[44]

In another study, researcher M. Fahim and colleagues also found that zinc supplementation reduced the size of the prostate and benign prostatic hyperplasia symptoms in the majority of volunteers.[45]

If zinc had been taken with vitamin E, selenium, flaxseed oil, and saw palmetto berry extract, would the recovery rate have been much higher?

Zinc has numerous relationships with male sexual development and function all through a male's life. Zinc deficiency in childhood leads to impaired development of the male sex organs and secondary sexual characteristics. In adulthood, zinc is vital to the testicles and for testosterone production. Even a marginal zinc deficiency can lower a man's libido.[46]

Saw Palmetto Berries—Helps Enlarged Prostate.

Saw palmetto berries (*Serenoa repens*) come from the saw palmetto palm trees that are native to the Atlantic seaboard, from South Carolina to Florida. They bear fruit that has a long folk history of use as an aphrodisiac and sexual rejuvenator.

Recent studies on the saw palmetto fruit have shown that the berries have about 15 percent saturated and unsaturated fatty acids and sterols that have been found not only to reduce prostatic swelling, but also to stimulate immune function. Clinical trials have shown repeatedly that saw palmetto extract results in a significant decrease in prostate size, improvement in urinary flow, less residual urine, and relief of other prostate symptoms.[47]

I appeared on a Trinity Broadcasting Network television program with a panel of doctors, including Dr. Julian Whitaker, and discussed prostate problems. Dr. Whitaker went into great detail about the importance of saw palmetto extract. He explained that enlarged prostates result from hormone fluctuations that convert testosterone to dihydrotestosterone (DHT). Testosterone by itself isn't the problem, testosterone produces good muscle mass, a lively libido, and a variety of other masculine characteristics. Rather, Dr. Whitaker contends, the conversion of testosterone to dihydrotestosterone causes the problem. The extract from the saw palmetto berry blocks that conversion.

Saw palmetto berry extract has had no side effects reported in any of the clinical trials. Detailed toxicology studies on the extract have been carried out on mice, rats, and dogs, and the extract has no toxic effects in these studies.

Studies of the saw palmetto extract have shown it to be effective in nearly 90 percent of patients, usually within a period of four to six weeks.[48]

Sadly, according to Dr. Whitaker, most men with prostate problems will never hear about saw palmetto berry extract. In 1990, the FDA rejected an application to have saw palmetto approved in the treatment of benign prostatic hyperplasia (BPH). Thus, even though clinical evidence is strongly in support of this natural extract for the treatment of enlarged prostate, manufacturers and distributors of the extract cannot make that claim on their product labels.

Dosage and Safety Information about Saw Palmetto.

To achieve full benefit from saw palmetto, I believe it is important for men to use an extract like the one used in clinical studies. Specifically, this is a fat-soluble saw palmetto extract standardized to contain 85–95 percent fatty acids and sterols. These extracts are available in pill form and the dosage recommended by both Andrew Weil, M.D., and Michael Murray, N.D., is 160 mg twice daily.[49]

Pygeum Has Been Used for Centuries

The powdered bark of pygeum (*Pygeum africanus*) has also been used for centuries as a treatment for urinary disorders. This herb has been proven in many studies to significantly improve troublesome prostate conditions.

In 1986 at the University of Genova, twenty patients with benign prostatic hyperplasia (BPH) received pygeum orally for two months. Within thirty days, these patients experienced a decrease in night time urination, and all the symptoms of BPH had decreased significantly within sixty days. Other human studies have confirmed the benefit of this herb with benign prostatic hyperplasia with no toxic side effects observed, even at large doses and prolonged use.

The scientist in France who isolated its active compound found the herbal preparation did in fact produce anti-inflammatory, anti-edema, and cholesterol lowering properties. Both animal and human clinical trials have shown this herb to promote the regression of symptoms associated with benign prostatic hyperplasia (BPH) with no toxic side effects observed, even at large doses and with prolonged use.[50]

The mode of function of pygeum is that it blocks the entry and breakdown of cholesterol in the prostate. This tends to encourage the production of certain prostaglandins, which exhibit an anti-inflammatory action.[51]

At this time there are many other research articles on pygeum and prostate function. You should be hearing more about the effectiveness of pygeum in the coming years.

Saw Palmetto—Pygeum Combination. Pygeum can be taken as a preventive (prophylactic), and can be used alone or in combination with saw palmetto berries.

Together they provide several synergistic mechanisms that help prevent or reverse benign prostatic hyperplasia. This combination is considered a safe and effective means of maintaining healthier prostate function into old age. Several combination products are available in your nutrition store.

Three Amino Acids
Important to the Prostate

The three amino acids of highest concentration in the prostate are *glycine, alanine,* and *glutamic acid.* Several studies have been conducted using this mixture in patients with enlarged prostates, and they experienced prompt relief. In one study involving forty-five men, researchers supplemented the diet with glutamic acid, alanine, and glycine. Ninety-five percent of the men reported that they had fewer trips to the bathroom during the night. Eighty-one percent said that the urgency to urinate had diminished, 73 percent had to urinate less often, and 70 percent reported a delayed need to urinate. These men took two, 360 mg capsules three times daily for two weeks, and thereafter, one capsule three times daily.[52]

Just how these amino acids work to help the prostate is unknown, but the effect may be related to glycine's role as an inhibitory neurotransmitter in the central nervous system. Amino acid therapy at this point is considered to be primarily palliative (providing relief but not a cure).

Other Nutritional Helps

Make sure you read Chapter 13 to help you find a balanced program. It is important that you are taking all of the antioxidants, vitamins and minerals in addition to what has just been suggested. Include the essential fatty acids, 1 to 2 tablespoons of fresh organic flax oil or 1 tablespoon of cod liver oil, and 3 to 6 evening primrose oil capsules. Panax ginseng increases testosterone levels while decreasing prostate weight.[53] Another herbal is horsetail (*Equisetum arvense*), noted for its help in reducing inflammation or benign enlargement of the prostate. It is also used with hydrangea (*Hydrangea arborescens*) which is highly effective in the treatment of inflamed or enlarged prostate glands.[54]

Raw glandular therapy (prostate tablets) have been shown in some cases to be very effective in the treatment of prostate problems.

Add soy products to the diet, as soy isoflavones are similar in structure to estrogen and testosterone.

Since the 1960s, bee pollen has also been used to help prostatitis and benign prostatic hypertrophy in Europe. Several double-blind clinical studies have shown its effectiveness, which may be related to its high content of plant flavonoids.[55]

A New Beginning

It's never too late to start a "health-improvement" program and develop a fresh, new-attitude toward life. If we hope to prevent disease and untimely aging, we must have respect for our bodies and provide it with the best nutrition possible for lasting, satisfactory performance at all times!

Chapter 13

*L*et's Put it
All Together
The Complete Lindberg Nutrition Program

"Your increased sense of well-being, your boundless energy, and the knowledge that you're practicing prevention are worth all the money in the world, a handsome reward for following a good nutritional program. Preventive medicine places most of the care of your body into your own hands."
—Gladys Lindberg

This chapter represents a comprehensive, balanced program incorporating the latest scientific and nutritional information. It has truly stood the test of time. I recommend it to you today as a program originated by my mother, Gladys Lindberg, one of the original pioneers of nutrition. It is a beginning point in developing your own personal nutritional program to stay on for the rest of your life. Remember, it's never too late to get started. **Let's make today your first day toward more vibrant health!**

Many people who come into our store bring with them a long list of health problems and symptoms. Nearly always their list includes feeling run down, irritable, and exhausted. They complain of having no energy. You probably have a list, too! After listening carefully, I often find myself using the same words I heard my mother say more times than I can count, *"I am not a doctor, and I cannot treat disease, but healthy people don't have that, so, let's make you healthy!"*

This program is designed to help you eat right—suggesting foods to eat and foods to avoid. It stresses the value of taking nutritional supplements to build sound health. It emphasizes the importance of proper digestion, assimilation, and regular elimination, and the need for sound rest at night. Exercise enhances a person's feeling of well being and it also should be a part of your health building program. There are a number of sound exercise programs you can follow. Find a moderate one and begin a regular routine of exercise.

Understanding Hypoglycemia

Many years ago, Mother began seeing individuals suffering from what was later classified as hypoglycemia. They had tried drugs, but the problem persisted. Hearing their complaints and learning of their dietary habits, she was prompted to study the problem. She reached the conclusion that there was too much sugar and devitalized, refined carbohydrates (white rice, white flour products, white sugar) in their diets.

What Causes Hypoglycemia? Of the specific illnesses related to sugar, hypoglycemia is perhaps the most common. The hypoglycemic's problem can be caused by inborn errors of metabolism (babies can be born with exhausted adrenals); may be acquired as a result of overindulgence in refined carbohydrates, alcohol, stimulants, and drugs; or may be triggered by stresses that exhaust the adrenal glands. And the physical problems have psychological manifestations.

The adrenal glands are stimulated when anything toxic enters the body. Coffee, caffeine, nicotine, alcohol, drugs and medications—all stimulate the production of adrenaline, which triggers the alarm reaction in the body. This alarm reaction stimulates the central nervous system through the thalamus and the hypothalamus to the pituitary gland, which manufactures a hormone called ACTH. The ACTH works on the outside core (adrenal cortex) of the adrenal gland to produce cortisone and about 55 other hormones.

Cortisone raises the blood sugar by pulling glycogen out of the liver, calcium out of the bones, and protein out of the muscles. In effect, you "cannibalize" yourself. When this alarm reaction becomes exhausted by years of overuse and runs out of material to make cortical hormones, then we may suffer from arthritis, asthma, and other degenerative conditions.[1]

The problem has not changed through the years. Almost everyone I see shows some evidence of one or many symptoms commonly associated with low blood sugar.

These symptoms are so multiple that Dr. Stephan Gyland, himself a victim of low blood sugar, treated 600 patients and compiled a long list of symptoms, along with the percentages of hypoglycemic's patients in which each of the symptoms occurred. Here is his list:

HYPOGLYCEMIA SYMPTOMS

Symptom	Percentage
Nervousness	.94
Irritability	.89
Exhaustion	.87
Faintness, dizziness, tremor, cold sweats, and/or weak spells	.86
Depressions	.77
Vertigo, dizziness	.73
Drowsiness	.72
Headaches	.71
Digestive disturbances	.69
Forgetfulness	.67
Insomnia	.62
Constant worrying, unprovoked anxieties	.62
Mental confusion	.57
Internal trembling	.57
Palpitation of heart and/or rapid pulse	.54
Muscle pains	.53
Numbness	.51
Indecisiveness	.50
Unsocial, asocial, or antisocial behavior	.47
Crying spells	.46
Lack of sex drive in females	.44
Allergies	.43
Lack of coordination	.43
Leg cramps	.43
Lack of concentration	.42
Blurred vision	.40
Twitching and jerking of muscles	.40
Itching and crawling sensations of the skin	.39
Gasping for breath	.37
Smothering spells	.34
Staggering	.34
Sighing and yawning	.30
Impotence in males	.29
Unconsciousness	.27
Night terrors, nightmares	.27
Rheumatoid arthritis	.24
Phobias, fears	.23
Neurodermatitis	.21
Suicidal intent	.20
Nervous breakdown	.17
Convulsions	.2 [2]

Go back through this list and put a check mark next to any symptom you may have.

Notice that nervousness, irritability, and exhaustion tend to be the most common indicators of an energy problem. It is alarming how many symptoms are primarily mental. Not only do you feel run down, but mentally you fall apart. We must always keep in mind that we cannot separate our minds from our bodies. They are part of the same chemical system!

Often individuals who suffer from low blood sugar think their problem is just "nerves" or that they have "an emotional problem" or a "psychosomatic illness." Although the hypoglycemic's problems are not psychological *in origin*, psychological problems are often part of the hypoglycemic's symptoms.

A Glucose Tolerance Test will reveal if a person's problems are due to low blood sugar. The six hour test must be administered by a physician specially trained to interpret the glucose tolerance curve. You start after an 8 hour fast, your blood is drawn and then you drink a large glass of sugar water—100 grams of glucose. For the test to be accurate, your blood should be analyzed every hour until symptoms appear. Then testing should increase to every half hour. Blood is typically drawn by the prick of a finger. I do not recommend you go through this procedure unless your symptoms are severe. I feel that if you have the symptoms, you can assume you have low blood sugar and should change your diet. However, ask your physician and follow his advice.

Right after drinking the sugar water for the test, your blood sugar immediately rises. Insulin is then secreted by your pancreas to prevent your blood sugar level from going too high. Then as the effect of the sugar wears off, your blood sugar drops. If you don't eat another meal or food within about 3 hours, then your adrenals must mimic the consumption of a meal by pulling all the same nutrients from your body. But if your adrenal function is low, they are not as effective at this task and consequently your blood sugar drops too low. This is when low blood sugar symptoms occur.[3]

Like body temperature, our blood sugar fluctuates within a "normal" range, often cited as from 80 to 120 milligrams per 100 cubic centimeters of blood. During active periods of the day your blood sugar level hovers around 140 on the same scale.

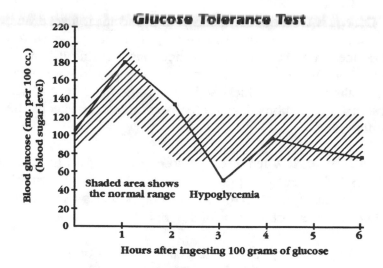

Glucose Tolerance Test

Hours after ingesting 100 grams of glucose

What Happens When Your Blood Sugar Falls

When the blood sugar falls rapidly to 60 or 70 milligrams, the symptoms are comparatively mild and may consist of slight headaches, faintness, muscular weakness, hunger, irritability, and perhaps a feeling of nervousness or tension. If it falls still lower, the symptoms become more severe, including headaches (even migraines), dizziness, fatigue, sweating, tremors, heart palpitations, marked irritability, and general nervousness. If the blood sugar continues to fall to 40 milligrams or lower, the sufferer can experience palpitations of the heart (a feeble but rapid pulse), and pallor will be more pronounced, until unconsciousness and convulsions occur.

Not only does your blood sugar level drop as your adrenals become exhausted but the amount of calcium in the blood is affected as well.

Calcium drops. When the adrenals are stimulated by stress, drugs, other stimulants and low blood sugar, they go into high gear and pull calcium out of your bones. The big muscles at the sides of your neck and head go into contractions, fluid gathers in the brain, and you may feel as if the top of your head is going to come off. You might feel shaky and tremble inside, or have "restless legs" and back aches.

Oxygen Decreases. When your blood sugar level drops, so does your supply of oxygen. You yawn (gasping for oxygen). You cannot concentrate. You doze off at meetings and find it hard to stay alert. Your blood carries oxygen to every cell in your body. Glucose is almost the only fuel used by the brain and central nervous system. The combination of glucose with oxygen keeps the brain functioning.

Salt is Lost. When blood glucose drops, salt is lost in the urine. It is salt that keeps the plasma in the blood vessels. When this salt is lost, the plasma becomes thinner and enters tissues it should not enter. Here is Mother's classic way of describing these conditions:

> When fluid goes into the brain, the condition is called migraine headache... When the fluid goes into the eyes, the condition is called glaucoma... when the fluid goes into the nose, you have a stuffy nose and the condition is called hay fever, sinus problems, post-nasal drip, or allergies . . . when the fluid goes into the middle ear, the condition is called Meniere's syndrome, and you experience ringing and noises in the ear, loss of hearing, and dizziness . . . when the fluid goes into the lungs, the condition is called asthma.

Such conditions as these may respond to a half-teaspoon each of *salt and baking soda* in an 8-ounce glass of warm water. You might want to add a teaspoon of honey. This mixture raises not only the sodium, but also your blood sugar level. It brings the adrenals out of shock and stimulates the thymus, which in turn will stimulate the tonsils, adenoids, and lymph glands and make antibodies. A child who suffers from asthma attacks in the early morning may find relief by taking the salt and soda drink before taking other measures. Giving the child some protein food a half hour later should help keep the blood sugar level up.

Your Lowest Ebb

If you have low blood sugar problems, your lowest ebb will probably be at three or four o'clock in the morning or afternoon.

Some people wake up then and cannot go back to sleep. The usual hypoglycemia symptoms are often compounded at night by irrational fears and nightmares. If this has been happening to you, then you might want to take a protein drink before you go to bed at night. Do the same when you wake up.

This early morning low ebb can actually become very serious. When the blood sugar, blood calcium, and blood oxygen levels drop, you may experience palpitations of the heart, rapid pulse, muscle pains, numbness (go back over the list). If you start to think this is a heart attack and fear sets in, then adrenaline may flood into the body and the heart could begin to pound harder still. A blood vessel can spring a leak as a result, causing a thrombosis (a blood clot within the vessel). If this condition progresses it may even cause a heart attack.

This could be prevented by keeping your adrenals healthy, the pancreas functioning properly, the diet low in refined carbohydrates and sugars, and the diet and lifestyle free of unnecessary stimulants.

Over Consumption of Sugar. It is hard to believe that the average person in the United States consumes about 130 pounds of sugar a year, or more than 2 pounds a week. That's more than one-third pound of sugar a day for every man, woman, and child! In reality, the average is much higher than that because infants and some adults don't eat very much sugar.

To demonstrate how quickly sugar adds up to equal one-third pound a day, my daughter Laura and I recently presented on a Trinity Broadcasting Network television program the quantity of hidden sugar in desserts. Laura counted out the teaspoons of white refined sugar into a bowl for each food as I relayed foods traditionally served at a child's birthday party:

Piece of chocolate cake (or cherry pie)	= 15 tsp
Large scoop of ice cream	= 6 tsp
Glass of chocolate milk or cola drink	= 9 tsp

With just these three foodless foods, we had a bowl full of 30 teaspoons of sugar! Would you give this bowl of sugar to your child or grandchild or even eat it yourself? Hardly. Yet we do so as a way of saying "I love you". But do you really? That is why hypo-glycemia conditions are so common and can be so severe.

Protein is the Best Nutrient to Eat in order to main-tain an even blood sugar level, because it is metabolized over a long period of time. An impressive 58 percent of protein can be con-verted to glucose if need be. Carbohydrates, on the other hand—particularly refined carbohydrates, such as cake, candy, soft drinks, white flour and sugar—are quickly metabolized, causing a rapid rise in blood sugar level. When refined sugar enters the blood-stream, insulin must flood to the rescue, to keep glucose levels from going too high.

Small Feedings Often. Most of us should have four to five feedings per day, rather than the standard three meals. Ideally these feedings should be spaced three to four hours apart, but no longer than four hours. This helps prevent your blood sugar level from dropping too low and keeps hypoglycemic symptoms from developing. It also gives your adrenal glands a chance to rest since food is used to raise blood sugar levels as opposed to stimulating your adrenals to keep blood sugar levels elevated.

Many people find that their health level improves immedi-ately when they shorten the time between feedings and eliminate as much sugar as possible from their diets.

The Lindberg Nutrition Program also emphasizes the value of protein-rich foods, the essential fatty acids, and complex carbo-hydrates that are natural and without man-made additives. This pro-gram is not a diet, per se, but rather, a program designed for better overall nutrition so that you can enjoy vibrant health the rest of your life.

Getting Started
on Your Nutritional Program

To get started, I always believe it is best to "start fresh." We need to establish an internal environment that allows for full assimilation of nutrients, and proper elimination. The product that helps with this is *Lactobacillus acidophilus*, for more information read the "Help for Elimination" section in this chapter.

The Importance of Breakfast

Breakfast is undoubtedly the most important meal of the day. How you "break the fast" from the night before actually determines the way you will feel the rest of the day. Your energy level in the afternoon hours is determined by what you had for breakfast.

I suggest that you have one of the four "breakfasts" described below. Remember, **"There is no excuse for leaving home without an adequate breakfast!"**

BREAKFAST #1

Consider eggs. Eggs are an excellent nutritional food, and may be included in your nutritional program several times a week. Eggs have received a lot of negative press in recent years, but they contain the best protein source, plus lecithin to emulsify the cholesterol in the yolk. Remember your hormones are made out of cholesterol. Eggs are a superior, complete food.

- Use fertile eggs if possible. You may scramble them, make an omelet or quiche, or eat them poached, soft boiled, or hard boiled. (Don't fry in shortening or margarine as this raises cholesterol levels!)
- Add whole-grain or multi-grain toast, a bagel, corn bread, or oat bran muffins for carbohydrates to burn as energy. Consider adding potatoes, brown rice, or granola (without added sugar) if your weight and appetite permits.
- Add fresh fruit and a beverage from the options described later.

NO bacon, sausage, ham, etc.

Note: Bacon, Ham or Sausage?

I suggest you avoid bacon, ham, and sausage for two reasons—their high fat content, and the chemicals which are added in the curing process (nitrate and nitrites), which many believe to be cancer-causing. Nitrites and nitrates also are found in most cured and smoked meats, hot dogs, salami, bologna, corn beef, and luncheon meats.

Researchers at the University of North Carolina at Chapel Hill discovered that youngsters who ate hot dogs once a week or more had twice the risk of brain tumors compared with non-hot-dog eating kids. Moreover, youngsters eating the most other cured meats, such as ham, bacon, and sausage, had an 80 percent higher risk of brain cancer. Children taking vitamins were less vulnerable to the brain cancer, suggesting that antioxidants countered the carcinogens in the cured meats.

Hot dogs have also been linked to childhood leukemia, according to researchers at the University of Southern California School of Medicine in Los Angeles. Youngsters eating more than twelve hot dogs a month had nearly ten times the risk of leukemia when compared to children who ate no hot dogs. The most likely culprits are nitrite and nitrate, which are used to cure the meat.

Eating sausage was linked to colon cancer risk in a Dutch research study.[4]

Recommended Breakfast Fruit

Less than 10 percent of Americans eat five or more servings of fruit and vegetables a day. It is amazing to know that more than half of Americans do not eat a single serving of fruit, vegetables or fruit juice on any given day. Breakfast is a good place to start.

To any of the breakfasts I discuss, add fresh fruit such as an orange, half a grapefruit, a melon wedge, a peeled apple, banana, pear, grapes, peaches, fresh berries, and so forth. Be sure to eat all of the white pulp of the citrus fruit to take advantage of the natural bioflavonoids naturally found there.

Eat a variety of fresh fruit each day—rather than canned fruit or juice. Use the dark colored berries, such as blueberries, blackberries, raspberries, strawberries, dark cherries, and Concord grapes. The dark colored fruit contains antioxidants and phytonutrients—*phyto* for plant. These substances have anti-cancer compounds.

Recommended Beverages

Beverages at breakfast may include any of the following:
- Pure water—filtered, spring, bottled—but not tap water in most cities.
- Non-homogenized milk, nonfat or low-fat, organic milk or certified raw if possible, whole goat milk is

excellent; children should have whole milk for proper hormone development.
- Soybean milk—soybeans are full of anticancer agents.
- Herbal teas of all varieties (which are caffeine free).
- Chinese green tea, which does contain caffeine. However, reports are showing it may be beneficial against certain tumors.
- Cultured milks, such as kefir, which is a delicious liquid yogurt, acidophilus milk, or buttermilk.
- Fruit juices should be diluted, but I recommend you eat whole fresh fruit instead, as the chewing helps digestion.
- Coffee substitutes made from grains are delicious drinks.
- Regular, organically grown coffee or water-processed decaffeinated coffee, depending on your general health condition.

Some people truly enjoy a cup of coffee and feel a need for this pick-up in the morning, as long as this coffee is not considered "breakfast." This program needs to be one that is "livable" so I don't recommend a complete denial of coffee for some people, but rather moderation. Most of the negative reports are usually associated with the amount of coffee that is consumed.

BREAKFAST #2

Fortified Protein Drink. My family's breakfast of choice is a protein shake! Through the years, this is the breakfast my family found to be most beneficial and "live-able" on a consistent daily basis. We usually have larger more traditional breakfasts on weekends, but during the week, fortified protein drinks keep us going and actually seem to give us more energy.

I will never forget our son, Douglas, saying to me when he was only in junior high school, "I can't think all the way to noon if I don't have my protein drink." Douglas recognized early in his life that he had a better attention span, could think more clearly, and was a better student if he had his protein drink. As a physician today, he is still drinking protein shakes for breakfast, and now giving them to his children.

I sent each of my children to college with a small refrigerator and a blender so they could make these drinks for breakfast. I knew they wouldn't eat the dorm breakfast or have time to go to the dining hall. Our oldest son, Gary, once said to me about the food at his college; "I don't know if this education is worth ruining my health." He played college soccer and it was an intensely competitive and demanding sport. The protein drinks were just what he needed to provide the extra nourishment his body required. Skip ahead a few pages to choose a protein powder and recipe that is best suited for your needs.

BREAKFAST #3
Natural Cereal. A nutritious balanced breakfast can also be achieved by using a variety of whole grain cereals and fortified milk.

* Oatmeal can be topped with oat bran, raisins, seeds, raw nuts, banana slices, or berries. In a study at the University of Kentucky, people with high cholesterol added 3-1/4 ounces of oat bran to their daily diet and lowered their cholesterol as much as 30 percent.
* Grains by themselves do not contain all of the essential amino acids, and thus, are not a complete protein, unless they are combined with other grains. To complete and increase the protein content of the cereal, use a fortified milk mixture. This can be made in advance and kept in the refrigerator for quick use.
* Add fruit and beverages from the recommended list.

Fortified Milk for Cereals
1 quart regular, low-fat milk or soy milk
1/2 cup powdered skim milk
   or whey protein powder
1 to 2 teaspoons vanilla extract
Blend together and chill for use as a cereal
   topping, or use in cooking the cereal.

BREAKFAST #4
Fortified Pancakes. Healthy pancakes or waffles are another great choice. Make sure these are fortified with soy flour or powdered skim milk and made with

whole grains. Try yogurt with fresh berries or sliced bananas as a topping. My family has also enjoyed pancakes and waffles topped with raw applesauce.

Raw Applesauce. Peel and cut up raw apples and put them in the blender with a little apple juice. Blend well. Crush and add several vitamin C tablets to prevent the apples from oxidizing (turning brown). You can also add other fresh fruit, such as strawberries, or yogurt to this mixture.

You might also top your pancakes or waffles with *pure* maple syrup diluted with water (so it is not as sweet). Don't use commercially marketed syrups that are loaded with sucrose and corn sweeteners. You may want to try sorghum, or use pure fruit jam sweetened with fruit juice. Be sure to read the labels closely.

Cook up the extra batter and have cold hotcakes as a "snack food." Children love these when they are topped with peanut butter.

Vitamin and Mineral Supplements

Take your vitamin and mineral supplements with or after breakfast. Vitamins and minerals should always be taken with foods or a protein drink for better digestion and assimilation. You can divide your supplements among your meals, or take them all after breakfast, depending how many you are taking.

Suggestions about vitamins and minerals are given later in this chapter.

Mid-Morning Feeding
(About 10:30 AM)

If you eat a very early breakfast, say at 5 or 6 AM, you may need to eat mid-morning. Too many hours between an early breakfast and lunch can cause symptoms of low blood sugar (hypoglycemia). Several snack suggestions are given under the mid-afternoon heading.

If you have a late breakfast, of course, you won't need this feeding. Try to space your feedings about three to four hours apart, throughout the day.

Luncheon Suggestions

It is very important that you eat a well-balanced lunch. Your serving size will depend on your weight and activity level. We always stress small feedings, often.

- A protein food—such as water-packed tuna, chicken, cottage cheese, yogurt, turkey, tofu or soy product, and so forth.
- A raw, dark green and yellow vegetable salad—using dark green lettuce, a variety of fresh vegetables; include cruciferous vegetables such as broccoli, cauliflower, and cabbage; tomatoes, avocados, carrots, sprouts, green or red peppers.
- A piece of fresh fruit.
- A whole grain product—such as a slice of multi-grain bread, a rice cake, a piece of corn bread, a bran muffin, or cooked brown rice.
- A beverage—herb iced tea, mineral water, etc.

If you have a protein drink as a mid-morning snack, eat a smaller lunch.

Mid-Afternoon Feeding
(About 3 PM)

A feeding at this time of the day staves off your lowest nutritional ebb, which is near four o'clock. Be sure to have a feeding before your blood sugar level gets too low. This feeding is an important key to feeling your best.

IMPORTANT: If you drink a protein shake at this time (see one of the "shake" recipes suggested for breakfast), you'll be amazed at how much better you will feel. Try it!

Suggestions for Mid-Morning & Mid-Afternoon Feedings

The following make excellent snacks.
- A protein shake (see recipe later in chapter)
- Cottage cheese with fresh fruit
- Half a tuna sandwich on whole grain bread or rice cake
- Apple with low-fat cheese

- Raw sunflower, pumpkin seeds or almonds
- Lowfat or nonfat yogurt with fresh fruit
- Whole-grain cereals
- A "green" drink—made with spirulina, wheat grass, barley grass, chlorella or a combination

Mid-afternoon and before bed are good times to eat whole-grain cereals, such as healthy granolas (no sugar added). I recommend these cereals as snacks, not as breakfast foods.

Dinner Suggestions
(5 to 7 PM)

Enjoy a leisurely dinner served in a calm, pleasant atmosphere, which aids in the digestion of foods. Be sure to eat a well-rounded meal, including a variety of fresh foods.

Many ethnic dishes are very nourishing and have lasted through the centuries. Some of these ancestral dishes would be considered "health foods" today. Yogurt and cultured products such as goat's milk cheese, a wide variety of unprocessed grains, legumes (such as a hearty lentil soup), sea vegetables (including kelp for the thyroid), fish soup, tofu, and many other dishes have high nutrient value. Learn about your ancestral dishes and incorporate them into your diet, but be sure to leave out the heavy fat and refined sugars.

Here are some menu suggestions to stimulate your creativity:

- **Salad.** A large fresh, raw salad using dark green lettuce or spinach, to which you add broccoli, cauliflower, carrots, grated raw beets, chopped purple or green cabbage, green or red peppers, cucumbers, zucchini squash, snow peas, radishes, celery, fresh mushrooms, cherry tomatoes, and alfalfa or bean sprouts. These vegetables are a rich source of carotenes and phytonutrients.

   Your salad dressing should have one tablespoon of essential oils, per person, such as olive or flax oil, with apple cider vinegar or balsamic vinegar and seasonings. There are many excellent salad dressings available in your nutrition store. Read the label and watch the fat content.

Preparing Salad
Ingredients in Advance

To save yourself time and to make salad preparation easier, make a huge salad with all the fresh greens and raw vegetables to last for several days. Cut the vegetables and tear the greens. Cover them with a damp towel or put them into air-tight bowls and refrigerate. This is a great time saver when preparing a balanced dinner, especially if you work, or if you live alone. Prepare enough to last several days. Be sure to add dressing only to the part of the salad that you will consume. Your salad is also ready for lunch time. Just add a chicken breast or water-packed tuna for a complete meal.

- **A protein food**—such as chicken, fish, turkey, eggs or tofu and moderate amounts of lean beef or lean lamb. Bake, broil, steam, or sauté. Be careful not to burn or blacken any of your meat on the barbecue grill. The Chinese method of cooking with a wok is quick and efficient. You can also combine protein foods and vegetables to make soups or stews, even adding whole-grain rice or lentils to the broth mixture.
- **Complex carbohydrates**—a serving of natural brown rice, baked potatoes, yams, lentils, beans, legumes, or moderate amounts of whole-grain pastas or multi-grain bread or muffins. If your fresh vegetables are not in your salad, have them for your complex carbohydrate. Carrots, string beans, zucchini squash, etc.
- **Fresh fruit** always makes an appropriate dessert. Pineapple and papaya are great for digestion and wonderful to serve after a meal. We sometimes freeze fresh blueberries, strawberries or bananas, then put them through our juicer or blender to make a wonderful after dinner natural sorbet.

Before Bedtime

If you eat your evening meal at around 5 or 6 PM, and don't retire until 10 or 11 PM, your stomach will be empty by bedtime. If you don't eat breakfast until the following morning, say about seven o'clock, you will have fasted for almost fourteen hours! That's a long time, nutritionally speaking for many people, especially those who are older, who are very thin, and those who have low blood sugar or diabetes. If you are having trouble sleeping, wake up exhausted, have nightmares or night terrors, wake up with palpitations of the heart or a rapid pulse rate, you may be suffering the effects of night time low blood sugar. Try adding an extra feeding around 9 PM or an hour before bed.

Young children and older people, especially, need this small extra feeding to help them sleep through the night, and to keep their bodies replenished with nutrients.

Teenagers who want to build muscle also can benefit from a protein drink at this time.

Many people find they feel better if they have a cup of one of the protein drinks, or eat a small snack, such as granola, yogurt, or cottage cheese with fresh fruit.

This before-bedtime feeding is not the time for sweets. Please: NO ice cream, cake, pie, sugared cereals, or other sugary foods before bedtime. They will only cause a greater drop in night time blood sugar and you may wake up feeling worse than if you hadn't eaten at all.

Remember this rule of thumb:
SMALL FEEDINGS OFTEN

Vitamin and Mineral Recommendations for Optimal Health

There are several excellent vitamin and mineral formulas in your nutrition store. We want to give you an idea of what potency to look for in a formula. Since we each have a great variance in size and weight, as well as differing medical histories, environments, and stress factors, you may need more or less of the items indicated below. The higher potencies of vitamins C, E, choline and inositol will not be found in most formulas. These extra nutrients can be added. Here is the range that will get you started.

Vitamin and Mineral Recommendations

1000 mcg=1 mg 1000 mg=1 gm
mcg=microgram mg=milligram gm=gram IU=International Unit

VITAMINS	OPTIMAL
Vitamin A (fish liver oil)	7,000–10,000 IU
Beta-Carotene	20,000–50,000 IU
Vitamin B1 (thiamin)	25–100 mg
Vitamin B2 (riboflavin)	25–100 mg
Vitamin B3 (niacin, niacinamide)	50–100 mg
Vitamin B5 (pantothenic acid)	100–200 mg
Vitamin B6 (pyridoxine)	50–100 mg
Vitamin B12 (cobalamin)	500–1,000 mcg
Biotin	50–200 mcg
Choline	500–1,000 mg
Inositol	500–1,000 mg
Folic Acid	400–800 mcg
PABA (Para-Amino Benzoic Acid)	50–100 mg
Vitamin C	1,000–6,000 mg
Vitamin D	400–800 IU
Vitamin E (d-alpha-tocopherol)	400–1,200 IU
Vitamin K	no supplement needed

MINERALS	OPTIMAL
Boron	1-3 mg
Calcium	1,000–1,500 mg
Chromium	200–400 mcg
Copper	2–3 mg
Iodine	150–300 mcg
Iron	10–18 mg
Magnesium	400–750 mg
Manganese	5–10 mg
Molybdenum	50–200 mcg
Phosphorus	not needed
Potassium (maximum allowed by law is 99 mg)	99 mg
Selenium	100–400 mcg
Zinc	30–50 mg

OTHERS	
Pycnogenols® or Grape Seed Extract	50–300 mg
Coenzyme Q 10	30–120 mg

In addition to the program above, here are some recommendations for additional help.

A Woman's Special Needs

Other nutrients that could be added to your vitamin and mineral formula depends upon a woman's individual need.

Women with menstrual problems should take higher amounts of vitamin B6, and evening primrose oil (three capsules, two times a day, which contains the essential fatty acids). Increase the B vitamins, choline and inositol, which support the liver, if you are having heavy periods. The ratio of calcium to magnesium should change from roughly 2 parts calcium and 1 part magnesium to equal amounts of both if you have PMS or hypertension in menopause.

Menopausal women with hot flashes may want additional herbs. Consider using dong quai, vitex, Siberian ginseng, ginkgo biloba, gotu kola, red raspberry, wild yam and others. There are many women's herbal formulas containing these herbs. You may wish to also consider wild yam cream, a source of natural progesterone.

Grape Seed extracts or pine bark extracts are always valuable for their anti-aging and antioxidant effects. There is a lot of great information on the hormones melatonin, DHEA and pregnenolone as anti-agers, so read Chapter 11 and see if you want to add any of these to your new program.

Another valuable antioxidant nutrient is CoQ10 for improvement of heart muscle, increased stamina and periodontal disease. CoQ10 also helps prevent free-radical formation by inhibiting lipid peroxidation, and most importantly, is anti-aging.

Additional Program for Men's Unique Challenges

After reading the Men's chapter, you may want to add to your program: saw palmetto and pygeum (for prostate health), yohimbe, ginkgo biloba (for memory and increased blood flow to extremities), and Korean ginseng, damiana and sarsaparilla (for impotence). Add coenzyme Q10 (for the heart) and grape seed extract or Pycnogenol® (for capillaries and antioxidant value). Make sure you include zinc with your mineral formula. The hormones DHEA, pregnenolone and melatonin may be of benefit.

Anti-Aging Program for Our Brain

You may want to include: CoQ10 (60–120 mg), melatonin (according to age), DHEA (according to need), phosphatidylserine (PS) (recommended 100–300 mg a day in divided doses), ginkgo biloba extract, acetylcholine (from quality lecithin granules). Pregnenolone is the new star for brain function. Also include extra vitamin B12 and the amino acid L-glutamine. Read more about 'brain' nutrients in Chapter 6.

A Person Under Extreme Stress

Add several liquid (organic) liver capsules daily, plus the herb milk thistle, to protect your liver. Take at least 2,000 to 4,000 mg of vitamin C, twice daily. Also, support your adrenal glands by taking extra B-complex vitamins, especially pantothenic acid (250 mg, once or twice daily) and adrenal glandulars. There are homeopathic products that can quiet you down and help you relax. Melatonin and herbs to help with sleep may also combat some of the emotional stress.

When You Need to Increase Immunity

Read Chapter 3 for various suggestions. Vitamins C, A, E, beta-carotene, zinc and selenium are all valuable to build your immune system. Raw thymus glandulars also support the immune system. The herbs echinacea and golden seal are immune stimulants and work as natural antibiotics. Several herbalists feel these herbs should be taken for approximately 10 days, then stopped for 5 to 7 days, then started again until you feel better. They should not be used by pregnant women. Astragalus and garlic may also help stimulate and improve immunity.

Aids to Help Digestion

The saying "you are what you eat" should actually be, "you are what you digest and assimilate." Even if you eat the best foods and take all the right vitamins, if you do not digest, assimilate and absorb the nutrients properly, you won't get the full benefit from them.

If you have trouble with digestion, take the following after each feeding or meal:

Betaine Hydrochloric Acid (HCl) with Pepsin. These tablets are designed to help your stomach digest protein, using the same digestive enzyme, pepsin. Pepsin breaks down protein into certain amino acids until pancreatic enzymes finish off protein digestion in the small intestine. The HCl converts pepsin to its active form.

How to take: Take them after each meal that includes protein. The usual suggestion is 2 to 4 depending on your need. Those who may have a special need for these tablets are: people past the age of forty; those with poor dietary habits; those who have been through years of stress and who have exhausted adrenal glands; those who are on high-protein diets; and those who have gas, indigestion and bloating.

Pancreatic Enzymes. Pancreatin is usually combined with bile which acts like the bile produced by the liver and secreted by the gall bladder to help emulsify and solubilize fats. Pancreatin contains three principle digestive enzymes—Protease (protein), Amylase (carbohydrates), and Lipase (fats). These enzymes are similar to the ones produced by a normal healthy pancreas. They assist in the digestion of protein, carbohydrates and fats in the small intestine.

How to take: The usual recommendation is for a person to take 2 to 4 pancreatic enzyme tablets. Those who may have a special need for this product are those who have consumed too much sugar over the years, individuals who are dieting, and people who have an excessive amount of carbohydrates and fats in their diet.

Combination Enzymes. As an alternative to the above, you might take a combination of digestive enzymes. These formulations generally have pancreatin, pepsin, betaine hydrochloride, plus papain from papaya and bromelain from pineapple, as well as other enzymes. These are usually lower potency formulas.

Help for Elimination Problems

A number of serious problems are related to infrequent or inadequate elimination. Cancer of the colon and rectum is the second most common form of cancer in the United States, with approximately 150,000 new cases reported each year, and upwards of 60,000 related death per year.[5]

Diverticulitis, hemorrhoids—occurring in half of all people over the age of fifty—irritable bowel syndrome, spastic colon, ulcerative colitis, and Crohn's disease are all colon-related problems. Most authorities feel these colon problems may be helped with good nutrition and proper bowel habits.

Dr. Ilya Metchnikoff, who received the Nobel Prize for his research, studied Bulgarian people who were more than one hundred years old. He found that they all had one thing in common: their bowels were acidic, just like those of a nursed baby. These people had been given no antibiotics, ate only natural foods, and had all been nursed for their first two or three years. For the rest of their lives, they drank a quart of yogurt nearly every day. Later investigation proved that the yogurt was simply providing the real hero, the friendly bacteria *acidophilus* that had been first established in nursing.[6]

Lactobacillus Acidophilus. My clients begin the nutrition program with a series of *Lactobacillus acidophilus* culture for at least six weeks. The large intestine normally contains this "friendly" bacteria and secretes acids that prevent the growth of "harmful" bacteria. Taking acidophilus in freeze-dried powder or liquid form will help re-implant and re-establish the favorable intestinal bacteria in your large intestine (colon). This bacteria is established originally in the intestines when a baby is nursed, and a person needs to maintain sufficient friendly bacteria in order for nutrients to be properly assimilated by the body.

When to take: Take 2 to 3 capsules of *Lactobacillus acidophilus* or other various strains of culture with a glass of water twenty minutes before breakfast and again before bedtime. Or follow the directions suggested on the label.

The intention is to get the culture past your stomach before the hydrochloric acid flows in to digest your breakfast, a process that tends to kill these "live and friendly" bacteria. Those with candida or other "yeast" associated problems should probably stay on acidophilus until the condition clears up.

Alfalfa Tablets. Alfalfa (*Medicago sativa*) binds and neutralizes various types of agents that are known to be carcinogenic to the colon. It is "nature's broom and deodorizer" which provides an excellent source of dietary fiber, chlorophyll, amino acids, and trace minerals. Overall, alfalfa is one of the most nutritious foods known.[7] Alfalfa has always been an important part of our health-building program.

How to take. Start with two to three alfalfa tablets and increase to six to ten, then take that amount twice a day. The optimal dosage may be twenty to thirty tablets taken throughout the day, until your bowels are regular. Then cut back to three or four tablets a day. The tablets may be taken at any time in a day and are relatively inexpensive.

Importance of Fiber. The National Cancer Institute has recommended that we each consume at least twenty-five to thirty-five grams of fiber a day. Fiber is either water-soluble (oat bran, apple pectin, guar gum, psyllium husks, and glucomannan) or water-insoluble (cellulose as wheat bran). The water-soluble forms absorb water, carrying added moisture through your bowels producing a softer stool. They also can carry toxins and harmful forms of cholesterol as well. Products containing psyllium tend to be the most popular.

Natural Herbal Laxatives. These are good for emergencies or to take on a trip, because they should only be used infrequently. *Cascara Sagrada* is one of the best herbs to use for chronic constipation, which is said to be non-habit-forming, helps in painless evacuations, and after extended usage, the bowels will begin to function naturally and regularly from its tonic effect.[8] It can be used alone or in combination with other herbs. *Senna* increases the intestinal peristaltic movements and has a strong laxative effect on the entire intestinal tract, especially the colon. Be careful to replenish your fluid levels since laxatives can cause a rapid loss of vital electrolytes, especially potassium.

Magnesium. One of the good side effects of too much magnesium is that it may act as a laxative. Magnesium can have a relaxing and toning effect on all muscles including the colon.

No Mineral Oil. Do NOT take mineral oil as a laxative. This undigested oil binds with the fat-soluble vitamins A, D, E, and K in the intestines where they are held captive, and are later excreted in the feces, thereby creating deficiencies of these vitamins.

Help for Sleep Problems

A number of herbal products are available to help those who want to wean themselves from synthetic, addicting sleeping pills and tranquilizers. These herbals are *non-habit forming*. They are not as powerful as drugs, which means that most people wake up feeling refreshed. These products are usually best taken an hour before bedtime.

Valerian Root. Valerian root has been used a great deal in Europe as a sleep aid. It is reputed to be a relaxant for nervous tension and act as a mild sedative or natural tranquilizer which is non-addictive. Try the extract form which is more concentrated.

Herbal Combination. These products often have other herbs included, such as **skullcap**, which is said to help control nervous disorders and relax the mind. **Hops** have a sedative effect, helps restlessness, and calms the nerves for insomnia. **Passion flower** is quieting and soothing to the nervous system, but does not bring on depression or disorientation. **Kava kava** is also a quieting herb used for nervousness and insomnia. It helps relieve cramping due to muscle spasms. Follow the label instructions on the bottles.

Herbal Teas. *Nighty Night®* and *Sleepy Time®* teas contain gentle herbal combinations that are naturally caffeine free. A hot cup of these mild herbal blends may help a person relax. **Chamomile** and **Passion Flower** teas are also helpful. Curl up with a good book and a cup of herb tea before bedtime and you will likely fall asleep easily and sleep more soundly!

Calcium and Magnesium. These two minerals promote natural sleep in some people. Many recall their mothers giving them a glass of warm milk before bedtime. Milk is a natural source of the amino acid tryptophan, as well as a good source of calcium.

A magnesium deficiency can cause over-excitement of the nervous system, which can lead to muscle spasms or cramps, even twitching of the muscles. Magnesium works as a nerve relaxer, and is necessary for the sending of nerve impulses for normal brain functions, as well as for sleeping.

Homeopathic Formulas. Several homeopathic formulas are found in nutrition stores to help with relaxation. They are a natural way to take the edge off restlessness and insomnia.

Melatonin. This is an exceptional sleep aid, which is particularly useful in overcoming jet lag. This hormone will help you sleep like a baby and may produce vivid dreams. Some report that it may also improve one's mood.[9] More information on the amount of melatonin to take in Chapter 11.

Protein Drinks

Here are some suggested protein drinks for breakfast, mid-afternoon or before bed.

Basic Super-Energy Drink Recipe

- 8 oz. certified raw milk, kefir, acidophilus milk, soy milk, nonfat milk, or diluted fruit juice
- 3 Tbs. protein powder—unsweetened (see suggestions in the section below)
- 1 Tbs. granulated soy lecithin
- 1 tsp. vanilla (optional)
- 1 tsp. natural sweetener—(see selection below)
- 1/2 frozen banana or 4–5 frozen strawberries
  (add several ice cubes if frozen fruit is not available)
  Blend all ingredients together and enjoy.

To make this drink even more power packed:
Add and blend in thoroughly one or two of the following optional ingredients:
- 1 Tbs. brewer's or nutritional yeast
- 1 tsp. of green powder (barley grass, spirulina, chlorella, wheat grass, or a combination of these)
- 1 Tbs. organic, cold-pressed flax seed oil (best vegetable source of linoleic and linolenic acids, which are essential fatty acids)
- 1/4 to 1/2 cup plain yogurt
- If you are milk intolerant or a strict vegetarian, use bottled water, diluted fruit juice, soy milk, or rice milk instead of cow's milk and use a soy based powder.

Suggestions for Choosing a Protein Powder

Not all protein powders are alike. It's important that you read the labels. At least four types of powders seem to be dominant today. These are used alone or in combination. It is a good idea to rotate between the various powders so there is less chance of developing an allergy. Sometimes we become allergic to foods we eat all the time.

Milk protein is from non-fat dry milk and calcium/potassium caseinate, which is a concentrated form of protein found in milk, minus the fat. It contains all the essential amino acids and is an excellent source of protein. It also contains natural milk sugar (lactose), to which some people are allergic or sensitive to.

Egg protein is from pure egg albumen, which is dried egg white. Egg white protein provides all twenty-two of the amino acids with a proper balance of essential amino acids. It is one of the most expensive, but an excellent protein source. Many will add a tablespoon of egg white powder to their favorite protein powder to boost the protein content.

Whey powder (or sweet whey) contains many of the vitamins and minerals of milk. In making cheese or cottage cheese, milk is separated into two parts—the milk solids and the whey, or milk liquid. Sweet whey is about 70 percent carbohydrate and the rest protein.

Some of the new whey powders use a special filtration and ion-exchange process to remove lactose for those who are intolerant to the lactose in milk. The protein content actually rises to almost 100 percent when the lactose is removed. These whey powders have been specially engineered and enzyme treated to be predigested (or hydrolyzed), for faster digestion and more complete absorption. They are good tasting, easy to mix, and contain all the essential and non-essential amino acids.

Manufacturers refer to a protein's Biological Value (BV), which is the amount of nitrogen (body protein in grams) that can be replaced by 100 grams of protein in an adult diet. The higher the BV of a protein, the higher the nitrogen retention. Proteins with the highest BV promote the most lean muscle gains.[10] Lactose removed whey has one of the highest BV's.

Soy protein is used as a base in many protein powder formulas and it is slightly less expensive than milk,egg white or lactose removed whey protein. The amino acid profile is not quite as good as the other three protein sources. Do not attempt to substitute soy *flour* for soy protein. The two are very different products. Soy flour must be heated for it to be assimilated by the body and raw soy flour has not been heat treated.

Dr. Stephen Barnes at University of Alabama at Birmingham, hails soy's *genistein* as a unique and incredibly promising inhibitor of breast and prostate cancer.[10] "So powerful is genistein, researchers see it as a potential new type of anti-cancer drug". For example, Dr. Ann R. Kennedy, University of Pennsylvania School of Medicine, finds that a protease inhibitor in soybean is so versatile against various cancers that she calls it "a universal cancer preventive agent."[11]

Asian women, who tend to have soy as part of their diet, do not have the cancers we Westerners do, and soy may very well be one of the reasons.

> "In addition to having an anti-cancer effect on cells, soybeans manipulate estrogen by blocking its ability to stimulate malignant changes in breast tissue. Thus, soybeans could help thwart both the occurance and spread of breast cancer in both pre-menopausal and postmenopausal women."[12]

Good news was reported in the *New England Journal of Medicine* which showed that soy protein selectively decreases the "bad" LDL (low-density) cholesterol and reduces serum triglycerides, without effecting the "good cholesterol"—the HDL (high-density) cholesterol. Many are turning to more soy products.[13]

No Added Sugars. Try to find a protein powder that does *not* contain sugar, corn syrup, dextrose or sucrose. If you can't find this powder at least make sure the form of sugar is not the first, second or third ingredient listed on the label. Most manufacturers know if it doesn't taste sweet people won't drink it. A small amount of fructose (fruit sugar) does not trigger the pancreas to release as much insulin, so a *small amount* of fructose may be included.

Other Ingredients to Consider

There are two ingredients that may be added to your protein powder. They are worthy of your consideration in choosing a protein powder.

Nutritional Yeast (Brewer's Yeast) has generous quantities of all the major B-vitamins (except B12), sixteen amino acids (which makes it a complete protein), and eighteen or more minerals, including selenium and a rich source of GTF chromium, which is not found in many foods. It greatly enhances the nutritional value of any food to which it is added! Originally made as a by-product of beer manufacturing, this yeast is now grown specifically to increase its nutritional quality compared to brewer's yeast.

One of the best known properties of nutritional yeast is its ability to increase energy. It should be used in conjunction with calcium supplements to offset its high phosphorus content. Nutritional yeast is dried, and is a different strain than the live yeast used in baking. It does not cause "yeast" infections or candida problems.

Lecithin is known to have an emulsifying action on fats, which helps keep the arteries free of cholesterol deposits. It is also a constituent of our brain and nervous systems. Lecithin contains a small amount of fat from soybean oil. Essential fatty acids are vitally important to dieters, since most people try to eliminate fat completely from their diets when they are trying to lose weight. Look for soy lecithin on the label of your protein powder, or better yet, just add it to your drinks.

Sweetening Your Protein Drinks

The following may be added to sweeten these fortified protein shakes:

- frozen concentrated orange juice or apple juice
- fresh or unsweetened frozen strawberries
- half of a ripe banana (a rich source of potassium)
- an apple or other fresh fruit—always peel your fruit unless it is organic
- sorghum or blackstrap molasses
- rice syrup, barley malt, fructose, date sugar or honey

- Stevia (*Stevia rebandiana*) is a natural herbal sweetener, claimed to be 50 to 60 times sweeter than sugar. Said to be safe for diabetics, hypoglycemic's and Candida sufferers. Is non-caloric, non-toxic and safe to use as a harmless sweetener.[14]
- Chocolate is one of the highly allergenic foods and it can be addictive to many people, so avoid this ingredient, especially with children.
- Do *not* use refined white sugar, corn sweeteners, or artificial sweeteners.

The Serenity Cocktail:
Gladys Lindberg's
Ultimate Protein Drink Formula

My mother experimented with and finally designed the Serenity Cocktail Powder when we were young. She first began to make this formula for us after she read about the many healthful properties in brewer's yeast (now called nutritional yeast) which she mixed into our milk. Then she added raw, defatted liver powder, which contained a powerhouse of nutrients.

When the value of lecithin was discovered, she added it as well. Lecithin is a fat metabolizer that helps clear the arteries and is important for the health of the heart. She knew, however, that nutritional yeast, liver, and lecithin are all high in the mineral phosphorus, but low in calcium, so she began to add other ingredients, including calcium, magnesium, and bone meal to balance the calcium-phosphorus ratio in the formula.

She added protein powder from powdered non-fat milk, egg whites, soy and whey—all of which are rich in trace minerals. Vitamin C was added, in part to prevent the mixture from oxidizing.

Mother named this powerful, complete formula for the "serenity" or inner calmness it gives to the body.

The powder has a mild, yeasty flavor. It may be sweetened with sorgum, molasses, frozen concentrated orange or apple juice, or fructose, which helps mask the flavor of some of the ingredients. It is designed for those who take nutrition seriously. It's the ultimate formula in the line of protein and nutritional powders. This formula has been used by countless people who are "on-the-go" to get them through their day in top form.

Recipe for the Serenity Cocktail Powder
A powerful Stress Formula

1 lb. protein powder (unsweetened)
1 lb. nutritional or brewer's yeast
1 lb. granulated soy lecithin
1 lb. powdered skim milk (non-instant)
1 lb. whey powder
8 oz. raw defatted liver powder (use if available)
8 oz. bone meal powder (or a form of powdered calcium)
1 oz. magnesium oxide powder
  (or crush 5 tablets of 250 mg chelated magnesium)
2 oz. vitamin C crystals
  (approximately 14 tsp. or 60,000 mg)
4–8 oz. fructose (or more, as desired, to taste)

Mix ingredients thoroughly in a large plastic or paper bag, turning the bag upside down repeatedly and shaking it well. When thoroughly mixed, store in a tightly sealed container. Makes over six pounds.

Each pound will provide approximately sixteen portions of three rounded tablespoons per serving. Each three-tablespoon serving of powder alone provides approximately:

Calories 110
Carbohydrates . . . . .10 grams
Protein . . . . .10 grams
Fat (as lecithin) . . . . .4 grams

By adding the mixture to milk, you add another 8 grams of protein.

To make a fortified shake from the Serenity Cocktail Powder:
  Put 1/2 pint (8 oz.) certified raw milk (if possible), or
    low-fat milk in the blender. Or use diluted juice, or
    soy milk.
  Add 1–3 tablespoons Serenity Cocktail Powder
  Add 1 tablespoon soy lecithin
  Add 1/2 frozen banana, or 3–4 strawberries,
    or 2–3 ice cubes
  Blend and enjoy

Making a Double Recipe. You may double this recipe and take half of the mixture to work in a chilled thermos for a mid-afternoon drink. If you choose to do this, be sure to add extra vitamin C to prevent the drink from oxidizing. You can use vitamin C crystals—1/4 teaspoon or 1,000 mg—or open a 1,000 mg capsule, or crush several tablets for each serving.

Other Suggestions. Until you become accustomed to the Serenity Cocktail Powder, add only one tablespoon of the dry mix to your shake. Over a period of several days, increase the amount to two or three tablespoons. To make the drink more flavorful, add a spoonful of concentrated frozen orange or apple juice, or sweeten it with honey, sorghum, blackstrap molasses, or more fructose.

A Review of the
Keys to Your Good Health

A great compliment about the Lindberg Nutrition Program has always been: "I can live with this."

We have simplified the program for just that reason—to help people improve their health using methods they can "live with" for the rest of their lives.

The program is helpful for every person in your family. If you have an eight-year-old child, a teenager, or an older parent living with you . . .use the same program except for making adjustments in the quantities of foods and supplements each person takes.

If you try this program for a couple of months, you will be amazed at the change in the level of vitality and health that you feel. Many of our clients have reported an almost immediate increase in their sense of well-being, their energy level, and the peace of mind they feel in knowing they are practicing preventive health care that can pay off in handsome dividends ten, twenty, thirty, and even more years into the future.

Good Health Do's and Don'ts

1. DO eat breakfast. Don't leave home without breakfast. If you are in a hurry, a fortified protein drink is an excellent way to start your day.

2. DO have a mid-afternoon feeding. It is critical to your maintaining an even blood sugar level throughout the day. You may need to eat a mid-morning snack if your breakfast time is early (5 to 6 AM). And you may need a snack before bedtime, again depending on your schedule. Try to space your feedings every three to four hours from the time you eat breakfast until the time you go to bed.

3. DO take your vitamins and minerals every day. I cannot stress enough their importance to your health. They make up for deficiencies in the diet and help protect you against the stresses of life. They are like a "health insurance policy" in many ways.

Be sure your mineral formula includes adequate amounts of calcium with magnesium in proper balance, as well as boron. Selenium is an antioxidant; chromium (GTF or picolinate) is to stabilize the blood sugar, important for diabetes, protects the heart, and helps with fat loss. Zinc is important for immunity and men's unique needs.

As you see all of the vitamins and minerals are important. Products sold in one or two-a-day tablet form may not contain adequate amounts of the minerals. There is not enough space to fit all the minerals into that few of tablets. To achieve adequate potencies, 6 to 8 capsules are desirable. Always take your vitamins and minerals with food for maximum digestion and assimilation.

4. DO eat your food in its natural form, if possible. This means fresh, whole fruit and vegetables eaten raw. If you must cook your vegetables, steam them, or use a wok. Use organically grown fruit and vegetables if they are available. Frozen foods are second best, avoid canned if possible. Eat five to six servings a day. Do not overcook or microwave your vegetables—both methods destroy enzymes.

Especially include the dark green and orange vegetables which are rich in carotenoids, natural antioxidants. Include as many of the deep colored vegetables as possible, such as tomatoes, red and green peppers, yams, and carrots. Also be sure to include the cruciferous vegetables—broccoli, cauliflower, cabbage, radishes, mustard greens, bok choy and Brussel sprouts—which are rich sources of a nitrogen-like compound called *indole*. The indole compound is believed to help deactivate excess estrogen in the body. If you have thyroid problems, eliminate the cruciferous vegetables. Read about the thyroid in Chapter 8.

Add large amounts of garlic and onion. The distinctive odor actually increases levels of enzymes that break down potential carcinogens and boost the activity of cancer-fighting immune cells. Scallions and chives are also good.

Add chili peppers, the hotter the pepper the more capsaicin it contains, which is great for the heart.

5. AVOID all refined carbohydrates. This means anything made with white flour and white sugar, including candy, cakes, donuts, pies, cookies, sugared cereals, white flour, white pasta, and so forth. These foods trigger and elevate blood sugar levels, increase triglyceride levels, slow down our immune system and cause weight gain.

6. DO use complex carbohydrates. Whole grain foods without preservatives are best—such as multi-grain breads, brown rice, whole-grain pasta, and whole-grain cereals. Use a variety of grains, such as oats, soy, rye, barley, millet, quinoa, spelt, and rice flours, not just wheat.

Also use legumes, such as beans, peas, lentils, and corn. Soybeans are the newest addition to cancer protectors. Soy contain a powerhouse of nutrients and other anti-disease agents able to battle aging and chronic diseases, such as cancer.[15] Be sure to read the labels on grain and cereal products.

7. DO fortify your baking products by adding soy flour and powdered skim milk to whole-grain pastry flour. This increases the protein value of the product but doesn't change the taste.

8. AVOID as many chemicals in your foods as possible. Artificial food colors and preservatives are synthetic additives. Read the labels carefully. Avoid sodium nitrite and nitrate, which are potential carcinogenic substances (cancer-causing). Products that contain sodium nitrate and nitrite can cause the formation of nitrosamines inside the stomach. Nitrosamines are chemicals that may cause virtually any type of cancer.[16] They are found in most cured and smoked meats, such as bacon, hot dogs, salami, corned beef, and luncheon meats. The fat content of these foods also tends to be high.

Most nutrition stores sell frozen chemical-free hot dogs and luncheon meats usually made from chicken or turkey meat. They also carry great veggi-burgers or hotdogs made with soy products that are a good source of protein. Give them a try!

9. AVOID all high-fat foods and deep-fried foods, which include French fries, fried onion rings and fried chicken. The smoking fat in deep-frying is part of their danger. Remove all white fat found on meats. Avoid margarine, shortening or cooking with white hardened (hydrogenated) fats, even if they say "cholesterol free." These foods are the curse of our modern civilization as far as I am concerned. Watch for the words hydrogenated vegetable shortening, and avoid this processed, hardened fat also.

10. DO use butter in small amounts. Butter is a good source of vitamins A and D. Sweet butter is unsalted and considered less processed and fresher. Butter can be blended with canola or flaxseed oil to extend it and make it more nutritionally valuable. Keep butter refrigerated. Use sparingly if your weight permits.

When preparing foods, use cold-pressed and unprocessed virgin olive oil or soy oil. Flaxseed oil (do not heat it) and canola oil are excellent and they contain the essential fatty acids, especially linolenic acid. Olive oil has been used for thousands of years and is mentioned often in the Bible.

DO store your oils in the refrigerator after opening. Never consume oil that smells rancid. Don't let oils heat to the smoking point—they can become carcinogenic (cancer-causing).

11. DO drink plenty of fresh pure water. This usually means bottled water, not city tap water. Some water filters are good, but be sure to change the filters often. We do not recommend distilled water, as the trace minerals have been removed.

12. AVOID "juice drinks" that actually have very little juice and lots of sugar and water. Children should *eat* the whole fruit not just drink the juice. Don't let your children drink soft drinks, whether regular or diet. They throw off the mineral balance in the body since soft drinks are high in phosphorus. The high phosphorus must be matched with calcium which is pulled from your bones, depleting calcium stores.

13. DO enjoy eggs as an excellent source of protein. Eggs are the most complete and perfect protein. They do contain cholesterol, but eggs also contain the cholesterol manager, lecithin, which monitors and adjusts cholesterol levels. Cholesterol is needed to make all our hormones—DHEA, estrogen, testosterone, progesterone, pregnenolone, etc. Try to find fertile eggs, grown and raised "cage free," which means the chickens and roosters are together and are capable of producing fertile eggs that will hatch.

14. DO include a variety of protein foods in your diet. Eat fish (tuna, salmon, halibut, etc.) often. I personally have eliminated the scavenger shell fish like lobster, crab and shrimp. Add poultry—chicken, turkey, and other fowl. If possible, AVOID meat and poultry products that have been fed synthetic hormones to speed growth. Look for hormone and antibiotic-free meat and poultry from organic producers. Red meat is an important source of heme iron (an easy assimilated form). Add soy protein foods to your diet. Try tofu, miso, tempeh and textured soy protein.

15. DO include a variety of dairy products from yogurt and cottage cheese to milk. Children and teens should not have non-fat dairy products. An essential part of a child's growth hormones are in the cholesterol of dairy products. Look for the organic milk, especially non-homogenized if possible. My children were given the certified-raw, whole milk which in my opinion, is a superior product.

16. AVOID artificial sweeteners as much as possible. Aspartame can cause a reaction, such as headaches, in many people. Especially avoid feeding these chemical sweeteners or products with sweeteners to children.

17. DO stop smoking. It's time to rejuvenate your heart and lungs! Also, you will be sparing your family from the effects of "second hand smoke."

18. AVOID ALL or reduce your alcohol consumption. Alcohol can be a destroyer of your liver and brain cells as well as lives and relationships.

19. DO use iodized sea salt from evaporated sea water. Sea water has the same mineral balance as our blood. People with low adrenals and low blood pressure actually need more salt in their diet. Avoid high sodium in processed, canned and frozen foods, especially if you have hypertension.

20. AVOID as many environmental toxins as possible. These negatively impact the immune system. Avoiding exposure to toxic chemicals is essential—such as bug bombs and insect sprays. Also avoid electromagnetic fields produced by microwave ovens, computers, radiant (electric) heating, glowing watches and clocks as much as possible. Protect yourself from as much "radiation" as possible, even if it seems to be in minute forms.

21. AVOID drugs as much as possible. Be sure to follow your physician's orders, but ask if you might try natural products to help you sleep, digest your food, assist you through menopause, or to help you with problems such as water retention or nervousness. If you can eliminate "non-essential" medications you will be making great strides towards better health! Be aware of the side effects of all medications you take.

22. DO exercise daily. A brisk walk before breakfast or after dinner is an excellent practice. The amount of exercise you do will depend to a great extent on your age and physical condition. Essentially, your body has five fundamental requirements: air, water, food, rest, and movement. Every organ benefits from exercise—the heart and circulatory (cardiovascular), respiratory, skeletal, and digestive systems. Get started and get moving!

23. DO get sufficient rest. If you are older, small cat naps are great. For those with trouble sleeping, try a calcium/magnesium supplement or a herbal or homeopathic product to help you get rest. Avoid using drugs to help you sleep or relax. They can be highly addictive.

24. DO make a decision for better health. Decide that you are going to be in excellent health. Your mental attitude and emotional state go a long way toward making excellent health a reality. Your mind has a powerful influence on your body's well-being, on your immune system, and on your level of energy.

25. DO develop your spiritual life, choosing to live spiritually the way your Creator designed you to live. The manufacturer's handbook, the Bible, states that we each need to rid ourselves of all bitterness, anger, hate, resentment, strife, and unforgiveness, since these are negative emotions that can contribute to disease. Scientific studies are bearing out this truth!

Adopt a spirit of love, joy, peace, patience, kindness, goodness, faithfulness, gentleness, forgiveness, and self-control. (Galatians 5:22–23) These attitudes can aid in building sound health!

Take charge of your health! Start doing today what it is that you know to do, and stay with the program, believing for the very best health possible! The Bible also says, "Beloved, I pray that you may prosper in all things and be in **health**, just as your soul prospers." (3 John 1:2) You have the potential to create a vital, more vigorous and healthy life than ever before. May you have God's abundant blessings throughout your journey!

Appendix

VITAMIN & MINERAL SUMMARY CHART

This chart provides you with a basic overview and description of all scientifically recognized vitamins and minerals. The following information is listed for each item.

Name: the name of the vitamin or mineral, along with its number or letter designation.

Fat-Soluble or Water-Soluble: Fat-soluble vitamins can be stored for longer periods of time in the body's fatty tissue and liver. Water-soluble vitamins must be taken into the body daily, as they are not stored over a long period of time.

Sources: the foods considered to be the richest natural sources for the vitamin or mineral.

What It Does: the major function in the body of a particular vitamin or mineral.

Deficiency Symptoms: the common symptoms people suffer when deficient in a particular vitamin or mineral.

Optimal Daily Amount: a range is given, aimed not only at achieving general health but abundant health. Our recommended amount is listed first. This is the amount that we believe through years of research and application will help a person achieve optimal health and longevity. In some cases, the potency range suggested is quite wide. This is because our individual differences, genetic code, family history, body size, activity and stress level, pollutant-exposure factors, and general levels of health tend to vary widely. Keep in mind, too, that these optimal daily amounts are the best recommendations we have at the present time. New scientific information may yield new recommended amounts. Note especially that these are the recommended optimal amounts for adults, not children. The U.S. Government's RDAs (recommended dietary allowances) are also listed.

UNITS OF MEASURE

Units of vitamins and minerals are measured in the following ways:

- Fat-soluble vitamins are measured in International Units (IU).
- Water-soluble vitamins and minerals are measured by:
    1,000 micrograms (mcg) = 1 milligram (mg)
    1,000 milligrams (mg) = 1 gram (gm)

Vitamins

VITAMIN A (Retinol)

Fat-Soluble

Sources: found only in animal sources, fish liver oils (as in cod liver oil), liver, milk, cream, cheese, butter, eggs.

What It Does: is required for all situations that have to do with vision and the eyes; builds resistance to respiratory infections; increases immunity, protects against cancer; prevents birth defects; helps with skin conditions and acne. Can be stored in the body.

Deficiency Symptoms: night blindness or loss of adaptation to the dark; dry eye disease; sty in the eye; increased susceptibility to infection; sinus and bronchial infections; drying out of skin and mucous membranes; loss of taste and smell which leads to loss of appetite; loss of vigor; defective teeth and gums; slowed growth.

Optimal Daily Amount: 7,000 to 10,000 IU.   RDA is 5,000 IU. We recommend a mixture of both vitamin A and beta-carotene.

BETA-CAROTENE (Provitamin A)

Fat-Soluble

Sources: yellow fruit, dark green, yellow and leafy vegetables, carrots, yams, cantaloupe, yellow squash, spinach, apricots, spirulina, wheat grass, alfalfa, barley grass, and over 400 carotenoids isolated from nature.

What It Does: important free-radical fighter for various forms of cancer; protects against ultraviolet damage; enhances immune system; many of the same functions as vitamin A. Beta-Carotene must be converted by the liver and the intestinal wall into useable vitamin A.

Deficiency Symptoms: intake of alcohol decreases beta-carotene in the liver; those with hypothyroidism and diabetes may have trouble converting beta-carotene into vitamin A.

Optimal Daily Amount: 20,000 to 50,000 IU. No RDA has been established. Non-toxic.

VITAMIN B1 (Thiamin)

Water-Soluble

Sources: yellow fruit, green and leafy vegetables, carrots, yams, cantaloupe, organ meats (especially liver), pork, dried beans, peas, soybeans, wheat germ, brewer's or nutritional yeast, egg yolks, poultry, fish and seafood, dried yeast, brown rice, rice husks or rice bran, whole grain products, oatmeal, nuts, most vegetables, milk, raisins, prunes.

What It Does: known as the 'morale' vitamin; converts carbohydrates (sugar) into energy; promotes growth; aids digestion and is essential for nerve tissues, muscles and heart; helps repel insects and mosquitoes, used in the treatment of alcoholics and drug addicts

Deficiency Symptoms: loss of appetite; fatigue; weakness; neuritis; muscle atrophy; head pressures; poor sleep; feeling tense and irritable; aches and pains; subjectively poor memory, difficulty concentrating; constipation; impaired growth; pins and needles sensation in the toes and 'burning' sensation in the feet; beriberi, which includes mental illness, paralysis of some eye muscles, foot drop and decreased sensation in the feet and legs. Alcohol consumption interferes with absorption of B1.

Optimal Daily Amount: 25-100 mg. RDA is 1.4 mg; additional 0.4 mg for pregnancy or lactation.

VITAMIN B2 (Riboflavin)

Water-Soluble

Sources: milk, cheese and yogurt are rich sources, along with liver, kidney, meat, poultry, fish, eggs, bran, wheat germ, lentils, beans, peanuts, soy beans, green leafy vegetables, fruit.

What It Does: helps convert protein, carbohydrates and fat into energy; protects against free-radical damage; necessary for cellular respiration and good vision, skin, hair and nails; physical exercise increases need.

Deficiency Symptoms: cracks and sores in the corners of the mouth; frayed or scaling lips; inflamed tongue with a purplish or magenta color; eczema or seborrhea; flaking skin around the nose, eyebrows, chin, cheeks, earlobes or hairline; oily appearance of nose, chin, and forehead with fatty deposits accumulating under the skin; bloodshot, watering, itching, burning, fatigued eyes with a keen sensitivity to light; increase in cataract formation; nervous symptoms such as "pins and needles" sensation, difficulty walking, muscular weakness, trembling and a lack of stamina or vigor; behavioral changes such as depression, moodiness, nervousness and irritability.

Optimal Daily Amount: 25-100 mg. RDA is 1.6 mg.

VITAMIN B3 (Niacin, Niacinamide, Nicotinic Acid, Nicotinamide)

Water-Soluble

Sources: lean meats, organ meats, fish, brewer's yeast, whole grains, nuts, dried peas and beans, white meat of turkey or chicken, milk, milk products.

What It Does: assists enzymes to break down proteins, fats, carbohydrates into energy; helps lower cholesterol levels, lowers triglycerides and other cardiovascular disorders; for the nervous system, maintains healthy skin, tongue and digestive tissues; plays a role in the production of bile salts, for synthesis of sex hormones; prevent or cures schizophrenia and some other mental disorders; alleviates arthritis.

Deficiency Symptoms: pellagra (symptoms include dermatitis, diarrhea, and dementia (mental disorders); bright red tongue, sore tongue and gums, inflamed mouth, throat and esophagus, canker sores, mental illness, perceptual changes in the five senses, schizophrenic symptoms, rheumatoid arthritis, muscle weakness, general fatigue, irritability, recurring headaches, indigestion, nausea, vomiting, bad breath, insomnia, small ulcers.

Optimal Daily Amount: 50–100 mg of niacinamide included in your daily B-complex supplement. To lower cholesterol, researchers use the niacin form, 250–1,500 mgs spread throughout the day. RDA is 20 mg.

VITAMIN B5 (Pantothenic Acid, Calcium Pantothenate, Panthenol)

Water-Soluble

Sources: brewer's yeast, liver, kidney, wheat bran, crude molasses, whole grains, egg yolk, peanuts, peas, sunflower seeds, beef, chicken, turkey, milk, royal jelly.

What It Does: vital for the adrenal glands and for production of cortisone, plays a role in creating energy from protein, carbohydrates and fats, helps synthesize cholesterol, steroids and fatty acids; for a healthy digestive tract; essential to production of antibodies; helps with arthritis and is an anti–inflammatory.

Deficiency Symptoms: burning sensation in the feet; enlarged beefy, furrowed tongue; skin disorders such as eczema's; duodenal ulcers; inflammation of the intestines and stomach; decreased antibody formation; upper respiratory infections; vomiting; restlessness; muscle cramps; constipation; sensitivity to insulin; adrenal exhaustion; physical and mental depression; overwhelming fatigue; reduced production of hydrochloric acid in the stomach; allergies; arthritis; nerve degeneration; spinal curvature; disturbed pulse rate; gout; graying hair.

Optimal Daily Amount: 100-200 mg in a B-complex supplement or up to 500 mgs in divided doses. RDA is 10 mg.

VITAMIN B6 (Pyridoxine, Pyridoxinal, Pyridoxamine)

Water-Soluble

Sources: brewer's yeast, sunflower seeds, wheat germ, liver and other organ meats, blackstrap molasses, bananas, walnuts, roasted peanuts, canned tuna, salmon.

What It Does: metabolizes proteins, fats and carbohydrates; forms hormones for adrenaline and insulin; makes antibodies and red blood cells; for synthesis of RNA and DNA; regulates fluids in the body; needed for production of hydrochloric acid; relieves carpal tunnel syndrome; helps with PMS symptoms; helps asthmatics; with magnesium helps prevent kidney stones.

Deficiency Symptoms: greasy, scaly dermatitis between the eyebrows, and on the body parts that rub together; low blood sugar; numbness and tingling in the hands and feet; neuritis; arthritis; trembling hands in the aged; water retention and swelling during pregnancy; nausea; motion sickness; mental retardation; epilepsy; kidney stones; anemia; excessive fatigue; nervous breakdown; mental illness; acne; convulsions in babies; newborn infants may develop crusty yellow scabs on the scalp called "cradle cap".

Optimal Daily Amount: 50-100 mg combined with a B-complex supplement. RDA is 2 mg.

VITAMIN B12 (Cobalamin or Cyanocobalamin)
Water-Soluble

Sources: organ meats, liver, beef, pork, eggs, whole milk, cheese, whole wheat bread, fish.

What It Does: metabolism of nerve tissue; protein, fat and carbohydrate metabolism, creates red blood cells, may stimulate appetite in children. An "intrinsic factor" must exist in the stomach for this vitamin to be absorbed.

Deficiency Symptoms: pernicious anemia including weakness, a sore and inflamed tongue that appears smooth and shiny, numbness and tingling in extremities, pallor, weak pulse, stiffness, drowsiness, irritability, depression, mental deterioration, senile dementia, paranoid psychosis, chronic fatigue syndrome, diarrhea, poor appetite, growth failure in children.

Optimal Daily Amount: 500-1,000 mcg with a complete B-complex vitamin. Sublingual form is best absorbed, with tablets placed under the tongue. RDA is 6 mcg.

BIOTIN
Water-Soluble

Sources: yeast, liver, organ meats, egg yolk, grains, nuts, fish.

What It Does: needed for maintenance of hair and skin, for brittle fingernails, sweat glands, nerves, bone marrow, normal bone growth; may help with Sudden Infant Death Syndrome (SIDS) or crib death.

Deficiency Symptoms: scaly dermatitis, inflamed sore tongue, loss of appetite, nausea, depression, muscle pain, sitophobia (morbid dread of food), pallor, anemia, abnormalities of heart function, burning or prickling sensations, sensitive skin, insomnia, extreme lassitude, increased cholesterol, depression of immune system.

Optimal Daily Amount: 50-200 mcg combined with B-complex. RDA is 3 mcg.

PABA (Para-Amino-Benzoic Acid)
Water-Soluble

Sources: liver, brewer's yeast, wheat germ, molasses, eggs, organ meats, yogurt, green leafy vegetables.

What It Does: stimulates intestinal bacteria which aids in production of pantothenic acid; coenzyme in making blood cells and metabolizing protein; important for skin health, hair pigmentation and health of intestines; may help with vitiligo, may restore gray hair to normal; used for many skin conditions.

Deficiency Symptoms: similar to symptoms caused by a folic acid or pantothenic acid deficiency; also vitiligo, fatigue, irritability, depression, nervousness, headache, constipation, and other digestive disorders.

Optimal Daily Amount: 50-100 mg included in a B-complex vitamin. No RDA has been established.

FOLIC ACID (Folacin, Folate)
Water-Soluble

Sources: deep, green leafy vegetables, liver, brewer's yeast, whole grains, bran, asparagus, lima beans, lentils, orange juice.

What It Does: for synthesis of RNA and DNA, for red blood cell production, metabolism of protein; increases the appetite; for production of antibodies; prevents neural tube defects and birth defects in babies; reduces susceptibility to infection.

Deficiency Symptoms: anemia, poor growth, weakness, an inflamed and sore tongue that may appear smooth and shiny, numbness or tingling in the hands and feet, indigestion, diarrhea, depression, irritability, pallor, drowsiness, a slow, weakened pulse; graying hair; mental illness; impaired wound healing; reduced resistance to infection; birth defects resulting in spina bifida and other neural tube defects, toxemia, insomnia, leg numbness and cramps in pregnant women, premature birth and after birth hemorrhaging, cervical cancer and dysplasia.

Optimal Daily Amount: 400-800 mcg combined with B-complex vitamin. RDA for men is 200 mcg; for women 180 mcg; for pregnant women 400 mcg.

CHOLINE
Water-Soluble

Sources: lecithin, brewer's yeast, fish, soybeans (tofu, tempeh, miso), peanuts, beef liver, egg yolk, wheat germ, cauliflower, cabbage.

What It Does: for transport and metabolism of fats and cholesterol in the liver; prevents cardiovascular disease; detoxifies the liver; for a proper functioning nervous system; part of the nerve fluid for nerve impulses; prevents and treats memory loss and diseases of the nervous system; influences mood and depression (manic-depressives); strengthens capillary walls, accelerates blood flow, thereby lowering blood pressure; aids in the treatment of gallstones.

Deficiency Symptoms: may cause high blood pressure, bleeding stomach ulcers, heart trouble, blocking of the tubes of the kidneys, hemorrhaging of the kidneys, hardening of the arteries, atherosclerosis, headaches, dizziness, ear noises, palpitations, constipation.

Optimal Daily Amount: 500-1,000 mg. No RDA has been established.

INOSITOL

Water-Soluble

Sources: lecithin, organ meats, wheat germ, whole grains, brewer's yeast, blackstrap molasses, peanuts, citrus fruit.

What It Does: with choline helps to metabolize fats and cholesterol in the arteries and liver; helps promote the body's production of lecithin; for growth and cell survival in bone marrow, eye membranes and intestines; with vitamin E may help nerve damage in certain forms of muscular dystrophy; in certain cases may prevent thinning hair and baldness; helps with brain cell nutrition; with choline may help with menstrual problems.

Deficiency Symptoms: none officially recognized; however, deficiency may cause constipation, eczema, abnormalities of the eyes, hair loss, high cholesterol.

Optimal Daily Amount: 500-1,000 mg. No RDA has been established.

VITAMIN C (Ascorbic Acid)

Water-Soluble

Sources: rose hips, citrus fruit and juices, strawberries, blueberries, cantaloupes, raw vegetables such as red bell peppers.

What It Does: a potent antioxidant to protect against cellular damage; formation and maintenance of collagen (the skin's "cement"), helps with wound healing and burns, especially those recovering from surgery; increases the absorption of iron and calcium; activates insulin; for a properly functioning nervous system; increases resistance to infections; raises HDL (good) cholesterol; helps protect from cardiovascular disease; prevents buildup of atherosclerotic plaque on the blood vessel wall; may help with cold and flu; may help with infertility; helps body produce interferon; for male fertility; protects us against industrial pollutants; for cataracts and other eye disorders; prevents bleeding gums; preventing many types of viral and bacterial infections; protects from many forms of cancer.

Deficiency Symptoms: bruising easily, bleeding gums, tooth decay, nose bleeds, swollen or painful joints, anemia, poor wound healing, lowered resistance to infection, general weakening of connective tissue, scurvy, easily fractured bones, weakened arteries rupture or hemorrhage, extreme muscle weakness, painful joints, wounds and sores will not heal.

Optimal Daily Amount: 1,000-6,000 mg depending on your need. RDA is 60 mg (slightly higher for pregnancy and lactation).

BIOFLAVONOIDS (Flavonoids, Rutin, Hesperidin, OPCs, Vitamin P)

Water-Soluble

Sources: white part (including the center part) and pulp of oranges, lemon and grapefruit; apricots, rose hips, cherries, grapes, green peppers, tomatoes, papayas, broccoli, cantaloupe and dark pigmented fruit and vegetables.

What It Does: decreases permeability and fragility of blood vessels and constricts the capillaries; protect vitamin C from oxidation; increases absorption of vitamin A; exhibits anti viral effects; are free-radical scavengers; natural antibiotic activity; may help ease pain of varicose veins; helps certain types of hemorrhoids; prevents bruising; may help relieve hot flashes; inhibits certain cataracts.

Deficiency Symptoms: edema or accumulation of fluid in the tissue, bleeding into the tissue (noticeable as red spots and splotches when it occurs close under the skin) resulting from fragile, faulty capillaries.

Optimal Daily Amount: 500-2,000 mg, depending on your need. No RDA has been established.

VITAMIN D (Ergocalciferol)

Fat-Soluble

Sources: sunshine (manufactured through your skin), fish liver oils such as cod liver oil, liver, egg yolks.

What It Does: enhances absorption of calcium and phosphorus; necessary for proper functioning of the thyroid and pituitary glands; improves psoriasis; maintenance of cell membrane fluidity.

Deficiency Symptoms: osteomalacia (softening of the bones) in adults, rickets in children, irritability, restlessness, fitful sleeping, frequent crying, heavy perspiration behind the neck in babies, delayed eruption of teeth, soft and yielding skull, bowed legs, knock knees, depressions in the chest, pigeon-chest deformity of the rib cage, swayback, overly prominent forehead causing the appearance of sunken eyes, delayed walking; may protect against colorectal and breast cancer.

Optimal Daily Amount: 400-800 IU from fish liver oil. RDA is 400 IU.

VITAMIN E (Tocopherol)
Fat-Soluble

Sources: wheat germ oil, soybean oil, safflower oil, peanuts, whole grains (wheat, rice, oats) green, leafy vegetables, cabbage, spinach, asparagus, broccoli, eggs.

What It Does: important for oxygen of the cells, preventing the oxidation of cells; may be useful in gangrene, coronary and cerebral thrombosis (clots), diabetes mellitus, congenital heart disease, arteriosclerosis, phlebitis, and other leg problems due to poor circulation; helps varicose veins; it is a powerful antioxidant, protecting against air pollution, damage against radiation; protects polyunsaturated oils from breaking down; prevents clotting in blood vessels; melts fresh blood clots, frees blood platelets for normal clotting of wounds; prevents strokes; normalizes the activity of ovaries in women, improving periods, preventing excessive bleeding, and vaginal dryness; prevents miscarriages, proper functioning of the sex glands, improves male sperm cells; strengthens the immune system; applied externally, it eliminates radiation burns, and reduces scarring; may help with non-cancerous breast cysts; protects against nitrosamines in foods; alleviates pain in osteoarthritis; may help relieve menopausal symptoms; increased stamina in athletes; improves action of insulin.

Deficiency Symptoms: may decrease survival time of red blood cells; faulty fat absorption; anemia in premature infants; degeneration of the brain and spinal cord; premature births and higher risk of miscarriage; decrease in sex hormones; higher risk of skin cancer.

Optimal Daily Amount: 400-1,200 IU. To obtain these potencies, you should use natural vitamin E supplements, as d-alpha tocopherol or the dry form, d-alpha tocopherol succinate. RDA is 30 IU.

VITAMIN K (Phylloquinone)
Fat-Soluble

Sources: yogurt, kefir, acidophilus milk, alfalfa, spinach, cabbage, cauliflower, tomatoes, pork liver, lean meat, peas, carrots, soybeans, potatoes, egg yolks.

What It Does: essential to blood clotting; for proper bone mineralization; has helped people with Crohn's disease and gastrointestinal disorders; for proper bone mineralization.

Deficiency Symptoms: hypoprothrombinemia (condition in which the time it takes for the blood to clot is prolonged), hemorrhages, bloody urine and stools, nosebleeds, miscarriages; deficiency in newborn babies results in bloody stools or vomiting (fairly common since newborns have no intestinal bacteria).

Optimal Daily Amount: Most vitamin and mineral supplements do not contain vitamin K as it is easily available in the diet and synthesized in the body. Consult your physician for further information on this vitamin. RDA for women is 65 mcg; 80 mcg for men.

Minerals

BORON

Sources: fresh fruit and vegetables.

What It Does: helps retain calcium in bone and prevents against calcium and magnesium loss through the urine; helps bone mineralization; prevents osteoporosis; increases estrogen naturally in postmenopausal women.

Deficiency Symptoms: none officially recognized.

Optimal Daily Amount: 1-3 mg daily combined with calcium, magnesium and all other minerals. No RDA has been established.

CALCIUM

Sources: milk, egg yolks, fish or sardines (eaten with bones), yogurt, soybeans, green leafy vegetables (such as turnip greens, mustard greens, broccoli, and kale), roots, tubers, seeds, soups and stews made from bones, blackstrap molasses, almonds, figs, beans.

What It Does: maintains acid-alkaline balance in body; normalizes contraction and relaxation of the heart muscles; for strong bones and teeth; protects against osteoporosis, rickets and osteomalacia; helps lower high blood pressure; lowers cholesterol and helps prevent cardiovascular disease; helps relieve backaches, menstrual cramps and may help you sleep more soundly; natural tranquilizer; helps prevent cancer, especially colorectal-cancer.

Deficiency Symptoms: nervous spasms, facial twitching, weak feeling muscles, cramps, rickets, slow growth in children, osteoporosis (porous and brittle bones), osteomalacia (a bone-softening disease), heart palpitations and slow pulse rate, height reduction, colon cancer.

Optimal Daily Amount: 1,000-1,500 mg with half to equal parts of magnesium. Some researchers say menopausal women need 1,500 mg, with added boron and magnesium. RDA is 1,000 mg daily for adults; 1,200 mg for pregnancy and lactation; 1,200 mg for males and females from age eleven to twenty-four.

CHLORIDE

Sources: most people obtain chloride from salt (sodium chloride) and salt substitute (potassium chloride), also found in large amounts in body.

What It Does: stimulates production of hydrochloric acid for digestion; maintains fluid and electrolyte balance; helps the liver.

Deficiency Symptoms: impaired digestion; loss of hair and teeth; rare as the body usually produces enough.

Optimal Daily Amount: The need nor the RDA has been established.

CHROMIUM

Sources: brewer's yeast, blackstrap molasses, black pepper, meat (especially liver), whole wheat bread and cereals, beets, mushrooms.

What It Does: helps stabilize blood sugar levels, therefore being effective against diabetes and hypoglycemia; lowers cholesterol; increases level of high-density lipoproteins (HDLs) in humans (shown protective against cardiovascular disease); increases lean muscle tissue while decreasing body fat.

Deficiency Symptoms: slowed growth, shortened life span, raised cholesterol levels, an array of symptoms related to low and high blood sugar such as diabetes and low blood sugar.

Optimal Daily Amount: 200-400 mcg of GTF (glucose tolerance form) taken with other minerals. Chromium polynicotinate (bound to niacin) and chromium picolinate (bound to picolinic acid) are natural forms. RDA has not been established. The National Research Council tentatively recommends 50-200 mcg to be effective.

COPPER

Sources: nuts, organ meats, seafood, mushrooms, legumes.

What It Does: with iron and protein it forms hemoglobin (red blood cells); forms melanin (pigment in skin and hair); helps form connective tissues such as collagen and elastin; helps lower cholesterol; helps prevent rancidity of fatty acids and maintains cellular structure; may help as anti-inflammatory against arthritis.

Deficiency Symptoms: anemia; loss of hair; loss of taste; general weakness; impaired respiration such as emphysema; brittle bones; chronic or recurrent diarrhea; hair de-pigmentation; low white blood cell count which leads to reduced resistance to infection; retarded growth; water retention; nervous irritability; high cholesterol; abnormal ECG patterns; development of ischemic heart disease; birth defects; miscarriage and neural tube defects; antacid use creates copper deficiency.

Optimal Daily Amount: 2-3 mg taken with zinc at a 10:1 or 15:1 ratio (zinc:copper). RDA is 2 mg.

FLUORIDE

Sources: usually added to our drinking water.

What It Does: necessary for formation of strong bones and teeth, may protect against osteoporosis.

Deficiency Symptoms: none.

Optimal Daily Amount: Don't take additional fluoride. Found in various toothpaste's and mouthwashes. No RDA has been established.

IODINE (Iodide)

Sources: seaweed (especially kelp), dulse, seafood, iodized salt and sea salt, eggs, garlic, turnip greens, watercress.

What It Does: stimulates the thyroid gland to produce thyroxin; protects against toxic effects from radioactive material; related to over a hundred enzyme systems such as energy production, nerve function and hair and skin growth; stimulates conversion of body fat to energy, regulating basal metabolic rate; relieves pain and soreness associated with fibrocystic breast; loosens clogged mucous in breathing tubes.

Deficiency Symptoms: goiter (characterized by enlarged thyroid gland which may thicken the neck, restrict breathing and cause bulging of the eyes); hypothyroidism (low thyroid); physical and mental sluggishness, poor circulation and low vitality; dry hair and skin, cold hands and feet, obesity; cretinism (characterized by physical and mental retardation in children born to deficient mothers); hearing loss.

Optimal Daily Amount: 150-300 mcg. RDA is 80-150 mcg. Liquid iodine for medicinal uses (as an antiseptic for wounds) should not be used orally.

IRON

Sources: liver, heart, kidney, lean meats, shellfish, dried beans, fruit, nuts, green, leafy vegetables, whole grains, blackstrap molasses.

What It Does: helps form red-blood cells called hemoglobin and myoglobin (red pigment in muscles); cures and prevents iron-deficiency anemia; stimulates immunity; helps with muscular and athletic performance; prevents fatigue.

Deficiency Symptoms: anemia (pallor, weakness, persistent fatigue, labored breathing on exertion, headaches, palpitation), young children suffer diminished coordination, balanced attention span, IQ, and memory; older children have poor learning, reading and problem solving skills; depressed immune system with decreased ability to produce white blood cells to fight off infection; concave or spoon like fingernails and toenails.

Optimal Daily Amount: RDA is 10 mg for men, 18 mg for women, and we feel this should be adequate. As a supplement, do not use inorganic iron (ferrous sulfate) which destroys vitamin E. Use organic iron (ferrous fumarate, ferrous citrate or ferrous gluconate).

MAGNESIUM

Sources: chlorophyll of all plants, figs, lemons, grapefruit, green, leafy vegetables, alfalfa, yellow corn, soya flour, whole wheat, peas, beans, brown rice, almonds, oil-rich nuts and seeds, apples.

What It Does: absolutely essential for life, a major mineral for the metabolism of glucose; production of cellular energy; to create protein; for nerve and muscle contraction; protective against cardiovascular disease; lowers high blood pressure; helps with PMS; helps kidney stones; for nervous system; important for people taking diuretics and digitalis.

Deficiency Symptoms: apathy, depression, apprehensiveness, confusion, disorientation, vertigo (a condition in which the room seems to spin around), muscular weakness and twitching, over-excitability of the nervous system which may lead to muscle spasms or cramps, insomnia, jumpiness, sensitivity to noise, irritability, poor memory, tremors or convulsions.

Optimal Daily Amount: 400-750 mg should be taken with twice as much calcium. RDA is 350 mg for men; 280 mg for women, plus 150 mg if pregnant or lactating. Large amounts of magnesium salts (3,000 to 5,000 mg daily) have a cathartic (laxative) effect.

MANGANESE

Sources: whole grains, wheat germ, bran, peas, nuts, green, leafy vegetables, beets, egg yolks, bananas, liver, organ meats, milk.

What It Does: required for vital enzyme reactions; proper bone development and synthesis of mucopolysaccharides; for help with osteoarthritis; required for many enzyme reactions; for normal functioning of the pancreas and for carbohydrate metabolism; to manufacture collagen; important part in the formation of thyroxin, a hormone secreted by the thyroid gland; for thymus gland function; may improve memory and reduce nervous irritability.

Deficiency Symptoms: weight loss; dermatitis; nausea; slow growth and color changes of hair; low cholesterol; disturbances in fat metabolism and glucose tolerance, deficiency suspected in diabetes; deficiency during pregnancy may be a factor in epilepsy in the offspring, myasthenia gravis (severe loss of muscle strength).

Optimal Daily Amount: 5-10 mg in combination with other minerals. No RDA has been established.

MOLYBDENUM

Sources: organ meats (liver, kidney), milk, dairy products, legumes, whole grains, leafy green vegetables.

What It Does: required for the activity of several enzymes in the body, a vital part of the enzyme responsible for iron utilization; helps prevent anemia; a detoxifier of potentially hazardous substances we may come in contact with; may be an antioxidant; protects teeth from cavities; aids in carbohydrate and fat metabolism.

Deficiency Symptoms: possible esophageal cancer in those that have molybdenum deficient soil.

Optimal Daily Amount: Optimal intake is still uncertain; 50-200 mcg (not mg). No RDA has been established.

PHOSPHOROUS

Sources: high-protein foods such as meat, fish, poultry, eggs, milk, cheese, nuts, legumes, bone meal; many processed foods and soft drinks preserved with phosphates adversely affect the body's calcium-phosphorous balance.

What It Does: essential for bone mineralization, for normal bone and tooth structure; involved in cellular activity; important for athletes and may help with muscular fatigue; important for heart regularity; needed for the transference of nerve impulses; aids in growth and body repair.

Deficiency Symptoms: muscle weakness (to the point of respiratory arrest), anemia, increased susceptibility to infection. The typical diet usually makes a phosphorous deficiency rare in the United States; those with kidney failure, or gastrointestinal diseases can have severe deficiencies; alcoholics and those taking antacids may be deficient.

Optimal Daily Amount: No supplementation needed as the diet should supply sufficient amounts. RDA is 800-1,200 mg for adults.

POTASSIUM

Sources: bananas, apricots, lettuce, broccoli, potatoes, fresh fruit and fruit juices, sunflower seeds, unsalted peanuts, nuts, squash, wheat germ, brewer's yeast, desiccated liver, fish, bone meal, watercress, blackstrap molasses, unsulfured figs.

What It Does: balances fluid with sodium inside the cells; for proper muscle and heart contraction; to assist red blood cells in carrying oxygen; helps stimulate water waste through kidneys; for proper carbohydrate metabolism; for energy storage in the muscles and liver; helps reduce high blood pressure; helps colic in babies; prevents heart attacks; helps allergies; important for those using diuretics.

Deficiency Symptoms: general weakness of muscles, mental confusion, muscle cramping, poor reflexes, nervous system disruption, soft, flabby muscles, constipation, acne in young people, dry skin in adults, severe deficiency leads to heart attack.

Optimal Daily Amount: 2,000-4,000 mg. Generally you get enough in foods. Athletes generally require more (3,000-6,000 mg) because of heavy perspiration. The maximum potency allowed by the government in supplement form is 99 mg. Discuss higher potencies with a physician. RDA is 2,000-2,500 mg.

SELENIUM

Sources: organ meats, tuna, seafood, brewer's yeast, fresh garlic, mushrooms, wheat germ, some whole grains.

What It Does: necessary for growth and protein synthesis; increases effectiveness of vitamin E, they are synergistic; an antioxidant for the cells to protect against oxygen exposure; protects against toxic pollutants for sexual reproduction; may reduce risk of cancer; helps against heart disease; reduces free-radical damage that causes aging; alleviates hot flashes and some menopausal symptoms.

Deficiency Symptoms: dandruff; enhanced damaging effects of ozone on the lungs; decreased growth; infant deaths associated with selenium and/or vitamin E deficiency; increased risk of cancer and heart disease.

Optimal Daily Amount: 100-200 mcg in high selenium areas; 100-400 mcg in low selenium areas. The Food and Nutrition board states that overt selenium toxicity may occur in humans ingesting 2,400-3,000 mcg. No RDA has been established.

SILICON (Silica)

Sources: flaxseed, steel cut oats, almonds, peanuts, sunflower seeds, onions, alfalfa, fresh fruit, brewer's yeast, dietary fiber.

What It Does: helps build connective tissue; most people take silica as a form of silicon, to help with hair, skin and nails.

Deficiency Symptoms: aging symptoms of skin (wrinkles), thinning or loss of hair, poor bone development, soft or brittle nails.

Optimal Daily Amount: We have no dietary recommendations. Adequate amounts are found in the diet. No RDA has been established.

SODIUM (Sodium Chloride, Salt)

Sources: sea salt, most foods from animal sources, shellfish, meat, poultry, milk, cheese, kelp, powdered seaweed, most processed foods.

What It Does: works with potassium to maintain proper fluid balance between cells; for nerve stimulation for muscle contraction; helps in keeping calcium and other minerals in the blood soluble; for weak muscles; stimulates the adrenal glands. High sodium usually accounts for high blood pressure. Aids in preventing heat prostration or sunstroke.

Deficiency Symptoms: They are rare since most foods contain sodium. However, symptoms include headaches, excessive sweating, heat exhaustion, respiratory failure, muscular cramps, weakness, collapsed blood vessels, stomach and intestinal gas, chronic diarrhea, weight loss, kidney failure, tuberculosis of kidneys, streptococci infections.

Optimal Daily Amount: rarely needed, an ordinary diet provides enough sodium. A gram of sodium chloride has been suggested for each kilogram of water ingested. RDA is 200-600 mg.

SULFUR

Sources: protein foods especially eggs, lean beef, fish, onions, kale, soybeans, dried beans.

What It Does: found in every cell of the body; helps nerves and muscles function properly, and normalizes glandular secretions; necessary for healthy hair, skin and nails; helps maintain oxygen balance necessary for brain function; the homeopathic supplement of sulfur helps with rashes and itching and other skin conditions.

Deficiency Symptoms: rare but may be excessive sweating, chronic diarrhea, nausea, respiratory failure, heat exhaustion, muscular weakness and mental apathy.

Optimal Daily Amount: a diet sufficient in protein should be sufficient in sulfur. No RDA has been established.

VANADIUM

Sources: fish, black pepper and dill seed are richest source, middle range is whole grains, meats, dairy products.

What It Does: in animal studies with diabetic rats, research showed it improved glucose tolerance and improved efficiency of insulin in the muscle cells. More research needs to be done.

Deficiency Symptoms: little known at this time, but high blood pressure and hardening of the arteries have been suggested.

Optimal Daily Amount: More needs to be known before we can suggest an amount. No RDA has been established.

ZINC

Sources: fresh oysters, herring, wheat germ, pumpkin seeds, milk, steamed crab, lobster, chicken, port chops, turkey, lean ground beef, liver, eggs.

What It Does: promotes wound healing; helps with acne; affects impotence in men, and aids in increasing sperm count; helps infertility; may help with prostate problems; for increasing immunity; for colds and flu; prevents hair loss; may help with some forms of cancer; helps with macular degeneration.

Deficiency Symptoms: fingernails with white spots or bands or an opaquely white appearance, loss of taste, smell and appetite, delayed sexual development in adolescence, underdeveloped penis and less full beard and underarm hair in boys, irregular menstrual cycle in girls, infertility and impaired sexual function in adults, poor wound healing, loss of hair, increased susceptibility to infection, reduced salivation, skin lesions, stretch marks, reduced absorption of nutrients, impaired development of bones, muscles and nervous system; deformed offspring; dwarfism.

Optimal Daily Amount: 30-50 mg (take with copper, a zinc:copper ratio of 10:1). RDA is 15 mg.

Notes

Chapter 1: Aging, Let's Slow it Down

1. Leonard Hayflick, *Scientific American* 218 (1968).
2. Gelfant, paper read at the Miami Symposium on Theoretical Aspects of Aging, February 7, 1974.
3. Dominick Buou, *The People's Guide to Vitamins and Minerals* (Chicago: Contemporary Books, 1980): 165.
4. Ruth Adams, *The Big Family Guide to All the Vitamins* (New Canaan, CT: Keats Publishing, 1992): 356.
5. James Braly and Laura Torbet, *Dr. Braly's Food Allergy and Nutrition Revolution*, (New Canaan, CT: Keats Publishing, Inc., 1992): 81.

Chapter 2: The Significance of Vitamins, Minerals and Herbs

1. Albert Szent-Gyorgyi, "How New Understanding About the Biological Function of Ascorbic Acid May Profoundly Affect Our Lives," *Executive Health*, Executive Publications, Rancho Santa Fe, CA: May 1978.
2. *Journal American Medical Association* 253:6 (February 8, 1985).
  • *Super Supplements* by Michael E. Rosenbaum, M.D. and Dominick Bosco, Signet Book, New American Library, New York 1987, p 249.
3. Gladys Lindberg and Judy McFarland, *Take Charge of Your Health*, (Harper and Row, San Francisco, 1982): 181.
  • *Prevention Magazine's Complete Book of Vitamins and Minerals*, New York: Wings Books, a division of Rodale Press Inc., 1988, 10-11.
4. *Take Charge of Your Health*, p 44.
5. Michael Robbins, The 1992 Top Ten Almanac, Workman Publishing, 1992.
6. Karolyn A. Gazella, "Nutritional Supplements: Protecting the Core of American Health" *Health Counselor*, (5:3): 27-31.
7. Paul Harvey, "Vitamins are a 'health hazard'? *Los Angeles Times Syndicate*, 1992.
8. *Journal of the American Medical Association* 226 (1991): 2847-2851.
9. Julian Whitaker, M.D., *The Whitaker Guide to Natural Healing*, Prima Publishing, Rocklin, CA, 1995, p 11.
10. Abram Hoffer, *Journal of Orthomolecular Medicine* 7:1 (First quarter 1992).
11. Ruth Adams, *The Big Family Guide to All the Vitamins*, Keats Publishing, New Canaan, CT, 1992, p 144.
12. Elizabeth Somer, *The Essential Guide to Vitamins and Minerals* (Harper-Perennial, division of Harper Collins Publishers, 1992).
13. Ashmead Dwayne, Ph.D., et al., *Intestinal Absorption of Metal Ions and Chelates*, Charles Thomas publisher, Springfield IL, 1985, p 4.
  • Frank Murray, *The Big Family Guide to all the Minerals*, Keats Publishing, Inc., New Canaan, CT, 1995.
14. *Herbal Gram* (12), Spring 1987, (Austin, TX: Herb Research Foundation and *The Journal of the American Botanical Council*.
15. Ibid.
16. Ibid.

Chapter 3: Building Immunity and Longevity with Antioxidants

1. Bruce N. Ames, "Understanding the Causes of Aging and Cancer," a paper presented at the Biological Oxidants and Antioxidants: New Developments in Research and Health Effects conference, Pasadena, CA, March 12-13, 1993.

-   Bruce N. Ames, "Oxidants, Antioxidants, and the Degenerative Diseases of Aging" *Proceedings of the National Academy of Science* 90:17 (1993): 7915-7922.

2. James Braly and Laura Torbet, *Dr. Braly's Food Allergy and Nutrition Revolution*, New Canaan, CT: Keats Publishing, Inc., (1992): 81.

-   J. Ward, "Free-radicals, antioxidants, and preventive geriatrics," *Australian Family Physicians* 23 (July 1994): 1297-1301.

3. D. Harman, "Free-radical Theory of Aging: History." In *Free-radicals and Aging*, eds. I. Ement and B. Chance. (Basel, Switzerland: Birkhauser Verlag, 1992).

-   D. Harman, "The Aging Process: Major risk factor for disease and death" *Proceedings of the National Academy of Sciences* 88(1991): 5360-5363.

-   D. Harman, "Aging: Prospects for further increases in the functional life span," *Age* 17 (1994): 119-146.

4. Sheldon Saul Hendler, M.D., Ph.D., *The Doctors' Vitamin and Mineral Encyclopedia*, Simon and Schuster, New York: 1990, p 49.

5. Regina Ziegler, "Carotenoids, vegetables, fruits, and risk of cancer" San Diego Conference, February 6-9, 1993.

-   G.H. Patterson, "Fruits and Vegetables in the American Diet: Data from the NHANES II Survey" *American Journal of Public Health* 80 (1990): 1443-1449.

-   K.A. Steinmetz, "Vegetables, Fruit, and Cancer—Part I: Epidemiology" *Cancer Cause Control* 2 (1991): 325-327.

-   Gladys Block, Ph.D., "Fruit, vegetables, and cancer prevention: A review of the epidemiologic evidence" *Nutrition and Cancer* 18 (1992): 1-29.

6. Prabhala, RH, "Influence of beta-carotene on immune functions" *Annals of the New York Academy of Science* 691 (December 31, 1993): 262-263.

-   Schroeder, D.J., "Cancer prevention and beta-carotene" *Annals of Pharmacotherapy* (April 28, 1994): 470-471.

7. Henkel, "Antioxidant Update," January/February, 1996.

-   Used with permission.

8. Ibid.

9. Gladys Block, Ph.D., "The data support for a role for antioxidants in reducing cancer risk," *Nutrition Reviews* 50 (1992): 207-213.

10. Gladys Block, Ph.D., "Fruit, vegetables, and cancer prevention: A review of the epidemiologic evidence" *Nutrition and Cancer* 18 (1992): 1-29.

-   Carper, Jean, *Stop Aging Now*, Harper Collins, 1995, p 170.

11. Gladys Block, Ph.D., "Epidemiologic Evidence for Health Benefits of Antioxidants." Paper presented at Pasadena, CA conference cited above.

12. B.E. Cohen and I.K. Cohen, "Vitamin A: ajunvant and steroid antagonist in the immune response" *Journal of Immunology* 3 (1973): 1376-1380.

-   Michael A. Weiner, *Maximum Immunity*, p 99.

-   *Nutrition and Cancer* 11 (1988): 207-217.

13. Sheldon Saul Hendler, M.D., Ph.D., *The Doctors' Vitamin and Mineral Encyclopedia*, p 42.

14. Michael A. Weiner, *Maximum Immunity*, p 98.

15. Ibid., p 99.

-   W.R. Beisel, R. Edelman, K. Nauss, and R.M. Suskin, *Journal of the American Medical Association* 245 (1981): 53-58.

16. *Journal of the National Cancer Institute* 73 (December 1984): 1463-1468.

- *The Doctors' Vitamin and Mineral Encyclopedia*, p 42.
- Michsche, M., et al., Stimulation of immune response in lung cancer patients by vitamin A therapy, *Oncology* 34: 234–238 (1977).
- Shikelle, R.B., et al., Dietary vitamin A and risk of cancer in the Western Electric study. *Lancet*, 2:1185, 1981.

17. Wald, N., Idle, M., and Boreham, J., (1980) *Lancet*, October 18, p 813.

- Hendler, *Doctors' Vitamin and Mineral Encyclopedia*, p 42.

18. Ibid.

19. *Journal of the National Cancer Institute* 73 (December 1984): 1463–1468.

20. Hendler, *The Doctors' Vitamin and Mineral Encyclopedia*, p 42.

- Michsche, M. et al., *Oncology* 34: 234–238 (1977).

21. Hendler, *The Doctors' Vitamin and Mineral Encyclopedia*, p 42.

22. Bendich A. and Langseth L., Safety of vitamin A, *American Journal of Clinical Nutrition* 49 (1989): 358–371.

23. Committee on infectious diseases, American Academy of Pediatrics, *Pediatrics* 91 (May 1993):1014–1015.

- Jack Challen, editor of *Nutrition Reporter,* Nov 1995.

24. Passwater, Richard, Ph.D., *The New Supernutrition,* Pocket Books, New York, 1991, pp 288–289.

25. A. Bendich and L. Langseth, "Safety of vitamin A," *American Journal of Clinical Nutrition* 49 (February 1989): 358–371.

26. Ibid.

27. Gladys Block, Ph.D., *Nutrition Reviews* 50 (June 1992): 207–213.

28. Jack Challem, "Vitamin A and Pregnancy: How Many People Will the Panic Injure?" *The Nutrition Reporter* 6 (November 12, 1995).

29. Committee on infectious diseases, American Academy of Pediatrics, *Pediatrics* 91 (May 1993):1014–1015.

30. Irwin Stone, *The Healing Factor* (New York): Grosset & Dunlap. 1972, p 72.

- Cameron and Pauling, *Cancer and Vitamin C,* p 114.

31. Ibid.

32. E. Cameron and L. Pauling. Warner Books. June 1981, *Cancer and Vitamin C,* p 114.

- Irwin Stone, *The Healing Factor* (New York): Grosset & Dunlap. 1972, p 72.

33. Irwin Stone, *The Healing Factor* (New York): Grosset & Dunlap. 1972, p 72.

34. Albert Szent Gyorgyi, "How New Understandings About the Biological Function of Ascorbic Acid May Profoundly Affect Our Lives!" *Executive Health* (May 1978).

35. Linus Pauling, *Vitamin C and Cancer,* The Linus Pauling Institute of Science & Medicine Newsletter reprint, Vol 1, Issue 2.

- Block, Gladys, Ph.D., "Beyond deficiency: New views on the function and health effects of vitamins," *The New York Academy of Sciences* (Feb 1992).

36. Cameron, E and Pauling. L., *Cancer and Vitamin C.* Warner Books, June 1981.

37. Schwitters, B., Masquelier J.. "OPC in Practice: Bioflavonols and their application." Alfa Omega, Rome, Italy. 1993.

38. Michael T. Murray. "PCO Sources: Grape Seed vs Pine Bark—a review and comparison," Botanical Report. *Health Counselor* 7:1.

- Richard Passwater and Chithan Kandaswami. *Pycnogenol*—*The Super Protector Nutrient* (New Canaan. CT: Keats Publishing, Inc., 1994): 7–8.

39. Richard Passwater and Chithan Kandaswami. *Pycnogenol*—*The Super Protector Nutrient* (New Canaan. CT: Keats Publishing. Inc.. 1994): 7–8.

40. Richard Passwater and Chithan Kandaswami, *Pycnogenol®—The Super Protector Nutrient* (New Canaan, CT: Keats Publishing, Inc., 1994): 7-8.

- Jacques Masquelier, "Pycnogenols®: Recent advances in the therapeutic activity of procyanidins" in *Natural Products as Medicinal Agents* (J.L. Beal and E. Reinhard, editors, Hippokrates Verlag Stuttart P., 1991):343-356.

41. Michael T. Murray, "PCO Sources: Grape Seed vs Pine Bark—a review and comparison," Botanical Report, *Health Counselor,* 7:1.

42. Hendler, *Doctors' Vitamin & Mineral Encyclopedia*, p 102.

43. Clark, Linda, *Nutrition & Cancer*, 1984, 6:13-21.

44. Meydani, Simin Bikbin, D.V.M., Ph.D., Effect of Vitamin E Supplementation on Immune Responsiveness of Healthy Elderly Subjects." Paper read at a seminar conducted by *The New York Academy of Sciences*, Nov 2, 1988.

45. *British Journal of Cancer* 49 (1984):321-324.

- *International Journal of Epidemiology* 17 (1988):281-286.

- *Journal of the American College of Nutrition* 4 (September–October 1985): 559-564.

46. Carlton Fredericks, *Look Younger, Feel Healthier* (New York: Grosset & Dunlap, 1972), p 136.

47. Kenneth H. Cooper, *Antioxidant Revolution* (Thomas Nelson, Nashville, 1994): 138-139.

48. *Mutation Research* 346 (April 1995): 195-202. Found in *Antioxidant Revolution* by Kenneth H. Cooper.

49. Selenium: A Quest for Better Understanding. *Alternative Therapies.* July 1996, Vol 2, No 4, pp 59-67.

50. Passwater, Richard, Ph.D., *Cancer Prevention & Nutritional Therapies*, Keats Publishing, New Canaan, CT., 1983, pp 59-67.

51. Passwater, Richard, Ph.D., *The New Supernutrition*, Pocket Books, New York, 1991, pp 124-125.

52. Clark, L.C., et al., Effects of Selenium Supplementation for Cancer Prevention in Patients with Carcinoma of the Skin. *JAMA*, Dec 25, 1996, 276(24): 1957-1985.

53. Lester Packer and Yuichiro Suzuki, "Alpha-Lipoic Acid and Inhibition of Gene Activating Transcription of HIV," Biological Oxidants and Antioxidants: New Developments in Research and Health Effects conference, Pasadena, CA, March 12-13, 1993.

54. J.T. Greenamyre, et al., *Neuroscience Letters* 171 (1994): 17-20.

- Richard A. Passwater, "Lipoic Acid, The Metabolic Antioxidant," *Good Health Guides* (New Canaan, CT: Keats Publishing, Inc., 1995): 1-47.

55. L. Packer, E.H. Witt, H.J. Tritschler, "Lipoic acid as a biological antioxidant," *Free-radical Biological Medicine* 19:2 (1995): 227-250.

56. B. Reschke, S. Zeuzem, C. Rosak, et al., "High-dose long-term treatment with thioctic acid in diabetic polyneuropathy," in Borbe and Ulrich (eds) *Thioctsaure* (1989): 318-334.

57. Richard A. Passwater, "Lipoic Acid, The Metabolic Antioxidant," *Good Health Guides* (New Canaan, CT: Keats Publishing, Inc., 1995): 1-47.

58. Beach, Gershwin, Hurley, 1982: Rosenbaum 1984: in *Maximum Immunity*, p 116.

59. Folkers, Karl, *Clinical Investigator* 1993; 71 (Suppl.): 51-54.

- Folkers, Karl, et al, *Biomedical and Clinical Aspects of Coenzyme Q.* Vol 6., Elsevier Publishing Co., New York, 1990.

- E. Bliznakof and G. Hunt, *The Miracle Nutrient Coenzyme Q 10*, Bantam, 1987.

- Lockwood, K., and Folkers, K., *Biochemical and Biophysical Research Communications* 199:1504-8, 1994. Found in Lindberg Nutrition newsletter written by Danny Wells.

60. Lockwood, Knud, M.D., *Biochemical and Biophysical Research and Communications* (July 6, 1995;212:172-177)

- Lockwood, Knud, M.D., *Biochemical and Biophysical Research and Communications* (March 30, 1994;199:1504-8)

- Karl Folkers, Ph.D., *Biochemical and Biophysical Research and Communications* (April

15, 1993;192:241-5)

61. D. Harman, "The Aging Process: Major risk factor for disease and death" *Proceedings of the National Academy of Sciences* 88 (1991): 5360-5363.

• D. Harman, "Aging: Prospects for further increases in the functional life span," *Age* 17 (1994): 119-146.

• Carper, Jean, *Stop Aging Now,* HarperCollins, New York, 1995.

62. Newsletter from the Linus Pauling Institute of Science and Medicine, Palo Alto, California.

63. Julius, M. Glutathione and Morbidity in a Community-based sample of elderly. *Journal of Clinical Epidemiology*, 1994; 47(9): 1021-26.

64. Carper, Jean, *Stop Aging Now*, HarperCollins, New York, 1995, p 124.

65. Ibid.

66. Braverman, E.R., Pfeiffer, C.C., *The Healing Nutrients Within*, Keats Publishing, Inc., New Canaan, Connecticut, (1987), p 99.

67. Jones, D.P., *Nutrition and Cancer* 1992; 17 (1):57-75.

68. Shabert, Judy, M.D., R.D., Ehrlich, Nancy, *The Ultimate Nutrient, Glutamine.* Avery Publishing Group, NY, 1994, p 51.

69. Shabert, Judy, M.D., R.D., Ehrlich, Nancy, *The Ultimate Nutrient, Glutamine.* Avery Publishing Group, NY, 1994.

70. *Cancer* (Vol. 52, 1983), 70-73.

71. Gae Weiss and Shandor Weiss, *Growing and Using Healing Herbs*, Emmaus, PA: Rodale Press, 1986, 64-65.

• *Longevity, Anti-Aging Herbs: The Proven Disease Fighters*, April 1991.

72. *Cancer* (52) 1983: 70-73.

73. Jack Ritchason, *The Little Herb Encyclopedia*, Pleasant Grove, UT: Woodland Health Books, 1994: 14.

74. Sheldon Saul Hendler, *The Doctors' Vitamin and Mineral Encyclopedia*, New York: Simon and Schuster, 1990, 279.

75. Michael T. Murray, N.D., *Healing Power of Herbs*, Rocklin, CA, Prima Publishing, 1992, pp 86-88.

76. Daniel B. Mowrey, *Herbal Tonic Therapies*. New Canaan, CT: Keats Publishing Inc., 1993, pp 107-109.

77. Michael Murray, *Healing Power of Herbs*, Rocklin, CA, Prima Publishing, 1992, pp 80-84.

78. Phillip N. Steinberg, "A Wondrous Herb from the Peruvian Rainforest," *Townsend Letter for Doctors* (An Informal Letter Magazine for Doctors Communicating with Doctors) 130: May 1994.

• "Plant Metabolites: New compounds and anti-inflammatory activity of Uncaria tomentosa," *Journal of Natural Products* (54:2) May/June 1991: 453-459.

• "The alkaloids of uncaria tomentosa and their phagocytosis increasing effects," *Planta Medica* (51) 1985: 419-423.

79. Brent W. Davis, "A New World Class Herb for AK Practice" (Summer 1992).

• "Phytochemical and biological research on uncaria tomentosa," *Buil Soc Ital Biol Sper* (65:6) 1989: 517-520.

80. *Take Charge of Your Health, p 20.*

• Paavo Airola, M.D., Ph.D., *Every Woman's Book* (Phoenix: Health Plus, Publishers 1979) pp 440-442.

81. Hendler, Sheldon, M.D., Ph.D., *The Doctors' Vitamin & Mineral Encyclopedia*, p 315.

• Vogel, G., A Peculiarity among the flavonoids: silymarin, a compound active on the liver. *Munich Proceedings of the International Bioflavonoid Symposium.* 1981, pp 461-480.

82. Ritchason, Jack, *The Little Herb Encyclopedia*, p 146.

Chapter 4: Mirror, Mirror on the Wall

1. Eric Braverman with Carl Pfeiffer, *Healing Nutrients Within*, (New Canaan, CT: Keats Publishing, 1987): 91.

2. Gladys Lindberg, Judy Lindberg McFarland, *Take Charge of Your Health* (San Francisco: Harper & Row, 1982), p 67.

3. Roger J. Williams, Ph.D., *Physicians Handbook of Nutritional Science*, C.C. Thomas, Springfield, MO. (1974) as found in *The Big Book of Vitamins* by Ruth Adams, Keats Publishing, Inc., New Canaan, CT, 1992, p 183.

4. Ibid.

5. R. Kuttan, et al., *Experientia* 37 (1981): 221-223.

6. Lindberg Newsletter, December 1995 by Danny Wells.

• Brown, Royden. *Bee Hive Product Bible*. Garden City Park, N.Y.: Avery Publishing Group, Inc., 1993.

7. Murray, Frank, *The Big Family Guide to all the Minerals*, Keats Publishing Inc., New Canaan, CT, 1995, pp 345-350.

• E.M. Carlisle, "The Nutritional Essentiality of Silicon", *Nutrition Review* 40 (1982): 193-198.

8. Frank Murray, *The Big Family Guide to all the Minerals*, Keats Publishing Inc., New Canaan, CT, 1995, pp 345-350.

• Jack Ritchason, *The Little Herb Encyclopedia*, 3rd ed., Woodland Health Books, Pleasant Grove Utah, 1994, pp 121-122.

9. Robert Erdmann, Ph.D., *The Amino Revolution*, A Fireside Book by Simon & Schuster, Inc., New York 1987, p 194.

10. Eric Braverman with Carl Pfeiffer, *Healing Nutrients Within*, (New Canaan, CT: Keats Publishing, 1987): 91.

11. Carl C. Pfeiffer, Ph.D, M.D., *Mental and Elemental Nutrients*, Keats Publishing, Inc. New Canaan, CT, (1975), pp 84-85 (Note: in the body, cysteine will readily convert to cystine, and vice versa, so for the sake of convenience I will refer to either as cysteine.)

12. H.L. Newbold, M.D., *Mega Nutrients for Your Nerves*, Peter H. Wyden/Publisher, New York, 1975, p 299.

13. Roger Williams, *Nutrition Against Disease*, Bantam Books, New York, 1971.

14. Hans Selye, *Calciphylaxis*, University of Chicago Press, Chicago, IL, 1962.

• Tuchweber, B., et al., *American Journal of Clinical Nutrition* 13, 238, 1963.

• Adelle Davis, *Let's Get Well*, A Signet Book, New York 1972, pp 115, 130.

15. Melvyn R. Werbach, M.D., *Nutritional Influences on Illness, A Sourcebook of Clinical Research*, Third Line Press, Tarzana, California 1993, pp 265-269.

• Stewart, J.C.M., et. al., Treatment of severe and moderately severe atopic dermatitis with evening primrose oil (Epogram): a multi-center study. *J Nutr Med* 2:9-15, 1991.

• Allsion, J.R., The relation of deficiency of hydrochloric acid and vitamin B-complex in certain skin diseases. *South Med J* 38:235-241, 1945.

16. Ibid.—Werbach

17. Ibid.—Werbach

18. C.N. Ellis, et al., *Journal of the American Academy of Dermatology* 29 (September 1992): 438-442.

N. Kurkcuoglu, F. Alaybeyi, "Topical Capsaicin for Psoriasis," *British Journal of Dermatology* 123(4):549-50, October 1990.

19. *The American Medical Association Encyclopedia of Medicine*, editor Charles B. Clayman, M.D. Random House, New York, 1989.

20. Wright, Jonathan, M.D., *Dr. Wright's Guide to Healing with Nutrition.* Erasmus, PA, Rodale Press, 1984.

• Frank Murray, *Better Nutrition*, "Acidophilus: The Friendly Bacteria," Jan 1987.

21. *Take Charge of Your Health*, p 233.

22. Adelle Davis, *Let's Get Well*, pp 134-135.

23. Sheldon Saul Hendler, M.D., Ph.D., *The Doctors' Vitamin and Mineral Encyclopedia*, A Fireside Book, New York 1990.

24. Lendon Smith, M.D., *Feed Yourself Right*, Dell Publishing Co., Inc. New York, 1983, pp 363-367.

25. U.S. Pharmacist 15 (12): 27.

   • Burton Goldberg Group, *Alternative Medicine*, for information on all types of skin disorders.

26. Information about all deficiency symptoms can be found in Gladys Lindberg and Judy Lindberg McFarland, *Take Charge of Your Health*, (San Francisco: Harper & Row, 1982): 184-241.

27. Eric R. Braverman, with Carl Pfeiffer, *The Healing Nutrients Within*, p 91.

   • J. H. Buchanan and M. S. Otterburn, "Some structural comparisons between cysteine-deficient and normal hair keratin" *IRCS Med Sci* 12 (1984): 691-692.

28. Louise Tenney, *Today's Herbal Health*, Woodland Books, Provo, Utah (1983), p 21.

29. Zia Wesley-Hosford, *Fifty & Fabulous* (Rocklin, CA: Prima Publishing, 1995).

30. Lindberg Newsletter, December 1995 by Danny Wells.

   • Royden Brown, *Bee Hive Products Bible*. Garden City Park, New York: Avery Publishing Group Inc., 1993.

31. Ibid. —Lindberg and R. Brown

32. Editors of Prevention Magazine Health Books, *Age Erasers for Women* (Rodale Press, Inc., 1994): 487.

33. Laden and Spitzer, "Identification of a natural moisturizing agent in skin" *Journal of Soc Cosmet Chemists* 18 (1967): 351-360, found in Durk Pearson and Sandy Shaw, Life Extension (New York: Warner Books, 1982): 53,33.

34. P. Belaiche, "Treatment of Vaginal Infections of Candida Albicans with the Essential Oil of Melaleuca Alternifolia" *Phylotherapie* 15 (1985).

   • E. Pena, "Melaleuca Alternifolia Oil, Uses for Trichomonal Vaginitis and Other Vaginal Infections" *Obstetrics and Gynecology* (June 1962).

   • M. Walker, "Clinical Investigation of Australian Melaleuca alternifolia Oil for a Variety of Common Foot Problems" *Current Podiatry* (April 1972).

Chapter 5: Our Windows to the World

1. "The Eye: Window to the World", by Lael Wertenbaker and Editors of U.S. News Books Washington, D.C., Division of *U.S. News & World Report*, Inc., p 7.

2. The *American Medical Assoc Encyclopedia of Medicine*, Medical Editor, Charles B. Clayman, M.D., Random House, New York. 1989.

3. Pauling, *How To Live Longer and Feel Better*. 1986, p 208.

4. S.M. Bouton, Jr., Vitamin C and the Aging Eye. *Arch Intern Med* 63:930-45. 1939.

   • Muhlmann, V., et al., Vitamin C Therapy of Incipient Senile Cataract. *Arch Oftalmol B Aires* (1939) 14:552-75.

5. Adams, Ruth, *The Big Family Guide to All the Vitamins*, Keats Publishing, 1992, p 241.

6. G.E. Bunce, "Nutrition and Eye Disease of the Elderly." *Journal of Nutritional Biochemistry* 5 (February 1994): 66-76.

7. Ruth Adams, *The Big Family Guide to All the Vitamins*, Keats Publishing, New Canaan, CT, pp 424-425.

8. *Science News*, Allen Taylor of the USDA Human Nutrition Research Center on Aging in Medford, MA. Volume 135.

9. S.D. Varma, D. Chand, Y.R. Sharma, J.F. Kuck, Jr., R.D. Richards, "Oxidative Stress on Lens and Cataract Formation," *Current Eye Research* 3:35-57.

- P.F. Jacques, et al., "Antioxidant status in persons with and without senile cataract," *The Archives of Ophthalmology* 106(3):337-40, (1988).

10. *The Archives of Ophthalmology* (February 1991).

11. Robert Azar, Prevention (July 1983): 99-103 as found in Melvyn Werbach, *Healing Through Nutrition* (HarperCollins Publisher, 1993): 71.

12. E. Cheraskin M.D., W.M. Ringsdorf, Jr., E.L. Sisley, *The Vitamin C Connection*, NY: Harper & Row, 1983.

13. G. B. Brietti, "Further Contributions on the Value of Osmotic Substances as Means to Reduce Intra-Ocular Pressure," *Ophthalmological Society of Australia* 26: 61-71.

- M. Virno, et al., "Oral Treatment of Glaucoma with Vitamin C," *The Eye, Ear, Nose, and Throat Monthly*, 46: 1502-1508.

14. *An American Medical Association Encyclopedia of Medicine*, p 658.

15. Melvyn Werbach, *Healing Through Nutrition*, 114.

16. L. Levine, *Journal of Behavioral Optometry* 3 No. 5(1992):115-119.

17. *Physician's Desk Reference* 46th ed. Montvale, NJ: Medical Economics Data 1992.

18. Jack Ritchason, *The Little Herb Encyclopedia*, Woodland Health Books, Pleasant Grove, Utah 1994, pp 24-25.

19. *The Little Herb Encyclopedia*, pp 98-99.

20. Michael Murray, N.D., Joseph Pizzorno, N.D., *Encyclopedia of Natural Medicine*, Prima Publishing, Rocklin, CA. 1990, pp 408-409.

21. Seddon, Johanna M., M.D., et al., "Dietary Carotenoids, Vitamins A, C and E and Advanced Age-Related Macular Degeneration." *Journal of the American Medical Association* 272(18):1413-1420, Nov 9, 1994.

22. Tufts University, *Diet & Nutrition Letter* 12 :11 (January 1995).

23. New Antioxidant defends against free-radical damage. *Nutrition News*, 1989.

24. Werbach, M.R., M.D., Murray, M., N.D., *Botanical Influences on Illness: A sourcebook of clinical research*. Tarzana, CA: Third Line Press, 1994.

25. American Council on Collaborative Medicine, Nov 1995, Vol 1, Issue 8, *Antioxidants and Anti-Aging—The Fight Against Free-Radicals*. Joyce McBeth, R.N., CN Editor.

26. A.R. Gaby, M.D. and J.V. Wright, "Nutritional Factors in Degenerative Eye Disorders: Cataract and Macular Degeneration" *Journal of Advancement on Medicine* 6:1 (Spring 1993), 27-39.

27. Bunce, G.E., Ph.D., "Nutrition and Eye Disease of the Elderly." *Journal of Nutritional Biochemistry* 5:66-77, February 1994.

- Schalch, Wolfgang, "Carotenoids in the Retina—A Review of Their Possible Role in Preventing or Limiting Damage Caused by Light and Oxygen," *Free-Radicals and Aging*, pp 280-298, 1992.

- Seddon, Johanna M., M.D., et al., "Dietary Carotenoids, Vitamins A, C and E and Advanced Age-Related Macular Degeneration." *Journal of the American Medical Association* 272(18):1413-1420, Nov 9, 1994.

28. Wolfgang Schalch, "Carotenoids in the Retina—A Review of Their Possible Role in Preventing or Limiting Damage Caused by Light and Oxygen" *Free-Radicals and Aging*, 1992: 280-298.

29. Gladys Lindberg & Judy McFarland, *Take Charge of Your Health*, Harper & Row, 1982, pp 188-189.

30. Carlton Fredericks M.D., *The Prevention and Cure for Common Ailments & Diseases*. A Fireside Book, Simon & Schuster, New York, NY, 1982, p 58.

31. *Take Charge of Your Health*, p 184.

32. *The Doctors' Vitamin and Mineral Encyclopedia*, p 199.

33. *Take Charge of Your Health*, p 65.

34. *The Doctors' Vitamin and Mineral Encyclopedia*, pp 224-225.

35. W.H. Bates, *The Bates Method for Better Eyesight Without Glasses*. New York: Henry Holt & Co., Owl Books, 1981.

Chapter 6: Anti-Aging Nutrients for the Brain

1. Harvey B. Simon, M.D., *Staying Well*. Boston: Houghton Mifflin Co., 1992, pp 74-79

2. Ibid.

3. Ibid.

4. Crook T.H., et al., Recalling names after introduction: changes across the adult life span in two cultures. *Dev Neuropsycho* 1993; 9: 103-13.

• Youngjohn J.R., et al., Test-retest reliability of computerized everyday memory measures and traditional memory tests. *Clin Neuropsychologist* 1992: 6:276-86.

• R.J. Ivnik, et al., Traditional and computerized assessment procedures applied to the evaluation of memory change after temporal lobectomy. *Archs Clin Neuropsychol* 1993: 8: 69-81, as presented at the NNFA lecture in Nashville, TN, July 1996.

5. K. Kreitsch, et al., "Prevalence, presenting symptoms, and psychological characteristics of individuals experiencing a diet-related mood disturbance." *Behavioral Therapy* (19) 1988: 593-604.

6. A.F. Subar, et al., "Folate intake and food sources in the US population," *American Journal of Clinical Nutrition* (50) 1989: 508-516.

• M.T. Abou-Salen and A. Coppen, "The biology of folate in depression: Implications for nutritional hypotheses of the psychoses," *Journal of Psychiatric Research* 20, 1986: 91-101.

• P.S.A., Godfrey, et al., "Enhancement of recovery from psychiatric illness by methylfolate," *Lancet*, (336) 1990: 392-395.

• M.I. Botez, et al., "Neuropsychological correlates of folic acid deficiency: Facts and hypotheses, in M.I. Botez, E.H. Reynolds, Eds. *Folic Acid in Neurology, Psychiatry and Internal Medicine*, New York: Raven Press, 1979.

7. Lindberg Newsletter July, 1996 by Danny Wells reported on Weil, A. *Dr. Andrew Weil's Self-Healing; Relieving Depression Simply*. Watertown, MA; Thorne Communications, Inc., 1:8, 1995.

8. Eric R. Braverman M.D. and Carl C. Pfeiffer Ph. D., *The Healing Nutrients Within*, New Canaan, CT: Keats, 1987, 59.

9. Sheldon Saul Hendler, M.D., *The Doctors' Vitamin & Mineral Encyclopedia*, Simon & Shuster, New York, 1990, pp 228-234.

10. Eric Braverman M.D., p 59.

11. Carlton Fredericks, Ph.D., *Program for Living Longer*, A Fireside Book, Simon & Schuster, 1983.

• Sheldon Saul Hendler, M.D., *The Doctors' Vitamin and Mineral Encyclopedia*, Simon & Shuster, New York, 1990, pp 232-234.

12. Eric Braverman M.D., p 191.

13. O. Frank, et al., Superiority of periodic intramuscular vitamin injections over daily oral vitamins in maintaining normal vitamin titers in a geriatric population. *American Journal of Clinical Nutrition* 1977: 30: 630.

14. Abram Hoffer, M.D., Ph.D., *Orthomolecular Medicine for Physicians*. New Canaan, Conn.: Keats Publishing, Inc., 1989, pp 149-152.

15. Ruth Adams, *Big Family Guide to All the Vitamins*. Keats Publishing, Inc., New Canaan, CT, 1992, pp 127-128.

• Hoffer, A., *Niacin Therapy in Schizophrenia*, Springfield, IL, Charles C. Thomas, 1962.

16. A. Hoffer, H. Osmond, Treatment of schizophrenia with nicotinic acid: a ten-year follow up. *Acta Psychiatr Scand* 40: 171-189, 1964.

17. H. Osmond, A. Hoffer, Massive niacin treatment in schizophrenia: review of a nine-year study. *Lancet* 1: 316-319.

18. M.I. Botez, et al., "Neuropsychological correlates of folic acid deficiency: Facts and hypotheses, in M.I. Botez, E.H. Reynolds, Eds. *Folic Acid in Neurology, Psychiatry and Internal Medicine*, New York: Raven Press, 1979.

- Eric R. Braverman and Carl C. Pfeiffer, *The Healing Nutrients Within*, New Canaan, CT: Keats, 1987, 59.

19. James S. Goodwin, M.D., On Nutrition & Memory, *Executive Health Report*, October 1984.

20. T.E. Pary, "Folate Responsive Neuropathy," *La Presse Medicale*, Jan 29, 1994; 23(3): 131-137.

21. Jonathan V. Wright, M.D., Alan Gaby, M.D., *Nutrition & Healing*. Vol 2, Issue 3, March 1995, p 9.

22. Sheldon Hendler, M.D., Ph.D., *The Doctors' Vitamin and Mineral Encyclopedia*, Simon & Schuster, New York, 1990, p 69.

- Beck, W.S., Cobalamin and the nervous system (editorial). *N Eng J Med* 318:1752-1754, 1988.

23. Garcia, C.A., Reding, M.J. and Blass, J.P., "Over diagnosis of dementia" *J Am Ger Soc*, 1981, 29, pp 407-10.

- Dommisse, J., "Subtle vitamin B12 deficiency and psychiatry: A largely unnoticed but devastating relationship?" *Medical Hypothesis* 34:131-140, 1991.

- "Vitamin B12 deficiency often overlooked," University of Colorado Health Sciences Center, *News*, June 30, 1988.

24. G.M. Craig, C.Elliot, and K.R. Hughes, "Masked vitamin B12 and folate deficiency in the elderly" *Br J Nutr*, 1985, 54, pp 613-19.

25. Michael Murray, N.D., *Encyclopedia of Natural Medicine*, p 133.

26. C.J.M. van Tiggelen, et al., "Assessment of vitamin B12 status in CFS." *Am J Psychiatry*, 1984; 141:136. as found in the Wright and Gaby newsletter.

27. Jonathan V. Wright and Alan R. Gaby. *Health & Healing*. Vol 2, Issue 3, March 1995.

28. L.L. Rogers and R.B. Pelton, "Effect of Glutamine on IQ Scores of Mentally Deficient Children, *Texas Reports on Biology and Medicine*, Vol 15, No 1, pp 84-90, (1957).

29. L.L. Rogers, R.B. Pelton, and R. Williams, "Voluntary Alcohol Consumption by Rats Following Administration of Glutamine," *Journal of Biological Chemistry*, Vol 214 (No 2): 503-506, (1955).

30. Werbach, M.D., *Healing Through Nutrition*, HarperCollins, New York, 1993, p 15.

31. J.B. Trunnell and J.I. Wheeler, "Preliminary Report on Experiments with Orally Administered Glutamine in Treatment of Alcoholics" *ACS*, Houston, Dec 1955.

32. L.S. Young, et al., "Patients Receiving Glutamine Supplemented Intravenous Feedings Report an Improvement in Mood." *JPEN 17* (1993): 422-427.

33. Pelton, Ross, R.Ph., Ph.D., and Pelton, Taffy Clarke. *Mind Food and Smart Pills*, New York, Doubleday, 1989.

34. Ibid.

35. Gebner, A., et al., "Study of the Long-term Action of a Ginkgo Biloba Extract on Vigilance and Mental Performance as Determined by Means of Quantitative Pharmaco-EEG and Psychometric Measurements." *Arzneimittelforschung* Vol 35, No 9, p 1459.

- Murray, Frank, *Ginkgo Biloba*, New Canaan, CT., Keats Publishing, 1993, pp 15-21.

36. Warburton, D.M., "Clinical Psychopharmacology of Ginkgo Biloba Extract." *La Presse Medicale*. 1986, Vol 15, No 31, p 1595.

37. Dr. G.E. Schuitemaker, Gingko Against Senility, a Dutch and German magazine *Orthomolecular*, 1988. A publication of the European Institute for Orthomolecular Science.

38. Intermittent Claudication: Trental vs. Ginkgo biloba extract. *Amer J Natural Medicine*, Jan/Feb 1995: 2(1): 10-13.

39. Christopher Hobbs, *Ginkgo: Elixir of Youth*. Botanica Press. Santa Cruz, CA 1995, p 57.

40. Sheldon Saul Hendler, M.D., Ph.D., *The Purification Prescription*. New York: William Morrow and Co., Inc., 1991, pp 61-63.

41. Ibid.

42. Sheldon Saul Hendler, M.D., Ph.D., *The Doctor's Vitamin and Mineral Encyclopedia*. Simon & Schuster, New York, 1990, p 263.

43. Richard Passwater, Ph.D., *The New Supernutrition*, Keats, New Caanan, CT, pp 55-56.

44. Parris M. Kidd, Ph.D., *Healthy & Natural Journal*. Phosphatidylserine and Aging. Vol 2. Issue 3,

45. T.H. Crook, et al., 1991. "Effects of phosphatidylserine in age-associated memory impairment." *Neurol*, 41:644–649.

46. Ibid.

47. B. Cenacchi, et al., 1993. "Cognitive decline in the elderly: A double-blind placebo controlled multi-centered study on efficacy of phosphatidylserine administration." *Aging Clin Exp Res*, 5: 123–133.

48. Ibid.

49. Palmieri, G., et al.,, 1987. "Double-blind controlled trial of PS in subjects with senile mental deterioration." *Clin Trials Journal*. 24:73–83.

50. Dean Ward, M.D., John Morgenthaler, Steven Fowkes, *Smart Drugs II, The Next Generation*, Health Freedom Publications, Menlo Park, CA. 1993, pp 91–93.

51. C. Cipolli and G. Chiari. Effetti della L-acetilcarnitina sul deterioramento mentale dell'anziano: primi risultati (Effects of L-acetylcarnitine on mental deterioration in the aged: initial results). *Clin Ter* 132(6 Suppl):479–510, 31 March 1990. as found in *Smart Drugs II*.

52. R. Bella, R. Biondi, R. Raffaele and G. Pennisi. Effect of acetyl-L-carnitine on geriatric patients suffering from dysthymic disorders. *Int J Clin Pharmacol Res* 10(6): 355–60, 1990.

53. A. Scrofani, R. Biondi, V. Sofia, F. D'Alpa, A. Grasso and S. Filetti. EEG patterns of patients with cerebrovascular damage. Effect of L-acetylcarnitine during sleep. *Clin Trials J* (United Kingdom) 25(Suppl. 1): 65–71, 1988.

54. T. Fulgente, M. Onofrj, Del Re M.L., F. Ferrancci, S. Bazzano, M.F. Ghilardi, and G. Malatesta. Laevo-acetylcarnitine (Nicetiel (R)) treatment of senile depression. *Clin Trials J* (United Kingdom) 27(3): 155–63, 1990.

• G. Garzya, D. Corallo, A. Fiore, G. Lecciso, G. Petrelli, and C. Zotti. Evaluation of the effects of L-acetylcarnitine on senile patients suffering from depression. *Drugs Exp Clin Res* (Switzerland) 16(2):101–6, 1990.

• C. Villardita, P. Smirni, and I. Vecchio. N-acetylcarnitine in depressed elderly patients (L'Acetil carnitina nei disturbi della sfera affettiva dell'anziano). *Eur Rev Med Pharmacol Sci* (Italy) 6(2): 341–44, 1984.

• E. Tempesta, L. Casella, C. Pirrongelli, L. Janiri, M. Calvani, L. Ancona. L-acetylcarnitine in depressed elderly subjects. A cross-over study vs. placebo. *Drugs Under Experimental Clinical Research* 13(7): 417–23, 1987.

55. E. Sinforiani, M. Iannuccelli, M. Mauri, A. Costa, P. Merlo, G. Bono and G. Nappi Neuropsychological changes in demented patients treated with acetyl-L-carnitine. *Int J Clin Pharmacol Res* 10(1–2): 69–74, 1990.

• Bonavita E. Study of the efficacy and tolerability of L-acetylcarnitine therapy in the senile brain. *Journal of Clinical Pharmacology, Therapy, and Toxicology* 24:511–6, 1986.

• E. Bonavita, D. Bertuzzi, J. Bonavita and A. Marani. L-acetylcarnitine (L-Ac) (Branigen) in the long-term symptomatic treatment of senile dementia. Optimal treatment times and suspension periods. *Clin Trials J* (United Kingdom) 25(4): 227–37, 1988.

56. M. Passeri, D. Cucinotta, P.A. Bonati, M. Iannuccelli, L. Parnetti and U. Senin Acetyl-L-carnitine in the treatment of mildly demented elderly patients. *Int J Clin Pharmacol Res* 10(1–2): 75–9, 1990.

57. Bowman B.A.B., Acetyl-carnitine and Alzheimer's disease. *Nutrition Review* (USA) 50(5): 142–4, 1992.

• M.G. Rai, G. Wright, L. Scot, B. Beston, J. Rest, and A.N. Exton-Smith. Double-blind, placebo controlled study of acetyl-L-carnitine in patients with Alzheimer's dementia. *Current Medical Research and Opinion* 11(10): 638–47, 1990.

• M. Sano, K. Bell, L. Cote, G. Dooneief, A. Lawton, L. Legler, K. Marder, A. Naini, Y. Stern and R. Mayeux. Double-blind parallel design pilot study of acetyl levocarnitine in patients with Alzheimer's disease. *Arch Neurol* (United States) 49(11): 1137–41, Nov 1992.

58. M.C. Cabrero Lahuerta and M.Crotes Blanco. Current treatment of Alzheimer's disease (Aproximacion al estado actual del tratamiento de la demencia senil tipo Alzheimer). *Cienc Med* (Spain) 9(3): 82–7, 1992.

- G. Cazzato, L. Bonfigli, M. Pasqua and F. Iaiza. Long-term treatment with acetyl-L-carnitine in patients suffering from dementia of the Alzheimer's type (Trattamento a lungo termine con L-acetilcarnitina in pazienti affetti da demenza di Alzheimer). *Neurol Psichiatr Sci Um* (Italy) 10(2): 201–15, 1990.

59. Dean Ward, M.D., John Morgenthaler, Steven Fowkes, *Smart Drugs II, The Next Generation*, Health Freedom Publications, Menlo Park, CA. 1993.

60. William Regelson, M.D., and Carol Colman, *The Superhormone Promise*, Simon & Schuster, N.Y., 1996.

61. Flood, J.F., Morley, J.F., Roberts, E., "Memory Enhancing Effects in Male Mice of Pregnenolone and Steroids Metabolically Derived From It." *Proc Nat Acad Sci USA* 89:1567-71, 1992.

62. *Complete Book of Vitamins & Minerals for Health*, p 208.

63. Braly, James, and Torbet, Laura, *Dr. Braly's Food Allergy and Nutrition Revolution*, New Canaan, CT., Keats Publishing, 1992, p 153.

64. Pfeiffer, Carl C., et al., "Stimulant Effect of 2-Dimethyl-l-aminoethanol: Possible Precursor of Brain Acetylcholine." *Science.* 1957, Vol 126, pp 610–611.

65. H.B. Murphree, et al., "The Stimulant Effect of 2-Dimethylaminoethanol (Deanol) in Human Volunteer Subjects." *Clinical Pharmacology and Therapeutics.* 1960. Vol 1, pp 303–310.

66. Ross Pelton, M.D., Ph.D., *Mind Food and Smart Pills*, Doubleday, New York, First Edition, August 1989, pp 76–79.

67. William, Regelson, M.D., and Carol Colman, *The Superhormone Promise*, Simon & Schuster, New York, 1996, p 53.

68. Editorial, "Problems with prescription drugs among elderly" *Am Fam Phys*, 1986, 28, p 236.

69. Murray & Pizzorno, *Encyclopedia of Natural Medicine*, p 128.

70. Ibid.

71. C. Wells, Dementia, F.A. Davis, R.D. Terry, and R. Katzman, "Senile dementia of the Alzheimer type", *Ann Neurol*, 1983, 14, pp 497–506.

- R.G. King, "Do raised brain aluminum levels in Alzheimer's Dementia contribute to cholinergic neuronal deficits?" *Med Hypoth*, 1984, 14, pp 301–6.

- Hershey, C.O., Hershey L.A., Varnes, A., et al., "Cerebrospinal fluid trace element content in dementia: clinical, radiologic, and pathologic correlations." *Neurol*, 1983, 33, pp 1,350–3.

- J.M. Candy, J. Klinowski, R.H. Perry, et al., "Aluminosilicates and senile plaque formation in Alzheimer's disease," *Lancet*, 1986, i, pp 354–7.

72. I. Klatzo, et al., *Journal of Neuropathol Exp Neurol*, 24(1965):187–199.

73. Sara Benum, "Brain Disorders—No longer are they viewed as Irreversible," *Medical Nutrition*, Summer 1978:24–29.

74. William Regelson, M.D. and Carol Colman, *The Superhormone Promise*, pp 54–55.

75. "Smoking Over a Pack a Day Seen as Risking Alzheimer's," *The New York Times*, June 23, 1986.

Chapter 7: You Gotta Have Heart

1. Matthias Rath, M.D., *Eradicating Heart Disease*, Health Now, San Francisco, CA, 1993.

2. Broda Barnes, M.D., and Lawrence Galton, *Hypothyroidism: The Unsuspected Illness*. Thomas Y Crowell Co., NY (1976) pp 168–169.

3. Cathy Pinckney and Edward R. Pinckney, *The Patient's Guide to Medical Tests*. (New York: Facts on File Publishers, 1986): 83–85.

- Richard Passwater, *The New Supernutrition*, Simon & Schuster, NY 1991.

- Stephen Langer, *Solved: The Riddle of Illness*, Keats Publishing, New Canaan, CT, p 99.

4. Robert C. Atkins, M.D., *Dr. Atkins' Nutrition Breakthrough* (New York: Morrow, 1981), pp 213-214.

- Passwater, *Supernutrition for Healthy Hearts*, pp 37-38, 318-319.
- Jeffery Bland, *Your Health Under Seige: Using Nutrition to Fight Back* (Brattleboro, VT: The Stephen Greene Press, 1981), pp 62-63.
- Linus Pauling, "Vitamin C and Heart Disease," *Executive Health*, January, 1978.

5. H. Lommis, Preferential Utilization of Free Cholesterol from High-Density Lipoproteins for Biliary Cholesterol Secretion in Man," *Science*, April 7, 1978, pp 62-64.

6. Cathy Pinckney and Edward R. Pinckney, *The Patient's Guide to Medical Tests*. (New York: Facts on File Publishers, 1986): 83-85.

7. *American Journal of Clinical Nutrition* 53 (January 1991):326S-334S.

8. Richard Passwater Ph.D., *The New Supernutrition*, Simon & Schuster, Inc, NY, 1991, p 139.

9. Richard Passwater Ph.D., *The New Supernutrition*.
   - *Solved: The Riddle of Illness*, p 99.

10. L. Pauling M.D., *How to Live Longer and Feel Better*, W.H. Freeman & Co., NY, 1986, p 195.

11. Carlton Fredericks Ph.D., "Hotline to Health," *Prevention* (January 1975):97.

12. Richard Passwater Ph.D., *The New Supernutrition*, Simon & Schuster, Inc, NY, 1991, p 139.

13. J. Yudkin, *Lancet* 2, 155, 1957.
    - A.M. Cohen, *American Heart Journal* 65, 291, 1962.
    - M.A. Antar, et al., *American Journal of Clinical Nutrition* 14, 169, 1964.

14. John Yudkin, *Sweet and Dangerous* (New York: Peter H. Wyden, 1972):91.

15. Manuel Tzagournis, "Triglycerides in Clinical Medicine," *The American Journal of Clinical Nutrition* (August 1978).

16. Manuel Tzagournis, "Triglycerides in Clinical Medicine," *The American Journal of Clinical Nutrition* (August 1978).

17. Matthias Rath, M.D., *Eradicating Heart Disease*, Health Now Publishers, San Francisco, CA, 1993, p 101.

18. *Annals of Nutrition and Metabolism* (May-June 1984): 186-191.

19. Shutes, E.V., *The Heart & Vitamin E*, The Shute Foundation for Medical Research, London, Canada, 1969.
    - Shute, W.E., Taub, H.J., *Vitamin E for Ailing and Healthy Hearts*. Pyramid House, NY, 1969.
    - Shute, W.E., *Vitamin E Book*. Keats Publishing, New Canaan, CT, 1978.
    - Ruth Adams, *The Big Book on Vitamins*," Keats Publishing, New Canaan, CT.

20. Cardiovascular Research 25:2 (February 1991):89-92.

21. Richard Passwater, Ph.D., *The New Supernutrition*, Pocket Books, New York, 1991.

22. Shutes, E.V., *The Heart & Vitamin E*, The Shute Foundation for Medical Research, London, Canada, 1969.
    - Shute, W.E., Taub, H.J., *Vitamin E for Ailing and Healthy Hearts*. Pyramid House, NY, 1969.
    - Shute, W.E., *Vitamin E Book*. Keats Publishing, New Canaan, CT, 1978.
    - Ruth Adams, *The Big Book on Vitamins*, Keats Publishing, New Canaan, CT.

23. Howard N. Hodis, et al., *Journal of the American Medical Association* 273 (June 21, 1995): 1849-1854.
    - "Vitamin E Seems to Benefit Heart, Two Studies Show," *The New York Times*, Nov 19, 1992.

24. E. Fred Gey, et al., "Inverse Correlation Between Plasma Vitamin E and Mortality from Ischemic Heart Disease in Cross Cultural Epidemiology," *American Journal of Clinical Nutrition*, 53 (January 1991): 326-334.

25. I. Jialal, "The effect of dietary supplementation with alpha-tocopherol on the oxidative modification of low density lipoprotein," *Journal of Lipid Research* 6 (1992): 899-906.

26. I. Jialal, "The effect of a-tocopherol supplementation on LDL oxidation and vitamin E: a dose response study," *Arteriosclerosis, Thrombosis and Vascular Biology* 15:2 (1995): 190-198.

27. Ibid.

28. *Research* 49 (1988): 393–404.

29. Charles Hennekens, Presentation to *The New York Academy of Sciences*, February 1992.

30. Ibid.

31. *Lancet* 346 (July 1995): 57–81.

32. Matthias Rath, M.D., *Eradicating Heart Disease*, Health Now, San Francisco, CA, (1993), pp 42–46.

33. *Proceedings of the National Academy of Sciences* USA, August 1990.

- Rath & Pauling, (1991) "Solution to the puzzle of human cardiovascular disease: Its primary cause is ascorbate deficiency, leading to the deposition of lipoprotein(a) and fibrinogen/fibrin in vascular wall." *Journal of Orthomolecular Medicine* 6:125–134 (1991).

34. The Linus Pauling Institute of Science and Medicine Newsletter, March 1992.

- M.Rath, M.D., "Lipoprotein(a)—a reduction by ascorbate." *Journal of Orthomolecular Medicine* 7:73–80.

35. The Linus Pauling Institute of Science and Medicine Newsletter, March 1992.

- M.Rath, M.D., "Lipoprotein(a)—a reduction by ascorbate." *Journal of Orthomolecular Medicine* 7:73–80.

36. Linus Pauling Ph.D., *How To Live Longer and Feel Better.* W.H. Freeman and Co, NY, 1986, p 152.

37. The Linus Pauling Institute of Science and Medicine Newsletter, March 1992.

- Rath, M. and Pauling, L. A Unified Theory of Human Cardiovascular Disease Leading the Way to the Abolition of this Disease as a Cause for Human Mortality. *Journal of Orthomolecular Medicine* (1992) in press.

38. Emil Ginter, M.D., "The Effects of Ascorbic Acid on Humans in a Long-Term Experiment," *International Journal of Vitamin Nutrition Research*, Vol 47, No 2.

- Ginter, E. Vitamin C in the Control of Hypercholesteremia in Man, in Vitamin C: *New Clinical Applications in Immunology, Lipid Metabolism, and Cancer,* ed. A. Hanck. Hans Huber, Bern, pp 137–152 (1982).

39. R. Norden, *International Journal on Microbiology* 3:425, 1984.

40. A. Bordia and S.K. Verma, *Clinical Cardiology* 8(10):552–554, Oct 1985.

41. Karl Folkers, et al., *Biomedical and Clinical Aspects of Coenzyme Q,* Vol 6. (New York: Elsevier Publishing Co., 1990).

- Bliznakov, E.G., and Hunt, G.L., *The Miracle Nutrient Coenzyme Q 10*, Bantam Books, New York, 1987.

- Folkers, Karl. Co-chairman's Opening Remarks, *Fifth International Symposium on Biomedical and Clinical Aspects of Coenzyme Q*, 1987.

- K. Folkers, P. Langsjoen, Y. Nara, K. Muratsu, J. Komorowski, P.C. Richardson and T.H. Smith, *Biochem Biophys Res Comm* 153, 888–896 (1988).

- S.A. Mortensen, S. Vadhanavikit, K. Nuratsu, and K. Folders, "Coenzyme Q 10: clinical benefits with biochemical correlates suggest a scientific breakthrough in the management of chronic heart failure," *International Journal of Tissue Research* 22:3 155–162.

- Karl Folkers "Contemporary Therapy with Vitamin B6, Vitamin B12 and Coenzyme CoQ10," *Chemical and Engineering News*, 64: 16 (April 21, 1986): 27–30, 55–56.

42. Karl Folkers (Priestly Medal Address) Contemporary Therapy with Vitamin B6, Vitamin B12, and Coenzyme Q 10. *Chem & Eng News* (April 21, 1986) 64 (16) 27–30, 55–56.

43. Karl Folkers, et al., *Biomedical and Clinical Aspects of Coenzyme Q,* Vol 6 (New York: Elsevier Publishing Co., 1990).

44. Bliznakov, E.G., and Hunt, G.L., *The Miracle Nutrient Coenzyme Q 10*, Bantam Books, New York, 1987.

45. Newsletter from the Linus Pauling Institute of Science and Medicine, 440 Page Mill Road, Palo Alto, CA, 94306.

- Karl Folkers, et al., *Biomedical and Clinical Aspects of Coenzyme Q*, Vol 6 (New York: Elsevier Publishing Co., 1990).

46. S.A.Mortensen, S.Vadhanavikit, K.Nuratsu, and K.Folkers, (1990) Coenzyme Q 10: Clinical Benefits with Biochemical Correlates suggesting a scientific breakthough in the management of chronic heart failure. *International Journal of Tissue Research* 22:3, 155-162.

47. Ibid.

48. Ibid.

49. Antony W. Linnane, Center for Molecular Biology and Medicine, Monash University, Clayton, Australia.

50. International Clinical *Nutrition Review*, 2:3 (1982): 14.

51. O. Ghidino, M.Azzurro, A.Vita, and G. Sartori, "Evaluation of the therapeutic efficacy of L-carnitine in congestive heart failure," *International Journal of Clinical Pharmacology, Therapy and Toxicology* 26 (1988): 217-220.

52. Morton Walker, *The Chelation Way*, Garden City Park, NY: Avery Publishing Group, Inc., (1990):211.

53. A. Cherchi, C.Lai, F.Angelino, et al., "Effects of L-carnitine on exercise tolerance in chronic stable angina: a multicenter, double-blind, randomized, placebo controlled crossover study" *Int J Clin Pharm Ther Toxicol*, 1985, 23, pp 569-72.

   * Orlando, G. and Rusconi, C., "Oral L-carnitine in the treatment of chronic cardiac ischaemia in elderly patients" *Clin Trials J*, 1986, 23, pp 338-44.

   * T. Kamikawa, Y. Suzuki, A.Kohayashi, et al., "Effects of L-carnitine on exercise tolerance in patients with stable angina pectoris: *Jap Heart J*, 1984, 25, pp 587-97.

   * Kosolcharoen, P., Nappi, J., Peruzzi, P., et al., "Improved exercise tolerance after administration of carnitine" *Curr Ther Res*, 1981, 30, pp 753-64.

   * Pola, P., Savi, L., Serricchio, M., et al., "Use of physiological substance, acetyl-carnitine, in the treatment of angiospastic syndromes" *Drugs Exptl Clin Res*, 1984, X, pp 213-17.

54. O. Ghidino, M.Azzurro, A.Vita, and G. Sartori, "Evaluation of the therapeutic efficacy of L-carnitine in congestive heart failure," *International Journal of Clinical Pharmacology, Therapy and Toxicology* 26 (1988): 217-220.

55. Cherchi A, et al., Effects of L-carnitine on exercise tolerance in chronic stable angina: A multicenter, double-blind, randomized, placebo-controlled, crossover study. *Int J Clin Pharm Ther Toxicol* 23:569-72, 1985.

   * Orlando G and Rlusconi C: Oral L-carnitine in the treatment of chronic cardiac ischaemia in elderly patients. *Clin Trials J* 23:338-44, 1986.

   * Kamikawa T, et al., Effects of L-carnitine on exercise tolerance in patients with stable angina pectoris. *Jap Heart J* 25:587-97, 1984.

   * Pola P, et al., Use of physiological substance, acetylcarnitine, in the treatment of angiospastic syndromes. *Drugs Exptl Clin Res* X:213-7, 1984.

   * Folkers K and Yamamura Y (eds): Biomedical and Clinical Aspects of Coenzyme Q 10, Vols 1-4, Elsevier Science Publishers, Amsterdam. Vol 1:1977, Vol 2:1980, Vol 3:1982, Vol 4:1984.

   * Littarru G.P., Ho L., and Folkers K.: Deficiency of coenzyme Q10 in human heart disease: Part II. *Int J Vit Nutr Res* 42:413. 1972.

   * Kamikawa T, Kobayashi A. Yamashita T, et al., Effects of coenzyme Q10 on exercise tolerance in chronic stable angina pectoris. *Am J Cardiol* 56:247, 1985.

56. Whitaker, Julian, M.D., *Dr. Whitaker's Guide to Natural Health*, 1995, p 157.

57. Sheldon Saul Hendler, *The Doctors' Vitamin and Mineral Encyclopedia*, 157.

58. L.T. Iseri, "Magnesium and Cardiac Arrhythmias. Magnesium 5:111-126.

   * L.T. Iseri and J.H. French, "Magnesium: Nature's Physiologic Calcium Blocker," *American Heart Journal*, 109:188-193.

59. A. Dudley and R. Solomon, "Magnesium, myocardial ischaemia and arrhythmias: the role of magnesium in myocardial infarction. *Drugs* 37 (1989): 1-7.

   * Sheldon Saul Hendler, *The Doctors' Vitamin and Mineral Encyclopedia*, p 159.

60. H.S. Rasmussen, et al., "Intravenous Magnesium in Acute Myocardial Infarction," *Lancet 1* (1986): 234-235.

61. Richard Passwater, *The New Supernutrition*. (New York: Pocket Books, 1991): pp 144-146.

62. Ibid.

63. Karl Folkers, "Contemporary Therapy with Vitamin B6, Vitamin B12 and Coenzyme Q 10," *Chemical and Engineering News*, 64: 16 (April 21, 1986): 27-30, 55-56.

64. *Journal of the American Medical Association*, Vol 274, No 13, 1995.

• *Cardiovascular Research* 25:2 (February 1991): 89-92.

65. Richard Passwater, *The New Supernutrition*. (New York: Pocket Books, 1991): p 147.

66. Sheldon S. Hendler, M.D., Ph.D., *The Doctors' Vitamin and Mineral Encyclopedia*. New York: Simon & Schuster, 1990, p 130.

67. USDA Quarterly Report of Selected Research Projects, July 1 to Sept 30, 1992.

68. Ibid.

69. Jancin Bruce, "Try Niacin Yourself and Improve Patient Rapport," *Family Practice News* (November 1, 1995): 18.

• Canner P.L., et al., Fifteen year mortality in Coronary Drug Project patients: Long-term benefit with niacin. *J Am Coll Cardiol* 8, 1245-1255, 1986.

70. Passwater, Richard, *The New Supernutrition*, p 182.

71. *Journal of Lipid Research* 22:22-36.

72. Abraham Hoffer, "The News About Niacin is Good News," *Your Good Health* (February 1984).

73. John P. Clearly, "Niacin Deficiency Disease," *Medical Tribune* (January 1, 1987).

74. Murray, M., *Encyclopedia of Nutritional Supplements*, p 93.

• Welsh A.L., and Ede M., Inositol hexanicotinate for improved nicotinic acid therapy. *Int Record Med* 174, 9-15, 1961.

• El-Enein A.M.A., et al., The role of nicotinic acid and inositol hexaniacinate as anticholesterolemic and antilipemic agents. *Nutr Rep Intl* 28, 899-911, 1983.

• Sunderland G.T., Belch J.J.F., Sturrock R.D., et al., A double blind randomized placebo controlled trial of hexopal in primary Raynaud's disease. *Clin Rheumatol* 7, 46-49, 1988.

• O'Hara J., Jolly P.N., and Nicol C.G., The therapeutic effect of inositol nicotinate (Hexopal) on intermittent claudication: A controlled trial. *Br J Clin Practice* 42, 377-383, 1988.

75. *Take Charge of Your Health*, pp 88-90.

76. Gary W. Evans, American Societies for Experimental Biology in New Orleans, March 21, 1989.

77. Richard Passwater, *The New Supernutrition*, 179.

78. Louise Tenney. *Today's Herbal Health*. Provo, UT: Woodland Books, 1992.

79. Michael Murray, N.D., *Encyclopedia of Natural Medicine*. Rocklin, CA: Prima Publishing, 1990, p 146.

80. The *Lancet II* (1969): 800, 962.

• *Journal of Traditional Chinese Medicine* 6 919860:117.

• *American Chemistry Society* 106 (1984): 82-95.

81. Ibid.

82. Julian Whitaker *Health & Healing* 6:2 (February 1996).

• Sanders, T.A.B., "Cod Liver Oil, Platelet Fatty Acids, and Bleeding Time," *Lancet* 1 (1980): 1189.

83. Michael Murray, *Encyclopedia of Nutritional Supplements*, 1996.

84. M. Sugano, et al., *Annals of Nutritional Medicine* 30 (1986): 289-299.

85. T. Syckner and P.O. Wester, *British Medical Journal* 286 (1983): 1847.

86. Lecture at the National Nutritional Foods Association convention in Las Vegas, Nevada, 1995.

87. Nelson, M.E., et al., *Am J of Clin Nutr* 43: 910-916 (1986).

Chapter 8: Are You Cold When Everyone Else is Warm?

1. Ratcliff, J.D., "I am Joe's Thyroid." *Reader's Digest*, Pleasantville, NY, March 1973.

2. Broda Barnes, *Hypothyroidism: The Unsuspected Illness* (New York: Thomas Y. Crowell Company, 1976).

   • Stephen Langer, *Solved: The Riddle of Illness*, (New Canaan, CT.: Keats Publishing, Inc., 1995): 15.

   • David Shefrin, N.D., Seminar for Broda Barnes research Foundation, Fall Physician Teaching Seminar, Sep 22-24, 1995, Scottsdale, AZ.

3. A.S. Jackson, "Hypothyroidism." *Journal of the American Medical Association* (1957): 121-165.

4. Murray Israel M.D., *The Thyroid-Vitamin Approach to Cholesterol, Atheromatosis and Chronic Disease*: A Ten Year Study New York: The George Press, Inc. 1960.

5. Ibid.—Israel

6. Ibid.—Israel

7. Ibid.—Israel

8. Broda O. Barnes and Lawrence Galton, *Hypothyroidism: The Unsuspected Illness*, Thomas Y. Crowell Co., New York 1986, p 43.

9. Ibid.

10. Ibid.

11. Braverman and Pfeiffer, *Healing Nutrients Within*, (New Canaan, CT: Keats Publishing, Inc., 1987): 51.

12. Dr. Julian Whitaker's *Health & Healing* newsletter May 1994.

   • Harby, K. New practive guidelines urge thyroid screening. *Medical Tribune*, Jan. 19, 1995.

13. Ibid.

14. Braverman and Pfeiffer, *Healing Nutrients Within*, (New Canaan, CT: Keats Publishing, Inc., 1987): 51.

15. Murray Israel M.D., *The Thyroid-Vitamin Approach to Cholesterol, Atheromatosis and Chronic Disease:* A Ten Year Study, New York: The George Press, Inc. 1960.

16. Alan Gaby, M.D., *Preventing and Reversing Osteoporosis*, Prima Publishing, Rocklin, CA, 1994, p 143.

17. Peat, Ray Ph.D., "Thyroid: Misconceptions," *Townsend Letter for Doctors*, No 124, Nov 1993, pp 1120-1122.

   • Balch, James, F., M.D. and Phyllis A. Balch, C.N.C., *Prescription for Nutritional Healing*. Garden City, NY: Avery Publishing Group, Inc., 1990, pp 213-214.

   • Goodhart, Robert S., M.D., and Maurice E. Shils, M.D., *Modern Nutrition in Health and Disease* (6th ed.). Philadelphia: Lea & Febiger, 1978, 406, 473.

18. Broda O. Barnes and Lawrence Galton, *Hypothyroidism: The Unsuspected Illness*, Thomas Y. Crowell Co. New York, 1976, p 176.

   • Murray Israel, *The Thyroid-Vitamin Approach to Cholesterol Atheromatosis and Chronic Disease: A Ten Year Study*, New York: The George Press. (1960).

   • Murray Israel, M.D., "An Effective Therapeutic Approach to the Control of Atherosclerosis Illustrating Harmlessness of Prolonged Use Of Thyroid Hormone in Coronary Disease, in *American Journal Digestive Diseases*, 22:161-168, 1955.

19. Murray Israel M.D., *The Thyroid-Vitamin Approach to Cholesterol, Atheromatosis and Chronic Disease: A Ten Year Study*, New York: The George Press, Inc. 1960, p 9.

20. Gladys Lindberg and Judy Lindberg McFarland, *Take Charge of Your Health*, Harper & Row, San Francisco 1982, p 223.

21. Michael Murray, M.D., *Encyclopedia of Nutritional Supplements*, Prima Publishing, Rocklin, CA, 1996.

22. Dalonen, J.T., et al., "High Stored Iron Levels are Associated with Excess Risk of Myocardial Infarction in Eastern Finnish Men," *Circulation*, 1992, pp 86, 803-811, 1992.

Chapter 9: If the Pressuse is Up, Let's Turn it Down!

1. M.H. Alderman, "Which antihypertensive drugs first—and why," *JAMA* 267 (1992): 2786–2787.

2. Paul Raeburn, Associated Press, "Doctor's: Popular drug isn't working," *The Daily Breeze*, November 20, 1995:A1–A7.

- Julian Whitaker, *The Whitaker Guide to Natural Healing* (Rocklin, CA: Prima Publishing, 1995), 11.

3. Carlson Wade, "A Nutritional Approach to Lowering Blood Pressure" Better Nutrition, Feb. 1987.

4. S.Ackley, E. Barrett-Conner and L. Suarez, Diary Products, calcium and blood pressure. *The American Journal of Clinical Nutrition*, 38:457, 1983.

- Norman Kaplan, M.D., "Non-drug treatment of hypertension" *Annals of Internal Medicine*, March 1985, 102:359–373.

5. Charles Clayman, M.D., *The American Medical Association Encyclopedia of Medicine* (New York: Random House, 1989): 188.

6. Langer, Stephen, M.D., "Don't Gamble with Hypertension," *Better Nutrition for Today's Living*, (Nov 1995): 48–52.

7. Charles Clayman, M.D., *The American Medical Association Encyclopedia of Medicine* (New York: Random House, 1989): 948.

8. Charles Clayman, M.D., *The American Medical Association Encyclopedia of Medicine* (New York: Random House, 1989): 948.

9. Hendler, Sheldon Saul, M.D., Ph.D., *The Doctors' Vitamin and Mineral Encyclopedia*. New York: Simon and Schuster, 1990, p 176.

- Horowitz, Nathan, "Dietary Potassium Is Said To Protect Against Stroke," *Medical Tribune*, Aug 17, 1989, p 6.

10. Ibid.

11. Khaw, Kay-Tee, M.D., and Barrett-Connor, Elizabeth, M.D., "The Association Between Blood Pressure,Age and Dietary Sodium and Potassium:A Population Study," *Circulation* 77:53–61, 1988.

12. Khaw Kay-Tee and Barrett-Connor E., Dietary Potassium and stroke-associated mortality:A 12-year prospective population study. *New England Journal of Medicine* 316:235–240, 1987.

- Khaw, Kay-Tee and Thom S., Randomized double-blind cross-over trial of potassium on blood pressure in normal subjects. *Lancet*. 2:1127–1129, 1982.

13. McLaughlin, Lloyd. "USDA Finds Salt and Potassium Intake Ashew in Adult Diets," *USDA News*, Dec 19, 1984.

14. Hendler, *The Doctors' Vitamin and Mineral Encyclopedia*, p 182.

- Nutrition Search, Inc., *Nutrition Almanac*, McGraw-Hill 1984.

15. Hendler, *The Doctors' Vitamin and Mineral Encyclopedia*, p 182.

- Nutrition Search, Inc., *Nutrition Almanac*, McGraw-Hill 1984.

16. F. P. Cappuccio, et al., "Epidemiological Association Between Dietary Calcium Intake and Blood Pressure: A Meta-Analysis of Published Data," *American Journal of Epidemiology* 142:9 (1995): 935–845.

17. *Science* 224 (June 29, 1984):12–17.

18. Lieberman, Shari and Burning, Nancy, *The Real Vitamin and Mineral Book*,Avery Publishing Group Inc., Garden City Park, N.Y. 1990. as excerpted in *American Journal of Clinical Nutrition* 42 (July 1985):12–17.

- S.Ackely, Barrett-Conner E and Suarez L., Dairy products, Calcium and Blood Pressure. *The American Journal of Clinical Nutrition*, 38:457, 1983.

19. Dyckner,T and Wester, P.O., *British Medical Journal* 286:1847, (1983).

20. Ruddell, H., et al., "Effect of magnesium supplementation in patients with labile hypertension." *Journal of the American College of Nutrition*. 6:445, 1987.

21. Ibid.

* L.M. Resnick, R.K. Gupta, and J.H. Laragh, "Intracellular free magnesium in erythrocytes of essential hypertension: Relation of blood pressure and serum divalent cations." *Proc Nat Acad Sci* 81:6511, 1984.

22. *International Journal for Vitamin and Nutrition Research* 54 (1984):343–347.

23. *American Journal of Clinical Nutrition* 48 (November 1988):1226–1232.

24. D.A. McCarron, C.D. Morris, H.U. Henry and J.L. Stanton, (1984) Blood Pressure and Nutrient Intake in the United States. *Science* 224:1392–1398 (as seen in) *Eradicating Heart Disease* by Matthias Rath.

25. *Nutrition Research* 3 (1983):653–661.

26. Michael Murray and Joseph Pizzorno, *Encyclopedia of Natural Medicine* (Rocklin, Ca., Prima Publishing, 1990, p 382.

27. K. Folkers, T. Watanabe, and M. Kaji, "Critique of coenzyme Q10 in biochemical and biochemical research and in ten years of clinical research on cardiovascular disease", *J Mol Med*, 1977, 2, pp 431–60.

* K. Folkers and Y. Yamamura, (eds), Biomedical and Clinical Aspects of Coenzyme Q, Vol 4, *Elsevier Science Publishers*, Amsterdam, 1984.

28. Berger, Stuart, M.D., *How to Be Your Own Nutritionist*. New York: Avon Books, 1987, p 92.

29. *Atherosclerosis*, Vol 49, 1983 and *Circulation*, March 1983.

30. *Lancet* II (1969):962, and *Lancet* II (1969):800.

* *Journal of Traditional Chinese Medicine* 6 (1986):117.

31. Bill Gottlieb, *New Choices in Natural Healing* (Emmaus, PA: Rodale Press,, 1995): 361.

32. Stephen Langer, M.D., contributing writer to *Better Nutrition for Today's Living*, November 1995, "Don't Gamble with Hypertension."

33. Pizzorno Murray, *Encyclopedia of Natural Medicine*, p 383.

34. Stephen Langer, "Don't gamble with hypertension," *Better Nutrition for Today's Living*, (November 1995): 48–52.

35. Bill Gottlieb, *New Choices in Natural Healing*, 363.

36. Mikel A. Rothenberg, M.D., *Dictionary of Medical Terms*, Barron's Educational Series, Inc., 1994, New York.

37. Adelle Davis, *Let's Get Well*, Signet, Published by the Penguin Group New York 1972, pp 278–279

38. Jonathan V. Wright, M.D., with Alan R. Gaby M.D., *Nutrition & Healing*, May 1996, Vol 3, Issue 5, p 12.

Chapter 10: When the Weather Changes, Do Your Joints Ache?

1. J. Williams Roger, *Nutrition Against Disease*, New York: Pitman Publishing Corp., 1971:122–123.

2. Michael Murray and Joseph Pizzorno, *Encyclopedia of Natural Medicine*. (Rocklin, Calif.: Prima Publishing, 1990): 337.

3. M. Gabor, "Pharmacologic effects of flavonoids on blood vessels," *Angiologica* 9 (1972): 355–374.

* J. Kuhnau, "The flavonoids. A class of semi-essential food components: their role in human nutrition," *World Review Nutrition and Dietetics* 24 (1976): 117–191.

* B. Havsteen, "Flavonoids, a class of natural products of high pharmacological potency," *Biochemical Pharmacology* 32 (1983): 1141–1148.

4. M. Gabor, "Pharmacologic effects of flavonoids on blood vessels, *Angiologica* 9 (1972): 355–74.

* J. Kuhnau, "The flavonoids: A class of semi-essential food components: their role in human nutrition," *World Review Nutrition and Dietetics* 24 (1976): 117–191.

- B. Havsteen, "Flavonoids, a class of natural products of high pharmacological potency," *Biochemical Pharmacology* 32 (1983): 1141–1148.
- E. Middleton, "The flavonoids," Trends in Pharmaceutical Science.

5. *American Medical Association Encyclopedia of Medicine*, Random House: NY, 1989, p 653.

6. Michael Murray and Joseph Pizzorno, *Encyclopedia of Natural Medicine*, 339.

7. M. Murray, *Encyclopedia of Nutritional Supplements*, Prima Publishing, Rocklin, CA, 1996, p 469.

8. William Regelson, M.D., *The Superhormone Promise*, pp 94–98.
- Van Vollenhoven, Ronald T., et al., "An open study of dehydroepiandrosterone in systemic lupus erythematosus," *Arthritis Rheum*, 37:1305–10, 1994.

9. J. Greenwood, Jr., "Optimum Vitamin C Intake as a Factor in the Preservation of Disc Integrity," *Med Annals of Dist of Columbia* 33 (1964): 274.
- J. Greenwood, Jr., "Intervertebral Disc Lesions: Adjuncts to Conservative, Operative and Postoperative Management." Proceedings of the Third International Congress of Neurological Surgery. Copenhagen, *Exerpta Medical*, p 807, abstract 1965.
- J. Greenwood, Jr., "On Osteoarthritis, the 'Wear and Tear' Disease . . . Can Vitamin C Help?" *Executive Health* 16:7 (April 1980).
- A. B. Houssay, et al., "Ascorbic acid concentrations in different periods of experimental arthritis in rats," *Acta Physiol Latino Am* 16 (1966): 43.
- B.C. Ballabio and G. Sala, "Research on arthritis treatment," The *Lancet* 258 (1950): 644.
- R. Gallini and B. Grego, "Chorionic gonadtropin and ascorbic acid in experimental arthritis of the rat," *Sperimentale* 101 (1951): 169.
- R. J. Williams and G. Deason, "Individuality in vitamin C needs," *Proc Nat Acad Sci* 57 (1967): 1638.

10. Alan Gaby, M.D., *Preventing and Reversing Osteoporosis*, pp 157–172.

11. J. M. Ellis, et al., "The Effect of Pyridoxine Therapy in the Management of Carpal Tunnel Syndrome," *Proceedings of the National Academy of Sciences* 79 (1982): 7494–7498.

12. *Proceedings of the National Academy of Sciences* (81), November 1984.
- J. M. Ellis, "Treatment of carpal tunnel syndrome with vitamin B6," *Southern Medical Journal* 80 (1987): 882–884.
- John M. Ellis, *The Doctor Who Looked at Hands* (New York: Vantage Press, 1966).
- P.C. Amadio, "Pyridoxine as an adjunct in the treatment of carpal tunnel syndrome," *Journal of Hand Surgery* 10 (1985): 237–241.
- M.L. Kasdan and C.J. James, "Carpal tunnel syndrome and vitamin B6," *Plastic and Reconstructive Surgery* 80 (1987): 882–884.
- J.M. Ellis, et al., "Response of Vitamin B6 Deficiency and the Carpal Tunnel Syndrome to Pyridoxine," *Proceedings of the National Academy of Sciences USA* 79 (1982): 7479–7498.

13. *Take Charge of Your Health*, p 24.

14. Carl Pfeiffer, *Mental and Elemental Nutrients*. (New Canaan, CT: Keats Publishing, Inc., 1975): 452.

15. Richard Follis, Jr., *Deficiency Disease*. (Springfield, IL.: Charles C. Thomas Publishers, 1958).

16. Carlton Fredericks, *Arthritis: Don't Learn to Live With It*, pp 97–98.

17. Ibid.

18. Linus Pauling, *How to Live Longer and Feel Better*. (New York: W. H. Freeman and Co., 1986): 25.

19. Ibid.

20. Ibid.

21. Carl Pfeiffer, *Mental and Elemental Nutrients* (New Canaan, CT: Keats Publishing, Inc., 1975): 454–455.

22. Ibid.

23. Robert Bingham, "The Conquest of Arthritis by Nutritional therapy," *Arthritis News Today*, July 1980.

- R. Bingham, *Fight Back Against Arthritis*, (Desert Hot Springs, CA: Desert Arthritis Medical Clinic, 1984).

- R. Bingham, "New and Effective Approaches in the Prevention and Treatment of Arthritis," *Journal of Nutrition* 28 (1976): 38–47.

- R. Bingham, "Arthritis News Today," Arthritis and Health News 1-5:1-65 (1978-1983). *Arthritis Patients Association*, Yorba Linda, CA.

24. W. Kaufman, "The Use of Vitamin Therapy to Reverse Certain Concomitants of Aging," *Journal of the American Geriatrics Society*, 3:11 (November 1955): 927–936.

- J.L. Kalliomaki, et al., "Urinary excretion of thiamin, riboflavin, nicotinic acid, and pantothenic acid in patients with rheumatoid arthritis," *Acta Med Scand* 166 (1960): 275.

- L. Pauling, *How to Live Longer and Feel Better*, 204.

- W. Kaufman, "Niacinamide, A Most Neglected Vitamin." *International Academy of Preventive Medicine* 8 (1983): 5–25.

- W. Kaufman, "Niacinamide therapy for joint mobility: Therapeutic reversal of a common clinical manifestation of the 'normal' aging process," *Conn St Med J* 17 (1953): 584.

- L. D'Agostino, "The vascular or erthremic effect of nicotinic acid upon various portions of the body of men in health and various diseases," *Acta Vitaminol 1* (1947): 130.

25. Carlton Fredericks, *Arthritis: Don't Learn to Live With It*, p 126.

- John Ellis, "Review of B6" A Physician's Handbook on *Orthomolecular Medicine* (New York: Pergamon Press, 1977): 60–63.

- J. Ellis, *Free of Pain: A Proven and Inexpensive Treatment for Specific Types of Rheumatism* (Brownsville and Dallas, TX: Southwest Publishing, 1983).

- J. M. Ellis and J. Presley, *Vitamin B6, the Doctor's Report* (New York: Harper and Row, 1973).

- A. Hoffer, "Treatment of arthritis by nicotinic acid and nicotinamide," *Can Med Assoc J* 81 (1959): 235.

26. Ibid.

27. Ibid.

- J. M. Ellis and J. Presley, *Vitamin B6, the Doctor's Report* (New York: Harper and Row, 1973).

28. J. Aaseth, et al., research paper presented at the Second International Symposium on Selenium in Biology and Medicine, May 1980.

29. *Scandinavian Journal of Rhematology* 14 (April-June 1985): 97–101.

30. *Biological Trace Element Research* 7 (May-June 1985): 195–198.

31. Richard Passwater, *Supernutrition*, pp 253–254.

32. Pujalte, J.M., et al., Double-blind clinical evaluation of oral glucosamine sulphate in the basic treatment of osteoarthrosis. *Curr Med Res Opin* 7, 110-114, 1980.

- Drovanti A, et al., Therapeutic activity of oral glucosamine sulfate in osteoarthrosis: A placebo-controlled double-blind investigation. *Clin Ther* 3, 260-272, 1980.

33. O'Ambrosia, E. et al., Glucosamine sulfate: a controlled clinical investigation in arthritis. *Pharmatherapeutica* 1991; 2:504-8.

34. Murray, M., *Encyclopedia of Nutritional Supplements*, p 342.

35. *Healing Through Nutrition*, Melvyn Werbach, M.D., HarperCollins, NY, (1993), p 284.

- Vaz, A.L., Double blind-clinical evaluation of the relative efficacy of ibuprofen and glucosamine sulfate in the management of osteoarthrosis of the knee in out-patients. *Curr Med Res Opin* 8, 145-149, 1982.

36. G. Crolle and E. D'este, "Glucosamine sulfate for the management of arthrosis: a controlled clinical investigation," *Curr Med Res* Opin 7 (1980): 104–114.

- M.J. Tapadinhas, I.C. Rivera, A.A. Ginamini, "Oral glucosamine sulfate in the management of arthrosis: report on a multi-center open investigation in Portugal," *Pharmatherapeutica* 3 (1982): 157–168.

- E.D. D'Ambrosia, B. Casa, R. Bompani, G. Scali, M. Scali, "Glucosamine sulfate, a controlled clinical investigation in arthrosis," *Pharmatherapeutica* 2 (1982): 504-508.
- Murray, M., *Encyclopedia of Nutritional Supplements*, p 342.
37. W. Lane, "Shark Cartilage and the Pain of Arthritis," *Explore!* 3 (1992): 23.
38. *Alternative Medicine: The Definitive Guide*. The Burton Goldberg Group, Future Medicine Pub., Puyallup, WA, 1994, p 535.
39. J.F. Prudden and L.L. Balassa, "The Biological Activity of Bovine Cartilage Preparations," *Seminars in Arthritis and Rheumatism* 4 (1974): 287-321.
40. Ibid.
41. M. Murray and J. Pizzorno, Jr., *Encyclopedia of Natural Medicine* (Rocklin, Prima Publishing, 1991): 447-453.
- P.A. Sunkin, "Treatment of rheumatoid arthritis with oral zinc sulfate," *Agents Action Supp* 8 (1981): 587-596.
42. D. M. Williams, "Copper deficiency in humans," *Seminars in Hematology* 20 (1983): 118-128.
43. T.H. Lee, et al., "The Effect of Dietary Enrichment with Eicosapentaenoic and Docosahexaenoic Acids on In Vitro Neutrophil and Monocyte Leukotriene Generation and Neutrophil Function," The *New England Journal of Medicine* 312:19 (May 9, 1985): 1216-1224.
44. J. Kremer, et al., *Clinical Research* 33 (1985):A778.
45. J. Kremer, A.V. Michaelek, L. Lininger, et al., "Effects of manipulation of dietary fatty acids on clinical manifestations of rheumatoid arthritis" The *Lancet* (January 26, 1985):184-187.
- J.N., McCormick, et al., The *Lancet* 2 (1977): 508.
46. Ibid.
- L. Cleland, et al., *Journal of Rheumatology* (15) October 1988: 1471-1475.
- The *Lancet* (January 26, 1985): 184-187.
- *Annals of Internal Medicine* 106 (April 1987): 497.
- *Journal of Immunology* 134/3 (March 1985).
47. J. N. McCormick, et al., The *Lancet* 2 (1977): 508.
48. J. Belch, et al., *Ann Rheum Digest* 47 (October 1988): 94-104.
- Bingham, *Fight Back Against Arthritis*.
49. J. Rosen, W.T. Sherman, J.F. Prudden, G.J. Thorbecke, "Immuno- regulatory Effects of Catrix," *Journal of Biological Response Modifiers* 7 (1988): 498-512.
- J. Heinerman, *Science of Herbal Medicine* (Orem, UT: BiWorld Publishers, 1984): 97.
50. Lindberg Newsletter, June 1993, "Wonderful Chlorophyll" written by Danny Wells.
51. P.N. Steinberg, "Uncaria Tomentosa (Cat's Claw) a Wondrous Herb from the Peruvian Rain Forest," *Townsend Letter for Doctors* (May 1994).
52. J. McBeth, *American Council on Collaborative Medicine* 2:2 (March 1996).
53. M. DeVos, "Articular Disease and the Gut: Evidence for a Strong Relationship between Spondylarthropy and Inflammation of the Gut in Man," ACTA *Clinica Belgica* 45:1 (1990): 20-24.
54. Robert Bingham, "Yucca Extract," *The Journal of the Academy of Rheumatoid Disease* 2:1 (1990): 20.
- R. Bingham, "Yucca Plant Saponin in the Management of Arthritis," *Journal of Applied Nutrition* 17 (1985): 45-51.
- R. Bingham, "Yucca in the Treatment of Hypertension and Hypercholesterolemia," *Journal of the American Academy of Applied Nutrition* 30 (1978): 3-4.
55. Michael Murray and Joseph Pizzorno, *Encyclopedia of Natural Medicine*, p 339.
56. Jack Ritchason, *The Little Herb Encyclopedia*, (Pleasant Grove, UT: Woodland Health Books, 1994): 73-74.

57. Ibid., p 259.

58. Robert Bingham, "The Conquest of Arthritis by Nutritional therapy," *Arthritis News Today*, July 1980.

   • R. Bingham, *Fight Back Against Arthritis*, (Desert Hot Springs, CA: Desert Arthritis Medical Clinic, 1984).

   • R. Bingham, "New and Effective Approaches in the Prevention and Treatment of Arthritis," *Journal of Nutrition* 28 (1976): 38–47.

   • R. Bingham, "Arthritis News Today," Arthritis and Health News 1-5:1-65 (1978-1983). *Arthritis Patients Association*, Yorba Linda, CA.

59. Norman Childers, "A Relationship of Arthritis to the Solanacaea (Nightshades)," *Journal of the International Academy of Preventive Medicine*, (November 1982): 31-37.

60. Seminars in Arthritis and Rheumatism 23, *Supplement* 3 (1991): 48-52.

61. Gordon Thomas, Dr. Issels and His Revolutionary Cancer Treatment, (New York: Peter H. Wyden, Inc., 1973): 85.

62. R. Bingham, *Fight Back Against Arthritis*.

Chapter 11: Anti-Aging Therapies

1. Richard Hodes, "The National Institute On Aging and Their Position on Growth Hormone Replacement Therapy in Adults," *The Journal of American Geriatrics Society* 42 (1994): 1208–1211.

2. Richard Hodes, "The National Institute On Aging and Their Position on Growth Hormone Replacement Therapy in Adults," *The Journal of American Geriatrics Society* 42 (1994): 1208–1211.

3. W. Regelson, C. Colman, *The Superhormone Promise* Simon & Schuster, 1996, p 41.

4. Beth M. Ley, *DHEA—Unlocking the Secrets to the Fountain of Youth*, by BL Publications, Newport Beach, CA (1996), pp 28-29.

5. M. Kalimi, and W. Regelson, *The Biological Role of Dehydroepiandrosterone*, de Gruyter, New York, 1990.

   • Regelson, W., Loria, R., Kalimi, M., Dehydroepiandrosterone (DHEA) The "Mother Steroid" I: Immunologic Action. *Ann NY Acad Sci* 719: 553-563, 1994.

6. A.G. Schwartz, L. Pashko, and J.M. Whitcomb, "Inhibition of tumor development by dehydroepiandrosterone and related steroids, *Toxicol Path* 14 (1986): 357-362.

   • R. M. Loria, et al., Protection against acute lethal viral infections with the native steroid dehydroepiandrosterone (DHEA)," *Journal of Medical Virology* 26 (1988): 301-314.

   • A. Schwartz, et al., "Dehydroepiandrosterone: An anti-obesity and anti-carcinogenic agent," *Nutr Cancer* 3:1 (1981): 46-53.

   • A.G. Schwartz, L. Pashko, and J.M. Whitcomb, "Inhibition of tumor development by dehydroepiandrosterone and related steroids, *Toxicol Path* 14 (1986): 357-362.

   • R. M. Loria, et al., Protection against acute lethal viral infections with the native steroid dehydroepiandrosterone (DHEA)," *Journal of Medical Virology* 26 (1988): 301-314.

   • J.E. Nestler, et al., "Dehydroepiandrosterone reduces serum low density lipoprotein levels and body fat but does not alter insulin sensitivity in normal men," *Journal of Clinical Endocrinology and Metabolism* 66 (1988): 57-61.

   • T. Sunderland, et al., "Reduced plasma dehydroepiandrosterone concentrations in Alzheimer's disease," (Letter) *Lancet* 2 (1989): 570.

   • J.F. Flood and E. Roberts, "Dehydroepiandrosterone sulfate improves memory in aging mice," *Brain Research* 448 (1988): 178-181.

7. Russel J. Reiter, et al., "A review of the evidence supporting melatonin's role as an anti-oxidant," *Journal of Pineal Research* 18 (1995): 1-11.

   • Life Extension Report, "DHEA Replacement Therapy." Vol 13, No 9, Sep 1993.

8. M.E. Reff, Schneider, E.L., "Biological markers in aging." Bethesda HIH Pub., 1980; 82-2221.

9. M. Kalimi, and Regelson, W., *The Biological Role of Dehydroepiandrosterone*, Walterde Gruyter, New York, 1990.

10. Regelson, W., Kalimi, M., Loria, R. Dehydroepiandrosterone (DHEA): the precursor steroid: introductory remarks. In: *The Biologic Role of Dehydroepiandrosterone* (DHEA). Kalimi, M., Regelson, W., Eds., New York: Walter de Gruyter, 1990, pp 1–6.

11. *Science News* 19(3):39, 1981.

12. Gaby, Alan, M.D., *Preventing and Reversing Osteoporosis*, Prima Publishing, Rocklin, CA, 1994, pp 157–172.

13. N. Orentriech, et al., "Age changes and sex differences in serum dehydroepiandrosterone sulfate concentrations throughout adulthood," *Journal of Clinical Endocrinology and Metabolism* 59 (1984): 551–555.

   • Yen, S.S., Morales A.J., Nolan Nelson, J.C., "Effects of replacement dose of dehydroepiandrosterone in men and women of advancing age." *J Clin Endocrinol Metabl* 1994, June 78(6):1360–7.

   • Regelson, W., *The Superhormone Promise*, Simon & Schuster, New York, 1996, pp 47–48.

14. D. L. Coleman, R.W. Schwizer, and E.H. Leiter, "Effect of genetic background on the therapeutic effects of dehydroepiandrosterone (DHEA) in diabetes-obesity mutants and in aged normal mice," *Diabetes* 33 (1984): 26–32.

   • G.B. Gordon, D.E. Bush, and H.F. Weisman, "Reduction of atherosclerosis by administration of dehydroepiandrosterone," *Journal of Clinical Investigation* 82 (1988): 712–720.

   • W. Regelson, R. Loria, and M. Kalimi, "Hormonal intervention, buffer hormones or state dependency: The role of dehydro-epiandrosterone (DHEA), thyroid hormone, estrogen and hypophysectomy in aging," *Annals of the New York Academy of Science* 521 (1988): 260–273.

15. T. Sunderland et al., Reduced plasma dehydroepiandrosterone concentrations in Alzheimer's disease (Letter). *Lancet* 2:570, 1989.

   • Roberts, E. et al., "Effects of Dehydroepiandrosterone and its Sulfate on Brain Tissue in Culture and on Memory in Mice." *Brain Research*, 1987, 406: 357–362.

16. C.R. Merril, M.G. Harrington and T. Sunderland, 1990. Reduced plasma dehydroepiandrosterone concentrations in HIV infection and Alzheimer's disease. *In the Biological Role of Dehydroepiandrosterone*, edited by M. Kalimi and W. Regelson, 101–105. New York: de Gruyter.

   • Gaby, A., *Preventing and Reversing Osteoporosis*, p 158.

   • Nordin, B.E.C., et al., 1985. The relation between calcium absorption, serum dehydroepiandrosterone, and vertebral mineral density in postmenopausal women, *Journal of Clin Endocrinol Metab* 60:651–657.

17. Regelson, W., *The Superhormone Promise*, pp 50–51.

   • Baulieu, E.F., Robel, P., Neurosteroids: A new brain function? *J Steroid Biochem Mol Biol* 37: 305–430, 1990.

   • Majewska, M. "Neuronal Actions of DHEA. Possible Role in Brain Development, Aging and Memory," *Ann NY Acad of Sci* 774:111–120, 1995.

18. Loria, R.M., et al., Protection against acute lethal viral infections with the native steroid dehydroepiandrosterone (DHEA). *Journal of Medical Virology*. 26:301–314, 1988.

19. R. Klatz, Goldman, R., *Stopping The Clock*, Keats Publishing Inc., New Canaan, Connecticut 1996, p 62.

   • O.A. Khorram, L.Vu, S.S.C. Yen, "Activation of Immune Function by Dehydroepiandrosterone (DHEA) in Age Advanced Men," *J Geront*, in press. 1996.

20. F. Feo, R. Pastale, Glucose-6-phosphate dehydrogenase and the relation of dehydroepiandrosterone to carcinogenesis. In: *The Biologic Role of Dehydroepiandrosterone (DHEA)*. Lalimi, M., Regelson, M., Eds., New York: Walter de Gruyter, pp 331–360, 1990.

21. R.D. Bulbrook, J.L. Hayward, C.C. Spicer, Relation between urinary androgen and corticoid excretion and subsequent breast cancer. *Lancet* 2:395–398, 1971.

- J.Adams, and J.B. Brown, Increase in urinary excretion of estrogen on administration of dehydroepiandrosterone sulphate to an adrenalectomized, oephorectomized patient with breast cancer. *Steroidologic*, 2:1–6, 1971.

- Schwartz, A.G.; Pashko, L., and Whitcomb, J.M., Inhibition of tumor development by dehydroepiandrosterone and related steroids. *Toxicol Path* 14:357–362, 1986.

22. A.G. Schwartz, L.L. Pashko, Cancer chemoprevention with the adrenocortical steroid dehydroepiandrosterone and structural analogs. *J Cell Biochem Suppl* 1993:17G:73–9.

- A.G. Schwartz, "Inhibitions of spontaneous breast cancer formation in female C3H (Avy'a) mice by long-term treatment with dehydroepiandrosterone." *Cancer Res* 1979; 39: 1129–1132.

23. A.G. Schwartz, Whitcomb, J.M., Nyce, J.W., Lewbart, M.L., Pashko, K.K., Dehydroepiandrosterone and structural analogs: a new class of cancer chemopreventive agents. *Adv Cancer Res* 1988:51:391–424.

24. W. Regelson, *The Superhormone Promise*, p 73.

- C.W. Boone, G.H. Kelloff, W.E. Malone, Identification of candidate cancer chemopreventive agents and their evaluation in animal models and human clinical trials: a review. *Cancer Res* 1990 Jan 1:50(1)2–9.

- G. B. Gordon, L.M. Shantz, P.Talalay, Modulation of growth, differentiation, and carcinogenesis by dehydroepiandrosterone. *Adv Enzymology Regulation* 26: 355–382, 1987.

- L.A. Hastings, L.L. Pashko, M.L. Lewbart, A.G. Schwartz, Dehydroepiandrosterone and two structural analogs inhibit 12-0-tetradecanoylphorba-13-acetate stimulation of prostaglandin G2 content in mouse skin. *Carcinogenesis* 9:1099–1102, 1988.

25. A. Schwartz, et al., "Dehydroepiandrosterone: An anti-obesity and anti-carcinogenic agent," *Nutr Cancer* 3:1 (1981): 46–53.

- Jakubowiez, D. J., Beer, N.A., Nestler, J., "Disparate Effects of Weight Reduction by Diet on Serum DHEAS Levels in Obese Men and Women," *J Clin Endoc Metab* 80: 3373–76, 1995.

26. M.P.Cleary, The antiobesity effect of dehydroepiandrosterone in rats. *Proc Soc Exp Biol Med* 1991 Jan: 196(1):8–16.

- Cleary, M.P., Shepherd, P., Jenits, B., "Effect of dehydroepiandrosterone on growth in lean and obese Zucker rats." *J Nutr*, 1984;114:1242–1251.

- M.P. Cleary. The role of DHEA in obesity. *The Biologic Role of Dehydroepiandrosterone (DHEA)*. Kalimi, M., Regelson, W., Eds., New York: Walter de Gruyter, pp 281–298, 1990.

27. A. Schwartz, et al., Dehydroepiandrosterone: An anti-obesity and anti-carcinogenic agent. *Nutr Cancer* 3 (1):46–53, 1981.

28. Alan Gaby, M.D., *Preventing and Reversing Osteoporosis*, Prima Publishing, Rocklin, CA, 1994, pp 157–172.

- J.F. Mortola, and Yen, S.S.C., The effects of oral dehydroepiandrosterone on endocrine-metabolic parameters in postmenopausal women. *J Clin Endocrinol Metab* 71:696–704, 1990.

29. Alan Gaby, M.D., *Preventing and Reversing Osteoporosis*, Prima Publishing, Rocklin, CA, 1994, pp 163–171.

30. Ibid.

31. P.N.Sambrook, et al., 1988. Sex Hormone status and Osteoporosis in Postmenopausal Women with Rheumatoid Arthritis. *Arthritis Rheum* 31:973–978.

- Gaby, Alan, M.D., *Preventing and Reversing Osteoporosis*, Prima Publishing, Rocklin, CA, 1994, p 166.

32. Ibid.

33. R.G. Crilly, D.H. Marshall, B.E.C. Nordin, 1979. Metabolic effects of corticosteroid therapy in post-menopausal women. *Journal Steroid Biochem* 11:429–433.

34. E. Barrett-Connor, et al., A prospective study of dehydroepiandrosterone sulfate, mortality, and cardiovascular disease. *New England J Med* 1986, 315:1519–1524.

35. Mitchelle, L.E., et al., Evidence for an association between dehydroepiandrosterone sulfate and non-fatal, premature myocardial infraction in males. *Circulation* 89:89–93.

- Hendler, S., M.D., *Doctors' Vitamin and Mineral Encyclopedia*, p 371.
36. Regelson, W., *The Superhormone Promise*, Simon & Schuster, New York. 1996, p 80.
37. Regelson, W., *The Superhormone Promise*, Simon & Schuster, New York. 1996, p 49.
- G. B. Gordon, D.E. Bush, H.F. Weisman, "Reduction of atherosclerosis by administration of DHEA," *Journal of Clin Invest* 1988, 82:712-720.
38. Interview with Dr. Ray Sahelian on DHEA, in *Nutritional News*, Vol 10, No 4, July 1996.
39. Regelson, W., *The Superhormone Promise*, Simon & Schuster, New York. 1996, pp 88–89.
- J. Mortola, and S.S.C. Yen." The effects of oral dehydroepiadrosterone on endrocrine-metabolic parameters in postmenopausal women." *J Clin Endoerinol Metab* 71:696-704, 1990.
- P.R. Casson, et. al., "Oral dehydroeplandrosterone in physiologic doses modulates immune function in postmenopausal women." *Amer J Obstet Gynecol* 1993, 169; 1536.
40. Ibid.—Regelson, p 89.
41. A. Gaby, *Preventing and Reversing Osteoporosis*, p 164.
42. Ibid. Gaby, pp 168–169.
43. J. Whitaker, *Dr. Whitaker's Guide to Natural Healing*, Prima Publishing, Rocklin, CA, 1995.
- Arlene J. Morales, Effects of Replacement Dose of Dehydroepiandrosterone in Men and Women of Advancing Age, *Journal of Clinical Endocrinology and Metabolism*, Vol 78, No 6, 1994.
44. *Life Ext Rep*. Vol 13, No 9, Sept 1993, p 70, Saul Kent, Editor/Publisher.
45. Joyce McBeth, "Melatonin Madness," *American Council on Collaborative Medicine* 1:6 (September 1995).
- Kent, Saul, Life Extension Reports, "How Melatonin Comgats Aging," *Life Extension Magazine*, December 1995, pp 10-27.
46. Russel J. Reiter, et al., "A Review of the Evidence Supporting Melatonin's Role as an Anti-oxidant," *Journal of Pineal Research* 18 (1995): 1-11.
- Russel J. Reiter, et al., *Melatonin*, Bantam Books, New York, December 1995.
47. Walter Pierpaoli and William Regelson, *Melatonin Miracle* NY: Simon & Schuster, 1995, pp 57-58.
48. Walter Pierpaoli and William Regelson, *Melatonin Miracle* NY: Simon & Schuster, 1995, pp 57-58.
49. Walter Pierpaoli and William Regelson, *Melatonin Miracle* NY: Simon & Schuster, 1995, p 59.
- Russel J. Reiter, "The Pineal Gland and Melatonin in Relation to Aging: A Summary of the Theories and of the Data," *Experimental Gerontology* 30:3,4 (1995): 199-212.
50. Ibid.
51. Joyce McBeth, "Melatonin Madness," *American Council on Collaborative Medicine* 1:6 (September 1995).
- Lissoni, P., Megegalli, S., Barni, S., and Frigerino, F. "A Randomized Study of Immunotherapy with Low-Dose Subcutaneous Interleukin-2 Plus Melatonin vs. Chemotherapy with Cisplatin and Etoposide as First-Line Therapy for Advanced Non-Smal Cell Lung Cancer." *Tumori* 1994; 80:464-67.
52. A.O. Massion, et al., *Medical Hypothes* 44:1 (1995): 39-46.
- L.D. Chen, et al., *Cancer Letter* 91:2 (1995): 153-159.
53. G. Praast, et al., *Experientia* 51:4 (1995): 349-355.
- Walter Pierpaoli and William Regelson, *Melatonin Miracle* NY: Simon & Schuster, 1995.
54. J.J. Reiter, *Rev Environ Health* 10:3,4 (July-December 1994): 171-186.
55. Steven J. Brock and Michael Boyette, *Stay Young the Melatonin Way*, (NY: Dutton—Penguin Group, 1995).
- Sahelian, Ray, M.D., "Melatonin: The Natural Sleep Medicine," *Total Health*, August 1995, Vol 17, No 4, p 30.
- Zhdanova, I.V., Wurtman, R.J., and Schomer, D.L., "Sleep-inducing Effects of Low Doses of

Melatonin Ingested in the Evening." *Clinical Pharmacology and Therapeutics* 1995; 57; 552-558.

56. Walter Pierpaoli and William Regelson. *Melatonin Miracle*, p 161.

57. Walter Pierpaoli and William Regelson, *Melatonin Miracle*, p 162.

58. *Dictionary of Medical Terms for the Nonmedical Person*, Hauppage, NY, 1994, p 174.

59. *Alternative Medicine*, The Burton Goldberg Group, Future Medicine Pub, Inc., Puyallup, WA, 1994, p 668.

60. Rodriguez Calle, E.E., Contes, R.J., Manacle-McMahill, H.L., Wun, M.J., Heath, C.W. Jr., Estrogen Replacement Therapy and Fatal Ovarian Cancer. *Am J Epidemiol* 1995;141:828-835.

61. *Primary Care & Cancer*, June 1991, reprinted with permission from *The Cancer Bulletin*, Volume 42, Number 6, 1990. The publication of M.D. Anderson Cancer Center.

62. American Cancer Society, Cancer Facts and Figures 1991

63. Follingstad, A.H., 1978. Estriol, the forgotten estrogen: *JAMA* 239-:29-30.

• Gaby, A., *Preventing and Reversing Osteoporosis*, pp 131-133.

64. Fredericks, Carlton, *Breast Cancer: A Nutritional Approach* (New York: Grosset & Dunlap, 1977).

65. Woman's International Pharmacy, "Most asked questions about natural oral progesterone." Your source for information by Women's Health Connection.

• Lee, John, M.D., *What Your Doctor May Not Tell You About Menopause*. Warner Books, Time Warner, NY, 1986, p 89.

66. Regelson, W., M.D., *The Superhormone Promise*, p 178.

67. Woman's International Pharmacy, "Most asked questions about natural oral progesterone." Your source for information by Women's Health Connection.

• Dr. John Lee, *What Your Doctor May Not Tell You About Menopause*, Warner Books, Time Warner, New York, NY, 1986, p 89.

• Hargrove, J.T., Maxon, W., Wentz, A.C., "Absorption of oral progesterone is influenced by vehicle and particular size" *American Journal of Obstetrics and Gynecology*, Oct 1989.

68. Dr. John Lee, *What Your Doctor May Not Tell You About Menopause*, Warner Books, Time Warner, New York, NY, 1986, p 89.

69. Fredericks, Carlton, Ph.D., *Breast Cancer: A Nutritional Approach*, Grosset & Dunlap, A Filmways Co. Publishers, NY, 1977, pp 5-6.

70. Betty Kamen, Ph.D., *Hormone Replacement Therapy, YES or NO?* Nutrition Encounter, Inc., Novato, California, 1993.

71. Morton Walker, *The Chelation Way* (Garden Park, NY: Avery Publishing Group, Inc., 1990): 93.

• Gary Null, "Chelation Therapy: One of Medicine's Best Kept Secrets," *OmniMedicine* 16:2 (November 1993).

• Robert C. Atkins, *Dr. Atkins Health Revolution* (Boston: Houghton Mifflin Co., 1988): 219.

72. Ibid.

73. Personal Conversation with Dr. Casdorph in Long Beach, CA.

74. Gary Null, "Chelation Therapy: One of Medicine's Best Kept Secrets," *OmniMedicine* 16:2 (November 1993).

75. Robert C. Atkins, *Dr. Atkins Health Revolution* (Boston: Houghton Mifflin Co., 1988): 219.

• E.Y. Chein, M.D., Palm Springs Life Extension Institute pamphlet, Palm Springs, CA.

76. K. Schmid and J. Stein (eds), *Cell Research and Cell Therapy* (Thoune, Switzerland: Ott Publishers, 1967): 19.

77. Ibid.

• K. Schmid and J. Stein (eds), *Cell Research and Cell Therapy* (Thoune, Switzerland: Ott Publishers, 1967): 19.

78. Telephone conversation with Dr. Tom Smith.

- The Burton Goldberg Group, *Alternative Medicine—The Definitive Guide* (Payullup, WA: Future Medicine Publishing, 1993).

79. Dr. Niehan's original clinic, Clinic La Prairie, is in Geneva, Switzerland.

- Dr. Smith's International Clinic of Biological Regeneration has an American information office: P.O. Box 509, Florissant, Missouri 63032. (800) 826-5366.

- The International Society for the Application of Organ Filtrates, Cellular Therapy, and Onco-Biotherapy may be contacted through Robert Bosch Strasse, 56a, D-6906, Walldorf, Germany. 06-2-227-6330.

80. P. Cazzola, P. Mazzanti, and G. Bossi, "In vivo modulating effect of a calf thymus and lysate on human T lymphocyte subsets and CD4+/CD8+ ratio in the course of different diseases," *Curr Ther Res*, 42 (1987): 1011-1017.

- R. Genova and A. Guerra, "Thymomodulin in management of food allergy in children," *Int J Tissue Reac* 8 (1986): 239-242.

- G. Valesini, V. Barnaba, M. Levrero, et al., "Clinical improvement and partial correction of the T-cell defects of acquired immunodeficiency syndrome (AIDS) and lymphadenopathy syndrome (LAS) by a calf thymus lysate," *Eur J Clin Oncol* 22 (1986): 531-532.

- A. Fiocchi, E. Borcella, E. Riva, et al., "A double-blind clinical trial for the evaluation of the therapeutic effectiveness of a calf thymus derivative (Thymomodulin) in children with recurrent respiratory infections," *Thymus* 8 (1986): 831-839.

Chapter 12: Men's Unique Challenges

1. *The American Medical Association Encyclopedia of Medicine*, Medical Editor Charles B. Clayman, M.D., Random House, New York, 1989.

2. *Dictionary of Medical Terms,* Mikel A. Rothenberg, M.D., Charles F. Chapman, Barron's Medical Guide-Educational Series, Inc., 1994.

- *The American Medical Association Encyclopedia of Medicine*, Medical Editor Charles B. Clayman, MD, Random House, New York, 1989.

3. H.L. Newbold, *Mega-Nutrients for Your Nerves*, Peter H. Wyden Publishers, New York, 1975.

4. Ibid.

5. Edmund Chein, M.D., J.D., *Testosterone—Male Menopause (Andropause)* article in a book from the Life Extension Institute, Palm Springs. 2825 Tahquitz Canyon Way, Suite A, Palm Springs, CA 92262.

- Heller, C., Myers, G., "The Male Climacteric its Symptomatology, Diagnosis and Treatment." The *Journal of the American Medical Association,* 1994.

6. Ibid.—Chein

- Davidson, J.M., Chen, J.J., Crapo, L., Gray, G., "Hormonal changes and sexual function in aging men," *J Clin Endo & Metab* 57:71-79, 1983.

- Gouchie, C., Kimuro, D., "The relationship between testosterone levels and cognitive ability patterns," *Psychoneuroendocrinology* 16:323-334, 1991.

7. Ronald Hoffman, M.D., Medical Director of the Hoffman Center for Holistic Medicine in Manhattan, New York. *New Life* July/August. "Testosterone: The New Longevity Drug?"

8. Ibid.—Chein

- J.S. Tenover, "Androgen Administration to Aging Men." *Endocrinol and Metab Clinics of North America* 23:877-88, 1994.

9. Dr. Gerald Phillips, Department of Medicine at Columbia University, *Atherosclerosis and Thrombosis*, Vol 14, No 15, May 1994.

- Edmund Chein, M.D., JD., *Testosterone—Male Menopause (Andropause)*.

10. J.R. White, et al., Enhanced sexual behavior in exercising men. *Arch Sex Behav* 19:193-209, 1990.

11. Edmund Chein, M.D., J.D., *Testosterone—Male Menopause (Andropause)*.

- *Atherosclerosis and Thrombosis,* Vol 14, No 5, May 1994, Department of Medicine at Columbia University.

12. Ibid.

13. Gail Sheehy, "Endless Youth," *Vanity Fair*, June, 1996.

14. Regelson, W., *The Superhormone Promise*, Simon & Schuster, New York, 1996, p 123.

15. Daniel Rudman, M. D., "Effects of Human Growth Hormone in Men Over 60 Years Old," The *New England Journal of Medicine*, Vol 323, No 1, July 5, 1990, pp 1-6.

16. Ibid.

   • Daniel Rudman, M.D., "Growth hormone, body composition, and aging." *J of the Amer Ger Soc*, 1995.

   • Rudman, D., Kutner, M.H., Rogers, C.M., et al., "Impaired growth hormone secretion in the adult population: relation to age and adiposity." *J Clin Invest* 67: 1361-69, 1981.

17. Dr. Ronald Katz, *Grow Young with HGH*, Harper Collins, Publisher, New York, NY, 1997, p 5.

18. Regelson, W., *The Superhormone Promise*, Simon & Schuster, New York, 1996, p 203.

19. Regelson, W., *The Superhormone Promise*, Simon & Schuster, New York, 1996, p 203.

   • Schwartz, A. G., Fairinan, K. K., Pashko, L. L., "The Biologic Significance of Dehydrolprandrosterone," In: *The Biologic Role of Dehydrolprandrosterone (DHEA)*. Kalimi, M., Regelson, W., Eds., New York, Walter D. Gruyter, pp 7-12, 1990.

20. Klatz, Ronald, Goldman, Robert, *Stopping the Clock*, Keats Publishing, Inc., New Canaan, CT, 1996, p 19.

21. Edmund Chein, M.D., "Living Younger Longer with Hormone Replacement Therapy," Radio interview with host Ron Dotner, on cassette tapes, 1995.

22. Klatz, Ronald, Goldman, Robert, *Stopping the Clock*, Keats Publishing. Inc., New Canaan, CT, 1996, p 19.

23. Ibid. p 11.

24. *Health Counselor*, Sept/Oct 1991. By Michael T. Murray, N.D.

25. W. Regelson, *The Superhormone Promise*, Simon & Schuster, New York. 1996, p 49.

26. W. Regelson, *The Superhormone Promise*, Simon & Schuster, New York. 1996, pp 118-119.

   • R.D. McLure, R. Oses, M. L. Ernst. "Hypogonadal Impotence Treated by Transdermal Testosterone" *Urology* 37: 224-228, 1991.

27. Robert Erdmann, Ph.D., Meirion Jones. *The Amino Revolution*, A Fireside Book—Simon & Schuster Inc., New York , 1989, pp 164-165.

28. Ibid.—Erdmann

29. Ibid.—Erdmann

30. Richard A. Passwater, Ph.D., *The New Supernutrition*, Pocket Books a division of Simon & Schuster New York, 1991, p 82.

31. Sheldon Saul Hendler, *Doctors' Vitamin and Mineral Encyclopedia*, pp 214-215.

   • Schachter A., et. al., Treatment of oligospermia with the amino acid arginine.
   J Urol 110:311-313, 1973.

32. Ruth Adams, *The Big Family Guide to All the Vitamins*, Keats Publishing, New Canaan, CT, 1992, p 299.

33. K. Reid, et al., "Double-blind trial of Yohimbine in Treatment of Psychogenic Impotence," *Lancet* II:8556 (August 22, 1987): 421-423.

   • Eberhard Kronhausen and Phyllis Kronhausen, *Formula for Life*—Science Rediscovers a Natural Aphrodisiac (NY: William Morrow and Co., 1989): 551-557.

34. Ibid.—Reid

   • Jack Ritchason, *The Little Herb Encyclopedia*, Woodland Health Books, Pleasant Grove, UT, 1994, p 263.

35. J. Geller, "Overview of benign hypertrophy," *Urology* 34: Suppl. (1989): 57-68.

   • R. Sikora, M. Sohn, F.J. Deutz, D. Rohrmann, W. Schafer, "Ginkgo biloba extract in the therapy of erectile dysfunction," *Journal of Urology* 141 (1989): 188A.

36. Donald J. Brown, N.D., *Herbal Prescriptions for Better Health*, Prima Publishing Rocklin, CA, 1996, pp 253-257.

- Jonathan V. Wright, M.D., *Nutrition & Healing*, 1:2 (September 1994): 3,8.

37. S. Shibata et al., Chemistry and pharmacology of *Panax Econ Med Plant Res* 1:217-84, 1985.

38. Donald J. Brown, N.D., *Herbal Prescriptions for Better Health*, Prima Publishing Rocklin, CA, 1996, pp 253-257.

39. Sheldon Saul Hendler, *Doctors' Vitamin and Mineral Encyclopedia*, pp 291-292.

- Ritchason, Jack, *The Little Herb Encyclopedia*, Woodland Health Books, Pleasant Grove, Utah, p 70.

40. Ritchason, Jack, *The Little Herb Encyclopedia*, Woodland Health Books, Pleasant Grove, Utah, p 70.

41. J. Geller, "Overview of benign prostate hypertrophy," *Urology* 34: Suppl. (1989): 57-68.

42. Sheldon Saul Hendler, *The Doctors' Vitamin and Mineral Encyclopedia*, p 198.

43. Julian Whitaker, M.D., *The Prostate Report*, 20.

44. I.M. Bush, "Zinc and the Prostate." Paper read at the annual meeting of the American Medical Association, Chicago 1974.

45. M. Fahim, et al., "Zinc Treatment for the Reduction of Hyperplasia of the Prostate," *Federal Proc* (35) 1976, 361.

46. Richard Passwater, *The New Supernutrition*, New York: Pocket Books, 1991, 79.

47. G. Champlault, J.C. Patel, and A.M. Bonnard, "A double-blind trial of an extract of the plant Serenoa repens in benign prostatic hyperplasia," *Br J Clin Pharmacol*, 1984, 18, pp 461-2.

- A. Tasca, M. Barulli, A. Cavazzana, et al., "Treatment of obstructive symptomatology caused by prostatic adenoma with an extract of Serenoa repens. Double-blind clinical study vs. placebo," *Minerva Urol Nefrol* 1985, 37, pp 87-91.

- C. Boccafoschi, and S. Annoscia, "Comparison of Serenoa repens extract with placebo by controlled clinical trial in patients with prostatic adenomatosis," *Urologia*, 1983, 50, pp 1,257-9.

- Braeckman, J., *Current Ther Res*, 1994; 55:776-85.

48. Julian Whitaker, M.D., *Dr. Whitaker's Guide to Natural Healing*. Prima Publishing, Inc., 1995, p 22.

47. Andrew Weil, M.D., *Spontaneous Healing*, Fawcett Columbine, New York, 1995, p 260.

- Michael T. Murray, *The Healing Power of Herbs*, Rocklin, CA.: Prima Publishing, 150-151.

- Michael T. Murray, *Natural Alternatives to Over-the-Counter and Prescription Drugs*, New York: William Morrow and Co., Inc., 215.

50. Lange, J., and Bardeaux, M., "Clinical Experimentation with V1326 in Prostatic Disorders." *Bordeaux Medical* 3, No 11 (Nov 1970), 2807-2808, In French.

51. Jack Ritchason, *The Little Herb Encyclopedia*, Woodland Health Books, Pleasant Grove, UT, 1994, pp 190-191.

52. F. Dumrau, "Benign prostatic hyperplasia: amino acid therapy for symptomatic relief." *Am J Ger*, 1962, 10, pp 426-30.

- J.M. Feinblatt, and J.C. Gant, "Palliative treatment of benign prostatic hypertrophy: value of glycine, alanine, glutamic acid combination," *J Maine Med Assoc*, 1958, 49, pp 99-102.

- From *Encyclopedia of Natural Medicine*, Murray & Pizzorno, p 483.

53. W.S. Fahim, J.M. Harman, T.H. Clevenger, et al., Effect of panax ginseng on testosterone level and prostate in male rats. *Arch Androl*, 1982.

54. Hoffman, D., *The New Holistic Herbal*. Rockport, MA, Elemart, Inc., 1991, pp 69-70.

55. Ask-Upmark, Prostatic and its treatment. *Acta Med Scand*, Vol 161, 1987, pp 355-367.

Chapter 13: Let's Put It All Together

1   Lindberg, G., McFarland, J., *Take Charge of Your Health*, pp 48-49.

2. Ibid.

- Carlton Fredericks, Ph.D., *Eat Well, Get Well, Stay Well*, Grosset & Dunlap, NY, 1980, pp 42-43.

3. *Take Charge of Your Health*, pp 48-49.

4. Jean Carper, *Stop Aging Now* (New York: Harper Collins, 1994), 222.

5. American Cancer Society, "Leading Sites of Cancer Incident and Deaths—1993 Estimates" found in *Cancer Facts and Figures*, 1993.

6. *Take Charge of Your Health*, Harper & Row, San Francisco, CA, 1982, p 109.

7. Jack Ritchason, *The Little Herb Encyclopedia*, Woodland Health Books, Pleasant Grove, UT, pp 5-6.

8. Louise Tenney, *Today's Herbal Health*, Provo, UT: Woodland Books, 1983, p 118.

9. Melatonin, Its Fundamental Immunoregulatory role in Aging and Cancer," *Annals NY Acad. Sciences* (521) 1988: 140–148.

10. Barnes, "Soybeans inhibit mammary tumor growth in models of breast cancer," *Mutagens and Carcinogens in the Diet* (Ed. M.W. Pariza, New York: Wiley-Liss, 1990).

11. Renner, *W-GmbH, Milk and Dairy Products in Human Nutrition*, Munich, Germany: Volkswirtshafticher Verlag, 1983.
   - M. Messina, "The role of soy products in reducing risk of cancer," *Journal of the National Cancer Institute* 83 (1991): 541–46.

12. Jean Carper, *Stop Aging Now* (New York: Harper Collins, 1994), 222.
   - Ronald Klatz, Robert Goldman, *Stopping the Clock*, Keats Publishing Inc. New Canaan, Connecticut, 1995.
   - M. Messina, "The role of soy products in reducing risk of cancer," *Journal of the National Cancer Institute* 83 (1991): 541–46.

13. James Anderson, "Meta-Analysis of Effects of Soy Protein Intake on Serum Lipids in Humans," *New England Journal of Medicine* 333 (August 3, 1995): 276-282.
   - C.R. Sirtori, "Soybean protein diet and plasma cholesterol: from therapy to molecular mechanisms," *Annals of The New York Academy of Sciences* 676 (1993): 188-201.

14. Ritchason, Jack, *Little Herb Encyclopedia*, p 227.

15. Jean Carper, *Stop Aging Now* (New York: Harper Collins, 1994), 222.
   - Ronald Klatz, Robert Goldman, *Stopping the Clock*, Keats Publishing Inc. New Canaan, Connecticut, 1995.
   - M. Messina, "The role of soy products in reducing risk of cancer," *Journal of the National Cancer Institute* 83 (1991): 541–46.

16. W.C. Yu, "Diet and high risk of stomach cancer in Shandong, China," *Cancer Research* 48 (1988): 3518-23.
   - Weisburger, J.H., *Mutagens in Food: Detection and Prevention*, ed. H. Hayatsu (Boca Raton, FL: CRC Press, 1991).
   - Jean Carper, *Stop Aging Now* (New York: Harper Collins, 1994), 222.

Index